The Pirate Myth

The image of the pirate is at once spectral and ubiquitous. It haunts the imagination of international legal scholars, diplomats and statesmen involved in the war on terror. It returns in the headlines of international newspapers as an untimely 'security threat'. It materializes on the most provincial cinematic screen and the most acclaimed works of fiction. It casts its shadow over the liquid spatiality of the Net, where cyber-activists, file-sharers and a large part of the global youth are condemned as pirates, often embracing that definition with pride rather than resentment. Today, the pirate remains a powerful political icon, embodying at once the persistent nightmare of an anomic wilderness at the fringe of civilization, and the fantasy of a possible anarchic freedom beyond the rigid norms of the state and of the market. And yet, what are the origins of this persistent 'pirate myth' in the Western political imagination? Can we trace the historical trajectory that has charged this ambiguous figure with the emotional, political and imaginary tensions that continue to characterize it? What can we learn from the history of piracy and the ways in which it intertwines with the history of imperialism and international trade? Drawing on international law, political theory, and popular literature, *The Pirate Myth* offers an authoritative genealogy of this immortal political and cultural icon, showing that the history of piracy – the different ways in which pirates have been used, outlawed and suppressed by the major global powers, but also fantasized, imagined and romanticised by popular culture – can shed unexpected light on the different forms of violence that remain at the basis of our contemporary global order.

The Pirate Myth: Genealogies of an Imperial Concept will therefore be of immense interest to those working and researching in law, politics and history.

Amedeo Policante is Assistant Professor of Political Theory and International Relations at the University of Nottingham.

Law and the Postcolonial: Ethics, Politics, & Economy

Series edited by
Prof Denise Ferreira da Silva
Queen Mary, University of London
Dr Mark A. Harris
La Trobe University, Melbourne
Dr Brenna Bhandar
SOAS, University of London

Law and the Postcolonial: Ethics, Politics, & Economy seeks to expand the critical scope of racial, postcolonial, and global theory and analysis, focusing on how the global juridico-economic apparatus has been, and continues to be, shaped by the colonial and the racial structurings of power. It includes works that seek to move beyond the previous privileging of culture in considerations of racial and postcolonial subjectivity to offer a more comprehensive engagement with the legal, economic and moral issues of the global present.

Titles in this series include:

State Violence and the Execution of Law
Biopolitical Caesurae of Torture, Black Sites, Drones
Joseph Pugliese

The Pirate Myth
Genealogies of an Imperial Concept
Amedeo Policante

Forthcoming:

Puerto Rico and the Origins of U.S. Global Empire
The Disembodied Shade
Charles R. Venator-Santiago

Genocidal Democracy
Neoliberalism, Mass Incarceration, and the Politics of Urban Gun Violence
John D. Marquez

Postcolonial Capitalism
Justice, Global Labour and Racial Violence
Denise Ferreira da Silva and Rashne Limke

The Pirate Myth

Genealogies of an Imperial Concept

Amedeo Policante

Routledge
Taylor & Francis Group
LONDON AND NEW YORK

First published 2015
by Routledge

2 Park Square, Milton Park, Abingdon, Oxon OX14 4RN
711 Third Avenue, New York, NY 10017, USA

a GlassHouse Book

Routledge is an imprint of the Taylor & Francis Group, an informa business

First issued in paperback 2016

British Library Cataloguing in Publication Data
A catalogue record for this book is available from the British Library

Library of Congress Cataloging-in-Publication Data
A catalog record has been requested for this book
Policante, Amedeo, author.
The pirate myth : genealogies of an imperial concept / Amedeo Policante.
pages cm—(Law and the postcolonial)
Includes bibliographical references and index.
ISBN 978-1-138-79731-4 (hardback)—ISBN 978-1-315-75722-3 (ebk) 1. Piracy (International law)—History. 2. Piracy—Law and legislation. 3. Piracy—Prevention—Law and legislation. 4. Terrorism—Prevention—Law and legislation. 5. Cyberterrorism—Law and legislation. I. Title.
KZ7212.P65 2015
364.16'4—dc23 2014027674

ISBN 978-1-138-79731-4 (hbk)
ISBN 978-1-138-21130-8 (pbk)

Typeset in Baskerville
by RefineCatch Limited, Bungay, Suffolk

Contents

Acknowledgements

The Ship of Thinking should never follow a straight course. This is, at least, a lesson that the journey described in the following pages has incessantly imparted unto me. When it is time to embark on a new adventure, we gather as many detailed maps as we can find; we pore over the travelogues of celebrated wanderers of the past; we draw elaborate routes, which promise to deliver us to the other, unknown shore. This gives us that sliver of audacity that is necessary to set sail. And yet, the Ship of Thinking is always led astray by uncharted winds, by unexpected currents, by sudden tempests followed by weeks of becalmed sea. We find ourselves chasing alluring sirens, only to be chased by monsters of the deep. If we are lucky, the Ship of Thinking is continuously hijacked, swerved and deflected from its course. Paradoxically, this is the only way in which the ship can cruise. Thinking is always a relational, responsive and deeply dysfunctional activity. Thinking is always a dialogue, a response, a continuous exchange with our surroundings. Far from being a solitary activity, it is a journey defined by the friends we meet on the way, each diverting the course of our projected voyage in a unique and sometimes indescribable way. The friends who have intervened in the creative odyssey behind this book are many, and each of them had a decisive role in determining the course of my journey. To each of them goes my most sincere gratitude. First of all, I would like to thank Saul Newman, without whose help this exploratory mission would have hardly set sail. His friendship and support have been a joy and a constant source of inspiration. I am also eternally – sometimes financially – indebted to the motley crew that has shared with me the many seasons of this journey: Davide Bradanini, Yari Lanci, Martina Tazzioli, Rhys Williams, Giulia Bazzanella, Marta Fioni and Alessandro Inglima have been a true brethren of the South-Eastern Shore. I would also like to thank Sandro Mezzadra, Peter Fitzpatrick, Michael Dillon, Alberto Toscano, Sanjay Seth and James Martin for their invaluable advice and support. I am greatly indebted to many people at the University of Nottingham, whose support has given me the opportunity to spend some more time putting together these pages: Michael Connors, Trevor Parfitt, Joshua Snider, Guy Burton and Francesco Stolfi have been a precious sustenance in distant lands and frenetic times. This book would not have been possible without the constant support of my family, which is also the greatest source of my imagination. These pages are also dedicated to their immense, lacustrine *joie de vivre*. Finally, and most importantly, this book is dedicated to my comrade Rosa Sansone with whom I have shared the countless moments that gravitate around the composition of this book, making each of them an exhilarating adventure in itself.

Note

A simple etymological curiosity indissolubly ties together pirates and Empire, opening up a space of interrogation regarding the constitutive relationship they secretly entertain with each other. According to the *American Heritage Dictionary of English Language*, the word pirate has its origins in 'Middle English from Latin *pirata*, from Greek *peirates*, meaning "attacker" or "adventurer", from *peiran*, to attempt, to risk, to try. [...] From Indo-European root *per-* from which derive the modern English words: fear, peril, empire and pirate'. Empire and pirates appear then intimately held together in an embrace, which is filled with fear, peril and terror. We have thus a tripartite relationship in which terror is the stigmata that leaves a trace both on the pirate and on Empire. The unpredictability of pirates, and the might of empires, certainly terrorize; but at the same time both Empires and pirates are themselves terrorized, so that they define themselves by the fact of putting themselves at risk in order finally to overcome terror. But what is this terror that pirates and empires overcome in order to qualify as what they are?

We may hypothesize that pirates as outlaws become what they are in the moment in which they step outside the boundary of the law so to constitute an exterior to it. And yet, as Giorgio Agamben has convincingly shown, to step or to be pushed outside the law is not to be thoroughly alien to it. Rather, as any child knows, outlaws are easy prey of emperors, and their lives have no further value than that of being thoroughly disposable: they may be killed with impunity. Undeniably, pirates are figures of terror: narratives on piracy overflow with monstrosity, violence and death; narratives on piracy also often end with hangings. The defeated pirate, chained, powerless, unarmed and waiting to be executed, comes to symbolize the overcoming of fear, which is nothing but the definition of Empire.

Empire in fact is originally, and most fundamentally, the name for whoever protects us against the pirate. Upon the naming of the pirate, in fighting it and finally in celebrating its triumph over it, Empire erects itself. There is no Empire without a pirate, a terrorizing common enemy, an enemy of all. At the same time, there is no pirate without Empire. In fact, pirates as outlaws cannot be understood in any other way but as legal creatures. In other words, they exist only in a certain extreme, liminal relationship with the law. In a similar way in which we cannot think of criminals without posing immediately the problem of a broken law and a police state, to reflect on pirates inevitably leads to the question of Empire. It seems, therefore – and this is our initial hypothesis – that the very essence of Empire calls the pirate into being, and that the pirate can exist only in a strict relationship with Imperial formations.

Introduction

This book has as its subject piracy and its relation to Empire. It is the result of several years of research and a long-term engagement with the fields of legal history, international relations and political theory. I tried to trace the significance of the figure of the pirate and to highlight how throughout modernity it has represented the image of an untameable outside against which the state, Empire and finally humanity have been called into action. The fundamental question that has oriented this study is: how did a marginal figure such as the pirate come to be defined as the first enemy of the human race? And more generally: how did the pirate come to host fantasies of an outside at once desired and feared, an outside that sets itself in contrast with the order of the state, of civilization and even of life itself? When did sea-robbers begin to be portrayed as monstrous beings against which all states must coalesce? Why, at a certain point in history, did European states decide collectively to appropriate, organize and subject to the legal yoke the oceans of the world? And why, after its conception, has the classical image of the pirate continued to hold a special place in the Western political imagination, becoming an inexhaustible source of analogies, which have targeted the most diverse subjects?

The figure of the pirate has mediated Western understandings of nineteenth-century Malay rovers and twenty-first-century Islamic terrorists; it has been evoked to characterize and condemn Barbary corsairs, African slave-traders, anarchist agitators, German submarines and denationalized German Jews. What is the rhetorical, strategic and political function served by the figure of the pirate? Why, throughout the centuries, have empires always claimed the burden of protecting humanity from pirates and from 'those who are like pirates'? And why today does the figure of the pirate seem at once heroic and reprehensible, exotic and banal, timeless and ever-changing, archaic and contemporary? Are there pirates among us today? And who are they? Considering the scope of these questions, which I hope will become clearer throughout the chapters, I would be hard pressed to confine my writing to any field of traditional academic study. As soon as one starts to reflect on the history of piracy, the fields and subfields of research that may be taken into consideration begin to proliferate in an anarchic fashion, creating a challenge that soon threatens to disrupt the enthusiasm of even the most well-disposed of researchers, and risks bringing about rapid dissatisfaction with the ways in which the topic has been approached in the past.

A pirate library

This chaotic threat – the apparent impossibility to confine the pirate to the historic, literary or mythical field – reflects itself in the fragmentary nature of the existing literature on piracy. Although a cursory bibliography of the texts dedicated to the topic seems to indicate a growing field, constantly enriched by a steady stream of more or less serious reflections on the issue, it is hard to say if a field exists at all, and if it is in fact possible to bring together what often appears as little more than a collection of studies on the most disparate issues, only kept together by this vague word that evokes contradictory images and feelings. The pirate escapes representation, and yet it keeps cropping up at the margins of a whole series of discourses, often concerned with equally marginal social spaces: legal reflections on the status of the world's oceans and the place of Universal jurisdiction in modern international law (Kontorovich 2004; Goodwin 2006; Azubuike 2009); theoretical investigations on the origins of the modern state (Mathew 1924; Thomson 1994); historical studies on the world of merchant empires and the colonial era (Andrews 1984; Zahedieh 1986); anthropological treaties concerned with little-known non-Western people and the ways in which they have been understood and portrayed by European travellers, colonialists and merchants (Trocki 1979; Colchester 1989); excursions in early modern European literature and its fascination with the ambiguity of the much-celebrated cosmopolitan marauders of the seventeenth and eighteenth centuries (Williams 2001; Arnold 2007); and security reports, which expose in detail the ways in which maritime piracy continues to threaten global chains of production, distribution and consumption in an increasingly integrated world market (Panjabi 2009; Stavridis and LeBron 2010).

The list appears unending and singularly confusing. Confronted by it, we are left with a multiplicity of texts that although claiming a formal correspondence – all of them may start with a simple foreword 'this is a book about piracy' – do not compose a single discourse, and remain isolated and practically silent to each other. How to make sense of it? Is there a way to understand the subtle thread that unites Muslim corsairs and Christian renegades of the seventeenth century, cosmopolitan marauders of the eighteenth century, Malay traders resistant to English Imperialism in the nineteenth century, German U-boats responsible for disrupting neutral shipping in time of warfare, as well as contemporary Somali pirates and young Indian copyright violators defying a growing, global copyright regime? And if nothing seems to be common to these disparate figures apart from the condemnatory label that is attached to them, what is the historical and political significance of this label? What role does it serve? Who is its master and how has the pirate image changed its meaning, passing through history while being appropriated at every turn by different discursive regimes?

Marx (1988) once affirmed that the criminal is also productive, but what should we say of the pirate? Certainly, the world we inhabit in our everyday life has been profoundly shaped by the existence of criminals and of the authorities who define them, judge them, fight them and imprison them; similarly, the international system has been profoundly shaped by the existence of pirates and by the fight against them. According to Marx, 'the criminal produces not only crimes but also criminal law' (1988: 309). Similarly, as we will see, we might say that the pirate has produced a great deal of international law, giving an essential contribution to its development from the eighteenth century until today. The fact that our contemporary international criminal law was born in the fight against piracy is today universally recognized. 'Crime,' says Marx, 'through its ever new methods of attack on property, constantly calls into being new methods of defence' (1988: 310). Piracy, as a form of crime that attacks property where no sovereign authority can claim an exclusive jurisdiction, has called into being Universal jurisdiction: a doctrine that today is becoming more and more important and that allows all and every state to prosecute a particular crime.

But there are many other ways in which pirates have been singularly productive. Marx went as far as asking: 'if one leaves the sphere of private crime: would the world market ever have come into being but for national crime?' (1988: 309). As we will see, there are no doubts that the history of piracy is one of the fundamental chapters in the history of the formation of the world market. First of all, lawless plunder had a fundamental role in early Imperialist ventures and in the origins of the capitalist mode of production. In a second phase, the suppression of piracy, the monopolization of legitimate violence, the regulation of Imperialist plunder and the increasing juridification of the oceanic commons created some of the essential preconditions for the creation of global markets organized on the basis of a number of essential legal norms. The suppression of piracy appears as a constitutive moment in the transition to an ordered system of capital accumulation on a global scale. Without the eradication of piracy, without the emptying out of the oceans of the world and their transformation in an integrated plane for safe commercial circulation, without the imposition of an international law protecting property and the safety of maritime trade, contemporary processes of globalization would have been simply unthinkable.

The pirate, thus, has had an important role in the history of the international legal order, as well as in the history of the world market that has arisen and thrived in the interstices of that order. The fight between the pirate and those taking upon themselves the burden of enforcing international law has been a drama endlessly repeated on the stage of history. Marx aptly notices that it is upon the existence of the criminal that depends on the authority of 'the whole of the police and of criminal justice, constables, judges, hangmen, juries, etc.' (1988: 310). Over and over again in history, hegemonic forces have tried to legitimize their claims to some form of global Imperial authority by appealing to the existence of pirates. If there are international criminals threatening international society, disrupting the legal order that sustain the global economy, endangering the security of all humankind, then we will need a 'global police force' and some 'international criminal justice', 'judges trained in international legal thought', a whole Imperial bureaucracy and, maybe, a global emperor on top. As we will see, since the days of the Roman Empire, the claim to serve humanity, extirpating those who threaten its welfare, has played a fundamental role in Imperial rhetoric.

The pirate, in short, had an essential role in the authoritative discourses of sovereignty and the law. Even more than the common criminal, the pirate 'produces an impression, partly moral and partly tragic, as the case may be, and in this way renders a "service" by arousing the moral and aesthetic feelings of the public' (Marx 1988: 311). And yet the pirate has also been appropriated by other discursive forms, which often challenge and ironically turn upside down official discourses. To borrow Marx's ironic words, the pirate 'produces not only compendia on Criminal Law, not only penal codes and along with them legislators in this field, but also art, belles-lettres, novels, and even tragedies. . . . The criminal breaks the monotony and everyday security of bourgeois life' (Marx 1988: 309). The figure of the pirate has thus attracted the attention of historians and legal scholars, of philosophers and students of literature. The pirate has produced countless books, of the most diverse sort, it crops up in the most unexpected shelves of our libraries and it casts its volatile shadow on whole sections of them.

First of all, the pirate has occupied historians since ancient times. Today, the interested reader can find numerous monographs giving more or less detailed accounts of piracy in different historical and geographical contexts. Those interested in the pirates of ancient Mediterranean history may turn to scholarly authorities such as Sestier (1880), Ormerod (1996), Monaco (1996) and De Souza (1999). Accounts of the Muslim and Christian corsairs that operated throughout the medieval period and until the early nineteenth century have been offered by important historians such as Lane-Pool (1890), Fisher (1974), Braudel (1996) and Wilson (2003). The important role of the Elizabethan Sea-Dogs and, in general, of the Protestant corsairs who challenged the Christian legal order of the early sixteenth century has been exposed, for instance, by Andrews (2011), Lane (1998) and Earle (2005). The freebooters and buccaneers who swarmed the Atlantic of the seventeenth century have been a constant subject of research with outstanding works by Haring (1910), Latimer (2009) and, obviously, Exquemelin (1684). Countless historians have offered detailed portrayals and intelligent studies of eighteenth-century pirates; among them I relied greatly on Johnson (1724), Jameson (1923), Ritchie (1986), Rediker (2004) and Linebaugh and Rediker (2000). Those who fought and were condemned as pirates by the European Empires of the nineteenth century, unfortunately, received less attention. Still, there is a multitude of interesting and detailed works on specific pirate groups. For instance, those interested in the Malay communities that were persecuted as 'piratical' in the nineteenth century may rely on Tarling (1963), Warren (2007), Prange (2011) and the extremely interesting anthropological study by Colchester (1989).

The pirates of the twentieth century have received scarce attention by contemporary historians. In return, they have received an extraordinary consideration in the work of international legal scholars. Those interested in the evolution of the law of nations have been enthralled by the exceptional status suffered by the pirate in that particular discursive construction. Authorities such as James Edward De Montmorency (1919), George Finch (1937), Raul Genet (1938), Hersch Lauterpacht (1939) and Carl Schmitt (1937) have fiercely debated the figure of the pirate and how it is to be defined. This controversy continues to the present day, with a number of important contributions that have attempted to reflect upon the growing importance of the pirate figure as a source of international criminal law. The bibliography is extensive, but one might start investigating the issue taking into consideration the work of Kontorovich (2004), Burgess (2005), Simpson (2006), Greene (2008) and Thorup (2012). A growing debate has also arisen around the contemporary global mobilization against piracy, particularly in the Gulf of Aden: Panjabi (2009) and Onuoha (2009) have offered important contributions for an understanding of the significance of the issue.

In the last decade, the figure of the pirate has also attracted the attention of philosophers and political theorists. In *The Enemy of All* (2009), Daniel Heller-Roazen went further than anybody else in the attempt to reconstruct an intellectual history of the concept of 'enemy of humanity', starting from the Roman origins of the concept. This admirable work of scholarship focuses on the evolution of legal thought, and it is able to show in a clear and convincing way how the concept of the pirate as *hostis humani generis*, which finds its origins in the Universalism of Imperial Roman law, and continued to serve as a 'state of exception' capable of suspending the order of international law throughout the modern age. It is a study that may usefully complement Agamben's study of the similar category of *Homo Sacer* (1998).

Unfortunately, Heller-Roazen limits his analysis to the figure of the pirate in legal theory, without considering the ways in which legal forms are most often little more than symptoms of much deeper material constitutions. The author shows that the pirate has often been considered, from the Roman Empire and until today, 'the enemy of all'. Nevertheless, legal concepts assume a specific meaning only when they are inserted in a particular social context and, thus, I believe that he left aside what is most interesting: why did the pirate assume such a title in the first place? What material necessities do the legal formulation that brands the pirate as *hostis humani generis* respond to? How did different empires, with different ideas of what humanity is, transform the concept of the pirate as *hostis communis omnium*? Why, in the eighteenth century, was a forgotten concept of Roman Imperial law suddenly resuscitated by a number of international legal scholars? How, in the nineteenth century, was the concept transformed in order to support the civilizing projects of increasingly industrialized European empires? Why, in the twentieth century, was there a return to the centre of European history what had been for centuries a concept relegated to the colonial world? And why was the traditional concept of the pirate as *hostis communis omnium* replaced today by the modern formulation that portrays the pirate as *hostis humani generis*? Why today, finally, has the figure of the pirate assumed an unprecedented significance?

One of the fundamental aims of this work is thus to show that behind the apparent inertia that characterizes the history of the concept of the pirate in international law we must hear the roar of battles, the sound of clashes of power, the howls produced in the struggles to impose particular visions of the world. Juridical transformations effectively point toward changes in the material constitution of world power and order. I do not think it possible to understand the history of the figure of the pirate in international law without, at the same time, studying the power struggles that have shaped, to a large extent, that history. This is why I always try to unite intellectual history with the material, concrete histories of pirates and empires.

Genealogical methods

Symmetrically opposed to the fascinating abstraction of Heller-Roazen's work of intellectual history, most historical reflections have considered the pirate as a real, material and bodily figure which opposes the state, the merchant class and sometimes an entire human civilization, and whose bellicosity forces the thinker and the writer to take sides: you are either with the pirate or with the state, with the irregularity of the marauder or with the discipline of the navy, with the violence of the criminal or with the annihilating power of the state and its war-machines. The trap of moral discourse is immediately set and it is easy to slip from analysis to condemnation, from research to pamphleteering.

Examples on both sides are abundant: from the celebration of working-class struggle, mutiny and maritime radicalism that echoes through the historical works of Marcus Rediker (2004) and Peter Linebaugh (2000) to the condemnatory tones, sympathetic to the cleansing power of the English Navy of more traditional historians like Peter Earle (2005) and Angust Konstam (2008). In these works the pirate appears in full shape, provided with full historical detail and is a particular, well-defined historical figure; the work of the historian is to render that image as clearly as possible and maybe to judge on the actions, the morality and the immorality of what is described. What remains unclear is what a pirate really is, how it comes into being, how it is produced through a power-knowledge that individuates it and marks it as different from the simple merchant, or the highway robber, or the political enemy. More than being interested in writing once again the history of piracy, these pages are therefore dedicated to the task of uncovering the production of the pirate image in a series of related historical discourses, and to understand what role this image has served in supporting the claims to power of sovereigns, emperors and various international institutions.

I consider the pirate 'a legend', just as the 'infamous men' to whom Michel Foucault (1977) dedicated one of his most emotional pieces of writing. First of all, 'because as in all legends there is a certain ambiguity between the fictional and the real' (Foucault 1977: 162). And secondarily, since it is hardly possible to think of pirates without also reflecting upon the nature of Empire. After all:

> the power that watched these lives, that pursued them, that lent its attention, if only for a moment, to their complaints and their little racket, and marked them with its claw was what gave rise to the few words about them that remain for us. . . . All those lives destined to pass beneath any discourse and disappear without ever having been told were able to leave traces – brief, incisive, often enigmatic – only at the point of their instantaneous contact with power. So that it is doubtless impossible to ever grasp them again in themselves, as they might have been 'in a free state'; they can no longer be separated out from the declamations, the tactical biases, the obligatory lies that power games and power relations presuppose.
>
> (Foucault 1977: 161)

Sometimes, especially in popular literature, we might find the pirates speak back to those who condemn them, but even then:

> the brief and strident words that went back and forth between power and the most infamous existences doubtless constitute for the latter the only monument they have ever been granted: it is what gives them, for the passage through time, the bit of brilliance, the brief flash that carries them to us.
>
> (Foucault 1977: 162)

When one considers the juridical, literary, political and historical texts in which different subjects are condemned as pirates, it is necessary to keep in mind that these discourses not only refer to reality, but they are directly 'operative within it; that they form part of the dramaturgy of the real; that they constitute the instrument of a retaliation, the weapon of a hatred, an episode in a battle, the gesticulation of a despair or a jealousy, an entreaty or an order' (Foucault 1977: 160). When the representatives of Empire portray their violence as a service to mankind – and those who they eliminate as 'enemies of all', 'enemies of humanity' or 'enemies of the human race' – it must be remembered that:

> whatever their inaccuracy, their exaggeration, or their hypocrisy, . . . real lives were 'played out' in these few sentences: and this does not mean that they were faithfully represented but that their liberty, their misfortune, often their death, in any case their fate, were actually decided therein, at least in part. These discourses really crossed lives; existences were actually risked and lost in these words.
>
> (Foucault 1977: 161)

My methodology, my aim, my way of thinking is therefore neither historical, nor philosophical, neither literary nor scientific, but properly genealogical. As Michel Foucault has discussed in his early essay 'Nietzsche, Genealogy, History', the work of genealogy is first of all to investigate those elements which 'we tend to feel are without history' (1977: 146). This would include such things as sexuality, and other elements of everyday life, but also historical characters like the madman, the criminal and, I argue, the pirate. Genealogy is not the search of origins, and is not the construction of a linear development. Instead, it seeks to deconstruct the artificial unity imposed on the chaotic nature of history by language, discourse and power. Genealogical works therefore do not ask: 'What is the real nature of a particular subject?', nor do they attempt to preside in judgement over history; the aim is rather to understand how a particular concept has developed through time: genealogy follows the breaks, the ruptures, the invasions of power into language. Genealogy studies how knowledge – the words we use and the ideas we employ in discourse – is always to be understood as a weapon in an always-evolving matrix of power. Genealogy is first of all a history of the present.

Outline of the chapters

The first part of the book is dedicated to a study of the pirate figure as it appears in the context of various global orders from antiquity until the early eighteenth century. The second part follows the ways in which the spectre of eighteenth-century piracy continues to haunt modern international law, playing an important role in the history of European Imperialism, in the escalation to total war in the twentieth century, and today in the context of the war on terror. Each chapter is divided in three sections: the first introduces the fundamental characteristics of the global order under scrutiny; the second focuses on the ways in which the image of the pirate has been constructed in each historical period; and the third discusses some of the paradigmatic pirate figures of the age and examines their role in history, philosophy and literature. This linear mode of exposition is followed throughout the first and the second part, with only occasional variations. The aim is to contextualize systematically how and why particular individuals and groups were perceived and described as 'piratical' in a certain historical and geographical context. In this way, it becomes possible to consider the significant historical continuities that underlie different discourses that, throughout history, have made use of the concept of 'the pirate'; but also, it enables us to follow the ways in which the meaning of that same concept changed in passing from one global order to another. There is a sense in which pirates have always been with us and yet, beneath the superficial timelessness of the subject, we discover fundamental discontinuities, sudden turnarounds, discursive shifts that transform the meaning of what a pirate is supposed to be.

The first chapter introduces the main line of argumentation and analyses the structural relationship between the concepts of piracy and Empire. I do this through an investigation of how these two concepts were originally constructed in the context of Roman Imperial law. I discuss the reasons why they emerged almost simultaneously at the centre of a common discursive framework, and the many ways in which they mutually reinforced each other. First of all, I reflect upon the meaning of the concept of *imperium* as it was originally understood in ancient Rome. In the Imperial imaginary that was forged by the convergence of Greek cosmopolitanism and Roman hegemonic power, the world was sustained by what Aristotle called a *koinos nomos*, a Universal law of mankind. This is why the concept of *imperium* had probably its earliest and most consistent use in the particular space of commerce and cultural exchange that was the ancient Mediterranean. In this space, subtracted from all forms of *dominium*, possession and sovereignty, Rome presented itself as a bastion of peace and order, as the enforcer of the Universal law of nations (*ius gentium*) and as a steward, exercising jurisdictional rights in order to prevent abuses of the maritime commons rather than tracing lines of inclusion and exclusion. In the second section, I consider the origin and meaning of the figure of the pirate in Roman law, trying to understand the discursive framework that sustained its depiction as the 'enemy of all communities'. Finally, I explore the history of Roman persecutions against pirate communities in the Mediterranean, trying to understand the contemporary significance of the forgotten institution of the *persecutio piratarum*: a form of Imperial violence that claims to act, in the name of humanity at large, against a common enemy beyond international law.

The second chapter explores the evolution of the concept of Empire in the medieval *res publica Christiana* and the ways in which the figure of the pirate emerged once again in the context of an epochal conflict between Catholic Spain and the major Protestant countries, over the right to preach, trade and conquer in the lands of the New World. Supported by the authority of the Pope, the Spanish and Portuguese monarchies claimed an *imperium* over the Atlantic Ocean in order to protect and defend the evangelization of the Americas. Since they were acting in the name of the entire *res publica Christiana*, they considered the English corsairs who contested and attacked their mission to be pirates – i.e. enemies of the entire Christian system of international law. From the Spanish perspective, the excommunicated heretics who crossed the papal line of demarcation were not public enemies but *hostis communis omnium*. The pirates originated, sponsored and supported by Protestant nations were the vanguard of a new freedom outside the Universalism of the Christian legal order. They were a religious Other, who challenged not only Spanish interests but the unity of the entire Christian commonwealth. They were a revolutionary force of global historical significance insofar as they opened a rupture within the edifice of medieval law, a rupture in which a new order of international law moved its first steps.

The third chapter discusses the ways in which a new global order, based on a strict division between Europe and the New World, emerged in the second half of the sixteenth century. The conflict between the Spanish Empire and the Lutheran corsairs, which threatened to plunge the whole Christian community into an escalating civil war, was quarantined in a special zone: a zone of plunder in which 'might made right' and lawless plunder could take its place in a threshold between legality and illegality. With the *amity lines* of the seventeenth century, the international legal order continued to be centred in Europe, but now it suspended itself in the oceanic vastness beyond the line. The New World was therefore constituted as a 'free space' – that is, a space free from the restrictions of morality and the international legal order. The pirate here is not a criminal against international law – as it was in the early sixteenth century, as long as a Universal Christian legal order was recognized to exist – but strictly an outlaw, a freebooter. The chapter reflects upon the ambiguity of this classical figure. On the one hand, throughout the sixteenth and the seventeenth centuries, freebooting played a fundamental role in the primitive accumulation of European capital and it was tolerated and even sponsored by European states. On the other, the unleashing of private violence in the anomic spaces beyond the line often meant also the possibility of losing control of it. The exceptional status of the oceanic spaces beyond the line made them a dangerous space, where violence was omnipresent, relationships of power were often brutal, and trade was systematically intertwined with Imperialism, outright plunder and the kidnapping of slaves. But this exceptionality made them also a place of extraordinary freedom and recurrent rebellion, mutiny, insurrection: the turning upside down of traditional relationships of power. Thus, I look at the organization of the privateering ship as both an engine of primitive accumulation and as a capitalist heterotopia; but I also follow the rise and decline of the Caribbean Buccaneers: the disorganized rabble that, in the seventeenth century, inflamed the fantasies of the European public as the embodiment of a savage freedom.

In the fourth chapter, I concentrate on what has been defined by modern historians as the 'Golden Age of Piracy', covering approximately 1670 to 1720. In this half a century, an unprecedented military mobilization against piracy gradually unfolds. It is a play of cruelty and opposed terrors, which has the oceans of the world as its theatre, and the community of modern states against the last partisans of the sea as protagonists. The pirates of the Golden Age represent the last sentinels of a fading conception of the oceans as a space of absolute freedom, which was still dominant in the previous century. In the early eighteenth century, in fact, the exceptional spaces navigated by the lawless freebooter and the anarchic buccaneer progressively disappear. These paradigmatic figures of the space of exception, then, are forced either to enter the order of the state or to be declared enemies of the modern international system, at this point still solidly centred in Europe. Those freebooters who refused to discipline their hostility were therefore treated as systemic enemies of the emerging international order and hanged en masse as denationalized individuals, stripped of their rights. The construction of the capitalist world market, the reduction of the oceans into a hyperspace of commercial circulation, the erection of a modern community of interdependent states centred in Europe, all required the annihilation of the pirate and of its absolute freedom. In the final part, therefore, I discuss the closure of the Golden Age of piracy and its legacy, which pulses at the heart of modernity and international law.

The second part of the book is concerned with the ways in which the image of the pirate that emerged in the early-modern period captured the European imagination, and left a profound trace in the evolution of the modern international order. In a brief intermezzo, I discuss the profound fascination that the pirate character has exercised on the imagination of almost three centuries of readers and writers. I contemplate over the complex and often contradictory role of eighteenth-century pirate narratives, suspended between a moralizing celebration of the recurrent triumph of civilization over lawlessness and a carnivalesque enjoyment in the representation of clamorous transgressions. I look at the romantic celebration of the pirate as paradigmatic outlaw: a towering figure embodying the awe-inspiring resistance of wild nature against industrial civilization, of sublime individuality against collective discipline, of desire against reason, of dangerous freedom against the security of urban confinement. I point to the remnants of the pirate image in contemporary expressions of popular culture.

The fifth chapter is concerned with the ways in which the concept of the pirate continued to dwell in the colonial world of the nineteenth century. It is in the context of European Imperialist expansionism that the figure of the pirate continued to play an important role in global history, well after the end of the Golden Age of piracy. The same European states that recognized each other as equal members of a single civilization most often denied a similar recognition to extra-European polities. As a consequence, a number of extra-European groups were condemned as piratical on the basis of their attacks on European trade. The concept was singularly useful to Imperial rhetoric since, once labelled as pirates, native subjects could be persecuted as stateless outlaws and their destruction presented as a service to humanity and civilization. In particular, it was the British Empire that affirmed itself as a liberal power, enforcing a Universal right to free trade in the name of all people. The genocide of entire Malay communities was thus justified by their condemnation as 'piratical people', and even the statehood of important Malay sultanates was openly denied once they were portrayed as 'piratical states'. Similarly, in the Mediterranean, the Barbary States were gradually stripped of their traditional legitimacy and international recognition, depicted as insufferable pirates' dens, bombarded by the American and the British Navy, until the French Empire finally subjugated them. The application of an exogenous concept to the Barbary cities of North Africa played an important part in the erasure of a long, regional history of diplomatic exchange and international equality. The recurring condemnation of the North African cities as 'pirate states', of their acts of war as 'piracies', and of their corsairs as 'pirates' prepared the ground for European colonization.

The sixth chapter follows the post-colonial trajectory by which the modern concept of the pirate as 'enemy of the human race', which served an important role in the history of Imperialism, eventually travelled back to the European centre. I thus reflect on the collapse of the *jus publicum europaeum* through an investigation of the heated debates that accompanied the advent of 'total war' during the first half of the twentieth century. In particular, I scrutinize the frame of ideas of international legal scholars such as James Edward De Montmorency who, breaking with the classical tradition of international law, urged the condemnation of Germany as a 'pirate state' at war with whole mankind. More generally, I argue that the continuous evocation of the pirate spectre was vital for the early development of international criminal law, a view that is distinctly supported by even a cursory glance at the writings of cosmopolitan legal scholars such as Hans Kelsen, Georges Scelle and Hersch Leuterpacht. Since the pirate concept appeared as a unique anomaly in an otherwise state-centric international law – which evoked perspectives of Universal jurisdiction, global policing and humanitarian intervention – it became singularly significant in order to enable a gradual transition to a more cosmopolitan conception of the international legal order. In fact, by establishing an analogy with eighteenth-century pirates, states could subject *any* offence against international law to Universal jurisdiction, beginning with unrestricted submarine warfare.

The final chapter discusses the many ways in which the spectre of the pirate continues to guide contemporary transformations of international law, projecting itself over ever-changing subjects, taking newfangled clothes and names, disguising itself. First, I consider the essential role played by the figure of the pirate in the rhetorical and juridical construction of new 'enemies of the human race'. Both 'terrorists' and 'criminals against humanity' have been recently construed as *hostes humani generis* relying on a systematic analogy with classical pirates. In order to protect humanity from their threatening presence, new practices of global security have been introduced and fundamental norms of international law have been suspended, while 'humanitarian bombings', 'surgical strikes' and 'targeted killings' have been legitimized as exceptional but necessary measures. I follow some of the key historical moments in the genealogy of the contemporary concept of 'the terrorist' from the early twentieth century until today, focusing in particular on the discourses surrounding the persecution of 'anarchist terrorism', 'Palestinian terrorism' and 'Islamic terrorism'.

Finally, I look at contemporary perceptions of maritime piracy through an analysis of the recent global mobilization against Somali piracy. Prior to the rise of the pirate threat, no other issue could have brought the navies of the United States, the EU nations, NATO, China, Japan, Iran and Russia to identify a single common enemy and a single common cause. As opposed to the 'war on terror', the current global mobilization against pirates seems to be politically uncontroversial: a simple issue of global policing and international law-enforcing. The pirate, thus, continues to be the figure that most perfectly embodies the idea of an apolitical pest to be suppressed and removed. In the contemporary *persecutio piratarum,* even more than in the 'War on Terror', violence is not presented as a weapon in a confrontation between equal enemies, but as an instrument meant to serve and protect humanity. In this sense, we might be witnessing the first steps of a global biopolitical logic, which goes beyond traditional national paradigms.

Part I

Pirate figures (1400–1800)

Chapter 1

Persecutio piratarum

Pirate outlaws and the Roman Empire

The Roman Empire has been, throughout modernity, the paradigmatic Empire. Notwithstanding their innovations, all modern European Imperial formations looked back to the ancient world, and most of all to the Roman legacy, for inspiration and for a veneer of historical continuity. It was in the history of Rome that modern polities like Spain, France, England and then the United States found the language and the political model that today we associate with the word 'empire'. The Roman Empire always retained a fundamental role in the European imagination. In this sense, the Roman legacy profoundly shaped the ways in which modern international politics and modern international law developed, centuries after the collapse of Latin power. The Roman Empire remained an *Imperial model*, against which it was possible to compare and measure all other Imperial formations. In other words, following Maurice Duverger, we could say that there is a *concept of empire*, which rests essentially on a particular organisation of space and a consequent distribution of people in space (Duverger 1980: 1–12).

The term *imperium* itself originally described the sphere of executive authority possessed by Roman authorities, and it had marked sacral overtones. It was understood to exist side by side with the institution of *dominium*, which defined the exclusive possession of a territory by a community, or an individual. It was, therefore, from the beginning, something different from mere sovereignty over an enclosed space. It indicated a claim to rule and to exercise authority, even beyond the borders that defined one's exclusive possessions. The Roman people had certainly a vast dominion: an expanding collection of territories directly under their control, and over which only the laws of Rome had effectiveness. But they also claimed an *imperium* – that is, a claim to power – which extended well beyond their borders. Rome understood itself not only as a powerful polity, whose domination extended across a number of distant lands; it was also the centre of a civilization. For Roman philosophers such as Cicero, the *civitas* was the sole place of human flourishing; the walls that enclosed the city of Rome were the incubators of the most humane way of life ever achieved, the source of a form of culture and knowledge that was potentially Universal in scope.

Under the later Republic, and then increasingly during the Principate of Augustus, the concept of *imperium* became increasingly suffused with the cosmopolitan aspirations bred by a renovated Stoicism. For philosophers and statesmen, Rome represented the centre of a single Universal civilization, which would eventually include the whole of humanity under a single set of laws and regulations. Roman power could act according to its own particular interests, but it could also be a force in service of this higher cosmopolitan law. It was in the latter case, when Roman might was ostensibly deployed in the service of the cosmopolitan community, that Rome presented itself as an Imperial power. The most important instance of this form of Imperial interventionism is probably identifiable in the *persecutio piratarum*, an institution of Roman law that allowed Roman power to act in the Mediterranean – understood as a space subjected to Roman power and common to all people – as upholder of a Universal *ius gentium*.

In this chapter, therefore, I consider the role of the pirate figure in Roman law, Imperial theory and rhetoric. First of all, I give a brief presentation of the law of nations as they were understood in ancient Rome. I consider in particular why the Mediterranean Sea was understood as a space beyond Roman domination, and the ways in which interventions in this common space were justified as a service to the whole human community. I then consider the origin and meaning of the figure of the pirate in Roman law, trying to understand the discursive framework that sustained its depiction as the 'enemy of all communities'. Finally, I explore the history of Roman persecutions against pirate communities in the Mediterranean, trying to understand the contemporary significance of the forgotten institution of the *persecutio piratarum*: a form of Imperial violence that claims to act, in the name of humanity at large, against a common enemy beyond international law.

A Mediterranean *imperium*

The history of the Roman Empire, its growth from a small town on the Palatine Hill to the urban centre of an extended Imperial *dominium* that included most of the ancient Mediterranean, was intimately bound and influenced by its proximity to the sea. The Italian peninsula juts far out into the Mediterranean waters, effectively dividing the Mediterranean in two halves, the Eastern and Western Mediterranean. To the east lie the sites of the ancient Greek civilization, Crete, the Phoenician coast and the Middle East. To the west lie the southern coasts of France and Spain, the northern coast of Africa and the Straits of Gibraltar, known in ancient times as the extreme limit of the habitable world: the Pillars of Hercules. Inevitably the history of Rome, like the one of the Greek *poleis* of the ancient world, was profoundly shaped by the Mediterranean Sea. Nevertheless, Rome remained for a long time essentially a land-power. While the Mediterranean Sea formed a major focal point of Greek culture and civilization, Roman history and literature remained for a long time ultimately tied to the land.

Roman power was initially firmly rooted in the military might of its armies, and until the beginning of the First Punic War Rome had virtually no fleet under its control. According to Fik Meijer:

> The early Romans . . . starting out as a small agrarian community had taken only two centuries to gain ascendancy over the whole Italian peninsula. This had been achieved without a single ship and they had never even so much felt the want of a ship . . . When in 349BC Greek pirates approached the coast of Latium the Romans were unable to fit out a fleet to defeat them. Instead, they stationed soldiers along the coast to prevent the pirates from landing.
>
> (1986: 149)

A fleet was constructed only in the course of the century-long confrontation that opposed Rome to the maritime power of Carthage, which dominated the Mediterranean until the end of the second century BC.

In the last two centuries of the Roman Republic, after the defeat of Carthage, Mediterranean trade increased exponentially, and Rome became the centre of a vast trading network that brought to the port of Ostia riches coming from the Roman provinces of the Eastern and the Western Mediterranean. All provinces shipped cargoes to Rome, either as a yearly tribute or as a contribution to its thriving markets:

> Alexandria provided the Roman aristocrats with papyrus; Pergamum supplied parchment and coloured glass. Marble was shipped from the island of Paros as well as from Athens and Euboea. Purple-yielding molluscs and sponges were brought from the Eastern Aegean. Even ivory from India made its way to Rome, via Alexandria and Delos, as well as precious metals and stones.
>
> (Meijer 1986: 187–188)

Meanwhile, the Roman landholding elites in the Italian peninsula increasingly specialized in high-value crops such as wine and olive oil, which was exported throughout the Roman Empire. The growth of enlarged landing estates (*latifundia*) was based on the exploitation of slave labour. After each military campaign, thousands of slaves were brought to Italy in order to serve the needs of the landholding class: in 174 BC, the conquest of Sardinia ended with the capture of 40,000 slaves; in 167 BC, over 150,000 slaves were brought away from Epirus; in 146 BC, the destruction of Carthage resulted in the arrival of over 50,000 people on the Roman slave market (Harris 1999: 62–75). A Mediterranean market was thus formed in which slaves and grain poured into Rome, while the latter gradually became a net exporter of military power and high-value agricultural products (De Martino 1965: 113–124).

It is only at this point that controlling the sea became a fundamental requirement of Empire. The senatorial landholding class looked to the Mediterranean Sea for the promise of markets for the high-value crops grown in the Italian peninsula; the new emerging class of maritime merchants, the *equites*, considered the sea their main area of operation; the plebeians were increasingly reduced to a complete dependence from maritime trade for their very survival (Martin 1971: 51–54). De Martino (1965) shows how the availability of cheap grain from Sicily and the Eastern provinces contributed to the ruin of the small landholding class, which was the backbone of the Republic. In a vicious circuit, then, the commerce that was initially only economically convenient became vital since the cultivation of grain and basic foodstuffs in Italy was largely abandoned.

As the urban population increased in the second and first centuries BC – also as a result of the dispossession of large numbers of peasants, whose land was usually incorporated to larger estates cultivated by slave labour – grain imports became more and more necessary. Already during the second century BC the agricultural surplus yielded by the Italian peninsula did not suffice to feed the growing urban population in Rome. In order to support its over 800,000 inhabitants, Rome depended on the grain produced in its Mediterranean provinces. According to Meijer, by the end of the second century BC:

> the entire population of the city would require at least 175,000 tons of grain per year. Local production amounted to 20,000 tons at most, so that 150,000 tons had to be imported by sea. The average tonnage of freighters being 300 tons, a minimum of 500 grain ships must have reached Ostia every year in order to feed the Roman people.
>
> (1986: 191)

The growing importance of commerce, and of maritime transport in general, rapidly augmented the political power of the merchant class, and elevated the effective control of circulation in the Mediterranean Sea into a political issue of vital significance. The centrality of commercial circulation for the Roman economy soon posed the political issue of how to govern a smooth space, which in order to serve as a plane of circulation among different communities could not be simply occupied, fenced and closed off. The classical Roman understanding of the Mediterranean Sea as a social space had emerged during the century-long Punic Wars. Roman doctrine was originally based on a philosophical and juridical position critical of Carthage's hegemonic maritime power, which precluded free passage for Roman ships and at times severely limited its commercial exchanges. Against Carthage's maritime might, Roman jurists claimed that the Mediterranean could not be occupied by any single power. It was instead to be considered *res communis omnium*: a space common to all Mediterranean people. According to this conception, no one could be excluded from the Sea, and no single power could impose its laws over it (Reppy 1950).

After the defeat of Carthage, Roman law continued to consider the sea a commons shared by all communities, which could not be claimed by any single power. Nevertheless, it increasingly strived to regulate this 'common space' promoting certain particular uses of it, while actively discouraging others. As concluded by the British historian, Michael Fenn:

> the sea was held to be free to the common use of all men . . . There were claims to the right to exercise jurisdiction over some part of the sea, or to

> possess the *imperium*: yet this claim was not expanded into a claim involving any sort of property right to the sea itself, that is, the claim to *imperium* was not developed into a claim to *dominum*.
>
> (1925: 724)

And further: 'the Roman jurists, postulating a legal person which is created in agreement with the most recent jurist philosophy, regarded the coasts and the seas as being protected and guarded by the Roman people as "a sacred trust of civilization"' (1925: 726).

Although Roman power grew to the point of occupying most of the coasts surrounding the Mediterranean Sea, it never claimed exclusive ownership of the sea itself. Roman jurists continued considering the sea to be outside direct Roman domination. Yet they justified the use of Roman hegemonic power in order to prevent abuses of the Mediterranean commons, and to enforce the *ius gentium* defined as a set of laws common to all people (Gormley 1963). According to this conception, Rome acted as an Imperial power, insofar as it claimed to act not simply out of its own interest, but rather as the servant of a higher law, deemed common to all men. Historians of Rome have shown how the concept of *imperium* had its earliest and most consistent use in the particular space of commerce and cultural exchange that was the ancient Mediterranean (Rosello 1962). In this space, subtracted from all forms of *dominium*, possession and sovereignty, Rome presented itself as a bastion of peace and order, as the enforcer of the Universal law of nations (*ius gentium*) and as a steward: exercising jurisdictional rights in order to prevent abuses of common space, rather than tracing lines of inclusion and exclusion (Gormley 1963). As Philip Steinberg has noticed:

> [Rome] exercised its stewardship role as it saw fit, primarily toward the end of maintaining the Mediterranean as a space wherein its troops and goods could be transported among the far-flung reaches of the empire. Thus, to the casual observer, the Mediterranean appears to be 'Roman space'. But legal studies of Rome's ocean law clearly demonstrate that the Mediterranean was perceived and governed as a space distinctly outside the Roman state, even as it was recognized as a legitimate arena for the exercise of Roman power.
>
> (1999a: 259)

According to Hugo Grotius' reading of the classical sources:

> Those who say that a certain sea belonged to the Roman people explain their statement to mean that the right of the Romans did not extend beyond protection and jurisdiction; this right they distinguish from ownership. Perchance we do not pay sufficient attention to the fact that although the Roman people were able to maintain fleets for the protection of navigation

> and to punish pirates captured at sea, this was not done for Roman own right, but for the common right by which all free people enjoy the sea.
>
> (2001: 35)

This is significant because it allows us to distinguish clearly between *dominium* and *imperium* as two distinct technologies of power. In the classic Latin tradition, the first always relates to the land and essentially corresponds with what we currently understand as exclusive property and sovereignty; the second most often relates to the Mediterranean Sea and it is a power that evokes contemporary theories of global governance, security and control. *Dominium* essentially means control and effective occupation of the territory, the setting of firm boundaries, and the establishment of a law that regulates the occupation and distribution of the land. *Imperium*, on the other hand, is not affixed to a territory; it refers rather to a space of circulation that must be kept in motion. The principle of *imperium* in fact is not the law with its intimate relationship with the boundary, but security in a global space. As argued by W.P. Gormley, the origin of *imperium* was intimately related to the necessity to impose control and security over a common space, outside sovereign jurisdiction:

> Under the *ius gentium*, the sea was open to the legitimate use of everyone, it was *res communis*; still it was not in a state of anarchy or beyond effective control. . . . The Romans never hesitated to utilize military power in a completely ruthless manner once they determined that such action was desirable on behalf of the general welfare.
>
> (1963: 561)

In the last years of the Republic, Rome obtained absolute hegemonic power over the Mediterranean region and the whole area was increasingly integrated within a multiplicity of intertwining networks of commercial exchange. The Mediterranean ceased to be a space symmetrically opposed to the order of the city and of the tilled land, a zone of anti-civilization populated by monsters and gods and traversed by waves of absolute and persistent danger. The Mediterranean Sea, therefore, started to be conceived as a space that, although subjected to Roman domination, sustained and enabled the existence of urban life: an essential plane of transportation, a conveyor belt on which provincial governors and armies were expected to travel regularly outbound and North African grain ships were required to moor in the City's ports with clockwork regularity. The sea, thus, was conceived as a space naturally predisposed for free commerce, movement and circulation. The Universal *ius gentium* was considered to command respect of this freedom (Fenn 1925).

The sea was therefore considered a 'global commons', regulated by a Universal law of nations, which was deemed binding for all communities. Roman jurists often considered the *ius gentium* to be rooted in human nature and yet they insisted that it would require consistent enforcement to become effective in the regulation of common global spaces such as the sea (Pollock 1901). Roman power, in other words, was necessary for the transformation of the Mediterranean Sea into a vast transnational market, which would have completed the integration of all people under the benevolent hegemony of Roman Imperial power. In the process, Rome would have transformed itself from a mighty Republic bent toward military expansion, into an Imperial power responsible for the crafting and the maintenance of a Mediterranean *pax romana* (Parchami 2009: 13–59).

Those resisting (and thus endangering) the existence of a regulated common space resting on a Universal *ius gentium* were increasingly portrayed as enemies of all Mediterranean people. They could be thus suppressed by Roman power in the name of this emerging global Imperial order (Tarwacka 2009: 56–67). 'Since the sea was primarily conceived as a surface for the movement of troops and goods,' writes Steinberg, 'interventions in this space were not meant to conquer new territories but were centred on ridding the space of pirates and other oppositional forces that could impede the flow of goods and people' (2001: 66). Classic warfare punctuated the expansionist drive of an Imperialist Roman Republic. The persecution of pirates, instead, as I show in the next section, rapidly emerged as the paradigmatic form of violence of a consolidated Roman Empire, which understood itself as a force preserving international peace and enforcing the *ius gentium* in the name of all peoples.

The pirate as *hostis communis omnium*

According to Roman historians such as Lucia Monaco (1996) and Monique Clavel-Léveque (1976), the gradual problematization of piracy in the Mediterranean can only be understood in relation to the unprecedented importance that commerce took in the late Republican period. In the third century AD, the gradual transformation of the Roman economy led to a crisis of traditional forms of subsistence farming and to the emergence of a market-oriented economy, which was founded on the export of high-value crops produced in large estates tilled by slave labour. In this new socio-economic system, commerce was not simply a marginal phenomenon; instead it became essential to the maintenance of Roman civilization itself (Cavazzuti 2004). It is from the periphery of the Roman Imperial world, in fact, that most of the agricultural products arrived that were necessary to feed both the slave-labour, employed to produce high-value crops, and the plebeians, a growing urban population of dispossessed, often on the brink of revolt and kept content only by stable provisions of *panem et circenses* (Clavel-Léveque 1976).

The central role played by maritime commerce in the development of Roman civilization required the imposition of forms of governance, security and control over the sea-commons. Piracy, in particular, was identified as a practice whose eradication was necessary in order to make stable and secure the expanding networks of trade and communication that sustain urban life. As the foremost scholar of the international laws of piracy, Alfred P. Rubin, has written:

> it appears that there was a change in Roman conceptions under way. To label a group 'pirates' was not merely to classify their way of life . . . . By the time Plutarch wrote, there was an implication of impropriety to that way of life, . . . an antiquated way of life in a new commercial and political order, which could no longer countenance interference with trade in the Mediterranean Sea.
> (2006: 10)

As the importance of commerce grew, piracy became increasingly a practice that was not only unacceptable but actually considered inimical to Roman civilization.

The origins of the figure of the pirate as 'enemy of all', thus, must be traced back to the constitutional transformations that invested the Roman Republic in the second and first centuries BC. As Lucia Monaco (1996) has shown, the emergence of the figure of the pirate at the centre of the philosophy of neo-Stoic philosophers like Cicero might be read as an important symptom of these historical transformations, which participated in the adaptation of the ancient Roman Republic to its new Imperial role. The elaboration of the concept of the pirate within Roman legal thinking, in other words, was an essential part of a wider legal and political alteration. During the transition from a Republican to an Imperial constitution, Rome ceased considering itself as a political community among others; it became instead an Imperial power, imposing the observance of a sacred peace (the Pax Romana) and a Universal law (the *ius gentium*).

While wars of an earlier period were usually understood as symmetrical conflicts opposing Rome to another, equally legitimate, political community, during the Principate, Rome increasingly conceived itself as an Imperial power, enforcing the *ius gentium* against disqualified communities of pirates (Domingo 2010: 3–11). The Empire appeared simultaneously as a cosmopolitan power – whose might was at the service of a crystallized peace – as an enforcer of international law, and as a steward of the Mediterranean commons. Accordingly, Imperial military interventions were increasingly depicted as a service rendered to all Mediterranean communities, which were seen as a united front against those who endangered the stability of the overall order. As the Western half of the empire trembled under the invasions of the fourth century AD, Claudian could still write that Rome 'has received the conquered into her bosom, and like a mother, not an empress, protects the whole human kind, summoning those whom she has defeated to share her citizenship . . . We are all one people' (cited in Koebner 1961: 15).

The expansionist drive of the Roman armies thus became the iron hand with which to realize the cosmopolitan ideal that according to Plutarch had been envisioned by Zeno himself, the founder of the Stoic School:

> we all should live not in cities and regions, each distinguished by separate legal systems, but should regard all men as fellow neighbours and fellow citizens;

> there should be only one life and order as of a single flock feeding together on a common pasture.
>
> (cited in Baldry 1965: 159)

Certainly a critical spirit initially suffused cosmopolitan philosophy, which allowed the Stoic thinkers to criticise the exclusionary nature of particular institutions in the name of the fundamental unity of mankind. And yet cosmopolitanism also served as quintessential Imperial ideology, at least in the late Roman Republic. When the hegemonic power of the ancient world embraced cosmopolitan ideals, the *ius gentium* – that is, the particular Roman conception of the law of nations – 'became the embodiment of what Aristotle had called a *koinos nomos*, a universal law for all mankind . . . The civil law itself, which had been created by human reason out of an understanding of the natural law, was the human law, the *lex humanus*. Those who lived by it were, by definition, humans; those who did not, were not' (Pagden 1995: 20).

On this basis, the Roman philosopher and politician Cicero was one of the first and most influential thinkers to elaborate a cosmopolitan philosophy that had at its centre three elements: the affirmation of a Universal law binding all human communities; the elevation of the Roman Empire to the role of enforcer of this Universal law; and the justification of operations of eradication and suppression of those who, negating the validity of the *ius gentium*, endangered the unity of mankind. In the philosophy of Cicero, exposed most clearly in the *De Officiis*, we find a direct connection between a political conception of humanity as the wider community that includes all other communities, and the idea of the pirate as 'enemy of all' (Cicero 2006: 288). It is in this sense that Cicero quotes approvingly the historian Lucius Anneus Florus when he accused the pirates of breaking the bond that unites the human community: 'The Cilician pirates made the sea unviable and, interrupting trade, broke the pact that unites humankind' [*Cilices invaserant maria sublatisque commerciis, rupto foedere generis humani*] (2006: 73).

According to Cicero, there is a 'natural fraternity' that associates 'all members of the human race' (2006: 30). This natural fraternity is born of us sharing reason and speech, which engenders the possibility of communicating, and thus recognizing one another as members of the same species. This bond is further reinforced by the fact that all individuals and all communities share a number of things in common, which must be preserved free and open to all. Cicero writes:

> This, then, is the most comprehensive bond that unites together men as men and all to all; and under it the common right to all things that Nature has produced for the common use of man is to be maintained, with the understanding that, while everything assigned as private property by the statutes and by civil law shall be so held as prescribed by those same laws, everything else shall be regarded in the light indicated by the Greek proverb: 'Amongst friends all things in common.'
>
> (2006: 32)

From the existence of *res communis omnium*, such as the sea, derived a number of maxims like: 'Deny no one the water that flows by.' These maxims were considered by Cicero not to pertain to the *ius civile*, which regulated the life of the Roman Republic; they were rather part of the Universal laws of nations, which he saw as the juridical embodiment of nature (*natura, id est iure gentium*). The *ius gentium*, according to Cicero, is the only law that unites all people in a single 'human society' (*societas omnium inter omnes*) and it must be considered valid for all people, even if it is not written down (Cicero 2006: 20–30). This is why a number of authors have gone so far as considering Cicero 'the father of the law of nations' (Domingo 2010: 2). Cicero probably coined the term, but the concept rapidly established itself in Roman philosophy and law, so that the *ius gentium* is mentioned in the writings of Seneca and in Tacitus, 'and again in the jurists of the second century: Celsus, Gaius, Cervidius Scaevola. It is also found, in the beginning of the third century, in Papinian and Triphoninus – advisors to the Emperor Septimius Severus – and in Ulpian' (Domingo 2010: 9). According to Ulpian in particular, just as the *ius civile* was meant to regulate public life in the city, the *ius gentium* was meant to regulate the use of what is common to all peoples, including the high seas (*hoc solis hominibus inter se commune sit*) (Weinreb 1987: 45).

Those who violate these common rules that tie together the human community – understood as the sum total of all families, groups and nations – are thus considered by Cicero 'enemies of all'. Respect for the *ius civile* and the traditions of one's own people cannot justify actions against the *ius gentium* since those:

> who say that regard should be had for the rights of fellow-citizens, but not for those of foreigners, would destroy the universal brotherhood of mankind; and, when this is annihilated, kindness, generosity, goodness, and justice must utterly perish; and those who work all this destruction must be considered as wickedly rebelling against the immortal gods. For they uproot the fellowship the gods have established between human beings.
>
> (Cicero 2006: 221)

Naturally, this left open the fundamental question of what this *ius gentium* exactly commanded and who could legitimately interpret it. Moreover, what force could have been entrusted with enforcing that interpretation?

The consequences of 'breaking the pact that unites humankind' are not always clear in Cicero's writing. In the case of pirates, Cicero explicitly states that, since they imperil commerce and impede the Universal right to freely dispose of the Mediterranean commons, they are disqualified from the *ius gentium* and all agreements, promises, conventions and laws which may bind other people to them are to be considered void: 'We have laws regulating warfare, and fidelity to an oath must be observed in dealing with an enemy . . . ', and yet 'a pirate is not included in the number of lawful enemies, but is rather the common enemy of all, with him there ought not to be any pledged word nor any oath mutually binding' (2006: 288). Pirate communities such as the Cilicians, therefore, may have been considered excluded from the human community and punishable for their lack of respect for the common rights of all people to travel and trade freely in the Mediterranean. In light of their disregard of the *ius gentium*, Cicero considered the pirates *hostes communis omnium.*[1]

In fact, Cicero's wording closely follows Roman ordinances such as the *lex de pirates* of 101 BC, written almost 60 years before, which justified the Roman invasion of Cilicia as an extreme measure meant to protect the common right to trade and travel throughout the Mediterranean:

> Roman citizens and their Latin allies in Italy must be able to conduct their business affairs . . . without danger and they may be able to sail the seas in safety. . . . Cilicia was occupied by the Roman people for these reasons and not from love of power or gain.
>
> (Johnson et al. 2003: 60)

The *hostis communis omnium* may be ruthlessly persecuted since they are excluded from all communities and from all laws. If there was any doubt, Cicero invokes the debased condition of the 'enemy of all' when considering the condition of another man he believes, for different reasons, to have 'severed the ties of human society':

> As for the case of Phalaris, a decision is quite simple: we have no ties of fellowship with a tyrant, but rather the bitterest feud; and it is not opposed to Nature to rob, if one can, a man whom it is morally right to kill;—nay, all that pestilent and abominable race should be exterminated from human society. And this may be done by proper measures; for, as certain members are amputated, if they show signs themselves of being bloodless and virtually

1 It might be useful to stress that already at this point, Cicero did not define the pirates as *hostes humani generis* [enemies of the human race]. This was an expression repeatedly attributed to him by modern international legal scholars, but it must be considered a modern variation of Cicero's original expression. According to Cicero, pirate communities were considered by the Roman Empire as 'enemies of all' and not as 'enemies of the human race'. Cicero's expression, in other words, left undefined the nature of that inclusive community united by its common animosity against the pirate. Following his reasoning in works such as the *De Officiis* and the *Tusculanae Disputationes*, which are steeped in Stoic cosmopolitan ideals, it is clear that he considered the *ius gentium* to be a law binding together a Universal human society. Florus, who was known to Cicero, considered the pirates to have broken 'the common pact of humankind' (*rupto foederi generis humani*). Nevertheless, the most appropriate translation of the term *hostis communis omnium* may be 'enemy of all communities' since Cicero conceived human society as a 'community of communities', and the *ius gentium* as a law regulating interaction between human communities. Roman conceptions of humanity were profoundly different from those of modern writers who used the term *hostis humani generis*, and often translated it as 'enemy of the human race' (see for instance Story 1833: 82). According to the Romans, in other words, pirates were conceived as enemies of 'all communities', but they did not consider them enemies of the 'human race', defined as a biological community beyond nations.

> lifeless and thus jeopardize the health of the other parts of the body, so those fierce and savage monsters in human form should be cut off from what may be called the common body of humanity.
>
> (2006: 136)

In Cicero's writing it is consistently clear that it is Roman power that claims the right to interpret the *ius gentium*, single out the *hostis communis omnium* and 'cut it off from the common body of humanity'. In other words, it is Roman power that claimed an *imperium* in the Mediterranean world.

In Roman Imperial law, therefore, pirates are never qualified as *hostes rei publicae* and in relation to them there is never a formal declaration of war opening hostilities, or a triumph celebrating the victory over them (Tarwacka 2009: 61). This emerges clearly in the writing of Ulpian contained in the *Corpus Iuris Civilis*, today the most authoritative source for the student of Roman law. In the *Digest* – that comprises the second part of the collection which, at the time of its composition, was meant to be the sole source of law for the whole Roman Empire – it is reported that 'enemies are those upon whom the Roman people has declared war publicly or who have themselves declared war upon it: the rest are termed outlaws or pirates' (Mommesen et al 1954: 836). Similarly Pomponius wrote that 'enemies are those who have declared or against which we declare a public war; all others are robbers and pirates' (cited in Peters 2005: 283).[2]

Since communities deemed piratical were considered disturbers of a just Mediterranean peace, enforced and maintained by Roman power, they were not considered *hostes*; and since they were not *hostes*, who were still considered part of the *ius gentium*, but outlaws, the rules of war were not considered applicable to them. A number of authors, notably Phillipson in his magisterial history of international law in the ancient world, noted that:

> pirates, no matter how large their bands, and how organized they were, were not regarded as regular enemies, but as enemies of mankind; so that the usual formalities relating to the commencement of war, and the mitigations conceded in case of other belligerents were not held to be applicable to pirates.
>
> (1911: 375)

2 *Hostis* or *perduellis* was the name reserved to enemies against which Rome waged a just war (*bellum justum*), that is, a war declared according to the procedure described in the *ius fetiale*. The declaration of war presupposed that the opponent was recognized an independent polity, whose word was deemed honourable so that negotiations and peace agreements were always possible. The enemy was thus considered endowed with certain important rights that had to be respected even in time of war, in order to maintain the possibility of a future peace (Phillipson 1911). This was a conception that was increasingly inconsistent with the position of an Imperial power that was determined to impose its Pax Romana over the whole of the ancient world.

Similarly, the Polish scholar of Roman law Anna Tarwacka has recently argued: 'Cicero's expression *communis hostis omnium* carries implications in the sphere of the *ius gentium*. It means that the pirates should be pushed onto the margins of law by all organized societies, which should also unite in the fight against piracy' (2009: 41).

To sum up, we could again evoke Alfred Rubin's authority, according to whom:

> piracy to the Romans was a descriptive noun for the practices of . . . Eastern Mediterranean people whose views of law and intercommunity relations appear to have reflected a millennium-long tradition that had become an obstacle to Roman trade and inconsistent with Roman views of the world order under hegemony.
>
> (2006: 12)[3]

Since the late Republican period, and increasingly after the imposition of a Pax Romana throughout the ancient world, the Mediterranean Sea was considered as a common space in which all communities retained a right to travel and trade freely. Since pirates were accused of violating the *ius gentium*, they were branded as *hostis communis omnium*.

In the following section, I show how the persecution of piracy came to represent the paradigm of an Imperial form of discriminatory violence, whose logic is profoundly different from the one associated with classic international wars. I consider the *persecutio piratarum*, a very specific Imperial institution. The term denotes discriminatory operations of global policing, which are deemed to impose security over a common global space. These were operations that played a fundamental role not only at the material level but also (and especially) at the rhetorical and ideological levels: it is precisely by taking upon itself the burden of fighting those who were represented as 'common enemies of all human communities' that Rome claimed an Imperial role throughout the Mediterranean. Imperial ideologues such as Cicero could therefore present Imperial authority as

3 Although I consider Rubin's analysis at once valid and important, I regard as untenable his conclusion that piracy, although intolerable from the point of view of the Roman Empire, 'did not imply criminality under any legal system, Roman or law of nations' (2006: 13). It seems to me that piracy was not only suppressed and fought because judged 'improper' but that, increasingly, it was considered a breach in the *ius gentium*, which legitimated Roman intervention in the name of all Mediterranean communities. Cicero's comments, obviously, seem to point in this direction. Even more significant is the fact that in 67 BC, for instance, the law that trusted the *imperium* in the hands of Pompey was aptly called *lex de piratis persequendis*, which is usually translated as 'law for the effective prosecution of pirates'. This seems a correct translation since 'prosecution' derives directly from the Latin *persequor*, from which *persequendis*. The law therefore seems to imply that pirates were not simply fought but rather prosecuted against. My claim is that implicit there is already the idea of the Roman Empire as enforcer of a Universal *ius gentium* and of the pirates as Universal criminals excluded from all communities.

a benign presence, enforcing respect of the *ius gentium* throughout the ancient the world. In the words of Cicero: 'the Roman Empire maintained itself by acts of service, not of oppression. Wars were waged in the name of our allies. . . . Therefore, our authority should be called more accurately a protectorate over the whole world [*patrocinium orbis terrae*] rather than a dominion' (2006: 147–148).

Persecutio piratarum and the forms of Imperial peace

The fact that the Mediterranean was for a long time a space in which trade and plunder merged into one another, as variations of an unregulated sphere of intercultural contact and exchange, has been a widespread opinion for a long time, cultivated by a large swathe of historians of ancient times. This tendency is well summarized by Montesquieu's maxim in *The Spirit of the Laws*, according to which 'the first Greeks were all pirates' (2011: 339). Coleman Phillipson, whose study of ancient Greek conceptions of international law is highly credited, wrote: 'In the Homeric age the practice of piracy was looked upon as a creditable . . . means of enrichment' (1911: 33; Homer 2004: 25). Thucydides' *The History of the Peloponnesian War* is the *locus classicus* of this type of reflection:

> It should be explained that in early times both the *Hellenes* and the barbarians who dwell on the mainland near the sea, as well as those on the islands, practiced piracy . . . falling upon cities that were unprotected, and consisted of groups of villages, they pillaged them and got most of their living from that source. For this occupation did not as yet involve disgrace, but rather conferred something even of glory. This is shown by the practice, even at the present day, of some of the peoples on the mainland, who still hold it an honor to be successful in this business, as well as by the words of the early poets, who invariably ask the question of all who put in to shore, whether they are pirates, the inference being that neither those whom they ask ever disavow that occupation, nor those ever censure it who are concerned to have the information.
>
> (1962: 9)

According to this established view, then, piracy should be regarded as a central component of the ancient Mediterranean world, often integrating in an essential way the subsistence economy on which different people organized their existence. Aristotle, for instance, emphasized piracy as a widespread means of production: whereas some early inhabitants of the Mediterranean chose to be 'fishermen and others live by the pursuit of birds or wild beasts', he writes matter-of-factly, 'others support themselves by different forms of hunting. Some, for example, are pirates' (1996: 20). This fascinating image of pirate communities, dedicated to a nomadic form of life resistant to agricultural civilization, is present in the writings of numerous ancient historians. Ormerod, for instance, says of the Cilicians that 'by land, the poverty of the soil had forced them to become hunters and brigands rather than agriculturalists; the same pursuits were followed at sea' (1996: 14). Similarly, Strabo describes the peoples of Colchis, near the Black Sea who:

> by equipping fleets of *camarae* and sailing sometimes against merchant vessels and sometimes against a country or even a city hold the mastery of the sea. . . . And, when they return to their own land, since they have no anchorage, they put the *camarae* on their shoulders and carry them to the forests, where they live and where they till a poor soil.
>
> (1856: 224)

In light of these historiographical representations, we should ask how the figure of the pirate as an absolute enemy, and as a remnant of an anomic state of nature always threatening to return, has served as a recurrent trope in Imperial ideology. The first thing to do is to exorcise the evolutionary spectre that had been haunting historians from the days of Thucydides. We must observe the ideological role played by the notion that piracy, 'represents but the lingering remnants of what in a long bygone age had been the normal—one is tempted to say the natural—condition of humanity' (Avidov 1997: 7). This characterization sustained a central role in the ideology of the Roman Empire, which presented itself as the only bastion of peace and civilization in a Mediterranean world otherwise destined to collapse back into the anomic state of nature of mythical times.

Augustus, founder of the Roman Empire and its first Emperor, boasted among its greatest achievements the eradication of piracy from the Mediterranean. In his *Res Gestae*, he wrote: 'I made the sea peaceful and freed it from pirates' (*mare pacavi a praedonibus*) (Cesare Ottaviano Augusto 1991: 22). During his reign, the Roman Empire had completed the conquest of Egypt, Palestina and Panphilia, making the Mediterranean a sea completely surrounded by Roman territories, with the exception of a handful of allied, client states such as Mauretania, Lycia and Thracia. This was the beginning of an era of relative peace known as the Pax Romana. Despite wars of Imperial expansion continued on the Empire's outer frontier, especially against the Parthian Empire and the Germanic tribes of Northern Europe, the Mediterranean world remained at peace for more than two centuries. It is usually held by historians that since 29 BC – when the Roman Civil War of the first century was brought to an end by the victory of Octavius Augustus – until Marcus Aurelius' death in AD 180, no major war affected the Mediterranean area, which therefore enjoyed an unprecedented degree of stability and security (Parchami 2009: 31–58).

In this same period, piracy was ruthlessly eradicated in the Mediterranean. The eradication of piracy was often quoted in the context of laudations of Roman Emperors, who claimed to have imposed order and security in the Mediterranean to the advantage of all civilized people. The praise of Imperial peace was reinforced by the idea that trade brought a new prosperity throughout the Mediterranean, which had been previously endangered by the unruliness of pirate individuals, communities and nations. Thus Alexandrian Jews, in Philo's account of their embassy to Gaius, so described the Roman Emperor:

> This was the Caesar who calmed the storms that raged everywhere, who healed the common plagues of Greeks and non-Greeks, which originated in the south and east and spread to the north and west, scattering the seeds of chaos over all lands and seas between. This was the man who, not only loosed, but broke the chains which burdened and shackled the world. This was the man who removed open warfare and the unseen warfare of bandit attacks. This was the man who emptied the sea of pirate boats and filled it with merchantmen.
>
> (*Embassy to Gaius*: 145–146)

And, similarly, Egyptian merchants, at least in Suetonius's accounts, would enthusiastically salute Augustus for making trade safe and persecuting piracy throughout the Mediterranean Sea:

> . . . clad in white, garlanded and burning incense, heaped upon him best wishes and outstanding praise. They cried that it was through him that they lived, through him that they sailed and through him that they enjoyed liberty and good fortune.
>
> (*Lives of the Twelve Caesars*: 98.2)

In these passages, the eradication of piracy is presented as a fundamental aspect of the Imperial capacity to maintain peace and prosperity. Imperial peace is not only the result of the elimination of warfare between large, mutually recognizing polities; it depends also on the continuous suppression of unacceptable forms of behaviour. The suppression of piracy – which often implied the killing of pirate crews but also the extermination and forced resettlement of entire populations – was portrayed as a form of Imperial policing, which did not disrupt peace, but was rather a constitutive part of it. The claim to serve as an ever-necessary stronghold against the persistent threat of piracy, which could at any time cause the Mediterranean world to lapse back into savage anarchy and disorder, served for centuries an important role in the legitimation of Imperial authority and control. Cicero could therefore point to the persistent threat of piracy in order to argue in favour of increasing the size of the Imperial Navy, even after the ascension of Augustus to the Imperial throne:

> [Pompey] destroyed the pirates' fleets, their cities, their harbours and their refuges. He bestowed peace upon the maritime world through his great courage and incredible speed. Bet he never undertook, nor should he have undertaken, to be held responsible if a pirate ship should happen to

> appear again, somewhere. Therefore he himself, when he had already brought an end to all the wars on land and sea, nevertheless ordered the same cities to provide a fleet.
>
> (*Flaccus*: 29)

The military might of the Empire is credited to be necessary for the establishment, and then for the maintenance, of the basic conditions of civilized life, especially security for property and trade. The notorious verses of Horace, that quintessential Imperial poet, insist with clarity on this point, which is ever-present in Roman literature in any case. It is only under the firm authority of a single Empire that, throughout the Mediterranean, 'the ox roams the fields in safety, Ceres and kind Prosperity nourish the fields while, across a pacified sea, fly the merchants and sailors' (Horace, *Odes*: 4.5. 17–19). If in the Egyptian countryside livestock and crops flourish, then it is partly because the Roman Empire has embraced it under its protection. If, across the Mediterranean, trade flourishes and the merchandise produced in the provinces safely reaches the markets of Rome, this is partly because the Roman Empire continuously imposes its might over the sea, destroying those who disrupt the intricate networks of trade and transportation distributing goods, taxes and tributes.

The maintenance of Imperial peace, therefore, paradoxically justifies increased military spending, the construction of navies, and the relentless persecution of those who are deemed to endanger the established order. Imperial peace is not distinguishable from a state of war on the base of the *quantity* of violence it engenders, but rather on the base of the *quality* of violence it justifies. In their study of the Roman conception of the Emperor as *pacator orbis*, literally 'the global peace-enforcer', Attilio Mastino and Antonio Ibba insisted on the important ideological role played by the insisted portrayal of the ancient world as a pacified totality, subjected to a benevolent Roman hegemony:

> In Imperial propaganda the *pax* appeared as a divine gift or, better, as a gift from the only man who enjoyed eternal divine favour. Ovidius thus defined the Emperor *auctorem pacis*, the one who crafts the peace. . . . It was not by chance then that the deification of peace coincides with the deification of the figure of the Emperor: in a coin from 22 d.C Augustus is represented as the *fundator pacis*, the one who lies the foundations for peace, erected on a throne, on his right hand an olive branch, in his left hand the sceptre, symbol of power. . . . The peace was also called Pax Augusta not so much because it was created once and for all by Augustus, but because it was something constantly inherent to the functions of the Emperor. *Et vos orate, coloni, perpetuam pacem pacificumque ducem* wrote Ovidio, emphasizing not only the commingling of pax and imperium, but also the constant struggle of the Emperor, also named *pacificus dux*, in creating and preserving the peace.
>
> (2006: 3–6)

The Roman Empire thus legitimated its hegemony over the Mediterranean with the claim of keeping piracy in check, and championing civilization, peace and prosperity through the imposition of a form of policing over the maritime commons deemed proper according to the Universal *ius gentium*.[4] This seems to be a recurrent feature of Imperial ideology, rooted in a representation of international space as a thoroughly pacified and juridified arena in which violence can be only a disturbance of peace, or a form of peace-enforcement. 'As Thucydides, Livy, and Tacitus all teach us, along with Machiavelli commenting on their work,' write Hardt and Negri, 'Empire is formed not on the basis of force itself but on the capacity to present force as being in the service of right and peace' (2000: 15). This is why 'although the practice of Empire is continually bathed in blood, the concept of Empire is always dedicated to peace: a perpetual and universal peace outside of history' (ibidem).

The paradox, which becomes explicit in the thousands of pirates, slaves, bandits and rebels crucified in the name of the preservation of the *pax romana*, is that of the indistinguishability of war and peace from the point of view of the quantity of violence systemically produced. But while war presents violence as a clash between opposed normative systems, peace can only tolerate violence as either a threat to the dominant normative system or a force imposing it from above. The imposition of a *pax romana* did not mean the elimination of violence, but that the bloodshed, hostility and aggression in the Mediterranean world could only be described in two ways: as a threat to international law, performed by pirates as *hostes communis omnium*; or, specularly, as the prosecution of outlaw groups (*persecutio piratarum*) carried out by a global peace-enforcer (*pacator orbis*) in the name of all communities:

> Order and peace, the eminent values that Empire proposes, can never be achieved but are nonetheless continually re-proposed. The juridical process of the constitution of Empire lives this constant crisis that is considered (at least by the most attentive theoreticians) the price of its own development.
> (Hardt and Negri 2000: 16)

After the fall of the Roman Empire, other polities, often arching back explicitly to Roman Imperial law and rhetoric, claimed to act as enforcers of international law against pirate individuals and outlaw communities throughout the world; before the Roman principate, other polities had similarly credited themselves as benign

4 As Alexander Justice noticed in his *General Treatise of the Dominion of the Sea*, the Roman Empire could therefore deny that it had appropriated the Mediterranean, insisting that it would intervene in maritime affairs only as enforcer of the *ius gentium*. Antoninus Pius, Roman Emperor from 138 AD to 161 AD, accordingly maintained: 'I am Emperor of the Land, but the Law of the Sea', meaning by this that while controversies on land were always determined exclusively according to Roman law, Maritime Affairs remained subjected to the ancient Rhodian Law, which was part of the *ius gentium* (Justice 1724: 6–8).

Imperial forces in the Mediterranean world. Thucydides, writing at the end of the fifth century BC, suggested that the first Empire credited with the eradication of piracy among the ancients was the one ruled by King Minos of Crete. Greek and Roman historians often reported the ways in which the Minoan Empire suppressed piracy in the Aegean, praising this almost mythical precursor of Rome for promoting trade, and enforcing the law over the sea's vastness (Ormerod 1996: 80–85). Similarly, the Athenian Empire was often portrayed as a benign hegemonic force, enforcing law and order in the Mediterranean for the advantage of all Greek *poleis*. Its diminished power was therefore often portrayed as a catastrophic event for the city-states subjected to its hegemony, since it was directly linked by ancient historians to the resurgence of piracy in the Aegean (De Souza 1999: 189–198).

Later on, in the fourth century, the right to suppress piracy throughout the Aegean was contested among different *poleis*. In particular, as David Braund has noticed, 'the role of pirate-suppressor became a bone of contention between Athens and Philip II of Macedon. The struggle for this role indicates the larger imperial role which it implied' (1995: 201). The practical and symbolic significance of Imperial claims to the role of guardian of the commons and protector of the trade of all people is brought out in the speech *On the Halonnesos*. In this work by Hegesippus from the fourth century BC, the author warns the Athenians not to accept the offer made by Philip, Emperor of Macedonia, to suppress piracy on their behalf, because this would be an admission of weakness on their part, which would eventually lead to domination:

> With regard to the pirates, he [Philip] states that it is just that you and he together suppress those who commit evil acts by sea against you and him alike. That amounts to a bid that you set him in control of the sea. That is to admit that without Philip you are incapable of exercising the safe guardianship of the sea. All he is doing by this is calling upon you to recognize his authority.
>
> (2004: 142–143)

Hegessipus' fears were not altogether unfounded since, after the Macedonian Empire, the expanding Roman Empire strived to legitimize its newly achieved hegemonic role in the eyes of the Greek *poleis* presenting itself as a powerful bastion against piracy. According to David Braund:

> It is as part of this tradition that we should understand Cicero's remarks on Pompey's much-vaunted eradication of piracy from the Mediterranean. The suppression of piracy was part of the Roman Empire's beneficent patronage over the world. It was also a cause and legitimation of Roman imperialism and territorial expansion.
>
> (1995: 199)

A number of Roman military interventions, occupations and conquests were justified on the ground of being necessary for the eradication of piracy and the maintenance of free trade in the Mediterranean, including in the Balearics at the end of the second century BC, in Cyrene, in Syria, and in Cyprus (Monaco 1996: 112–114).

It is in this context that we can also understand the Roman occupation of Illyria in 229 BC, which marked the first time the Roman Navy crossed the Adriatic Sea to launch an invasion. According to William Harris, the main motivation behind Rome's military expedition against the Illyrians is to be found in the increasing importance of Adriatic trade and the subsequent Roman interest in controlling Mediterranean sea-routes (1985: 195–197). Roman sources insist that the Illyrians had long been in the habit of attacking Italian trading vessels, but the Romans ignored resulting complaints from the merchant classes, on the ground that the sea remained outside their power and jurisdiction. Only in 230 BC did Rome decide to send an embassy to investigate the case. The ambassadors 'were assured that the Illyrian monarchy meant no harm to Rome, but that it was not their custom to restrain their subjects from practicing piracy at sea. The ambassadors then told her that Rome would take steps to make the Illyrians reform their customs' (De Souza 1999: 76).

According to Roman sources, the Illyrians thus maintained a loose political structure in which the monarchy did not claim a monopoly over the projection of violence beyond the territories nominally under its control. Seafaring people, in particular, maintained their autonomy of action and judgment, something that was becoming unacceptable for Roman power. The result was the Roman invasion, which ended with the imposition of Demetrius of Pharo as a ruling client of Rome (Wilkes 1995: 160–163). Rome therefore justified the occupation of Illyrian territory with the necessity of imposing a more centralized political structure, which would maintain control over the use of violence and discipline the population of Illyria (Badian 1952).

According to Harris, 'these events should be allowed their plain meaning, no more and no less: from time to time the Senate was prepared to use the power of the state in favour of large groups of merchants' (1985: 65). We should add, nevertheless, how and why mercantile interests required the constant backing of Roman power. The invasion of Illyria exemplified the way in which the constant growth of merchant capital, the growing inter-dependence between Mediterranean polities, the transformation of the conditions of production and the formation of urban, 'civilized' societies depended on the conversion of sea-space into a smooth plane of circulation, a market-sphere regulated by a series of juridical norms (Fenn 1925). Therefore, decentralized forms of government like the one predominant on the Illyrian coast could no longer be tolerated. In order to support the new commercial economy – based on the exploitation of slave-labour in the Roman countryside and on the existence of a large property-less class in Rome – it became necessary to make sea-routes safe for large-scale commerce. Roman punitive expeditions often aimed at imposing respect for the constitutive norms of the emerging Mediterranean market to other polities, people and groups. Keith Hopkins has convincingly portrayed the fundamental role played by Roman hegemonic power in imposing the conditions necessary for the construction of a Mediterranean market that would stimulate a consistent economic growth in the first two centuries AD:

> For more than two centuries, the Roman peace more or less freed the inhabitants of the Roman world from major military disturbances: the Mediterranean was free of pirates, major roads were usually clear of brigands, tax burdens were by and large predictable. I do not wish to eulogize the grandeur of the Roman Empire. But it seems likely that these conditions allowed the accumulation of capital.
>
> (Hopkins 1983: 19)

Hopkins depicts the different ways in which Roman Imperial power reshaped conditions of life in the ancient Mediterranean world. New forms of political control contributed to the construction of an integrated Mediterranean market, which contributed to economic growth. We should nevertheless stress that economic growth did not necessarily mean growing human prosperity. At the opposite, as it may be obvious in an Imperial system, economic growth was highly (and increasingly) unequal. The construction of an integrated market contributed to the direct and indirect transfer of wealth from the provinces to Rome; moreover, it enabled the growth of market-oriented plantations tilled by enslaved multitudes, in place of traditional systems of subsistence agriculture. It is in these terms that Greg Woolf (1992) has convincingly argued that the Roman Empire should be viewed as an early form of world-system, with a core and a periphery, defined in both economic and political terms along the lines elaborated by Immanuel Wallerstein.

The Illyrian wars represented only the first in a long series of similar Roman interventions, which were justified as necessary for the extirpation of piracy from the Mediterranean. The Roman Empire consistently presented itself as a force protecting the trading peoples of the world. According to Polybius, when Roman military might crushed the Illyrians, punishing them for their piratical customs, it did so to protect not only Roman and Italian traders, but peaceful traders from all countries. The Greek *poleis* are thus portrayed by Roman sources as 'unanimously accepting Rome as the only effective safeguard for themselves against the future lawlessness' of the pirates, 'for the Illyrians were not the enemies of this people or that, but the common enemies of all' (Polybius 1922: 270). The portrayal of the Illyrian people as a multitude of *hostes communis omnium* played a central ideological role in Imperial rhetoric. It allowed Rome to present itself as a benign hegemonic force, serving the common good of all people with its extraordinary military might, and thus deserving to be accepted as the dominant force in the Mediterranean. Roman sources, thus, can effectively 'present Rome as acting in the interests of Italian traders and the Greek cities, protecting them against the "common enemy" in a fashion which seems more altruistic and . . . more suitable, for the future masters of the Mediterranean world' (De Souza 1999: 80).

The *lex de provinciis praetoriis* of 100 BC further articulated the Roman conception of piracy, making explicit that the suppression of threats to commerce in the Mediterranean was considered a constituent part of Roman *imperium* over this common space of circulation. The law justified the occupation of Cilicia as a necessary measure to establish control on the pirate bases present in the area, and invited the allies to fully cooperate with Roman military measures. According to De Souza:

> Here the Romans appear to be picking up on Polybius' suggestion that they have a *duty to protect* the Greeks against piracy, . . . the law articulates the Romans' assumption of the right to take aggressive, imperialistic measures in order to counter the threat of those whom they designate as pirates.
>
> (1999: 110–113, my emphasis)

The description of the pirates as 'enemies of all communities' specularly supported Rome's Imperial claim to act in the name of all Mediterranean communities. The theatricality of the pirates' execution described by Cicero in the *Verrine Orationes*, thus, was only the most exceptional part of an Imperial discourse that removed from sight the persistence of war and conflict in the Mediterranean world. After the *lex de provinciis*, Roman captives were often literally labelled as pirates, made to carry descriptive placards, and paraded through the provincial towns on their way to execution:

> One man, Publius Servilius, captured alive more pirates than all the previous commanders put together. And when did he ever deny to anyone the pleasure of seeing a captured pirate? On the contrary he displayed the most enjoyable spectacles of captives in chains. And so they came from all places, not just from the towns through which the pirates were being led, to behold that sight.
>
> (Cicero 1992: 5.66)

It must be stressed that the 'pirates' who were persecuted, captured and executed by Roman Imperial power were not only isolated individuals and small groups of desperate bandits. As Lucia Monaco made clear, the subjugation of a great part of the Mediterranean by the Romans, the widespread imposition of slavery and the expropriation of the small landholders throughout Italy and in other provinces 'nourished, a sort of social piracy to which were attracted impoverished communities, mutinous slaves, political exiles, rebels, dismissed sailors from the fleets of conquered cities, and other desperate people' (1996: 83; Garlan 1987). Nevertheless, these were not the only subjects of Roman *persecutio*; entire populations were labelled as 'piratical' and therefore condemned as inimical to commerce and civilization. The Cilicians, in particular, were represented as a lawless alternative to civilization, which posed a danger to Roman power in the Mediterranean. The portrayal proposed by Plutarch is worthy to be quoted in full, since it makes clear the ways in which entire populations could be considered inimical to commercial civilization, and thus exposed to the Imperial wrath:

> Even the wealthy, the aristocratic and would-be intellectuals took to piracy in order to gain a reputation. Pirates had bases and strongholds everywhere. The fleets which called there were remarkable for more than the strength of their crews, the skill of their helmsmen, the speed and dexterity of their ships, suited to their purpose. More appalling than their terror was their disgusting extravagance, with gilded sails and purple awnings and silver-coated oars, as if they reveled and plumed themselves upon their evil doing. The Roman Empire was disgraced by their flutes, strings and drinking along the entire Mediterranean coast, by their seizures of Imperial authorities and by their ransoming of cities. They plundered refuges and shrines previously inviolate. . . . They offered strange sacrifices at Olympus and performed secret rites. But the Romans took the brunt of their insolence. . . . The pinnacle of that insolence was this: whenever one of their victims protested that he was a Roman citizen and gave his name, they pretended to be awe-struck. They struck their thighs and threw themselves at his feet, begging for forgiveness. The victim would be taken in by their abject cowering. Then some pirates would put Roman shoes on his feet, while others clad him in a toga, so that there would be no further mistake. After having had their fill of mockery and pleasure, they would lower a ladder in the open sea and invite their victim to disembark and go his way in safety.
>
> (Plutarch 1923: 175–176)

In 67 BC, thus, Gnaeus Pompeius Magnus was invested with absolute Imperial power and enormous resources, and entrusted with the task of clearing the Mediterranean from pirates. The *lex de pirates persequendis*, also known as *lex de uno imperatore contra praedones istituendo* (law constituting one single emperor against the pirates) represented a fundamental breach in the constitution of the Roman Republic. The law constituted the first and most important rupture in the Republican tradition, and it was the foundation for a further centralization of power: 'Pompey was to be given not only the supreme naval command but what amounted in fact to an absolute authority and uncontrolled power over everyone,' writes Plutarch, and 'there were not many places in the Roman world that were not included within these limits' (1923: 179–180). The chosen *imperator* received almost the entire content of the Roman Treasury – 144 million sesterces – to pay for the military operations, which included building a fleet of 500 ships and raising an army of 120,000 infantry and 5,000 cavalry (Monaco 1996: 107). Such an accumulation of power was unprecedented and there was literally a riot in the Senate when the bill was debated. It was clear to many that the concentration of power advocated to be necessary for an effective suppression of the pirate threat would itself threaten the Roman Republic. The *lex de piratis* opened a state of exception that fatally subverted the institution it was supposed to protect.

Contemporary sources stress the threat posed by piracy to the grain supply as the decisive factor in the decision to confer extraordinary powers to Pompey, often blaming the enormous population of the city for the distress that resulted from even a brief interruption of maritime trade. According to Plutarch, who remains the foremost authority in the history of the period in question:

> the power of the pirates was felt in all parts of the Mediterranean, so that it was impossible to sail anywhere and all trade was brought to a halt. It was this that really made the Romans sit up and take notice. With their markets short of food and a great famine looming, they commissioned Pompey with extraordinary powers to suppress the pirates.
>
> (1923: 178)

The incredible power attributed to the pirates in Roman sources obviously magnifies the prestige of Pompey as the only man capable to control them, and of the Roman Empire as the only bastion of order in the Mediterranean. The demonization of the Cilicians, portrayed as lawless pirates in perpetual war against all civilized communities (*hostes communis omnium*), legitimized the destruction of the Roman Republic and the concession of extraordinary powers in the hands of the Emperor, while at the same time serving as a justification for a military campaign that invested the whole Mediterranean region. According to De Souza, 'the purpose of this catalogue of piratical disasters is to make the power of the pirates appear to be overwhelming and inescapable, so that the act of defeating them, and rendering the seas safe for Romans and their allies, assumes almost mythical proportions' (1999: 186).

Through the *persecutio piratarum*, the Roman Republic transformed itself into an Imperial power. Augustus became a divine figure, which had been capable to finally pacify the Mediterranean and unite all polities against the pirate menace. Even the Cilician pirates were largely resettled and reformed by Roman power since:

> even wild beasts put off their fierce and savage ways when they partake of a gentler mode of life, Pompey determined to transfer the men from the sea to land, and let them have a taste of gentle life by being accustomed to dwell in cities and to till the ground.
>
> (Plutarch 1923: 188)

Heretofore, as we have seen, Rome portrayed itself as the centre of a united and pacified Mediterranean world, conquered by military might and tamed by the imposition of a civilized way of life. In this cosmopolitan Empire finally ruled the *ius gentium*, interpreted and enforced by Roman power. For Roman writers such as Strabo, 'the march of Roman imperialism had been a civilizing and ordering process for the whole world' (cited in De Souza 1999: 203). The history of piracy, and the role it played in Imperial law and rhetoric before and after the rule of Augustus, shows that the pretence of having achieved an unprecedented peace throughout the Mediterranean could also be seen as a political instrument, which protects the victors and their spoils from the unruliness of the defeated: 'a weapon in an on-going war which presents itself as an instrument of the new peace' (Galli 2001: 3).

Chapter 2

The Christian Commonwealth

Pirates, heretics and inquisitors

In the sixteenth century, the Spanish conquest of America, the emergence of a vast Catholic Empire on both sides of the Atlantic and the growth of Protestant piracies against it prompted the forceful return of the same questions and perplexities that had been evoked over a thousand years before by Roman Imperial power. The accession of Charles V, Holy Roman Emperor and King of Spain, 'appeared to fulfil messianic hopes, both humanist and apocalyptic, of a new age presided over by a world emperor, with Jerusalem reconquered, Islam overthrown, and the New World subjugated and opened up for the penetration of Christianity' (Brading 1988: 101).

These sentiments were given poetic expression by Hernando de Acuna in verses addressed to the Emperor in the first years of colonization of the New World:

> Now approaches Lord, or now has arrived/The glorious age in which heaven shall proclaim/One shepherd and one flock alone on earth/. . . And now for its solace, the world awaits/One monarch, one empire and one sword/The world partly feels itself to be and completely hopes to be your kingdom/conquered by you in just war/For he to whom Christ has given his standard, Christ will give a second, happier day/on which he will conquer the land, having conquered the sea.
>
> (cited in Flynn 1966: 57–58)

At the beginning of the sixteenth century, the world seemed finally on the eve of being united in a single imperial cosmopolis that would abolish war and proclaim a Universal peace, uniting all humanity under the common Catholic Christian faith.

In the following chapter, I consider how Christian Universalism contributed to the construction of those resisting Spanish Imperial efforts as unjust enemies worthy to be branded as heretical pirates, outside the pale of the Universal Christian community under construction. The vision of a pacified humanity united under God, the Pope and the Emperor thus had, as its dark side, the declaration of a just war that was to be waged both against unrepentant Indians and those European renegades who decided to resist Christian Universalism. In the first part, I expose the ways in which the vision of a humanity finally united under a single Universal *res publica Christiana* justified and even required the declaration of a just war against those who refused inclusion in the Imperial project emanating from Europe.

In the second part, I focus on the gradual explosion of a violent confrontation between Catholic and Protestant nations over the right to preach and conduct commerce in the lands of the New World. I therefore expose the ways in which the Imperial ideology that supported early Spanish expansionism in the New World contributed to the radicalization of the European wars of religion, and to their potential expansion on both sides of the Atlantic. Supported by the authority of the Pope, the Spanish and Portuguese monarchies claimed an *imperium* over the Atlantic Ocean, in order to protect and defend the evangelization of the Americas. Since they were acting in name of the entire *res publica Christiana*, they considered the English privateers who contested and attacked their mission to be pirates – that is, enemies of the entire Christian system of international law. The global civil war that engulfed the Atlantic for over a century, therefore, represented a profound crisis of international law, which was increasingly incapable of serving as a limit to war and armed conflict.

Finally, I consider the systemic pressures which led, between the sixteenth and the seventeenth centuries, to the decline of the medieval *res publica Christiana*, a system of international law founded on the central distributive role of papal authority. What emerged in its place was a modern system of international law, which was initially characterized by the separation of Europe from the Atlantic wilderness, therefore reduced to a space of exceptional freedom beyond the law: a space in which might made right and plunder could function unimpaired as the secret engine at the heart of early-modern process of primitive accumulation of wealth and capital. The crisis of pre-modern international law brought about by the global civil war between Catholic and Protestant nations was therefore an essential precondition in the construction of the modern state system. The rupture of pre-modern international law, from a perspective rooted in the *res publica Christiana*, could only be caused by pirates at the margin of that same legal system. It could not be caused by a dynamic internal to that system of international law, but rather by the emergence of a new perspective and a new systemic enemy, prepared to challenge the entire structure of medieval international law. The pirates – who originated with, and were sponsored and supported by, Protestant nations – were the vanguard of a new freedom outside the Universalism of the Christian legal order. They took upon themselves the role of systemic enemies of the old system of international law; their crimes were not limited to the plundering of the Spanish wealth, they were instead contesting and destabilizing an entire international order. They were a revolutionary force of global historical significance insofar as they opened a rupture within the edifice of medieval law, a rupture in which a new order of international law could begin to take shape.

Imperium Christianus: Spanish Universalism and the conquest of America

> In 1502, on his fourth and final voyage, Christopher Columbus happened upon a great trading canoe just off the coast of Honduras. It was 'long as a galley', as Ferdinand, the Admiral's thirteen-year-old son recalled, and carved from one great tree trunk. Neither its twenty-five paddlers nor the richly clad men who appeared to be their masters offered any resistance as the Spaniards seized their craft, and they remained paralyzed with fright as the bearded strangers rifled through the cargo. It was only when some cacao beans were allowed to spill from their containers in the course of the looting that they momentarily forgot their fear, scrambling to retrieve them 'as if they were their eyes'.
>
> (Clendinnen 1987: 3)

In this remarkable passage from *Ambivalent Conquests*, Inga Clendinnen's investigation of the Spanish conquest of America, we catch not only a glimpse of the beginnings of European piracy in the Atlantic world, but also an early clashing of two vastly different value systems. The episode might be assumed as a synecdoche of what imperialism really means since, as Kris E. Lane already noticed in his seminal history of sixteenth-century piracy, 'a literal interpretation of our current legal and dictionary definitions of piracy could cast much of the European conquest of the Americas as piracy, "a grand larceny on or by descent from the sea"' (1998: 15). Looking at the history of Empire from the point of view opened by the narrative above means first of all accepting the semantic ambiguity that is at the very base of the piratical as a category, and accepting the pirate as a historical and literary figure.

In literature as in history, the pirate threatens to submerge all clear distinctions, being neither friend nor enemy, neither sovereign nor subject. It is not only that piracy is the secret name of Empire and the pirate is, like in St Augustine's famous anecdote, the mirror image of the most powerful emperor; even more radically the pirate wants us to question many of the certainties on which the very structure of our contemporary society is based. Certainly, it was a 'witty and truthful rejoinder', the one which the Bishop of Hippo attributes to a pirate, captured by Alexander the Great and sentenced to infamy and death. The king asked the pirate, 'What is your idea, in infesting the sea?' And the pirate answered, with uninhibited insolence, 'The same as yours, in infesting the earth! But because I do it with a tiny craft, I'm called a pirate; because you have a mighty navy, you're called an emperor' (cited in Mattox 2006: 25). Nevertheless, we should not be content to notice the ambiguous, uncanny proximity of pirates and emperors – a critical practice whose persisting significance Noam Chomsky has shown in his *Pirates and Emperors, Old and New* (2002) – but we should look at the ways in which that perilous proximity is constantly obscured and denied.

The conquest of America, the appropriation of the wealth of the New World, the destruction of the ancient civilizations of that land and the thousands of murders that made everything possible were not brought about with the cynical insolence of that imaginary pirate described by St Augustine. They were instead understood as part of a much larger just war, whose final aim was nothing but the inclusion of the New World within the Christian community. It is true, as Schmitt (2003) notes, that the discovery of America in 1492 was a revolutionary moment in the history of Europe and of the World. In that moment two worlds, up to that point separated by an unsurpassable wall of water, joined together. In that moment, Europe finally crossed the Atlantic border and it was confronted by a substantial alterity: another value system, another religious outlook, another social structure, another way of being human (Todorov 1984). In that moment a fundamental question was immediately posed, regarding the relationship that was to be established with this Other World: was it to be left to its own devices? Was it to be considered 'a state of nature' subtracted from the order of morality and the law? Or was it to be integrated in the Christian European order, of which it would slowly become a part under 'one monarch, one empire and one sword'?

As we have seen, the poetics of Hernando de Acuna envisioned the possibility of an integration of the New World within the medieval structure of international law. This is a perspective that looks not only to the past but also to the future. He has a sense of finality, a vision of an Empire embracing the whole of humanity: there will be a glorious age; there will be one shepherd and one flock; there will be a fulfilment of the emperor's 'holy zeal'; there will be a Christian legal order everywhere; there will be one monarch, one pope, one empire and one sword. Acuna emphasizes the future, and a just war that is directed towards what ought to be in the future, although the future is nothing but the extension of the past. The Spanish Empire, in other words, takes upon itself the task of subsuming the New World within the medieval order of international law that was characteristic of fifteenth-century Europe.

The papal bulls, *Aeterni Raegis* and *Inter Caetera*, released in the spring of 1493, declared the existence of a Universal mission, which the Spanish Empire was meant to perform in the name of the whole of Christianity and, in messianic terms, in the name of the whole of humanity. Pope Alexander VI, as spiritual head of the entire Christendom, traced a pole-to-pole line 100 leagues west and south of the Azores, establishing all of the lands west of that line as missionary zones under the control of the Spanish monarchy. In 1494, Portugal and Spain concluded the Treaty of Tordesillas by which they determined the boundary between their respective missionary zones. The boundary was a line drawn from pole to pole at a distance of 370 leagues from the island of Capoverde (Francalanci and Romanò 1994: 2). In Spanish this boundary line was referred to as the *raya* and it constituted the first global line, as it was traced with a perspective that took into consideration the whole world as a single smooth space open to Christian missionary expansion (Grewe 2000: 233). Nevertheless, the papal bulls did not pretend to give to the Spanish monarchy exclusive possession (*dominium*) of the lands west of the papal line of demarcation and of the ocean leading thereof. Instead, they entrusted the Spanish Empire with the task of converting the inhabitants of the occupied lands to the Christian faith. The Spanish rulers were invited to fulfil their obligation 'selecting a multitude of sincere, God-fearing, learned and capable missionaries' to instruct the natives in the Catholic faiths and to educate them in good morals (Grewe 2000: 101).

The appropriation of American land – and the parallel expropriation of the natives – was considered functional to the fundamental goal of converting the Indians, therefore enlarging the Christian Commonwealth. The announcement of:

> the Christian truth must proceed at the same pace as the military advance, so that conversion may allow the non-Christian to be saved . . . by becoming faithful subjects of the Christian kingdom. Such an optimistic vision considered human history as a gradual process towards a Christian kingdom covering the entire globe: once this goal is reached the time will be ripe for the effective realization of Christ's universal sovereignty also on earth, not only in heaven.
>
> (Lupieri 2011: 13)

Although this Universalist idea may seem astonishing, it should be remembered that 1492 had also been the year in which the *reconquista* of the Iberian peninsula had been completed, while the Teutonic Knights had gained stable control of Prussia and the Baltic Coast (recognizing the sovereignty of the Holy See on those lands, and receiving in return the possession of that same territory in the form of fiefdom, with the aim of favouring the conversion of the inhabitants to the Catholic faith).

The conquest of American soil by the Spanish Empire posed fundamental questions of legitimacy to the Scholastic school of thought that dominated Spanish universities. In this context, it was legitimised essentially on the basis of a global extension of the traditional medieval doctrine of just war. The conquest of America was understood as the continuation of the *reconquista* that had reaffirmed Christianity first in Rome, and then in the whole of Europe. Although the natives had never had any contact with Europe prior to the arrival of Columbus, they were immediately absorbed within the centrifugal tendencies of a European Christian history that was supposed to be Universal in essence. Paradoxically, it was not the discriminating thought of neo-Aristotelian theologians like Luis Sepulveda that presented the most damning argument against the Indians, but rather the more tolerant and humanist argument brought forward by Vitoria, who is still regarded as the most important thinker of the period and, arguably, a liberal thinker of international law *ante-litteram* (Scott 2000: 275–280).

The main thrust of Sepulveda's argument for a 'just war' being made against the Indians is carried by Aristotle's theory of natural slavery (Pagden 1987: 27–57). He proposed the inhumanity of the Indian race, which he considered more similar to anthropomorphic beasts than to civilized Europeans. Because of this 'racial difference', the Indians could not be considered rightful owners of the American riches; instead they could be freely captured, enslaved and exploited by the Spanish. To this neo-Aristotelian racism – that essentially applied the ancient opposition of Greek versus Barbarians to the new dichotomy opposing Christians versus Indians – Vitoria responded with a humanist philosophy that argued for the possibility of a rightful Spanish war against the Indians, even if they were to be considered thoroughly human and on an equal footing with the Spanish *conquistadores* arriving in those lands. Eventually, the Pope, with an appropriate bull signed in 1537 with the title *Sublimis Deus*, officially declared that the *Indios* were human beings with a soul. The legal problems then became how the Catholic sovereigns could justify the subjugation of the Indians and the appropriation of their land (Lupieri 2011: 10).

Vitoria's recognition of the humanity of the Indians ends up being the very base on which lies not only the *possibility* of conquest, but in fact the *moral duty* of a forceful Spanish intervention aimed at the punishment and subjection of the Indians. In Vitoria's view, the Spanish were essentially messengers, 'ambassadors of Christianity'. In 1493 the Spanish king had been chosen by the Pope to bring the divine Word over the Atlantic, and to the people on those distant lands. The Spanish, on the basis of the Universal right to communicate and trade (*titulus naturalis societatis et communicationis*) were therefore entitled to cross the sea, which is common to all people, and to establish their missions there; they were entitled to spread the Word of God, to commerce with the natives and to extract all the wealth that the natives treated as 'undivided common wealth' (Koskenniemi 2011: 112). It was only because Vitoria recognized the Indians' humanity that he could then condemn their sinful and unjust behaviour:

> ambassadors are by the law of nations inviolable and the Spaniards are the ambassadors of Christian peoples. Therefore, the native Indians are bound to give them, at least, a friendly hearing and not to repel them. This, then, is the first title which the Spaniards might have for seizing the provinces and sovereignty of the natives.
>
> (1917: 156)

Because they are to be included among the community of mankind, the Indians must be given the opportunity to convert. It is to further this universal right of mankind that the Spanish might conduct a just war against those who obstruct their missionary activity. The just war waged by the Spanish against those Indians who oppose their missionary activity is therefore – as all just wars in the Christian period were – only coincidentally a war of reprisal, meant to punish the evil inclinations of the Indians; it is, first of all, a war waged in the name of the interest of Christian humanity – and the Indians themselves. When the Indians opposed the Universal mission that the Pope entrusted to the Spanish, the latter then 'can make war on the Indians, no longer as on innocent folk, but as against forsworn enemies, and may enforce against them all the rights of war, despoiling them of their goods, reducing them to captivity, deposing their former lords and setting up new ones' (Eppstein 2012: 450).

It must be stressed that Vitoria's view is not particularly innovative in this sense. In fact, although in the past there had been constant disagreement on the legitimacy of fighting wars with the only aim of forceful conversion, most schools within the Catholic Church seemed to agree on the legitimacy of combating those who deliberately obstructed the missionary duty imposed by God on the Roman Church. Even Thomas Aquinas, while criticizing the crusading zeal that thought legitimate to impose spiritual faith through domination and conquest, considered necessary to fight for the right of free mission (*ius communicationis*). It was Thomas Aquinas' conviction that 'it was not the purpose of holy wars to convert the infidels by force. They should only be coerced into not obstructing the expansion of the Christian faith' (Grewe 2000: 52). For Thomas Aquinas, as for Vitoria, the Universality of the *res publica Christiana* is traversed by a fundamental distinction between a Christian Europe – organized hierarchically in a stereometric space that has at its apex the Pope, as the representative of God on Earth – and the non-Christian world. But this difference is not understood as permanent, eternal or even natural; it is instead transitory, because also the heretics and the heathen are destined to be converted and at last to receive the Word. Christian Universalism is therefore, from the beginning, objective and missionary, as testified by the commandment of Jesus Christ that demands to all Christians to spread the Word and become agents of a Universal community to come: *euntes docete*. This logic – according to which Christianity is a Universality which has the duty to fulfil itself – is the secret engine of an expansionary drive that cannot be stopped and that legitimates an endless 'just war' against those who oppose Christian missionary activity.

Vitoria's inclusion of the Indians in the Universal human community is therefore at once cosmopolitan and Imperial. If, according to Sepulveda, savages are nothing but animals and thus *can* be tamed and even killed if necessary, then according to Vitoria the fact that savages are fully humans means that they *must* be punished for breaching the Universal law, disrespecting the *ius communicationis* and subjecting the innocents to brutal and un-Christian laws. If for Sepulveda the *conquista* is in part shepherding, in part hunting, according to Vitoria, it is an action of justice, meant to include the New World into the expansive Universality of the Church and punish the enemies of humanity residing in the New World.

Christianitas afflicta: The Atlantic wars of religion

As we have seen, according to Vitoria, it was in the common interest of the *res publica Christiana* that the Spanish were given the right to travel to the Indies, to settle there, and to preach the Gospel. The mandate to spread the word of Christ in the Americas played a fundamental role not only in Vitoria's philosophy but, in general, in the whole system of international law elaborated during the expansion of late-medieval Christendom. From this perspective neither the nation nor the society of nations was the community of last instance. Over and above it, there was another community embracing sky and world, the Church in its totality, *una et tota ecclesia* (Grewe 2000: 120). The Universalism of medieval Christian international law was based on the image of a future Christian cosmopolis, whose realization could be obtained only through the systematic employment of the sword and the crozier, symbols of military and pastoral power (Policante 2012a).

It was this eschatological Universality of the Church that would justify the Spanish in their war against the Indians. Since it was in the common interest of the whole of humanity to overcome any resistance against the preaching of the Gospel, the forceful expansion of the Christian community could be presented at once as a just war and as a sort of humanitarian intervention *ante-litteram*. As Joseph Hoffner has argued in his important study of Scholastic philosophy, the realization of the Universality of the Church remained an essential justification for forceful expansion:

> Vitoria's system is clearly directed towards this goal. He attributes to the Christians the right to preach the gospel to all peoples, to overcome by force resistance against missionary activities, and to depose heathen princes. All these powers are destined to serve the ideal of the 'total Church'.
>
> (1969: 342)

Similarly, the centrality of the Holy See in the medieval structure of international law was based on the presupposition that the Pope had both the power and the duty to direct and coordinate all Christian nations, in such a way as to further their common interest. To this end, Pope Alexander VI tried to organize the integration of the New World in the international order, just as his predecessors had tried to direct the crusades that had punctuated the previous century. And yet, nothing demonstrates more clearly the irrevocable crisis of the *res publica Christiana* than a comparison of the great European expansion to the West in the sixteenth century, with the one that took place in the preceding century. Throughout the Middle Ages, the crusade remained (at least in principle) a common enterprise of the entire Christian community, which received its direction by papal authority and which gave meaning to the figure of a Christian Emperor, entrusted with the goal of fighting the common enemy of Christianity with armies drawn from all Christian nations. As noted by Carl Schmitt, during the Middle Ages the *imperium* was first of all 'a commission' entrusted to a particular crown, which was meant to serve the whole *res publica Christiana*, against forces that negated the very bases on which it existed (2003: 62).

We have seen how the concept of *imperium* originated in Roman law as a form of power exercised by Rome in the name of a wider human community; a power that often took the form of imperial interventions in the Mediterranean commons. The *persecutio piratarum* remained here the paradigmatic form of Imperial war insofar as it opposed an emperor acting in the name of humanity against pirates

– defined neither as enemies of a particular political power nor as criminals in relation to a particular legal system, but as 'enemies of all' – literally *hostis communis omnium*. In the Christian era, the concept of *imperium* developed in relation with the consolidation of a *societas Christiana*, standing high and above every single political power or local community. 'The *orbis terrarum*,' writes Pagden, 'thus became, in terms of the translation effected by Leo the Great in the fifth century, the *orbis Christianus*, which in turn, soon developed into the *Imperium Christianus*' (1995: 24). The Emperor thus became literally 'the sword of Christianity' and the crusade the paradigmatic form of Imperial war. The Emperor then always seemed to oppose whoever was deemed an Anti-Christ and an enemy of humankind, insofar as humanity itself was then a theological concept (Ullmann 1955: 212).

In medieval times, it was the authority of the Pope that guaranteed that a particular claim to *imperium* would be recognized by all crowns. It was the Pope who was meant to determine what was the common good of the whole Christian community and which crown could effectively serve it with its temporal power. In the vision expressed by the papal bulls tracing the *raya*, the conquest of the New World ought to take place according to the same ideal scheme. At that particular time, the Spanish king had been effectively entrusted with the title of Holy Roman Emperor and, subsequently, he was charged with the duty to organize the colonization of the American continent in the common interest of the whole *res publica Christiana*. It was evident that 'the persistent reliance in circles close to the Castilian court on the papal donation, and its continuing importance in the official historiography of the Spanish Empire, served to keep the continuity between the Spanish monarchy and the ancient *Christian Imperium romanum* firmly on the agenda', therefore stressing the legitimacy of the Spanish claim to the Americas against any other aspirant to the title (Pagden 1995: 32).

By the sixteenth century, nevertheless, Christianity was no longer the close-knit occidental community of the Middle Ages, united in a common faith and an ecclesiastical discipline under the twin authority of Pope and Emperor. The unity in faith had at this point already been shocked to its very foundations first by the Great Schism (1378–1417) – which, for almost half a century, excited wars among Christian princes, uprisings among the peasants and widespread concern over corruption in the Church – and then by the emergence of the Protestant Reformation, which led to a veritable schism in the Christian community. The Reformation carried with it profound institutional implications that gravely imperilled Christendom's survival. At the systemic level, it threatened the role of the Pope as a mediatory figure, thus undermining what had been the main mechanism for adjudicating international disputes among Christian nations. The order-maintaining capacity of canon law, in fact, depended on the recognition of the Pope as the unquestioned authority to interpret it and apply it to individual cases. When Luther opened the way to the possibility of criticizing the Pope's interpretation of canon law, he also placed a powerful instrument in the hands of those Christian princes who were ready to move against the authority of the Pope. The Reformation, moreover, inflamed popular, radical and millenarian impulses throughout Christendom, as evidenced by the Peasants' War and the Anabaptist seizure of Munster, and it opened a century and a half of European wars of religion, which were brought to a halt only with the conclusion of the Treaty of Westphalia in 1648.

It is only under the light of this crisis that it is possible to understand the particular role played, both practically and ideologically, by the pirate wars that opposed the Christian Emperor to the Protestant Nations throughout the sixteenth and seventeenth centuries. The Huguenot buccaneers, the Dutch freebooters and the Elizabethan Sea-Dogs not only refused to respect the orders imposed by papal authority, but started to prey on the Spanish colonies, assaulting the Spanish galleons returning from the New World filled with the gold and silver of the American continent. They crossed the papal line of demarcation and stole the precious metals with which, according to a Jesuit close to the Spanish court like José Acosta, 'God himself had carefully sown the New World . . . so as to facilitate Spanish settlement' and finance the Universal mission entrusted by the Pope to the Christian Emperor (Brading 1988: 121). Moreover, they interrupted trade, which 'like the natural resources with which God had blessed the Americas, was viewed as a reward for the efforts . . . to bring the Indians to a knowledge of God' (Pagden 1995: 34). They were therefore excommunicated from the Christian community, expelled from the Universal Church and treated by the Spanish Empire not as public enemies, but as foes of the entire Christian civilization and enemies of mankind.

Refusing to obey the papal dispositions, the Protestant corsairs endangered the welfare of the entire Christian community. In fact, it was only in the common interest of all Christianity that the Pope excluded some nations from travelling to the Americas, at least according to the Catholic perspective expressed by Vitoria:

> 'Now the Lord has laid a command on everyone concerning his neighbour' (Ecclesiasticus, ch. 17). Therefore it concerns Christians to instruct those who are ignorant of these supremely vital matters. . . . Although this is a task common and permitted to all, yet the Pope might entrust it to the Spaniards and forbid it to all others. The proof is in the fact that, although (as said above) the Pope is not temporal lord, yet he has power in matters temporal when this would subserve matters spiritual. Therefore, as it is the Pope's concern to bestow especial care on the propagation of the Gospel over the whole world, he can entrust it to the Spaniards *to the exclusion of all others*, if the sovereigns of Spain could render more effective help in the spread of the Gospel in those parts; and not only could the Pope forbid others to preach, but also to trade there, if this would further the propagation of Christianity, for he can order temporal matters in the manner which is most helpful to spiritual matters. And if in this case that is how spiritual matters would be best helped, it consequently falls within the authority and power of the supreme Pontiff. But it seems that in this case this is the course most conducive to spiritual welfare, because, if there was to be an indiscriminate inrush of Christians from other parts to the part in question, they might easily hinder one another and develop

> quarrels, to the banishment of tranquillity and the disturbance of the concerns of the faith and of the conversion of the natives.
>
> (1917: 156)

Following a similar logic, with the official aim to facilitate the Spanish mission in the New World, in *Inter Caetera* Pope Alexander VI forbade 'all persons of whatever rank under the threat of immediate excommunication, from crossing the papal line of demarcation for the purpose of trade or any other reason without the explicit consent of the Spanish King' (Grewe 2000: 231). This papal disposition was laid down only as a side note in the more general structure of the bull, and yet it would rapidly emerge as one of the most fundamental turning points in the history of modern international law. The decision would effectively accelerate the crisis of the *res publica Christiana,* already strained by the emergence of Protestantism and the conflicting interests of the major European powers.

After 1493, for the subjects of emergent maritime nations such as France, Holland and England crossing the *raya* would automatically mean not only to leave Europe but also to abandon, once and for all, the Universal Christian Commonwealth. To cross the *raya* meant to incur excommunication *latae sententiae* (automatic, incurred at the moment of committing the offence), thus deserting the *res publica Christiana* and its international legal order. It meant forsaking one's belonging to the medieval order of Europe and stepping out of its fundamental structure. We should not discount the significance, within the classical medieval framework, of what appears as a purely spiritual disciplinary measure. The *excommunication major*, the great ban of the Church,

> resulted not only in exclusion from all sacraments, from mass, from an ecclesiastical burial, from benefices, from election rights and from ecclesiastical jurisdiction, but resulted also in absolute exclusion from the community of the faithful, with the result that no one was permitted to communicate with the banned person and that temporal powers were obliged to outlaw him.
>
> (Grewe 2000: 113)

The linkage between ecclesiastical excommunication and imperial outlawry, therefore, is strictly genealogical. This means, first of all, that the concept of 'ban' and 'outlawry' is nothing but the secularization of the theological notion of excommunication. It means, furthermore, that excommunication meant, already in the medieval period, being banned from the Christian community and reduced to an outlaw status.

The liturgy of excommunication offers a clear vision of what excommunication meant in the medieval period. The ceremony, performed in the case where excommunication was applied to a sin that did not already imply automatic excommunication, involved a bishop, with 12 priests, reciting an oath on the altar:

> We separate him, together with his accomplices and abettors, from the precious body and blood of the Lord and from the society of all Christians;

> we exclude him from our Holy Mother, the Church in Heaven, and on earth; we declare him excommunicate and anathema; we judge him damned, with the Devil and his angels and all the reprobate, to eternal fire until he shall recover himself from the toils of the devil and return to amendment and to penitence.
>
> (Riggio 1950: 122)

After reciting these words, the bishop would ring a bell to evoke a death toll, close a holy book to symbolize the ex-communicant's separation from the church, and snuff out a candle, knocking it to the floor to represent the soul of the sinner being extinguished and removed from the light of God. To be excommunicated therefore meant being dead to the community and excluded from its secular and spiritual life (Vodola 1986: 12–24). The effects of excommunication were by no means confined to the purely religious spheres of life. Intercourse with the excommunicated individual was prohibited: he or she was to be shunned. All obligations toward him or her were to be considered severed: financial debt to a usurer was not to be respected, cultural gratitude to a condemned teacher should be forgotten, political allegiance to an excommunicated king was to be refused. Having been declared an outcast, 'he was considered to be infected with a contagious disease, hence contact with him was prohibited. . . . Excommunication was and is the juristic and concrete social exclusion from the corporate body of Christianity' (Ullmann 1955: 300).

Until the discovery of America, the papal power to dispose of the newly discovered parts of the world in order to further the common interest of Christianity was never seriously challenged. The struggle over this power and thus over one of the last foundations of the Christian order only came to a head as a result of the West Indian investitures of Pope Alexander VI, by way of which the Spanish attempted to ensure the primacy of their rights in America. The struggle that opposed the Spanish Empire to the Protestant nations – in particular the Dutch and the English, but also the French Huguenots – was not limited to a fight over who had the right to colonize the New World. Much more fundamentally it was a struggle over the very foundation of the *res publica Christiana*. In challenging the right of the Spanish to exclude other nations from the Indies, the Protestant pirates were in fact contesting the authority of the Pope to dispose of newly discovered lands in the common interest of all Christian people; and in challenging the authority of the Pope to decide for the common good of the *res publica Christiana*, they were in fact threatening to destroy not only Spanish interests, but also the entire political structure on which international law was based at the time.[1]

1 This is why, fundamentally, Protestant freebooters and buccaneers could only be pirates in the eyes of the Spanish Imperial authorities; although to a modern eye they might appear as privateers – insofar as they acted not for their own interest but as part of a wider struggle that opposed Catholic against Protestant nations. Based on this modern view, even a usually attentive reader of international law such as Carl Schmitt was pushed to refer to the Protestant buccaneers as 'partisans of the seas' in order to stress the

The demonization of Protestant corsairs and freebooters was a direct consequence of the Spanish claim that the forceful conquest of American soil was part of a Universal mission entrusted to Spain in the name of all mankind. The treatment of Protestant corsairs as pirates and enemies of mankind, therefore, was not a simple ideological move; instead it was an essential and non-negotiable part of the Spanish attempt to act as the last bastion of the crumbling Universal order of the medieval *res publica Christiana*. As Carl Schmitt did not fail to notice, the papal lines of demarcation were not global lines separating Christian from non-Christian territories, but internal divisions in an emerging global *societas Christiana*. This is why, according to Carl Schmitt, the Spanish treatment of all Protestant corsairs as pirates and enemies of humanity is the clearest proof of the persistence in the first half of the sixteenth century of a Christian Empire, albeit one in crisis:

> For the order of the land, the tyrant was the common enemy, just as, for the order of the sea, the pirate was the enemy of the human race . . . because he exercised a power contrary to order in an otherwise autarkic and autonomous system, was both the internal enemy of this system and the enemy of empire as the comprehensive spatial order. As long as they were consistent with historical reality, such universal and core concepts of enmity as tyrant and pirate not only obtained their meaning from, but affirmed the existence of the concrete order of the international law of an Empire.
>
> (2003: 56)

The reduction of both Indians and Protestant heretics to the status of enemies of mankind, whenever they were accused of impeding such a Universal mission, was therefore a persistent possibility. A number of Christian humanists looked with horror at the practices attributed to the Indians, at least as much as they condemned the inhumanity of the Lutheran corsairs (*corsarios luteranos*). Paradoxically, therefore, the more Christian culture seemed to widen the scope of humanity, the more in fact it was forced to condemn harshly those who did not behave according to the Christian idea of humanity.

difference between the Elizabethan Sea-Dogs and the thoroughly denationalized pirates of later times (1997: 42). But although this distinction may seem useful and true to the modern mind, it misses the fundamental point. What we must stress in order to understand the peculiarity of the institution of the pirate as *hostis communis omnium* is that the Protestant privateers of the sixteenth century were the common enemy of the crumbling order of the *res publica Christiana*, at least as much as the denationalized pirates of the eighteenth century emerged as the common enemy of a rising international society of states centred in Europe. Although the two terms of the opposition radically changed, the form of the opposition remained substantially unaltered. In other words, the concept of the pirate continued to refer to the common enemy of an Imperial order aspiring to encompass the whole world, although after the sixteenth century this order was not identified any more with the *res publica Christiana*, but rather with an international society of states centred in Europe.

> Bacon said the Indians were proscribed by nature itself as cannibals. They stood outside humanity (*hors l'humanité*) and had no rights. By no means is it paradoxical that none other than humanists and humanitarians put forward such inhuman arguments, because the idea of humanity is two-sided and often lends itself to a surprising dialectic.
>
> (Schmitt 2007a: 103)

In fact, even in Vitoria's writings – which otherwise stress the necessity of moderation in the conduct of just war and might seem to be open to the quintessentially modern idea that a war might be just on both sides – the idea is firmly retained that the Spanish were the holders of a Universal mission, whose fulfilment was in the interest of all mankind. All of Vitoria's arguments, concerning the right of the Spanish to fight a just war against Indians as well as the duty to punish Protestant heretics who attempted to reach the Indies against the explicit prohibition of the Roman Church, descended from the fundamental presupposition that there was a common interest of all mankind, and that this interest was served by the Pope (as vicar of Christ) and by the Christian Emperor (as sword of Christendom). The fundamental meaning of the historical figure of a Christian Emperor is thus to be sought in his duty to fight tyrants and pirates as common enemies of mankind.

Corsarios luteranos: Pirates and heresy

In *Land and Sea*, Carl Schmitt interprets the early history of Atlantic piracy in the sixteenth century as part of a global civil war traversing the Universality of the Christian Commonwealth centred in Europe. He describes the first pirates as part of a religious confrontation between Catholic and Protestant nations that would effectively erode the very foundations of pre-modern Christian international law.

> As long as Portugal and Spain, two Catholic powers, were not challenged from the outside, the Pope in Rome could issue legal titles, institute order in newly-conquered lands, and arbitrate between the conquering powers. . . . For a century or so, the Spaniards and the Portuguese would refer to the Papal concessions in their attempts to refute the claims raised by the French, the Dutch, and the English. . . . Notwithstanding, with the onset of the Reformation, the nations converted to Protestantism would openly contest the authority of the Roman pontiff. Thus the struggle for the ownership of the new Earth turned into a struggle between Reformation and Counter-Reformation, between the world Catholicism of the Spaniards and the world Protestantism of the Huguenots, the Dutch, and the English. . . . The dividing line traced by the Pope in 1493 marked the beginning of the struggle for the new fundamental order, for the new nomos of the earth.
>
> (Schmitt 1997: 55)

The privateers of the sixteenth and seventeenth centuries, according to Schmitt, played a fundamental role in this global civil war between two opposing religious sects: 'All those buccaneers and adventurers had a common, political enemy: the powerful Catholic Spain. . . . Thus, they would make the frontline of world history on the side of world Protestantism, and against the world Catholicism of the day' (1997: 57). Schmitt, therefore, identifies the surge in piracy and privateering with the emergence of the individualist ethos characteristic of the new Calvinist faith. The history of piracy, according to the German author, received its fundamentally radical inclination from the Puritanism of the Calvinist sect, which claimed the freedom of the individual to judge in a sovereign fashion where the good and the true lies. The crisis of the Christian commonwealth and the global wars of religion were thus fed by the same Calvinist spirit of piracy and sedition, by the belief that the individual can interpret the Word and individuate the just cause, as much and, in fact, better than any established authority:

> Calvinism was the new militant religion, perfectly adapted to the elemental thrust seawards. So it became the religion of the French Huguenots, of the heroes of Dutch freedom, and of the English Puritans. Every non-Calvinist would cringe from the Calvinist faith, and above all from the stern faith in the predestination of man for all eternity. In secular terms, the doctrine of predestination is the utmost elevation of the human conscience that claims to belong to a world other than the doomed and corrupted world. In modern sociological terms, it may be said that it is the highest degree of self-consciousness, characteristic of an elite assured of its social position and its hour in history. To put it simply, it is the certainty of salvation, and this redemption is the very meaning of the whole world history, eclipsing any other idea. Inspired by this certainty, the Dutch corsairs could sing their joyful hymn: 'The land will become sea, and so will be free!' . . . When in the sixteenth century the elemental energies started turning towards the sea, their success was such that they soon irrupted into the arena of world politics and its history.
>
> (Schmitt 1997: 61)

Only the Calvinist ethos, according to Schmitt, could give to the Protestant corsairs the self-assurance that was necessary to challenge the Universal authority of the Pope and the extraordinary power of the Spanish Empire. Only the certainty of salvation, and the belief in the validity of their own interpretation of the law, could give them the audacity to disobey the Roman Pope, accepting banishment from the Christian Commonwealth and the fact of being branded as opponents of everything their fathers had considered sacred and true.

This hypothesis, which Schmitt penned in 1942 – with a note complaining about the fact that the influence of Radical Protestant sects had been so far ignored by most historical studies on sixteenth century piracy – has received a new life since the publication of *Radical Pirates?* by the celebrated British historian Christopher Hill (1986: 161–187). In this short essay, the prominent historian of the English Revolution – probably without a direct knowledge of Schmitt's hypothesis – looked at the history of seventeenth-century piracy as part of the age of revolts and revolutions caused by the emergence of the rebellious spirit that had first exploded the authority of the Catholic hierarchy, and then had nearly brought to its knees the authority of the early modern state. Following the collapse of the English Revolution in 1660, Hill argued, the Caribbean was flooded with a 'floating population' of 'persecuted radicals' who 'carried with them ideas which had originated in revolutionary England' (1986: 162–163). In his *Liberty Against the Law* (1996), Hill argues that pirates were part of a 'silenced vagabond class', a new class of expropriated commoners who had no other choice but either to enter the wage economy or roam the earth as beggars, criminals and pirates: perpetual exiles, created by the emergence of private property and bourgeois law. Many of them would revolt against the early capitalist legal system appealing to their own judgment, just as the heretical corsairs of the previous century had appealed to their own interpretation of the Scriptures against the authority of the Pope. We can bring forward the hypothesis – standing on the shoulders of Schmitt's reading of sixteenth-century piracy and Hill's view on the pirates of the following century – that a similar spirit of rebellion ran through over two centuries of piracy. For all their stark differences, the Lutheran corsairs of the sixteenth century and the pirates of the seventeenth and early eighteenth centuries shared a common disposition to challenge the established hierarchies and their authoritative interpretation of justice, being in turn excommunicated or branded as *hostis communis omnium*.

What is certain is that the pirates of the early sixteenth century rapidly emerged as the most formidable foe of Spanish Imperial policy. In 1523, Diego Colon, son of Christopher Columbus, wrote to King Charles I complaining about the number of corsairs roaming the seas, trying to rob the Crown of its well-deserved and legitimate riches. Colon notices that these first pirates, or 'Lutheran corsairs' – as they were generally called by the Spanish – were mostly French, based in the Calvinist stronghold of La Rochelle (Gerassi-Navarro 1999: 13). The English and the Dutch soon joined their ranks, preying on the Spanish colonies in the Caribbean, but the French Calvinists were the true vanguard of this uprising against the Holy Roman Emperor and the entire structure of Christian international law. In fact, although historical research on the history of piracy in the early sixteenth century remains scarce, it is clear that French corsairs predominated in the first half of the sixteenth century. As a Catholic monarch, the French Francis I deeply resented the Vatican's favouritism toward Charles I of Spain, at that time serving the Christian Commonwealth as Holy Roman Emperor. His celebrated protest against Adam's will made explicit that he would not accept the partitioning of the world between Spain and Portugal, going as far as questioning the honesty of papal authority: 'The sun shines on me as well as on others,' he famously quipped, 'I should be very happy to see the clause in Adam's will which excluded me from my share when the world was being divided' (Hart 2001: 31).

In his hatred of Spanish Imperial authority, the Catholic monarch of France would find a precious ally in the Calvinist seamen of La Rochelle. The Calvinist corsairs were already active in the Atlantic Triangle in the period of Columbus' famous voyages; but it was after Cortés' conquest of Mexico (1519–1521) that large amounts of wealth began to flow back to Spain, giving them an unprecedented historical relevance. In the second decade of the sixteenth century, then, during the first war between France and Spain over the control of the Italian peninsula, Francis I gave explicit permission and full political backing to a Florentine navigator based in Dieppe to organize an expedition in the Atlantic in order to harass Spanish sea-lanes. As a result, in early 1522, Giovanni de Verrazzano, better known to the Spanish as Jean Florin, captured two Spanish caravels carrying most of the fabled Aztec treasures, which Hernán Cortés had plundered in the name of the Spanish Crown. By some account, the pirate's attack yielded 65,000 ducats in gold stolen from Montezuma's treasure, 150 kg of pearls from Cubagua and Margarita, together with a cargo of sugar from Hispaniola (Lane 1998: 18). This first assault on the Spanish Main was significant, not only insofar as it opened the door to the modern age of piracy as an alternative and profitable means of undermining Spain's imperial power, but also because it announced an important change in global history, as the Indies became a theatre for the European wars of religion, which had already started to destroy the stability of the Christian Commonwealth.

In addition to Jean Florin, among the most well-known French pirates operating in the Atlantic were: Roberto Baal, who attacked Cartagena, La Havana and Santiago; Jean Agou operating off the Calvinist centre of La Rochelle; Philippe Lorain and Gonneville of Honfleur, who attacked Portuguese settlements in Brazil and were regarded as traitors of Christian civilization for having allied with a band of *cimarrones*, escaped slaves in permanent war with the colonial militias (Merrien 2003). But the boldest and most punishing raids in the Spanish West Indies were probably those organized by Jacques de Sores and François Le Clerc – also known as Jambe de Bois, literally 'Wooden Leg' or 'Peg Leg' – who raided the Portuguese Island of Madeira in 1552, and Santiago de Cuba in 1554 (Villiers 2007: 5–24). Together the two Huguenots from Normandy brought havoc to Spanish colonial settlements, going as far as capturing Havana in 1555. The Protestant Corsairs were said to seize Spanish vessels at sea, but also descend on villages and ports; according to Spanish reports they raided churches and homes, harassing the civilians for intelligence on the location of Spanish treasures, persecuting the Catholic clergymen and provoking the Spanish militias.

By the end of the sixteenth century, pirates had become Spain's most feared commercial and political enemies. Direct losses to the *corsarios luteranos* were certainly not unbearable at the time, at least in terms of stolen bullion and disruption of trade. Nevertheless, the attacks shocked the self-assurance of Spain's

Imperial subjects, instilling doubts on the unassailable holiness of Spain's Universal mission in the New World. The Spanish claimed that, if they followed the teachings of the Church, since they were in the Americas as servants of Christ, they would be able to overcome any adversity and any adversary. The success of the Lutheran corsairs therefore remained almost inexplicable and a source of persistent bewilderment. In 1604, the epic poet Miramontes y Zuazola could still consider the terrible audacity and carelessness of Drake's successful piracies and write in astonishment:

> *Incomprehensible God! Did this pirate*
> *not erase from his brow the mark*
> *that rescues from original sin*
> *he who sails upon the Roman ship?*
> *Why allow then such sums of gold and silver*
> *to be taken from the Catholic Crown today?*
> *Your work, Lord, is indeed just*
> *with which you claim marvellous fame!*
> (cited in Gerassi-Navarro 1999: 53)

From the Spanish perspectives the excommunicated heretics who crossed the papal line of demarcation were not simply enemies but *hostis communis omnium.* They were a religious Other, who challenged not only Spanish interests but the unity of the entire Christian Commonwealth. It must be stressed that, from a perspective still rooted in the *res publica Christiana*, the modern distinction between pirates (unlicensed freebooters) and privateers (privately owned armed vessels provided with a commission from an official government authorizing the owners to use the ship against a hostile nation) was certainly understandable but neither central nor particularly significant. All foreigners crossing the papal line of demarcation (*raya*) without explicit Spanish consent were excommunicated heretics, endangering Spanish missionary activity in America and questioning the authority of the Catholic Church. According to the Spanish, they were neither pirates nor privateers but rather *corsarios luteranos*, a term that always retained a strong religious connotation.

The expression is in itself revealing of the conceptual framework in which the Spanish Imperial understanding of the Protestant pirates set its roots. The first *corsarios* defined as such were those sent by the Barbary cities of North Africa to attack Christian ships and coasts as part of a long history of mutual religious warfare in the Mediterranean. To a sixteenth-century Spanish ear, the novel term *corsarios luteranos* almost automatically referred to the more established term *corsarios islamicos*, which had been used for centuries throughout the Mediterranean. 'When the Spanish used *corsair*' writes Nina Gerassi-Navarro 'they were alluding to the attackers' heretical characteristics in addition to defining their political aggression' (1999: 61). Those caught beyond the *raya* were defined not by their nationality –

there is seldom reference in the documents of *corsarios inglés, francés* or *holandés* – but by their heretical beliefs.

Accordingly, they were most often judged by the Inquisition. This is hardly surprising, considering the automatic excommunication of all foreigners crossing the *raya,* since 'the function of the Inquisition in the New World was originally and first of all to prevent contact with heretics and other individuals believing in false doctrines who might have arrived in the Indies' (Lane 1998: 48). In this way, the fight against the Protestant freebooters was included within the larger Imperial discourse centred on religious conversion of the native people, deposition of the native authorities and their devilish and pagan cults, protection of the natives from contact with the infective heresies of excommunicated individuals and sects.[2] In 1570, for instance, 38 pirates from John Hawkins' crew were tried for heresy by the Inquisition in Mexico. John Oxenham, a companion of Drake in the 1570s – who had become infamous among the Spanish for having forged an alliance with rebellious *cimaronnes* and indigenous groups like the Cuna Cuna of Eastern Panama – was captured in 1576, tried for heresy, hanged and burnt on the stake. His trial was held in Lima in front of the Court of Inquisition and soon became widely discussed in England (Maltby 1971: 32).

In the sixteenth century, the Lutheran corsair emerged as a recurrent character also in Spanish literature. As stressed by a Spanish historian of sixteenth-century colonial literature:

> The presence of pirates in these colonial texts illustrates the cruelty and violence the heretics were known to commit, and also exemplifies the dangers facing all those who do not embrace the Catholic faith. . . . Pirates are barbaric and commit ungodly crimes because they are Lutherans, Protestant heretics. As such they must be punished and expelled from Spanish America.
>
> (Gerassi-Navarro 1999: 68)

In other words, the representation of the cruelty, selfishness and savage violence of the heretical pirates served a fundamental role in Imperial ideology. The condemnation of pirates and the colourful description of their crimes cast a dark light on the Protestant faith, but most of all, it allowed the Spanish Empire to

2 According to Merriman, 'in the Inquisition the Empire possessed a weapon of defence as characteristically Spanish as the piracies of the sea-rovers were English' (1962: 268). According to Pauline Croft, although 'at no time did the Spanish government attempt to manipulate the Inquisition directly', the clergy played a central role in the judgment of Lutheran Corsairs (1972: 267–268). According to Horder, Spanish authorities 'found it convenient to turn over to the Inquisition any of the hated British who fell foul of them in Spain, and have them dealt with as heretics rather than as pirates or vagrants' (1975: 270).

represent itself as the last bastion of Christianity and protector of humanity. The pirate appears as the contrapuntal concept of Empire. The Lutheran Corsair is *hostis communis omnium*, at least as much as the Holy Roman Emperor is 'the sword of Christendom', a force in service of the Universal Christian Commonwealth. The violence of the heretical corsairs, in fact, threatens the Spanish as much as the natives, the faithful servants of the Church as much as the black slaves. As a result, the whole of humanity is invited to unite against them, under the guidance of the Catholic Crown of Spain.

Silvestre de Balboa Troya y Quesada's poem *Espejo de paciencia*, written in Cuba in 1608, represents well this ideological concept of the pirate, which would continue to serve a central role in a variety of Imperial discourses in the following centuries. The poem describes with horror the assault on the town of Yara by Gilberto Giron, a Calvinist pirate from the north of France. The corsair is portrayed robbing the pacific Spanish settlers. He amasses wealth, but he does not forgo the kidnapping of the elderly Catholic bishop, imprisoning and torturing him. The cruelty of the heretical pirate against this man of 'exemplary life', 'good deeds' and 'pure blood' cannot pass unnoticed and finally the whole community unites as a single body, confronting the heretical pirates and rescuing the clergyman (Quesada 2011: 42). The unrestrained greed and the savage violence of the Calvinist corsair is hateful to all the racial and social components of colonial society, which finally discovers itself united in a single front under the banner of Christianity and Empire. At last, a black slave, suitably named Salvador, kills the heretical corsair and saves the Catholic bishop, becoming a hero for the settlers as much as for the natives. Not only the Spanish but also the black slaves and the aboriginal Indians can recognize the devilish injustice of the pirate so that they finally set aside their differences to defend the colony. Paradoxically, therefore, the pirate emerges as the most powerful agent in the realization of that Imperial Universalist vision he is set to deny. As anticipated by St Augustine, it is only in the struggle against the enemy of Christian humanity that the latter appears to realize itself.

This religious discourse on piracy, which characterized the pirate as a faithless heretic and an enemy of all true Christians, would remain central to the Spanish national imagination well beyond the sixteenth century. Francis Drake would eventually emerge as the most recurrent embodiment of the terrible violence and devilish power of the new Anglo-Saxon Protestant nation and of its heretical creed. In fact, after Pope Pius V had issued the excommunication of 'Elizabeth, the pretended Queen of England and the servant of crime', all English subjects had been released from their allegiance to the English crown (Grewe 2000: 156). After the bull *Regnans in Excelsis*, issued on 25 February 1570, all Christians who continued to obey the orders of the heretical tyrant were therefore considered equally damned. According to the Catholic Church and the Holy Roman Emperor, therefore, the English more than the French were *by definition* corrupt. 'Their country has refused obedience to the Holy Father' and their nation had thus become, in the words of a sixteenth century chronicle, 'hateful to the world and to God' (Miramontes y Zuazola 1978: 44).

In poems such as Juan de Castellanos' *Discurso de el Capitan Francisco Draque* or Miramontes y Zuazola's *Armas Antartica*, Drake is portrayed as a dragon, an heretical beast, unrestrained in his greed and merciless in his cruelty. He is shown pillaging Catholic churches and cathedrals, burning cities, torturing Spanish whites, killing black slaves and innocent Indians, robbing the rich and the poor without distinction. As shown by Gerassi-Navarro's brilliant study of the Drake myth in Spanish early-modern literature, the heretical pirate 'is always the embodiment of a force bringing chaos to the well-framed world dictated by the Church in the Spanish colonies' (1999: 54). The demonization of Drake, then, is not only aimed at condemning the violence of English privateering, but also 'can be read as coetaneous re-enactement of the religious struggle against Protestantism, a struggle in which the cosmic order that Catholicism had established had to be reconfirmed. This provides the rationale for situating all pirates among the heretics (1999: 55).'

It is most significant therefore that, in the first poem that describes Drake in this fashion, the heretical corsair is made to state with great clarity that which had become, after the first half of the sixteenth century, the main justification for English piracies in the New World. In Castellanos' *Discurso de el Capitan Francisco Draque*, the English corsair takes centre stage and, answering to those who accuse him of breaching the laws of Christianity, he openly questions the legitimacy of the Spanish Empire and the validity of its laws in the New World:

> *Since you have such great understanding*
> *clarify for me this doubt:*
> *Did Adam order through any testament*
> *that Spaniards be the only ones to profit?*
> *Show me where this is written*
> *and I at once will resign my right,*
> *but if it be the contrary,*
> *let he who can take the most.*
> (Castellanos 1921: 42)

Drake's words are a poetic synthesis of the legal doctrine of the 'amity lines', sponsored in the sixteenth century by Elizabethan England and promoted for the first time with the Treaty of Cateau-Cambresis (1559). The doctrine, which would become hegemonic in the seventeenth century, radically challenged the Universalism of Christian Scholasticism. It attacked the notion that a Universal international law could be said to exist and, instead, argued for a strict separation of the European continent from the New Word. The *raya* that, as we have seen, represented the first *global line* of world-historical significance was therefore transformed in an *amity line*. It was no longer an ordering device within the Universal order of the Christian community, but rather the extreme frontier at which international law ended and anomy began.

After the Treaty of Cateu-Cambresis, international law suspended itself 'beyond the line' allowing for unrestricted plunder by all European nations. Following Drake's words, the institution of amity lines was meant to 'let he who can, take the most' of the wealth of the Americans. It prefigured a space of free plunder, which was meant to remain isolated 'beyond the line', so to conserve peace, order and certainty of property rights within the European Continent. In the seventeenth century, it was in this world 'beyond the line' that piratical plunder would express itself ruthlessly as the secret engine propelling Europe towards capitalist modernity and America towards colonial subjection. In a state of exception at the heart of modern international law, piracy would be the first capitalist enterprise and plunder the true name of the primitive accumulation of capital.

Chapter 3

Zones of plunder

Piracy and primitive accumulation

The Spanish Empire remained, at least until the end of the sixteenth century, the most formidable bastion of a crumbling Universal order centred around the twin institutions of a Christian Pope and a Christian Emperor. The law of nations, accordingly, remained the legal order of an expanding Christendom. On the one hand, the medieval law of nations was a fully developed legal order of the Christian–Occidental legal community. On the other hand, there was a Universal order of mankind based on the idea that every man and every nation was originally and essentially part of Christendom; even the wickedest men are children of God. This distance, nevertheless – between the historical roots of the *res publica Christiana* in a closely linked Occidental community of Christian nations, and the boundless destiny of Christianity that was to embrace all men on Earth – was not a conceptual contradiction or an unsurpassable aporia but an *eschatological horizon*. Christianity was at once European and Universal, rooted in a specific historical tradition and destined to all men. It was, in other words, the common foundation of a closed, geographically defined *res publica Christiana* but also the Truth that Christians had the right and the duty to bring to all men.

Modern international law is rooted in the fundamental crises of this Universal Christian order. A *cosmological crisis*, first of all, caused by the 'Copernican Revolution' that displaced the Earth from the centre of the universe. A *geographical crisis*, caused by the discovery of a New World that displaced the center of European power from the Mediterranean Sea to the Atlantic Ocean. But also a *cultural crisis*, caused by the encounter with the American Other that threatened to submerge the Universality of Christianity in the relativism of a plurality of moral and legal orders. A *theological crisis* caused by the Lutheran Reform that questioned the philosophical foundations and the institutional centers of the old order. An *economic crisis* caused by the beginning of the enclosure movement and the expropriation of the commons, which would cause the destruction of the medieval agricultural economy. And finally, a *political crisis* caused by the Lutheran corsairs and their refusal to respect the attempt by the Spanish Empire to exclude all other nations from the New Word.

In this chapter, I discuss the ways in which this threatening disorder was kept at bay from the mid-sixteenth century and how it contributed to produce a new global order based on a strict division between Europe and the New World. In the first part, therefore, I discuss the transformation of international law and the spatial imagination in the late sixteenth century. I consider the Spanish–French Treaty of Cateau-Cambresis an important event, insofar as it discarded for the first time the Christian Universalist spatial imagination, still dominant in the sixteenth century, and it introduced in its place a strict division between Europe and the New World. While the papal line of demarcation, the so-called *raya*, portioned a global space that remained governed by a single Universal law centred in Rome but valid throughout the world; the *amity lines* of the seventeenth century were the first global lines of division, because they no longer partitioned a single undifferentiated space, but rather established a radical difference between the two sides of the line. The international legal order continued to be centred in Europe, although no longer in Rome, but now it suspended itself in the oceanic vastness beyond the line. The New World was therefore constituted as a 'free space' – that is, a space free from the restrictions of morality and the international legal order. A zone of plunder in which 'might made right' and lawless plunder could take its place in a threshold between legality and illegality.

In the second part, I consider the centrality of plunder in the global processes of primitive accumulation of capital that led, in the seventeenth century, to the creation of the foundations of the modern state and the capitalist mode of production. Plunder had a fundamental role in allowing the accumulation of wealth in international capitals such as London, Amsterdam and Paris, therefore stimulating the process of urbanization and the definitive crisis of the traditional peasant economy based on production for subsistence. Moreover, plunder coupled with mercantilist principles enabled the swelling of state finances and the construction of the bureaucratic and military apparatus necessary to sustain the emerging capitalist mode of production. Finally, plunder contributed to the expropriation of the colonized and the destruction of entire traditional economies and networks of trade: a global process of primitive accumulation that contributed to the formation of a global uprooted class of proletarians dependent on wages and the world market for their survival.

In the third part, therefore, I consider the intermix of trade and plunder that fuelled early merchant-capitalist empires; moreover, I look at the legal instruments that were used in order to regulate the use of private violence in the colonial world, thus making it profitable for the state and the metropolitan capital that funded it. I look at the organization of the privateering ship as both an engine of primitive accumulation and as a capitalist heterotopia, a machine in the service of the accumulation of wealth and a paradigmatic social space. Finally, I introduce some of the tensions and contradictions of this particular form of imperialist power. The unleashing of private violence in the anomic spaces beyond the line often opened the possibility of losing control of it. The reduction of the extra-European world to an anomy in which primitive accumulation and widespread plunder may be maximized – and circumscribed, thus preserving the 'sanctity' of property within Europe – also meant that the very same freedom to expropriate might be sometimes turned against the imperialist states that legitimated it.

Beyond the line: Imperialism and the state of exception

Piracy in the Indies began with an act of rebellion, a collective insurrection against the hierarchical order of the medieval Christian Commonwealth. It was first of all an act of disobedience: crossing the internationally sanctioned border beyond which only Spanish subjects had the right to live, trade, preach, plunder and settle. Hundreds of traders and adventurers from all over Europe – relying on the individualist and rebellious spirit promoted first by the Lutheran reform and then by the new Calvinist, Quaker and Anabaptist faiths – decided to cross the first global line, exposing themselves to papal excommunication and imperial outlawry. By the middle of the sixteenth century, the European Wars of Religion had firmly reached beyond the papal line of demarcation, where they took the form of a violent clash between the Lutheran corsairs – mainly from France, Holland and the British Isles – and the Catholic subjects of the Spanish Empire. The animosity was so engrained that the expression 'No peace beyond the line' rapidly became a catchword, widely known by the public as much as by the official diplomatic services. In the 1684 English edition of *Buccaniers of America* one could still find stated with absolute conviction: 'We know that no peace could ever be established beyond the line, since the first possession of the Indies by the Spaniards, till the burning of Panama' (Exquemelin 1684: 3). This line, to which Exquemelin felt he could refer without any further clarification, was known in diplomatic circles with the name of 'amity line'.

This was a novel concept, which at first simply stated an historical fact: that the papal line of demarcation – although originally meant to be 'a mere internal division between two land-appropriating Christian princes' (Schmitt 2003: 54), which recognized the Pope as an authority legitimated to settle their conflicts and apportion the world in separate exclusive 'missionary zones' – had rapidly become a contested line, beyond which a permanent warfare between outlawed corsairs and the Spanish Empire perpetuated itself. Gradually, it became a principle firmly rooted in sixteenth-century international law, explicitly affirmed by Protestant nations, and grudgingly accepted by the Spanish Empire. As Carl Schmitt made clear in his seminal *The Nomos of the Earth*:

> the amity lines initiated with the Spanish-French Treaty of Cateau-Cambresis (1559) . . . were an important part of European international law during the 17th century. The principle they established remained in force for the whole epoch, i.e. that treaties, peace, and friendship applied only in Europe, to the old world, to the area on this side of the line.
>
> (2003: 90)

The 1559 peace treaty, marking the end of over 65 years of power struggles between France and Spain, established a number of regulations and codes of international law, but explicitly suspended itself west of the first meridian. Outside Europe, there would be neither peace nor certainty of property, neither a common accepted law nor a criminal who could break it. The principle established for the first time in 1559 would be repeated several times in the late sixteenth and early seventeenth centuries. In the Treaty of Vervins between France and Spain in 1598, for instance, it was agreed that the peace should not hold good south of the Tropic of Cancer and west of the meridian of the Azores. Beyond these two lines – here unequivocally called 'les lignes de l'enclos des Amitiés' or 'the lines which enclose friendship' – no law would be valid (Haring 1910: 52). In 1614, thus, the French Queen Regent Marie de Medici could openly refuse to prosecute English subjects accused of piracy by Spanish authorities. In rebutting Spanish demands, she could base her claims on what was by now a long-established tradition:

> 'The Spanish ambassador has no right to reclaim property taken by my son's subjects beyond the line, since there has never been any kind of peace between the subjects of the two crowns in those waters, as can be verified by all the treaties since the time of Francis I. And no matter how many times negotiators from both sides have met, they have never found any resolution of this particular difficulty, except to agree verbally and by word of mouth that, however many hostile acts occur beyond the meridian of the Azores to the west, and the Tropic of Cancer to the south, there shall be no occasion for complaints and claims for damages, but whoever proves the stronger shall be taken for the lord.'
>
> (cited in Mattingly 1963: 149)

The origin of modern international law, therefore, is to be found in the irreversible disintegration of the Universal claims that had sustained the late-medieval *res publica Christiana* and the emergence of a new legal doctrine, which fundamentally discarded the idea that Justice and Truth were transcendental notions whose validity cannot depend on time and space. For the first time, it was accepted – although only secretly and never officially by the Spanish Empire – that law and morality were not Universal values but spatially determined institutions. Such a division challenged all traditional intellectual and moral principles. The then-popular maxim 'Beyond the equator there are no sins' is echoed in the famous passage of Pascal's *Penseés* written in the mid-seventeenth century: 'Three degrees of latitude upset the whole jurisprudence and one meridian determines what is true . . . It is a funny sort of justice whose limits are marked by a river; true on this side . . ., false on the other' (1966: 46).

The amity lines represented a fundamental caesura, separating Europe from the colonial world and effectively defining the latter as an empty space subtracted from the law. It was first of all the result, as affirmed by Carl Schmitt and confirmed by statements like the one above by Marie de Medici, of the crisis of the *res publica*

Christiana and the subsequent impossibility to organize the European appropriation of American space on the basis of a common enterprise on the model of the medieval crusade. 'At this line', writes Schmitt:

> Europe ended and the New World began. At any rate, European law ended here. . . . Beyond the line only the law of the stronger applied. Different from rayas the amity lines defined a sphere of conflict between contractual parties, precisely because they lacked any common presupposition and authority. The only matter they could agree upon was the freedom of the open spaces that began beyond the line.
>
> (2003: 93)

The Treaty of Cateau-Cambresis made explicit European imperialism's underlying spatial conception. Europe defined itself as an increasingly civilized space, regulated by the growing edifice of international law and its strictly limited conception of war, and yet its identity remained dependent on the existence of a state of nature, an anomic space lurking beyond its coasts, a space in which might made right, and every man was a wolf to all others.

While in Europe the age of primitive accumulation was rapidly being followed by the establishment of a severe legal code protecting the new social order (Marx 1976: 896–904), beyond the line 'might should make right, and violence done by either party to the other should not be regarded as in contravention of treaties' (Grewe 2000: 523). It is easy to see how such a principle worked as a form of state of exception at the heart of early international law; a state of exception that would validate violent forms of primitive accumulation, imperialism and exploitation without putting in question the overall validity of international law itself. As Eliga Gould has shown, in the seventeenth century and to a degree also in the following century:

> both metropolitan and colonial writers accepted an image of Britain's Atlantic periphery as a region 'beyond the line,' a zone of conflicting laws where Britons were free to engage in forms of violence and exploitation that were unacceptable whether in Britain proper or in Europe's law-bound state system.
>
> (2003: 482)

The early history of piracy – and its use by European imperialist powers in order to extract wealth from the colonial world – had as its theatre precisely this space of exception, opened at the heart of modern international law. 'The fact that the lines gave free rein for looting,' writes Schmitt:

> especially to English 'privateers' is understandable and generally recognized. . . . And also the fact that the thoroughly Catholic King of France aligned himself with dangerous heretics and wild pirates, freebooters

> and buccaneers against the Catholic King of Spain can be explained only by the fact these pirate raids were undertakings beyond the line.
>
> (2003: 93)

Until the eighteenth century, international law was characterized by a strict separation between the European continent – which became considered more and more as a single legal system in which property was recognized internationally and violence was rigidly regulated – and the extra-European world, which remained essentially free for appropriation. In brief, throughout the sixteenth and seventeenth centuries, the validity of the *ius gentium* would come to an end at the meridian of the El Hierro island. Beyond that, plunder was neither legal nor illegal but simply suspended on a threshold between legality and illegality.

The sixteenth-century amity line is the becoming-visible of the founding threshold of modern international law. In relation to the law, certainly, one can only think in terms of legality or illegality. And yet this already presupposes a previous categorical gesture, which divides what enters the realm of the law and what escapes it. To capture this distinction, the Spanish language neatly differentiates between the *legal*, the *illegal* and the *alegal*. This perfectly captures the awareness that the language of legality may present itself as Universal, but it is in fact a socially-constituted form of language based on a central organizing principle.[1] The central dichotomy on which legal language organizes reality, therefore, 'leaves out a whole social territory where the dichotomy would be unthinkable as an organizing principle, that is, the territory of the lawless, the a-legal, the non-legal, and even the legal or illegal according to non-officially recognized law' (De Sousa Santos 2007: 5). The line that separates the realm of the law from the realm of the outlaw therefore grounds and precedes the dichotomy between legal and illegal which organizes the world on this side of the line.

This is why Proudhon's quip 'Property is theft!' (1994: 13) remains an irresolvable paradox. Does not theft, asked Marx, 'defined as a forcible violation of property', already 'presuppose the existence of property'? (1955: 169). Max Stirner posed a similar question:

> Is the concept 'theft' at all possible unless one allows validity to the concept 'property'? How can one steal if property is not already extant? What belongs to no one cannot be *stolen*; the water that one draws out of the sea he does not *steal*.
>
> (1995: 223)

1 Lafargue rightly complained: 'Hobbes and the philosophers who speak of natural right, natural religion, natural philosophy are lending to Dame Nature their notions of right, religion and philosophy, which are anything but natural. What should we say of the mathematician who should attribute to nature his concepts of the metric system and should philosophize on the natural meter and millimetre? Measures of length, laws, gods and philosophical ideas are of human manufacture; men have invented them, modified them and transformed them, according to their private and social needs' (1975: 177).

Property and theft, in other words, are rooted in the same soil, from which they cannot be eradicated; they are legal concepts, which are valid only where law rules. Beyond the line, in the state of exception that precedes and grounds the law, there is neither property nor crime, only freedom and struggle. The pirate here is not a criminal – as was the case in the early sixteenth century as long as a Universal Christian legal order was recognized to exist – but strictly an outlaw, a freebooter. While in Europe it made sense to distinguish between authorized privateers and criminal pirates, beyond the line the distinction was moot, and the lawless freebooter and the anarchic buccaneer dominate the scene.

Through the particular dispositif of the amity line, the world 'beyond the line' was for the first time included in the Euro-centric system of modern international law, but its inclusion was from the beginning paradoxical. The New World entered international law as a space beyond the law. The funding gesture of international law is thus an exclusive inclusion, through which the norm is applied to the exception simply in no longer applying, in withdrawing from it. At the heart of international law, the history of Imperialist plunder reveals a state of exception. As noted by Giorgio Agamben, in fact, 'the state of exception is thus not the chaos that precedes order, but rather the situation that results from its suspension. In this sense, the exception is truly, according to its etymological root, taken outside (*ex-capere*) and not simply excluded' (1998: 18). The space of exception in which modern piracy has its roots reveals itself as the fundamental localization of international law. It is on the threshold between order and anarchy, between the anomic realm of the buccaneer and the disciplinary order of the law, between the chaotic practices of imperialist plunder and the iron laws of the market in its contemporary form, that much of international law is played. The exception, to quote again Agamben's insightful analysis of the concept:

> does not limit itself to distinguishing what is inside from what is outside but instead traces a threshold between the two, on the basis of which outside and inside, the normal situation and chaos, enter into those complex topological relations that make the validity of the juridical order possible.
>
> (1998: 19)

The establishment of explicit amity lines beyond which freedom is absolute and human behaviour is *alegal* is therefore a rather complex operation that is at the very foundation of modern international law. There is a fundamental difference between the anomy of the ancient sea and the one established with the tracing of modern amity lines. The Ocean, for the man of antiquity and still in the Middle Ages, was a space wholly unexplored, an empty expanse, threatening, alien, unknown and hostile. Diodorus Siculus held that Hercules moved Spain and Africa closer to each other, forming the Pillars of Hercules only to hinder the monsters of the Atlantic Ocean from entering the Mediterranean. Certainly Plato imagined the lost realm of Atlantis beyond those Pillars, but only to place it once and for all in the realm of the Unknown. Even according to the Renaissance tradition the Romans engraved *Nec plus ultra* on the Pillars of Hercules in order to warn sailors and navigators to go no further. Odysseus in his Mediterranean wanderings never dared beyond the Pillars of Hercules, and when he did, in Dante's medieval imagination, he not only lost his life but his soul was damned for eternity. In short, the Ocean remained, until the fifteenth century, a paradigmatic space of myth and alterity: a space populated by gods and monstrous beasts, but barred to man. And yet, from the end of the fifteenth century, the Atlantic Ocean is no longer the space of myth, but a space of law and history, of trade and piracy. The motto of the Spanish Empire would be, from now on, *Plus Ultra*, signalling this overcoming of all mythical limits. The Ocean slowly abandoned the realm of mythology in order to gain a space in the modern treaties of international law: but only as a space beyond the law. With the establishment of amity lines, international law opened up within itself a space where it claimed to be permanently suspended.

This act of exclusionary inclusion represents a revolutionary moment. It determined, to a very large extent, the elemental imaginary that is at the base of modern political theory in its classical form. The work of Thomas Hobbes, in particular, is usually considered as symbolizing a fundamental turn in the history of European political thought (Galli 2001: 40–49). The origins of the modern state, according to Hobbes, are rooted in the attempt to overcome a state of nature in which everything can happen and freedom is absolute. The state is an artificial social machine, and its erection is the historical moment in which men leave behind the anarchy of nature in order to achieve security and discipline. Since everything in the state of nature is subject to open struggle, before and beyond the state there can be neither security nor property, 'and which is worst of all, continual fear, and danger of violent death: and the life of man, solitary, poor, nasty, brutish and short' (Hobbes 2010: 124). The ideological core of Hobbes' theory of the state has influenced modern political theory and determined, to a great extent, the course of international law. His negative ontology is at the base of an ideology that portrays the historical institutions of the modern state as strictly irreplaceable or, better, replaceable only with a form of anarchy that resembles a 'war of all against all'.

The hegemony of Hobbesian thought, nevertheless, can only be fully understood if we relate it not only to its ideological function, but also to the extent in which it reflected the image of the world that was emerging in the sixteenth century. The Hobbesian opposition between a savage state of nature 'where everything is permitted' and a closed space of civilization where rules apply was in fact the naturalization of the historical caesura operated by the Treaty of Cateau-Cambresis. As Schmitt writes:

> For Hobbes the state of nature is a domain of werewolves, in which man is nothing but a wolf among other man, just as 'beyond the line' man confronts other men as a wild animal. The axiom *homo homini lupus* has a long history . . . however in the 16th and 17th centuries, the formula acquired a concrete

> meaning with the amity lines, because now it was localized – it acquired its own space, recognized by Christian European governments, and thereby an unmistakable identity. Hobbes obviously was influenced not only by the creedal civil wars in Europe, but also by the image of the space beyond the law that Cateau-Cambresis established to exist in the great oceans and, beyond them, in the colonial world. His state of nature is a no man's land but this does not mean it exists nowhere. It can be located, and Hobbes' locates it, among other places, in the New World beyond the line.
>
> (2003: 96)

According to Hobbes, therefore, the alternative to the state is nothing but the world of freebooting, anarchy and perpetual warfare that the European empires had engendered in the New World. The paradox is that the vision of nature inaugurated by Hobbes, and holding a central place in the way politics has been thought in Europe since then, had its roots not so much in a scientific study of nature – as in Lewontin (Lewontin et al. 1985) – or in an anthropological study of how societies without state actually organize themselves – as, for example, in Graeber (2004) – but rather in the feral image offered by the development of early merchant capital in the anomic spaces 'beyond the line'. In the state of nature imagined by Hobbes, there can be neither law – since 'where there is no common power, there is no law', and a law cannot 'be made till they have agreed upon the person that shall make it' – nor security of property – 'there be no propriety, no dominion, no *mine* and *thine* distinct; but only that to be every man's that he can get, and for so long as he can keep it' (Hobbes 2010: 127).

Fitzpatrick correctly notices that in the sixteenth century, 'savagery came to be widely viewed as a general prelude to "civil society", the main instances continuing to be the savages of the New World "dispersed like wild beasts, lawless and naked"' (1992: 73). But it must be stressed that this characterization of the savages of the New World was not the result of detailed ethnographic studies, but rather of a preconception about the meaning of 'anarchy' and the 'state of nature', which reflected only the recent history of European imperialist struggles. For instance, Hobbes affirms the equivalence of the 'state of nature' with the absence of a feared 'common power', when an established commonwealth comes 'to degenerate into a civil war' (Hobbes 2010: 126). However, this description did not reflect the conditions of any savage tribe, but rather those of sixteenth-century Europe, then tormented by a civil war originated by the collapse of the Christian Commonwealth. In Hobbes' world, freedom means war and nature means omnipresent danger. Ironically, it was according to this paranoid vision of nature – that was really grounded in the image of what absolute freedom beyond the line meant for the acquisitive machines of early-modern European empires – that the savages 'beyond the line' were constructed as lawless predatory subjects in need of missionary teaching and civilizing imperial sovereignty.

The state of exception that lies at the heart of international law, therefore, was not only central in legitimating imperialist plunder; it also produced a paranoid vision of nature that continues to legitimize the institutions of the modern state, even today. At the domestic level, the terror of what the collapse of the state could mean has legitimized the most brutal repression of dissent, the most horrific genocide of minorities and the most scientific forms of torture, imprisonment and encampment.[2] At the international level, the most futuristic forms of warfare and violence are employed to suppress any space outside the state in the deployment of operations of 'state-building and 'peace-enforcing'. International law remains committed to a spatial imaginary founded on the distinction between a normal space in which law rules and exceptional spaces in which international law is suspended. As we will see, in fact, although the collapse of modern colonialism in the twentieth century resulted in the expansion of the international system from its European core to the whole globe, new spaces 'beyond the line' – subtracted from international law and therefore open to exploitation, plunder and direct international intervention – appear anywhere a 'failed state' is said to exist (Gordon 1997).

Plunder as primitive accumulation

The state of exception, in international law as in constitutional theory, is always at once a rupture in the texture of the legal system and the space in which sovereign violence can operate freely, so to transform the existing conditions and

2 Schmitt himself sees a connection between the early-modern suspension of international law 'beyond the line' and the mechanism of invocation of the state of exception at the domestic level. 'The . . . construction of a state of exception, of so-called martial law, obviously is analogous to the idea of a designated zone of free and empty space' (2003: 98). It is, first of all, in the new spaces beyond the line, in fact, that sovereign power is left unrestrained by traditional limits. In England, for instance, 'the King's power was considered to be absolute on the sea and in the colonies, while in his own country it was subject to common law and to baronial or parliamentary limits' (ibidem). The invocation of the state of exception or the imposition of 'martial law' is thus, first of all, a form of endo-colonization. Not only beyond the line, but within the modern state itself the law is suspended and the power of state sovereignty is revealed in its naked form. Beyond the line, in the spaces in which international law suspended itself, the sovereign could only be the strongest pirate, his power and freedom unrestrained. In the space of exception, equally, the sovereign has no legitimacy but only naked power and absolute freedom. In the anarchy created by the suspension of the law, everyone is exposed to the naked power of the strongest. And yet, as we will see, this absolute freedom can always, and it was in fact, appropriated by other powers, put to other uses, made dangerous even to the sovereign itself. It is in this sense that Fredric Jameson can think of the 'maritime state beyond the line' as 'a kind of spatial equivalent of the Bakhtinian carnival' (2005: 202). This is, incidentally, a lesson – and an emancipatory potential – that Agamben, in his otherwise precious *Homo Sacer*, seems to overlook. In assuming the camp, rather than the ocean 'beyond the line', as the paradigm of the state of exception, Agamben risks to forget that anarchy is where we are left exposed to the unmediated violence of the strongest, but it is also a place in which other freedoms, different from those to kill, to exploit and to plunder, could be and were experienced.

prepare a new order (which sometimes is nothing but the restoration of the old order). In addition to thinking of the exception as a negation of the norm, one must think of the norm as the becoming-normal of the exception. Plunder in the colonial world took place in a state of exception that negated, once and for all, the Universality of Christian international law; however, the wealth arriving in the ports of Europe would be soon registered and recognized as legitimate property. Plunder, piracy, theft – what originally had been a violent rupture – systematically becomes legal property. Beyond the line, all property is contested and yet, as Marie de Medici wrote to the Spanish King, 'whoever proves the stronger shall be taken for the lord' (cited in Mattingly 1963: 149). The state of exception, in other words, is an arena 'designated for tests of strength' (Schmitt 2003: 99), but once the line is crossed, the stronger shall be accepted as legitimate lord. The stronger freebooter 'beyond the line' becomes the legitimate holder of property on this side of the line. As Negri once pointed out, 'in the capitalistic economy, that excessive and founding political act that is the exception finds its equivalent in the act of original accumulation, of taking possession' (2008: 98).

More precisely, the state of exception is the legal form in which primitive accumulation can be realized. In Europe itself, only the rupture of traditional medieval norms could allow the transition to a new legal order. The long-standing relations of traditional use surrounding land – free pasture, common ownership of water springs and woods – were first suspended and breached, then new conditions were forced into being and recognized as the norm. What was, for the peasants who were rooted in the old medieval normative system, nothing but a crime – a subtraction from the commons in breach of traditional norms – eventually became the accepted norm. 'Landed property became absolute property; all the tolerated "rights" that the peasantry had acquired or preserved were now rejected by the new owners who regarded it simply as theft' (Foucault 1979: 85). In short, violence is 'the midwife of every old society which is pregnant with the new' (Marx 1973: 912), but every new order must negate the law-making violence that founds it, in order to establish itself as the norm.

Marx stresses over and over that the origins of capitalism are to be found in the interplay of imperialism and domestic original accumulation. There is a complex dialectical relationship between colonial predations and endogenous colonization; between the permanent state of exception 'beyond the line' and the temporary state of exception that, in countries like England, permitted the revolutionary transformation of the social structure. One could read causation from both sides: was imperialism the continuation of primitive accumulation on a global scale? Or rather was it early plunder 'beyond the line' that provided the model that was successfully applied in England, as Schmitt seems to suggest? Both statements seem partial, since they constitute only one side of a two-sided dialectical relationship. On the one hand, the expropriation of the commons in England contributed to the displacement of thousands of people who were then employed as labour power for colonial predatory ventures. On the other hand, the increasing opportunities for transnational exchange, forced or peaceful, created by the opening of new colonial markets stimulated the formation of a domestic economy organized for exchange (Policante 2012d).

As Marx makes clear in his efforts to account for the origins of the structural inequalities that sustain and fuel the relentless functioning of our contemporary, worldwide mode of production and consumption, lawless plunder is nothing less than capitalism's secret law and forgotten foundation. For Marx, 'the modern history of capital dates from the creation in the 16th century of a world-embracing commerce and a world-embracing market' (1976: 247). He saw 'the discovery of gold and silver in America, the extirpation, enslavement and entombment in mines of the aboriginal population, the beginning of the conquest and looting of the East Indies, the turning of Africa into a warren for the commercial hunting of black-skins' as 'the rosy dawn of the era of capitalist production' (1976: 915). In fact, behind the early colonial efforts of the European powers lay the need to finance the tremendous economic necessity of the newborn centralized systems of government, essential for capitalist development to happen. Without gold, silver, cotton and human beings coming from faraway lands, it would have been impossible to finance the institutional system that eventually paved the way for industrialization and development.[3]

Throughout the sixteenth and the seventeenth centuries, freebooting played a fundamental role in the primitive accumulation of European capital, and it was tolerated and even sponsored by the English, Dutch and French states, which would later be at the forefront of the Industrial Revolution of the nineteenth century. The British experience of piracy, for instance, began as a wing of semi-official government policy. In perpetual war against the mighty Catholic empires of Spain and Portugal, Protestant England granted special permits ('letters of marque') allowing private adventurers to explore, trade and prey upon the treasure ships of the enemy, as they sailed back to Europe heavy with silver and gold. Drake, Grenville, Raleigh and Morgan earned themselves a special place in British national memory since they played a central role in propelling London towards the Industrial Revolution. In fact, the first great wave of English marauding in the Atlantic, the vanguard of the British Imperial epoch, was a series of business ventures, always legitimated rather than commanded by a monarch whose power was more symbolic than material (Lane 1998: 33–62).

3 It must be stressed that primitive accumulation – that is, plunder, a form of accumulation based on the violent subtraction of means of production and livelihood – although necessary to the origin of the modern mode of capitalist production, cannot be relegated to the past. In fact, even today, side by side with capitalist accumulation proper – based on economic forms of compulsion that relegate violence only to the conservative role of protecting already-established forms of legalized property – forms of primitive accumulation based on the direct use of violence continue to play a role. Putting emphasis on this continuous character of primitive accumulation, Bucharin, on the eve of the first World War, could write an influential short essay titled 'The Imperialist Pirate State' (1916) just as, more recently, the Marxist geographer David Harvey advanced the notion of 'accumulation by dispossession' as the dynamic form of *The New Imperialism* (2005).

In order to understand the role played by plunder in the sixteenth and seventeenth centuries, we must turn to the dynamics proper to merchant capitalism. The immensely powerful trading companies of early modern Europe were instrumental in imposing favourable terms of trade to colonized nations, gradually integrating their economies within an emerging global market. At the end of the seventeenth century, the East India Company, a quasi-private, pre-colonial agency, handled more than half of British trade, and the fortunes that it generated for its shareholders were beyond imagination. The Dutch, the English and, to an extent, also the Portuguese and the French Empires, started off essentially as public–private partnerships in which merchant capital directly organized and projected military violence on a global scale. Most often, state institutions limited themselves to indirectly legitimizing the piratical violence of private entrepreneur, sanctioning their takings as legitimate and lawful once back in Europe. English, French and Dutch privateers distinguished themselves from criminal pirates (on this side of the line) and lawless freebooters (beyond the line) for their possession of letters of marque and reprisal, which was a government licence explicitly authorizing a person – known as a privateer – to attack and capture enemy vessels and bring them before admiralty courts for condemnation and sale. The wealth thus produced was reinvested in further maritime enterprises, with a fraction of it going to the sovereign's finances through direct and indirect taxation.

Markets in such a mercantilist pre-capitalist world were not metaphorically 'conquered' by means of cheap products on peaceful merchant fleets, but instead seized very tangibly and physically by warships and shining cannon balls. As pointed out by Marx, early merchant-capitalist Empires such as those organized by the Dutch East India company, the English South Sea Company and the French Compagnie de l'Occident not only 'exploit the difference between the prices of production of various countries' but 'the quantitative ratio in which products are exchanged is . . . arbitrary. . . . [C]ommercial profit not only appears as out-bargaining and cheating, but also largely originates from them' (Marx 2007: 388). The maintenance of 'arbitrary terms of exchange' could only be maintained in a situation of effective monopoly where competition was ousted and the rigidity of demand was consequently higher. Competition, therefore, instead of being based on production-efficiency and declining costs of production, took frequently the form of naval conflicts and increasing military expenditure. This is why Marx saw a structural connection between the development of merchant capital in Europe and the appearance of widespread practices of piracy and plunder on an unprecedented scale:

> Merchant's capital, when it holds a position of dominance, stands everywhere for a system of plunder, so that its development among the trading nations of old and modern times is always bound up with violent plunder, piracy, the taking of slaves and subjugation of colonies.
>
> (Marx 2007: 390)

The use of private maritime violence, in the form of privateering or legalized piracy, was an important tool of early European empires. As Janice Thomson

(1994) has shown, plunder was an integral part of a political-economic system structured around the principles of mercantilism. Early European states were able gradually to increase their institutional power through the systematic taxation of the wealth produced by private capital investments in overseas expeditions that usually were both commercial and piratical. Highly favourable terms of trade were most often backed by force, while traditional trading networks were systematically condemned as illegitimate, and subsequently destroyed by the superior military prowess of the European chartered companies. Since it represented their most significant advantage, Europeans made frequent use of maritime violence both against competing merchant groups – in order to disrupt commercial networks and therefore gain a dominant position – and against Asian states, in order to pry open port cities and improve trading conditions (Clulow 2009: 72).

In the sixteenth century, substantial returns were produced by preying upon the Atlantic arteries of the Spanish colonial empire, which had then begun systematically to exploit the American continent. Only in the last two decades of the century did over 76 English expeditions make their way to the Caribbean, at least once or several times, with the open intent of plundering the colonial riches extirpated from the colonial soil, and the indigenous body, by the Spanish Imperial system (Andrews 1984: 49). In the last 20 years of the sixteenth century, the value of prize money brought to England from the Caribbean alone ranged between £100,000 and £200,000 per year[4]. By the early seventeenth century, England obtained most of its bullion through Spain, either directly by way of freebooting beyond the line or indirectly through illegal trade with Spanish colonial subjects. By the second quarter of the century, 'raiding and plundering became the norm, and represented what seemed to be the extent of English capabilities, attracting considerable capital from the investing community' (Beckles 2001: 218).

Until the second half of the seventeenth century, the capital risks of investment in privateering adventures remained high, especially on account of the lack of a convenient base for English plundering in the Caribbean. The capture of Jamaica, following Cromwell's Western Design of 1655, greatly extended the possibility for profit. Freebooting was the key to early Jamaican economic development. From the second half of the sixteenth century, the Royal African Company's records show a steady stream of silver from the West Indies to London, which averaged £447,000 a year in the 1680s and helped balance trade with the Baltic and the East (Zahedieh 1990). This was despite the fact that most of the profit was invested in Jamaica where the wealth subtracted from the Spanish fuelled the development of the plantation system. 'Port Royal', writes Zahedieh, 'grew rich "out of the Spaniard purse": the profits of trading and looting were used to build up Jamaica's plantations' (1986: 211).

In an admirable work, drawing copious evidence from state papers, mercantile accounts and correspondence, shipping records, inventories and property deeds,

4 In order to imagine a modern-day equivalent for these sums one may consider that the annual wage of skilled construction craftsmen in London at the end of the sixteenth century would amount to a maximum of £12 to £19 a year (Rappaport 1989: 221).

Nuala Zahedieh has investigated the establishment of Jamaican sugar planting. She found that 'the bulk of the necessary capital was not obtained from the mother country. Capital was locally generated through the profits of a lucrative illicit trade based on plunder and contraband in the Spanish Empire' (1986: 205). Huge investments in capital were necessary in order to lay the bases of the modern plantation economy.

> To create the plantations, everything had to be brought over from other continents: the masters – white settlers; the labour force – black Africans (since the Indians of the coastal regions did not long survive the shock of the conquest); the plants themselves, except for tobacco. Along with the sugar cane, the techniques of sugar production had to be imported.
>
> (Braudel 1992: 273)

But where did the capital necessary for the establishment of the modern plantation originate? How were the slaves who would till the Jamaican ground eradicated from their soil? What was the origin of the riches that motivated and paid their captors?

The mechanism is clearly reflected in Taylor's list of the island's 'principal gentlemen and planters', which sums up a detailed government-funded study of the sugar industry in 1688. Almost without exception, their debt to the Spaniards is apparent. The most telling example was Henry Morgan, the most celebrated of the privateers, who built up a substantial plantation with 122 'negroes', valued at £5,263 on his death (Zahedieh 1986: 221). Far from supporting Adam Smith's theory that empire was a cost and burden on the mother country, the history of Jamaica provides a good example of Imperialism as plunder. As was already clear in the seventeenth century, outlaw freebooting served a fundamental role in the history of primitive accumulation. Through it, writes Hanson in 1683, England was able to drain some of 'the benefit of the Spanish gold and silver mines', without the 'labour and expense of working them' (1792: 11).

'Corsairs-capitalists' and outlaw buccaneers

During the Middle Ages, private violence was not always condemned; it was admitted as a form of law enforcement in a political reality conditioned by the lack of an effective judiciary capable of guaranteeing the enforcement of legal claims (Throop and Hyams 2010). Nevertheless, the law of feudalism, with its reliance on just violence as a means to punish evil and protect the divine order of the world, was gradually weakened and eventually erased by the emergence of an organized judicial system and an effective monopoly of legitimate violence in several European territories, which would finally consolidate in the form of the modern European state. Feuds were gradually forbidden and private warfare was substituted by the recourse to centralized courts of law, whose judgment was to be enforced only by state forces (Grewe 2000: 105). Already in the sixteenth century, therefore, a sharp distinction started to form between the order of the state, in which subjects were dispossessed of their right to vengeance and reprisal, and an international space, in which relationships between private subjects were always mediated by the public institutions of the state to which they belonged. As a result, any space for lawful revenge and reprisals was gradually annihilated. Bodin, in his classic *De Rei Publica*, considered the origins of the modern monopoly of violence as the result of the concentration of 'droits de marque ou de represaillés' in the sovereign ruler (1992: 46–89).

Only in the high seas, where the power of the state to mediate relationships between private subjects remained weak and ineffective, did the medieval institution of lawful revenge develop into a regulated regime, whose two central institutions were the so-called 'letter de marque et de represaillés' and the institution of 'general reprisals' in the form of privateering (Grewe 2000: 115). From the fifteenth century, therefore, a tendency emerged towards the growing separation between an international legal order of the land, based on the absolute centrality of the institution of the state with its monopoly on international violence, and a maritime order of the sea, in which power remained much more dispersed and private actors retained a relative autonomy from the state to which they belonged. At sea, merchants had to resort to forms of self-help throughout the Middle Ages. Naturally, this gave rise to forms of uncontrolled and uncontrollable piracy, as merchants had only to claim to have been victims of wrong treatment by a foreigner to obtain the right to claim damages from all the wrongdoer's countrymen. This often-manipulated practice came under the control of a strengthened public authority early in the seventeenth century (Grewe 2000: 202).

What remained widespread was the use of 'general reprisals', meaning official documents by which a king allowed his subjects to take all possible retaliatory measures against enemy ships. So-called *privateers* were private ships, authorized by a legitimate authority to perform violence at sea in the name of the state. This practice characterized the specific form taken by maritime warfare at least until the end of the eighteenth century. In fact, 'privateering' had a fundamental role in the history of the modern state and, especially in England, it contributed decisively to the financing of early state-building. Already in the first half of the sixteenth century, England's maritime life was so suffused with private marauding that it was widely referred in Europe as 'a nation of pirates' (Senior 1976: 1–12). In the sixteenth century, the coasts of Dorset, Cornwall and Wales developed thriving local economies based on plunder, and a number of noble families accrued much of their wealth by organizing and supporting piracy at sea.

The Killigrews, a Cornish family of immense local power, whose influence spread out to Wales and Ireland, were probably the most notorious local supporters of piracy. From the early days of Elizabeth's reign until 1598, the hereditary governors of Pendennis Castle were the centre of a vast network of sea-riding that fed mainly on coastal trade between Spain, Portugal, the north of France and Ireland.

> It was their support of the pirates that led to the elaborate system of harbours of sale and harbours of refuge that were organized for piracy under

> Elizabeth. . . . John Killigrew was a recognized leader. His uncle Peter had sailed the Irish seas as a rover. His mother, Lady Killigrew, was accused of leading a boarding party at Falmouth and murdering a factor in a Hanseatic ship for the sake of two barrels of Spanish pieces of eight.
>
> (Mathew 1924: 340)

Carl Schmitt singled them out 'as a handsome example of the predatory capitalism of the golden age, in its early stage':

> The Killigrews embody in an exemplary way the home front of the great age of piracy that saw the fulfillment of a thirteenth-century English prophecy: 'The lion's cubs will turn into fishes of the sea.' At the end of the Middle Ages, the lion's cubs were tending sheep in the main, and the fleece, sold in Flanders, was processed there into cloth. It was only in the sixteenth and the seventeenth centuries that this nation of shepherds recast itself into a sea-roaming nation of privateers, into 'children of the sea.'
>
> (1997: 55)

This early piratical capitalism developed in the late sixteenth century, when long-distance commerce and violence most often went hand in hand. European trade outside the old Continent 'was not generally an amicable affair; there were no international courts in which to enforce contracts. . . . Often demand had to be encouraged, and prices were agreed upon under duress from the stronger party. Might made prices right' (Lane 1998: 36). The Elizabethan Sea-Dogs amassed immense wealth not only by participating in the illegal slave trade – often forcing their trade both on the Africans as well as on the Spanish – but also through unmitigated plundering, often motivated by 'gentlemanly revenge'. In the late sixteenth century, 'piracy', writes the distinguished naval historian Nicholas Rodger, 'was not only an activity of marginal outcast communities . . . it was often an activity of the wealthy and well connected, privately and sometimes publicly backed by the Queen and her ministers' (1986: 345).

The celebrated adventures of John Hawkins, Richard Hawkins, John Oxenham, Francis Drake, Richard Grenville, Walter Raleigh, Martin Frobisher and Thomas Cavendish were all more or less successful joint-stock operations. Most of the ships were bought and fitted from London and the West Country, crossed the amity line and returned to have their profits registered as legitimate takings. Queen Elizabeth, while she publicly disavowed the outrages committed by the English freebooters, was often secretly one of the principal shareholders in their enterprises (Haring 1910: 21). A large share of profits (two-thirds in most cases) went back to the merchants and bankers who were financing the expedition. The rest was divided among the highest members of the crew, with most of the sailors often employed as wage-labourers. Similarly, the Dutch fitted privately financed ventures aimed simultaneously at trade, plunder and settlement beyond the line, which were most often affiliated to either the East India Company or the West India Company.

These joint-stock operations of plunder were paradigmatic forms of capitalist enterprise. As we shall see, the maritime work force was one of the first social groups to be thoroughly proletarianized – that is, expropriated and reduced to a complete dependence on wage-labour for survival. As a consequence, sailors often anticipated forms of strike – symptomatically, the use of the word first appeared in 1768, when rebellious sailors 'struck' the topgallant sails of merchant ships at the London main docks (Westover 1998: 371) – sabotage and overall insurrection that would become central elements in nineteenth-century working-class struggles around the world. For instance, when Piet Heyn returned in Amsterdam after having captured the entire New Spain treasure convoy of 1627, comprising valuables worth some 12 million florins, the shareholders enjoyed dividends of over 75%, while the underpaid sailors rioted in the streets of Amsterdam in the vain hope of receiving at least a part of the profit (Boxer 1965: 77).

In the sixteenth and seventeenth centuries, thousands of expropriated commoners were expelled from the English countryside, pouring into the urban conglomerates of London, Liverpool, and Bristol among others. There they were absorbed in the new disciplinary institutions: the manufacturing factory, the prison, but also – and especially – the ship. Thousands of property-less commoners became part of the swelling maritime working class, when they were pushed onto the ships that would colonize the world for England, bringing unheard wealth to its cities, opening new markets to its merchandise and contributing to its industrial expansion (Rediker 1989). Proletarian multitudes were pushed onto the enclosed space of the ship by the combined pressure of 'economic' and 'non-economic' compulsion; they were pushed to join the merchant navy by want, and they were often forced to join the Royal Navy by the press gang. In Elizabethan times, impressment as a form of recruitment was widespread, and with the introduction of the Vagrancy Act (1597), those who were identified as vagrants, unemployed and 'young without trade' were systematically drafted into service. This was a form of forced labour based on the legal power of the King to force men into military service, as well as to recruit volunteers. Moreover, seamen in the sixteenth century were not covered by Magna Carta and 'failure to allow oneself to be pressed' was punishable by hanging (Ennis 2002: 11).

The ship was the fundamental machine that allowed European expansion overseas, the primitive accumulation of capital and the growth of the modern state in Europe. In other words, as Carl Schmitt once pointed out, 'the ship is the core of human maritime existence, at least as much as the house is the core of its terrestrial existence' (1955: 161). It was thus with the aim of disciplining this fundamental European institution that the first legislation against mutiny was introduced in England in the early seventeenth century. The problem received attention at the highest levels of English law in 1615, when Sir Edward Coke presided over two cases in which mutiny was at issue. Since 'the Sea is excluded from common law and the Magna Charta provisions', writes Coke, 'the Admiral does not rule the sea' in Europe – and even less, as we have seen, beyond the line. Therefore, the ship was to be conceived as a floating fragment of country land in the midst of the anomic sea (Rubin 2006: 45). Although beyond the line there was neither law nor crime (and therefore imperialism, plunder and international struggle were unrestrained), class relationships within the enclosed space of the sea were still regulated according to traditional feudal law.[5] The new problems posed by the regulation of class struggle at sea could only be resolved by analogy, incorporating the governance of the ship within the traditional feudal framework: 'with English ships filling the role of floating English islands, merchant-captains filling the role of feudal masters, and sailors filling the role of servants and commoners' (Rubin 2006: 46–48).

Not only Foucault's *Stultifera Navis* but all early-modern ships shared a fundamentally ambiguous and paradoxical character. The sea is a space of freedom – 'navigation delivers man to the uncertainty of fate; on water, each of us is in the hand of his own destiny; every embarkation is potentially the last' (Foucault 2001: 8) – but it is also the ultimate space of danger, the demonic space par excellence. At sea, the workingman is confined to the ship, from which there is no escape, but on that floating prison he is 'delivered to the river with its thousand arms, the sea with its thousand roads, to that great uncertainty external to everything. He is a prisoner in the midst of what is the freest, the openest of routes: bound fast at the infinite crossroads' (Foucault 2001: 9). This is why the ship, more than the island, is the ultimate confinement; there is no escape from its discipline. It is a 'floating fragment of country land' with no space to hide. But, on the other hand, ships have always represented a means of escape, a radical line of flight from what is most nearby and usual. Hundreds of poor commoners – confined on merchant ships as indentured servants, wage-labourers and impressed sailors – rebelled, escaped and found a new freedom in the anarchy beyond the line.

> Out beyond the frontier, the state of Nature (i.e. no State) still prevailed – and within the consciousness of the settlers the option of wildness always lurked, the temptation to give up on Church, farm work, literacy, taxes, all the burdens of civilization and 'go to Croatan' in some way or another.
>
> (Bey 2003: 45)

5 In *A Search for Sovereignty: Law and Geography in European Empires*, Lauren Benton correctly notices that 'ships played a dual role as sources of order in the oceans: they were islands of law with their own regulations and judicial personnel, and they were representatives of municipal legal authorities – vectors of law thrusting into ocean space' (2009: 112). Nevertheless, she interprets the constitution of the ship as a 'legal island' to constitute a proof that scholars such as Carl Schmitt were incorrect in considering the amity lines fundamental institutions of sixteenth- and seventeenth-century international law. Looking at the myriad of ships crossing the oceans, each constituting a moving fragment of legal space, she concludes: 'the supposedly empty box of lawlessness, a legal void, was in fact full of law' (2009: 33). In fact, as Coke's writings clearly show, there was absolutely no contradiction between the idea that oceanic spaces beyond the line were legal voids and the conceptualization of ships as 'legal islands'. At the opposite, it was exactly the anomy of sixteenth-century oceans that demanded a new conceptualization of the ship as an enclosed legal space, subtracted from the anomy of the seas.

These renegade Europeans, along with marooned sailors and other marginal individuals, seem to have made up the core of the group that would later be called *the buccaneers*. Descriptions of communities of buccaneers appeared for the first time in seventeenth-century chronicles as hunters of feral cattle on the north coast of Hispaniola: 'their sustenance a kind of beef jerky grilled on a Taino-style wooden grate called a *boucan*. The French thus termed the jerky *viande bucanée* and the jerky-makers *boucaniers*' (Lane 1998: 97). Their origin is generally unknown, but certainly a number of them were drawn from the French settlers of the island of St Kitts, raided by the Spanish in 1616 (Exquemelin 1684: 49). They inhabited a forgotten region, abandoned by the Spanish after a first attempt to settle there in the early sixteenth century. Behind them the Spanish had left an empty land – the native population wiped out by disease, mine work, enslavement and forced migration – and an alien animal world composed of cattle, horses, hogs and dogs, first introduced by the Spanish and then left behind, growing in number in the absence of predators.

The Jesuit missionary, Father Du Tertre, in whose journal appears one of the first references to the buccaneers, writes about an 'unorganized rabble of men from all countries' who, as they 'would not suffer any chiefs':

> passed for undisciplined men. Who for the greater part had sought refuges in these places and were reduced to this way of life to avoid the punishment due for the crimes that could be proved against many of them. . . . I have seen some of these who had lived this miserable life for twenty years without seeing a priest or eating bread.
>
> (1671: 471)

According to the Spanish missionary, in general they were:

> without any habitation or fixed abode, but only rendezvoused where the cattle were to be found, and some sheds covered with leaves to keep off the rain and to store the hides of the beasts they had killed until some vessel should pass to barter with them for wine, brandy, line, arms, powder, bullets, and cooking vessels which they needed and which were the only movables of the buccaneers.
>
> (Du Tertre 1671: 475)

He described their way of life in the tone usually reserved to slaves and natives in need of fatherly correction, their communities made to appear similar to those composed by escaped slaves such as the maroons (Mackie 2005). These men, made famous by the Exquemelin best-seller *History of the Buccaneers of America* – first published in Amsterdam in 1678, by 1686 translated in German, Spanish, English and French and since then republished in countless editions – inflamed the fantasy of the European public, which was then living the traumatic transition to the conditions of modern urban life (Arnold 2007).

Exquemelin was a Fleming who travelled the West Indies from 1666 to 1674, joining the buccaneers in Tortuga and following some of their exploits. His own biography gives us a glimpse into the social composition of the buccaneering ommunities of Hispaniola and Tortuga. The Dutch author appears to have been sent to the Caribbean as an indentured servant of the French West India Company (Boucher 2007: 270). In Tortuga he was sold to the Lieutenant-Governor of the French settlement, at whose service he spent three years before being sold to a French surgeon in 1669. In the same year he was able to buy his liberty for 100 pieces of eight, to be paid in the following years. Burdened by this debt, 'being now at liberty, though like Adam when he was first created, that is, naked and destitute of all human necessities, not knowing how to get my living,' he determined to join the buccaneering community that at time was established on the island, among whom he worked as a barber-surgeon, while gathering material for his chronicles (Exquemelin 1684: 26). These provide the basis for most material on Caribbean buccaneering in the seventeenth century, the work of French missionaries in the West Indies such as Du Tertre, Labat and Charlevoix being almost the only other primary sources available.

It seems to be agreed by all primary sources that the early buccaneers had their source and nucleus in the hunters who dwelled the coasts of Hispaniola already in the early years of the century. The northern part of the island, after being abandoned by the Spanish, became an attraction from people on the run from French, English and Spanish authorities. As the case of Exquemelin shows, the conditions of life of indentured servants and impressed sailors on European ships and early colonial settlements made escape a recurrent event. Indentured bondage was an institution that developed side by side with the slave trade and it represented, to an extent, an alternative to it. It allowed unemployed, debtors and small offenders to sail to the West Indies paying their travel with a period of unpaid labour that would range from 18 months to seven years. They were 'veritable convicts, often more ill-treated than the slaves with whom they worked side by side, for their lives, after the expiration of their term of service, were of no consequence to their masters' (Haring 1910: 76).

During the 1630s, the numbers of buccaneers rose steadily, also because of the numerous refugees arriving from nearby French settlements, then under attack by the Spanish fleet. In the early 1640s, the Spanish tried to stop the inflow of unwanted migrants by setting fire to parts of Hispaniola and exterminating the wild cattle. This policy caused most of the hunters to move to the nearby island of Tortuga, off Hispaniola's northwestern coast. Here they started some small plantations, and a trade with French and British interlopers rapidly developed. From now on, nevertheless, the main source of revenue for the island's economy would be unrestricted plunder against Spanish vessels. In a turn that mimics Lewis Mumford's theories about the origins of ancient warfare, 'The hunters of cattle became hunters of Spaniards, and the sea became the savanna on which they sought their game' (Haring 1910: 89).

Exquemelin reports that when he first arrived in Tortuga, there were scarcely 300 buccaneers still engaged in hunting, all others being dependent on small farming and maritime marauding against the Spanish (1684: 41–42). Heretofore, until the end of the century, the buccaneers entered the history, and the mythology, of piracy in the West Indies. Philip Gosse went so far as calling Tortuga 'a buccaneer republic, where the seamen made their own laws and cultivated the land for sugar-cane and yams' (Gosse 2006: 11). While this may be a romantic overture, Exquemelin emphasized the extent to which early buccaneering expeditions and settlements were largely self-governed through what was called *la coutume de la côte*: 'a medley of bizarre laws which they had originated among themselves. . . . They based their rights thus to live upon the fact, they said, of having passed the Tropic, where, borrowing from the sailor's well-known superstition, they pretended to have drowned all their former obligations' (Haring 1910: 58).

By 1640, nevertheless, threatened by Spanish forces, Tortuga entered under the tutelage of the French monarchy. The population was mostly made up of French and Englishmen, along with a small number of Dutchmen. The decision was therefore the cause of a first split among the buccaneers along national lines. In the following year the island was re-conquered by the Spanish, who raided and destroyed most of the settlements. Although Tortuga would be soon retaken by the English, the buccaneers either turned to log cutting and wood trading from the island or moved to Jamaica, now under the control of the English. There they were soon enlisted in the service of privateering expeditions, which became larger and more organized throughout the 1660s and 1670s. Under the command of Henry Morgan, they enlisted hundreds of buccaneers who had previously been in Tortuga. These men, as we have seen, played a central role in the process of primitive accumulation of capital, which made possible the creation of the first sugar plantations in Jamaica (Latimer 2009).

Their success, nevertheless, also spelled their inevitable end (Policante 2012b: 30–45). As the Spanish Empire weakened under the combined attacks of the French, English and Dutch privateers; while the Protestant nations turned towards cultivating their newly acquired colonies, rather than preying on Spanish shipping lines, the historical trajectory of the buccaneers was arriving at a fundamental caesura. When, after the sack of Panama of 1671, Morgan was arrested for breaching the recently signed peace between England and Spain, the history of the buccaneers definitely came to an end. Although, once in London, Morgan would be knighted and awarded the title of Lieutenant-Governor of Jamaica, instead of being punished, still his arrest might serve as a historical turning point. In London, Morgan was honoured for his contribution to the two-century long battle that had finally brought to its knees the universal aspirations of the Spanish Empire. But when, in 1675, Morgan finally returned to Jamaica, he settled down as a plantation owner. There was no longer an exceptional space 'beyond the line', wholly subtracted from international law, in which the privateers and the anarchic buccaneers would dominate the scene. By the last quarter of the seventeenth century, international law was slowly penetrating the other side of the line, suffusing it with a new meaning. Soon the language of legality and illegality would force its way through the Atlantic, once again displacing and threatening the outlaw.

Chapter 4

Enemies of all nations

Piracy and the world-market

Throughout the sixteenth and seventeenth centuries, European imperialist expansion and the conduct of intestinal European warfare depended on thousands of privateers. Political theorists like Charles Tilly (1985), historians such as Jon Latimer (2009) and historical sociologists like Janice Thomson (1994) have argued convincingly that pirates, legitimated as privateers through the widespread use of *lettres de marque*, played an instrumental role in the violent processes inherent in state-building. Political economists like Karl Marx (1976) and economic historians like Nuala Zahedieh (1990) argued for the importance of piracy and maritime plunder in the dynamics proper to early modern commercial empires and for the accomplishment of primitive accumulation on a massive scale. Political theorists like Eliga Gould (2003) and legal scholars like Carl Schmitt (2003) have shown how piracy and imperialist plunder ultimately rested on a strict separation between Europe and the colonial world, with the latter effectively reduced to a permanent state of exception, at once included in and subtracted from modern international law.

And yet, as we have started to see, the reduction of the space 'beyond the line' to an anomy in which primitive accumulation and widespread plunder may be maximized also meant that the very same freedom to expropriate might be sometimes turned against the imperialist states that legitimated it. The exceptional status of the oceanic spaces beyond the line made them a dangerous space, where violence was omnipresent, relationships of power were often brutal, and trade was systematically intertwined with imperialism, outright plunder and the kidnapping of slaves. But this exceptionality made them also a space of extraordinary freedom and recurrent rebellion, mutiny, insurrection: the turning upside down of traditional relationships of power. The Atlantic Ocean in particular, in the seventeenth century, was really 'a place teeming with strange creatures, a place where sins proliferated and death was always present' (Rediker 2004: 135). The sea created a radical distance from the principal organizing institutions of modern life and it allowed freedoms that would have been (and often were) harshly condemned on European land.

In this chapter, therefore, I focus on the erasure of the amity lines in the early eighteenth century and the consequent construction of a world-market based on the Universal extension of international law and property rights. In the first part, I discuss the political and economic transformations that led to the suppression of the oceanic borderland, and the subsequent construction of the modern oceans as a space of free commercial circulation. I argue that the Commercial Revolution, the establishment of systematic forms of exploitation of the colonies and the formation of entire national economies organized for commercial exchange, both demanded and presupposed the erasure of the amity lines and the organization of the oceans of the world into an immense commercial glacis, the first embodiment of the world-market.

In the second part, I discuss this necessary transformation of international law and the spatial imagination, which took place in the early eighteenth century. I consider the Treaty of Utrecht (1713) an important event insofar as it sanctioned the first collective appropriation of the oceans by the modern maritime and commercial states, and therefore the inclusion of the space beyond the line in a system of international law based in Europe. In the early eighteenth century, in fact, the exceptional spaces navigated by the lawless freebooter and the anarchic buccaneer progressively disappear. These paradigmatic figures of the space of exception beyond the line are forced either to enter the order of the state, supporting the evolution of the modern navy and the modern army, or to be declared enemies of the modern international system, at this point still solidly centred in Europe. Those freebooters who refused to discipline their hostility and put it at the service of a recognized state were therefore declared *hostis communis omnium*, denationalized systemic enemies to be fought by all nations.

In the third part, finally, I concentrate on what has been defined by modern historians as the 'Golden Age of Piracy', lasting approximately from 1670 to 1720. In this half a century, an unprecedented military mobilization against piracy gradually unfolds. It is a play of cruelty and opposed terrors, which has the oceans of the world as its theatre, and the community of modern states against the last partisans of the sea as protagonists. The pirates of the Golden Age represent the last sentinels of a fading conception of the oceans as a space of absolute freedom, which was still dominant in the seventeenth century. In the eighteenth century, they became an intolerable threat to commercial circulation and to the consolidation of an ordered system of exploitation of the colonial world. They were therefore treated as systemic enemies of the emerging international order and hanged en masse as denationalized individuals, stripped of their rights. The construction of the capitalist world-market, the reduction of the oceans to a hyperspace of commercial circulation, the erection of a modern community of interdependent states centred in Europe, all required the annihilation of the pirate and of its absolute freedom. To conclude, therefore, I discuss the closure of the 'Golden Age of Piracy' and its haunting legacy, pulsing at the heart of modernity and international law.

Freedoms of the sea: From global plunder to the world-market

Janice Thomson (1994) offers us what is probably the most detailed study of the extent to which early-modern sovereigns relied on the initiative of private subjects in order to deploy the violence necessary to erect global empires and appropriate the wealth of the extra-European world. She shows how the widespread use of mercenary forces by land and privateers at sea was fundamental to enable processes of primitive accumulation, intra-imperial warfare and violent dispossession. She is clear that 'to attain the wealth and power promised by overseas expansion, states empowered non-state actors to exercise violence' (1994: 67). In other words, as also suggested by Gilles Deleuze and Felix Guattari, the edification of the military might of the modern state was largely dependent on its ability to capture the nomadic war-machines that were initially autonomous from it (2004: 419–423). And yet Thomson is also attentive to the counter-effects of this particular form of imperialist power, insofar as the unleashing of private violence in the open spaces beyond the line also meant the possibility of losing control of it:

> The state would authorize privateering, which was legalized piracy, during wartime. When the war concluded, thousands of seamen were left with no more appealing alternative than indiscriminate piracy. The state would make some desultory efforts to suppress the pirates, who would simply move somewhere else. With the outbreak of the next war, the state would offer blanket pardons to pirates who would agree to serve as privateers and the process would start all over again . . . At the heart of these matters was the process of state-building. Privateering reflected the rulers' efforts to build state power; piracy reflected some people's efforts to resist that project.
>
> (1994: 154)

In the sixteenth and seventeenth centuries, the state of exception beyond the line made the Atlantic Ocean singularly apt not only to imperialist plunder but also to counter-practices that, in Christopher Hill's famous formulation, 'turned upside down' the existing relationships of power (1975: 1–12). It was a space of absolute freedom, which certainly means the freedom to expropriate, to exploit, to murder and to impose one's superior power, but also the freedom to escape, to rebel, to avenge and to break oppressive rules and abusive customs. In the midst of this absolute freedom, the ship was conceived as a floating fragment of land, on which the European political, social and legal hierarchies were transposed unchallenged. In the early seventeenth century, as we have seen, Coke understood mutiny as a form of petty treason, which challenged and threatened the chain of interlinked ties of allegiance that composed the complex pyramid of power characteristic of European late-medieval feudal societies. The ship was made into a disciplinary machine, at the service of merchant capitalist practices and lawless primitive accumulation in the form of privateering and plunder.

Dr Johnson famously observed that 'no man will be a sailor who has contrivance enough to get himself into a jail; for being in a ship is being in jail with the chance of being drowned . . . A man in jail has more room, better food, and commonly better company' (cited in Brewer 2002: 50). Recent maritime historiography has confirmed the degrading conditions in which the seafaring workmen were forced to labour well into the eighteenth century (Rediker 1989). Episodes of mutiny were regularly repeated, often in response to the brutality of life aboard privateers and merchant vessels. Mutiny was a very feasible alternative for many members of those multinational crews who were forced to enlist either by coercion or by want. There were many reasons why hundreds of seafaring working men decided to mutiny, take possession of their floating prison and – as wrote John Atkins, a surgeon aboard a privateer-turned-pirate-ship – 'go from plundering for others, to do it for themselves' (1970: 226).

The anomy of the oceans – their distance from the centres of morality, control and legal coercion that disciplined the working class in the cities of Europe – was thus not only an ideal theatre for imperialist plunder, but also a line of flight for enslaved Africans escaping their chains, indentured felons escaping servitude and property-less proletarians escaping exploitative working conditions aboard. This chaotic nature of early-modern oceanic spaces was tolerated and even encouraged by a number of European states, which relied on privateers and freebooters to channel away from the Spanish Empire at least a part of the wealth of the new world. For the English, French and Dutch early state-formations, in particular, the act of backing private plundering ventures had a number of fundamental advantages: it brought revenues to the state in the form of direct taxation on the goods carried back to home ports, it introduced cheap goods in portal towns, it supported local economies and – especially in early colonial settlements – it played a fundamental role in financing the development of plantation production and the early manufacturing industry. Moreover, it directed hostility against foreign shipping and away from domestic trade, and especially, it allowed the formation of a maritime working class that would play a fundamental role both in times of peace and war. Privateering was, in fact, a trade that produced not only wealth but also capable sailors skilled in seamanship and the fighting arts, both essential in a maritime space in which trade and violence were often profoundly intertwined. This was a notion that already in the late sixteenth century was so well known among the ruling classes of Europe that Sir Henry Mainwaring could write in a plea to the sovereigns of England for renewed support for plundering activities: 'The State may hereafter want such men, who commonly are the most daring and serviceable in war' (2008: 18).

During the seventeenth century, nevertheless, the political and economic conditions that had supported the creation of the amity lines and the open support for practices of systematic plunder started to change. The oceans gradually became one of the most important theatres of a developing world-market that had its centre in Europe, and particularly in England and the Low Countries. By 1716, the worldwide process of expropriation had already torn millions of people from their ancestral lands in Europe, Africa and the Americas. Masses of people flocked to the burgeoning commercial cities, where they either found work in the early manufacturing trade – as well as in the more established commercial and naval businesses – or they were forced to crime and vagrancy by their destitute conditions (Marx 1976: 873–942; Linebaugh 1991). Criminals were then forced into workhouses (Foucault 1979), pressed to join the Royal Navy or forced to migrate to the colonies as indentured servants.

Already by the late sixteenth century, the Royal Navy had established itself as England's greatest employer of labour, its greatest consumer of material and its greatest industrial enterprise (Linebaugh and Rediker 2000: 157). Aboard its ships worked seamen drawn from all over the world, most often dispossessed commoners eradicated from their land and forced to find themselves a living in the maritime ports; or otherwise indentured criminals, transported to the colonies and forced to labour in the Navy ships for 14 years in order to pay their debt to society. The crews of ocean-going ships were thus invariably cosmopolitan, a mix of men with no other property but their own labour, freed from traditional ties to society and the land in which they were born. On the decks of these moving factories, that were the true engine of the Commercial Revolution, laboured proletarians uprooted from many lands: Kru from the coast of West Africa served on naval ships and also the mercantile vessels engaged in the West African slave trade, while hundreds of Indian lascars and Chinese seamen served in the Royal Navy alongside Irish, English and Somalis (Killingray 2004). They were all, notwithstanding their cultural, linguistic and ethnic differences:

> free labourers, in the double sense that neither they themselves form part and parcel of the means of production, as in the case of slaves, bondsmen, & c., nor do the means of production belong to them, as in the case of peasant-proprietors; they are, therefore, free from, unencumbered by, any means of production of their own.
>
> (Marx 1976: 874)

It was these men who were making the Commercial and then the Industrial Revolution possible, mastering the armed sailing ships that were conquering the oceans of the world for Europe. As the celebrated historian Carlo Cipolla has remarked, the armoured ship, introduced in the sixteenth century, was the foremost instrument of modern European expansionism. It was:

> an extremely efficient mean, which allowed a relatively small crew to control immense quantities of natural energy and direct them toward the production of speed and destruction. The secret of the rapid and unexpected rise of Northern Europe to global dominance was all there. . . . Thanks to the revolutionary character of their armed vessels, the European

> states rapidly established their dominance over the oceans, but since their advantage was all in their cannons and their sails for over three centuries, until the end of the eighteenth century, their supremacy was valid only at sea.
>
> (Cipolla 1965: 120)

This is one of the reasons why, in the early eighteenth century, early political economists like William Petty would describe seamen as 'the very Pillars of any Commonwealth', since 'every Seaman of industry and ingenuity is not only a Navigator, but a Merchant and also a Soldier' (Petty 1899: 259). In the eyes of European political economists, the exceptional power assumed by the small and peripheral Dutch nation seemed to demonstrate the importance of controlling shipping and international trade, in order to master power and wealth: 'I have shewn,' writes the author of *Political Arithmetic*, 'how Situation hath given them Shipping, and how Shipping hath given them in effect all other Trade, and how Foreign Traffick must give them as much Manufacture as they can manage themselves, and as for the overplus, make the rest of the World but as Workmen to their Shops' (Petty 1899: 261). It was this course, according to William Petty, that any polity which wanted to acquire power and eventually global hegemony had to follow, including the rising British Empire.

In fact, while 'from the days of the Angevin kings to the time of the Cromwellian Protectorate, wool or woollen cloth constituted almost the whole of English exports' (Davis 1954: 150), from the second half of the seventeenth century the beginning of the plantation economy – founded in great part by violent plunder and wholly non-economic means of compulsion – gave an unprecedented impulse to English worldwide commerce. In the development of 'a world-wide network of trading transactions centred in London', writes Phyllis Deane, 'the West Indian islands, administered by a British plantation *elite* on the basis of a slave society, constituted the most valuable and intimate link' (1980: 55). Weapons, hardware and spirits from Britain were now shipped to West Africa and exchanged in the booming slave trade. The slaves were sold to the West Indian plantation elite, initially in exchange for plundered bullion, and then increasingly for sugar, tobacco and raw cotton. The gold was shipped to the East and Near East for tea, silk, coffee and spices, although these were paid for mainly by the profits produced by the monopolization of Asian trade routes. Asian goods were sold in Europe and funded the necessary intake of timber, hemp, pitch and tar – essential for naval stores – on top of Swedish and Russian iron.

'English trade routes,' writes Marcus Rediker:

> constituted the arteries of the imperial body between 1650 and 1750. They unified distant parts of the globe, different markets, and distinct modes of production. . . . They organized the flow of commodities and the movements of labor. These pulsing routes, stretching from one port city to the next, were

> the most elementary material structures of empire, indeed of the whole world economy.
>
> (Rediker 1989: 21)

In the seventeenth century, in short, the wheels of commerce had started to gather increasing speed, gradually engulfing the whole world into a complex trading network. The ship was the machine that allowed the creation of maritime corridors that led to far-away lands, giving birth to long-distance inter-oceanic trade. The cannon was the ancillary tool, which punctually intervened to clear up the path from awkward obstructions, unfashionable blockages and primitive resistances. As shown by Fernand Braudel, the transition to modern market societies was, from the very beginning, a global endeavour; although one that could establish itself only gradually in time: 'Men's activities, the surpluses they exchange, gradually pass through this narrow channel to the other world with as much difficulty at first as the camel of the scriptures passing through the eye of a needle. Then the breaches grow wider and more frequent, as society finally becomes a "generalized market society"' (1992: 26).

The Commercial Revolution paved the way to the Industrial Revolution, insofar as it reorganized the social structure of entire national economies for exchange in the world-market, making their populations dependent from international trade and their industries dependent from foreign markets. In order for the wheels of commerce to gather the necessary speed, nevertheless, it was first of all necessary to prepare the ground on which they could spin unimpaired. It was necessary, in other words, to transform the oceans of the world into an immense hyperspace of circulation, a safe and homogenous highway on which circulation could simply 'flow' in predictable ways, according to estimated costs and expected profit. This was a fundamental but rather gradual transformation.

During the Middle Ages, the Ocean had been perceived as a completely alien environment, a space of myth rather than a space integrated in the tale of human history. By the sixteenth century, the oceans were still perceived as a space of danger, strife and struggle: a space that, as we have seen, was now included within human history and human institutions – such as international law – but only as a wholly exceptional place. Mercantilist-era maps depicted the sea as a space subtracted to civilization, a wilderness dominated by threatening monsters and wild pirates. Early-modern literature portrayed the sea as a space that resisted civil authority and power: an untameable borderland, in which human conventions and established hierarchies are moot. Before the advent of the Commercial Revolution, cartography and literature – as well as modern political theory in the Hobbesian tradition – reproduced and reinforced the image of the oceans as a space of lawless plunder. A myth that, as we have already seen, was fundamental to early-modern international law.

With the closing of the seventeenth century and the beginning of the eighteenth, nevertheless, the observer can distinguish a gradual transformation of the image of the oceans in the European spatial imagination. The sea increasingly became an empty surface. Maps featuring brave seaman battling with sea monsters and the vagaries of nature are replaced by modern cartographies, fixed on a smooth commercial glacis, traversed by straight commercial vectors and trading routes. Oceanic travel begins to be described as a slow, drudging, middle passage between lands, dangerous at times but ultimately unremarkable. Gradually the image of the sea as a space of danger, struggle, piracy and savage freedoms slipped into the background, although it was never completely erased from collective memory. Maritime life became increasingly associated with commerce, global circulation and expanding possibilities for long-distance trade. It is the beginning of a new image of the sea that would become hegemonic in the nineteenth and twentieth centuries: the sea neither a space of myth nor as a space of exception, but the paradigmatic sphere of capital circulation.

Changing spatial representations in cartography and literature attended to changing material practices and shifting authoritative definitions of the role of the sea in official treaties, diplomatic documents and, ultimately, in international law. The expansion of commerce and the growing power of liberal ideology translated itself into further consideration for the interests of long-distance trade. The permanent state of exception in which state-sanctioned privateers, lawless freebooters and anarchic buccaneers found their historical stage was also the chief source of instability for long-distance trade. International networks of communication and transportation were systematically disrupted; merchant ships were forced to arm themselves, participating in an escalation of violence; the risks connected with capital investment in shipping was high; uncertainty meant high insurance costs and discontinuous flow of essential commodities. Moreover, the persistent risk of losing entire ships to maritime marauders reflected itself in a growing concentration of power in the hands of gigantic joint-stock companies, which mastered enough capital to sustain occasional losses of ships and cargoes without going bankrupt. These expanding shipping companies were more and more capable of pressuring governments into establishing legal and political conditions more attuned to the needs of merchant capital.

It is only in this particular context that it is possible to understand the extraordinary success of Hugo Grotius' plea for a Universal right to free trade in *Mare Liberum*. It is well known the extent to which this early work of the foremost Dutch international legal scholar embodied the general perspective of the large merchant companies that increasingly dominated the economy of the most important European maritime nations. In fact, the legal treatise had been promoted directly by the Dutch East India Company in order to support ideologically the systematic plundering of Spanish and Portuguese vessels. In particular, it was meant to excuse the plunder of a Portuguese ship captured by the merchant company in the Strait of Singapore in 1602 (Van Ittersum 2007).

In fact, when the wealth captured in that act of plunder was brought back to Amsterdam, Grotius defended the right of the Dutch merchants to attack the Portuguese Navy. Insofar as the Portuguese pretended to exclude other nations from travelling and freely trading in the oceans of the world, they abused natural law and were therefore justly attacked and punished by Dutch privateers. Despite the complexity of Grotius' argument, what guaranteed the lasting success of what remains one of the most celebrated landmarks of international legal scholarship was the fact that its rallying cry perfectly embodied the perspective and the spatial views of the new bourgeois classes (Sebastianelli 2012). The work became the manifesto of a louder demand for a Universal right to circulate freely on the high seas, which were promoted as a global commons from which no one could be excluded. In a sudden reversal, the Spanish and the Portuguese were condemned in the light of natural law, just as the Iberic empires had previously condemned the Lutheran corsairs in the light of the Universality of the Christian Commonwealth.

The publication of *Mare Liberum* in 1609 solicited a sustained debate among international legal scholars of the seventeenth century, concerning the status of the world oceans in international law. This debate – which is generally referred to as 'The Battle of Books' – is usually characterized as an exchange between two symmetrically opposite positions between those who, following Grotius, argued that the oceans were free to all and those who, following the English jurist John Selden, replied that states had the right to enclose and claim exclusive possession of limited areas of ocean space. The most common reading of this debate, nevertheless, obscures the fundamental fact that all parties eventually agreed on a fundamental point, which would become hegemonic in the early eighteenth century. Although Selden insisted that coastal waters could be claimed as exclusive dominions by modern states, in fact, he seemed to agree that in the immense vastness beyond direct control by any one state the ocean remained *res communis omnium*. In the high seas, therefore, power could legitimately operate only imperially, that is, in the name of all and only to protect the general right to free trade against pirates and unjust enemies. As Steinberg recently argued:

> Selden had little to say about areas of the sea that lay beyond effective state control; presumably, state intervention in these spaces was permissible only to the extent that it was implemented in order to facilitate the basic human right of navigation. Thus, although Selden did begin to push against the norm of stewardship in coastal waters, he appeared to be proposing for the deep seas a doctrine that, like Grotius's, extended the norm of stewardship from individual states to the community of states.
>
> (1999a: 258)

Indeed, behind the clamour of the scholarly battle, a principle of common *imperium* over the oceans of the world started to affirm itself. In the first years of the eighteenth century, the Dutchman Cornelius van Bynkershoek elaborated the synthesis that would definitely end the battle of books and that would find general acceptance among the legal scholars of the modern age: territorial state sovereignty extended only so far into the sea as the coastal batteries could shoot. *Ubi finitur armorum vis*. Still following this fundamental principle, on the eve of the French

Revolution, the Neapolitan diplomat Ferdinando Galiani calculated that the validity of the laws of Naples ended only three miles from his studio (1782: 421–424). The three-mile limit subsequently crystallized to the point of remaining essentially valid until today. Beyond that point, no single state could impose its own laws, and only international legal principles that were generally recognized could be considered valid.

This left open the fundamental question: who would have the right and the duty to interpret and enforce international law on the high seas? Grotius' main innovation was to propose that the holder of *imperium* – the subject in charge of acting in the name of humanity and entrusted with the right and the duty to enforce the law of nations in those spaces common to them all – would not be 'one state, as it was in Rome, or individual states in their respective spheres of influence, as it was under the Tordesillas system, but rather the community of states' (Steinberg 1999a: 260). This would be the principle gradually emerging in the eighteenth century, which would definitely supplant the amity lines, transform the legal regime of the world ocean according to the needs of international commerce, and radically transform the environment and the status of the lawless freebooter, now submerged by an international law that seemed to damn it in front of the whole world.

Making the world safe for property: The pirate as *hostis communis omnium*

The conclusion of the War of Spanish Succession in particular represented a decisive turning point in the history of piracy and, more generally, in the history of the modern capitalist world-system. In 1713, with the signing of the Peace of Utrecht and as a result of its growing maritime power, Britain gained the exclusive right to export slaves to the Spanish colonies. Thus it began the trade that would provide the spur for the plantation economy and eventually for the beginning of the Industrial Revolution. This was, in Carl Schmitt's words, 'a *caesura*', 'a world-historical event of revolutionary importance' (2003: 98). After the Treaty of Utrecht, the period of savage primitive accumulation and anomic warfare between opposed European empires for the spoils of the American continent was brought to a halt. The 'amity line' principle was forever abandoned, in order to construct and sustain a more ordered system of trade, whose twin pillars were exploitation of wage labour in Europe and exploitation of slavery in the colonial plantations.

'A whole new period of the *jus publicum Europaeum*,' writes Schmitt, 'began in 1713 with the Treaty of Utrecht' (2003: 181). The treaty, which sanctioned the conclusion of an international war that involved Spain, Great Britain, France, Portugal, Savoy and the Dutch Republic, signed the fundamental passage from 'an elemental to a systematic freedom of the Sea'. Before that date, in fact, the principle of international law commanding freedom of the seas meant essentially 'that the sea is impervious to human law and human order, that is a realm free for tests of strength'. After that date, 'this freedom was limited by the fact that state control over the privateers of its subjects became stronger, while the old style freebooters sank to the level of criminal pirates' (Schmitt 2003: 182). Gradually, after the second half of the seventeenth century, lawless plunder had become an outmoded form of accumulation. Buccaneers and freebooters were slowly marginalized, condemned and suppressed; privateers were subjected to increasing and more stringent controls. Eventually, the sea lost its exceptional status; it was integrated in the nascent state-based international system and made functional to its order.

Modern politics did not develop in a multiplicity of 'close commercial states', autarchic and completely independent from one another – as projected and auspicated, for instance, by Fichte (2012) – but by a system of commercial states, economically interconnected by a thick web of commercial exchanges, vectors of domination and migratory patterns, from which each state became increasingly dependent. The history of international relations has been often characterized by a territorial bias, leaving to the margin the particular spatiality of the oceans and the fundamental role they actually played in the evolution of the modern international order. The practice of territorial rule – the geometrical power consisting in tracing borders, rising fences and dividing up the land – logically requires the existence of a free space, at once a commercial plane of circulation and a military glacis, over which communication may be effectuated. Modernity is like the two-headed eagle painted on the banners of the Austro-Hungarian monarchy: it is composed of a geometrical order imposed on the land but also on a system of imperial security imposed on the sea. Therefore its origins should not be symbolized only by the Treaty of Westphalia, but also by the peace signed in Utrecht in April 1713. Paradoxically, a Westphalian system of independent states is dependent on the existence of a space of communication at once internal and external to it, an anarchic space whose disorder could not be completely ordered and which, yet, was increasingly surveyed, controlled and securitized. *Terra mare et contra mare terras terminat omnis*: the prose of Lucretius expresses with extraordinary lucidity the modern dialectics between land and sea.

But if Schmitt is correct to assume that 'the separation of firm land and free sea was the basic principle of the *jus publicum Europaeum*' (Schmitt 2003: 179; Schmitt 1941), we must add that the sea has been socially *constructed* as a smooth hyperspace of circulation (Lefèbvre 1991; Steinberg 1999b). Too often Schmitt seems to slip into the tendency to naturalize the distinction between land and sea, moving towards mythological thinking. But with the advancement of technology, and the invention of borders and lines of division that do not depend on any material support, nothing essential prevented the sea from being partitioned and thoroughly territorialized. With the introduction of the notion of 'territorial waters' – the coastal area subjected to national jurisdiction – parts of the sea have been already transformed into land: that is, they have been subjected to the same rule as the land. 'The sea, the archetype of the smooth space' wrote Deleuze and Guattari, 'has also been the archetype of all the striations of smooth space' (2004: 427). This area could have been progressively advanced to cover much of the surface of the world oceans, especially if we consider that the progress in the power of armaments today extends their power infinitely beyond the three mile limit established in the late eighteenth century.

The permanence of a freedom of the sea should then be understood not in terms of a technological limit, but in terms of a social construction of the ocean which aims at conserving smooth space as a surface of circulation in the service of striated space. The fundamental point is that the state needs the non-state, the land needs the sea, in order to serve as military and commercial glacis on which speed and circulation can be maximized. Deleuze and Guattari summarized it well in saying that one of the fundamental tasks of the state is not only to striate the space over which it reigns – as it has done, for instance, in the case of coastal waters – but also 'to utilize smooth spaces as means in the service of striated space':

> One of the fundamental tasks of the State is to striate the space over which it reigns, or to utilize smooth spaces as a means of communication in the service of striated space. It is a vital concern of every State not only to vanquish nomadism but to control migrations and more generally, to establish a zone of rights over an entire 'exterior,' over all flows traversing the ecumenon. If it can help it, the State does not dissociate itself from a process of capture of flows of all kinds, populations, commodities or commerce, money or capital, etc. There is still a need for fixed paths in well-defined directions, which restrict speed, regulate circulation, relativize movement, and measure in detail the relative movements of subjects and objects.
>
> (Deleuze and Guattari 2004: 385)

The ordering impulse of modernity seems to lead either to the colonization of smooth spaces: establishing clear differences and distinctions, imposing on them always the same grid, making appear one more independent state where before there was none; or to maintain smooth space in a subjugated, strictly functional role, making it a space of pure circulation. As pointed out by Mikkel Thorup: 'The story of modernity is also the story of the repression or taming of the borderland. . . . The indistinct space between states, which used to be wide, is finally reduced to a line on a map' (2006: 113). The space 'beyond the line', which represented a paradigmatic borderland, started to disappear in the eighteenth century. That extra-European space, which had been initially included in international law as a wholly exceptional space – in which 'might made right' and European states could freely perpetuate their conflicting activities of mutual plunder, ruthless exploitation of the territory and the native people, killing and genocide, without ever putting into question the general validity of international law and morality – was now gradually being either colonized (in the case of extra-European land), or made to serve the European state system as a pure space of circulation.

In both cases, there was resistance to integration. On one hand, countless native people resisted the integration of their land into the imperialist order of European states; on the other hand, pirates remained an obstacle to the reduction of the oceans into a smooth surface of circulation, necessary for an efficient process of expanded capitalist accumulation that would feed on the systematic exploitation of wage labour in Europe and of slave labour in the colonies.

Between 1660 and 1700, the advent of the Commercial Revolution led to a fundamental change in the way in which piracy was perceived by states (Rubin 2006: 100–101). While, even in the early seventeenth century, piracy was treated as a minor nuisance or even an exploitable source of private violence, in the early eighteenth century, it emerged as a central problem of international law. A new sensibility toward the importance of long-distance trade and a new interventionist stance by European powers – interested in imposing a minimum of law and order on the oceans of the world, making them safe for global processes of capital and commercial circulation – translated itself in a new image of the pirates, now portrayed as irredeemable outlaws and enemies of civilization. 'It is a sign of the growing importance of far-away colonies and in general of long-distance oceanic trade for the whole of Europe,' writes J.H. Parry 'the fact that the epoch of pirates and buccaneers had to be followed by the age of admirals' (1971: 112). The growth of a new model of colonial exploitation, organized around the space of the plantation, required the criminalization of piracy, the securitization of international transport and the juridification of long-distance trade.

Concerted efforts between all major European powers toward the goal of subjecting the oceans of the world to a stricter regime of law and order began in the last quarter of the seventeenth century, yet a series of international wars intervened, which slowed down the process. King William's War ended in 1697, immediately followed by the War of Spanish Succession that would end only in 1713 with the signing of the Treaty of Utrecht. Nevertheless, with the closing of the seventeenth century, we witness two symptomatic transformations. First, a series of new laws meant to eradicate piracy were passed in Britain, starting from 'An Act for the more effectual Suppression of Piracy' of 1699 and ending with the 'Piracy Act' of 1721, 'promising death to anyone who cooperated with pirates and the loss of wages and six months' imprisonment to those who refused to defend their ship' (Rediker 2004: 27). Second, a number of courts started to appeal to the Roman law principle according to which, pirates being *hostes communis omnium*, all states would have the right and even the duty to suppress them wherever they were found.

In *Rex v. Dawson* (1696), for instance, the English Admiralty Court sentenced to death 32 captured members of Henry Avery's crew, on the base of Universal jurisdiction. The sentence cited Grotius, Puffendorf and Vattel as the main scholarly authorities supporting universal jurisdiction, but added:

> There is no defect in the definition of piracy by the authorities. . . . The definition given by them is certain, consistent, and unanimous; and pirates

> being *hostes communis omnium*, are punishable in the tribunals of all nations. All nations are engaged in a league against them for the mutual defence and safety of all. This renders it the more fit and proper that there should be a uniform rule as to the definition of the crime, which can only be drawn from the law of nations, as the only code universally known and recognized by the people of all countries.
>
> (Cranch et al. 1820: 158)

As *hostis communis omnium*, the pirate was represented as a systemic enemy of the entire international system of states centred in Europe, forcing otherwise irredeemable Imperial rivals to cooperate. By the eighteenth century, it could be considered an established legal principle that the world's oceans lay beyond the rightful reach of any single sovereign power, and that free passage on that common space should be guaranteed to all. According to authorities like Gentili, Puffendorf and Emmerich de Vattel, who formulated some of the most quoted texts of international legal scholarship, the high seas remained free from the laws of any single states. Nevertheless, a series of international legal principles applied, which were meant to safeguard the common use of the oceans as an avenue for international trade. Those who dared to break the common law of nations were therefore to be considered 'common enemies of all nations', against whom pended a Universal jurisdiction. Any nation could single them out, prosecute them and dispose of them as it deemed proper. The principle was so often reiterated in the eighteenth and nineteenth centuries that, in 1927, Justice Moore could write in his conclusions to the *Lotus* case:

> Piracy by law of nations, in its jurisdictional aspects is *sui generis*. Though statutes may provide for its punishment, it is an offence against the law of nations; and as the scene of the pirate's operations is the high seas, which it is not the right or duty of any nation to police, he is denied the protection of the flag which he may carry, and is treated as an outlaw, . . . whom any nation may in the interest of all capture and punish.
>
> (cited in O'Connell 1982: 967)

The pirate represents a liminal and paradigmatic figure in international law, structurally connected with the evolution of the cosmopolitan concept of Universal jurisdiction. Jurisdiction is classically understood in relation to territory or nationality, a conceptualization that reflected a global order of separate sovereign states, each enjoying the exclusive power to judge within its territory over its citizens. At sea, a sovereign state has direct jurisdiction only over its own citizens and over foreign citizens aboard ships flying its flag, which are considered as detached pieces of floating territory. Pirates, nevertheless, were considered as denationalized subjects and were therefore exposed to the sovereign violence of all states. The pirate ship, equally, was considered as a territory subtracted from the jurisdiction of any particular state and, therefore, it could be attacked by all states.[1] Those considered pirates by European powers were excluded from the international community and subtracted from the protection of their state of origin. They could therefore be apprehended and killed with impunity by all nations.

A veritable state of exception in the international legal system of the *jus publicum europaeum* was introduced in order to facilitate the killing of denationalized pirates and the protection of private property beyond national boundaries. The erasure of the amity lines was followed by the collective appropriation of the oceans of the world by the European states, which mutually recognized each other as lawful members of the international community, yet excluded most of the extra-European polities. From then on, the pirate ship was projected as a 'floating space of exception', at least in as much as state ships were considered 'floating fragments of state-territory'. 'Since civilization was equated with being bound within the rules (and the space) of a territorial state,' writes Philip Steinberg, 'vessels not sailing under a national flag, as well as national vessels that were acting in a piratical manner and thereby were forfeiting the protection of a home state, were identified with the anti-civilization of the sea' (2001: 131). To be named a pirate meant, first of all, being stripped of one's belonging to communities recognized by international law: before the tragedy of the thousands of stateless Jews wandering Europe during the twentieth century, the pirate was the original and paradigmatic denationalized subject.

So construed, the principle of universal jurisdiction would allow European Navies to move against all people, anywhere on earth, who dared to interfere with commerce (Rubin 2006: 312). In 1696, for instance, the jury in *Rex v. Dawson* was instructed that:

> The King of England hath not only an empire and sovereignty over the British seas for the punishment of piracy, but in concurrence with other princes and states, an undoubted jurisdiction and power for the punishment of *all* piracies and robberies at seas, in the most remote part of the world; so that if *any* person whatsoever, native or foreign, . . . shall be robbed or spoiled in the narrow or other seas, . . . either on this or the other side of the line it is piracy within the limits of your enquiry, and cognizable by this court.
>
> (Cranch et al. 1820: 178)

1 Kenneth Randall has recently summarized a range of scholarly literature on the topic with the following words: 'By engaging in piracy, individuals and their vessels become denationalized. As an outlaw entirely outside any state's law, "the pirate has in fact no national character" Even if a pirate vessel flies a state's flag, it is a vessel over "which no national authority reigns" and "the protection of the national flag is forfeited". Both the pirate and the vessel are considered stateless. Because no state has any greater connection to pirates and their vessels than any other state, every state therefore has universal jurisdiction to capture and punish pirates' (1988: 793).

Universal jurisdiction, originally created in order to tackle the particular problem of disciplining the exceptional space of the high seas, entails the ability to punish offenders that have no connection to the state sitting in judgment. From the beginning, therefore, there existed a potentially explosive tension between an international system of independent states and the concept of Universal jurisdiction. How the fantasy of the pirate, as the enemy of humanity, lies at the very foundation of a subterranean current of Universalist international law, which maintained its presence even in the classic period of the *jus publicum europaeum*, can be illuminated by a cursory view of the privileged place held by the pirate since the very origins of the canon. In Ayala, Grotius, Pierino Belli, Baldus Ubaldus, Alberico Gentili, Emmerich de Vattel and, more recently, in important scholarly authorities such as Scelle and Lauterpacht, the pirate is not simply a criminal figure. The pirate is rather the constitutive exception; the extra-legal character without whom that body of legal thinking would not have been able to delimit itself in the first place (Cranch et al. 1820: 169–180).

Originally, nevertheless, this tension was downplayed, since the exercise of Universal jurisdiction was meant to complement (rather than challenge) the emerging international order of independent territorial states. Universal jurisdiction was originally introduced in order to open an avenue for the legal suppression of stateless rogues acting on the high seas, a zone free from sovereignty but which was necessary to subject to control. Universal jurisdiction began as an institution meant to allow a form of legalized violence, by European nations, in defence of international trade (Goodwin 2006: 941). It was meant to allow a global protection for property, especially over the oceanic commons, and to sanction those subjects who would not recognize its legitimacy. The main impulse behind the reaffirmation of Universal jurisdiction against piracy in the eighteenth century was not a neutral 'revival in cosmopolitanism' or 'the result of a scholastic rediscovery of the ancient tradition of Imperial Roman law', but the rather more profane interest 'to protect private property crossing national boundaries' (Rubin 2006: 31). The growth of a global market and the intercontinental dimension of modern European empires, in other words, were required to transform private property into a true *cosmopolitan right*, a legal institution whose respect might be enforced at a global level. Since then, the right to free trade, although doctrinally constructed as an alternative to war, has served as the primary base for a particular form of imperial interventionism, conceived as a counter-piracy operation in the name of all, whose history must be put into a strict relationship with the origin and the development of the world-market.

Michel Foucault suggested reading the history of piracy as part of the struggle for the elaboration of a global market, organized in terms of a number of legal principles. It is relatively well known how Foucault tried to study the historical relationship between the liberal project of establishing and securing a global market governed by the principle of free and unfettered competition, and the elaboration of a new law and a new system of governmentality, which would be concerned more with the control of circulation than with the defence of clear borders (Foucault 2009: 10 – 45). What has been less commented on is the ways in which Foucault has linked the evolution of this new system of liberal governmentality with a new spatial thinking originating in maritime law and which expressed, from its very origins, the necessity of a violence capable of carving out and maintaining a smooth hyperspace of flow, a space of free circulation:

> The history of maritime law in the eighteenth century was an attempt to think of the world, or at least the sea, as a space of free competition, of free maritime circulation, and consequently as one of the necessary conditions for the organization of a world market. The history of piracy – the way in which it was consequently used, encouraged, combated and suppressed etc. – could also figure as one of the aspects of this elaboration of a worldwide space in terms of a number of legal principles. In relation to the suppression of piracy we can say that there was a juridification of the world, which should be thought of in terms of the organization of a market.
>
> (Foucault 2008: 176)

If we must understand the making of the world-market as a process of juridification that gradually invested the whole world, the suppression of piracy represents the unfolding of the law-making violence that originally concurred to the imposition of its rule. The eradication of piracy had a central role in the advance of productivity in eighteenth-century shipping, and therefore in the Commercial Revolution that stimulated early industrial production in Europe (North 1968: 954). But this is a violence that cannot be considered archaic, and whose significance is not limited to a simple historical interest in the origins of the contemporary global market. Like primitive accumulation, or better, as an integral part of primitive accumulation, the extirpation of piracy is a violence that, in the words of Deleuze and Guattari, 'must posit itself as preaccomplished, even though it is reactivated every day' (Deleuze and Guattari 2004: 343). We may say that if the pirate as *hostis humani generis* represents a paradigmatic form of the exceptional status of the irredeemable life of the 'enemy of humanity', then the ancient Roman institution of the *persecutio piratarum* may be the paradigm of a persistent form of international violence, distinct from classical warfare, and concerned with the perpetual securitization of the world-market. In the next section, therefore, I look at the eradication of piracy in the early eighteenth century as a key moment in the formation of the global market and in the introduction of a form of global policing, which will continue to play a definite role in international relations throughout the nineteenth and the twentieth century.

The golden age of piracy

In the second half of the seventeenth century, private plunder and privateering beyond the line started to be perceived as an obstacle to the expansion of trade, the stabilization of the international markets and the construction of a more ordered form of capital accumulation that would be no longer based on the forceful extraction of wealth by non-economic means, but rather on the organized exploitation of both slave and waged labour. The necessity of capturing the sea and making it serve as a global plane of commercial and capital circulation required the erasure of the amity lines, the regulation of the absolute freedom of plunder 'beyond the line' and the suppression of freebooting. This is what Thomas Hobbes, the English theorist of the modern sovereign state, had most certainly understood. *Pace* Schmitt, it is not by mistake that Hobbes gave the name *Leviathan* to his 1651 treatise on the construction of the modern state. In making reference to the biblical monster of the seas, he pointed toward the necessity to project the ordering power of the state over the anarchic freedom of thalassic spaces. Hobbes dreamed of subjecting the sea to the order of the land, and therefore extending the international legal order – based on a multiplicity of independent sovereign states, each endowed with an absolute monopoly on the legitimate use of violence – over the whole earth.

With this general framework in mind, it is possible to make sense of the only explicit reference to piracy in *Leviathan*: 'Also amongst men, until there were constituted great Common-wealths, it was thought no dishonour to be a Pyrate or a Highway Theefe' (Hobbes 2010: 99). Hobbes makes no distinction between the land-based thief and the maritime thief, since both are destined to be stripped of their right to exist, when the space in which they roam is included in a 'great Commonwealth'. Already during the early seventeenth century, coastal waters were gradually annexed to the order of the emerging national commonwealths, the modern European states. The growth in power of central governments meant that they were increasingly capable to curb the independence of the local gentry, which had traditionally provided an umbrella for piracy. The attitude of the ruling elites, moreover, began to change when local systems of agriculture started to be increasingly channelled into the international market through the mediation of maritime commerce. In Britain the power of the Killigrews – which, as we has seen, was considered largely paradigmatic of early forms of organized plunder – was already in decline by the early seventeenth century, when a series of conflicts with the monarchy led to accusations of treason and the twilight of their noble house (Marsden 2011: 285–292).

As early as 1612, James I offered a General Pardon to all pirates who were prepared to surrender their 'means of plunder', allowing them to keep 'the entire fruition of whatsoever they were then possessed of'. The use of General Pardons contributed to early state efforts to erect a modern navy, which would be under direct monarchical control. From the first half of the seventeenth century, London merchants were pressuring the government for the construction of a more powerful navy, the organization of a system of maritime policing and the suppression of piracy. John Bland's seventeenth century counsel to the English monarchy titled *Trade Revived, Or, A Way Proposed to Restore, Increase, Enrich, Strengthen and Preserve the Decayed and Even Dying Trade of this Our English Nation* insists over and over on the necessity of suppressing the pirate coves of Cornwall and the South of Ireland

(1660: 1–59). In the second half of the seventeenth century, thus, the perfection of the Navy as a disciplined tool in the hands of the sovereign meant that maritime space could be more controlled, and trade more efficiently policed. During the second half of the seventeenth century, when the oceans 'beyond the line' were still a space in which freebooters and buccaneers could cultivate some freedom from state discipline, the British seas were already under centralized state control and pirates were being hanged at Wapping Execution Dock on the River Thames. Between 1713 and 1725, when piracy was seen as endangering trade throughout the Atlantic and the Indian Ocean, there are reports of only half a dozen pirates operating in British coastal waters, and all of these were quickly captured (Earle 2005: 31). In November 1724, when John Gow led a mutiny aboard the *George Galley* in a revolt against scarce provisions and ill treatment of the working sailors, his attempt to hide in his native Orkney Islands led to the immediate capture of the whole crew. In June 1725, his body was tarred and suspended over the Thames, in a silent admonition to the thousands of sailors passing on their way to London (Defoe 1725: 45–46).

The great oceans of the world, nevertheless, remained excluded from the control of any one commonwealth. Only in the eighteenth century was the space of exception 'beyond the line' systematically included in the international order. The oceans were captured by the international Commonwealth of modern nations and not by any single Leviathan. The pirate thus became the common enemy of the nascent community of modern, civilized states. In order to make the oceans of the world safe for international trade, European property rights could not remain land-based; instead their validity had to be abstracted and de-territorialized. If the age of plundering adventure was to give way to the age of merchant ventures, the absolute freedom of the seas could no longer be held. Henceforth, one of the main tasks of European states and their new navies would be to provide protection for international trade, receiving in return a stable flow of revenue from indirect taxation and custom duties. Growing cities would establish expanding trading networks, which would sustain urban life through a regulated flow of foodstuffs and other essential staples from all around the world (Mumford 1968). The English governments, in particular, writes Peter Earle:

> would be committed to what has been called 'a grand maritime Empire', in which trade, shipping and the empire itself would be promoted, protected for the benefits of merchants and governments alike. . . . There was to be no place for pirates in this new world, no place for individualist marauders on the periphery of empire.
>
> (2005: 146)

In 1699, according to the Governor of Virginia, pirates had become 'a vermin in a commonweal and ought to be dangled up like polecats or weasel in a warren' (Thomson 1994: 106). It is symptomatic that the new Imperial motto chosen for the Bahamas in 1718, and unchanged until recently, would be: *Expulsis*

Piratis, Restituta Commercia – 'Pirates Expelled, Commerce Restored' (Storr 2004: 51–52).

Thus began the long history of counter-piracy operations that continue to this very day. The Herculean task of securing private property and unhindered commercial circulation over the immense vastness of the oceans of the world, in fact, has required a constant use of force and a never-ending theatrical display of disciplining violence, which remains inscribed in the very foundations of the contemporary world-market – a form of global policing violence, which originally enabled the carving of a hyperspace of circulation, and which must be reiterated over and over in order to maintain it. The eradication of piracy, in other words, was a foundational moment in the creation of the first and paradigmatic hyperspace of circulation: one of the most important moments in the history of modern global integration. The suppression of piracy appears as a constitutive moment in the transition to an ordered system of capital accumulation on a global scale. Without the eradication of piracy, without the emptying out of the oceans of the world and their transformation in an integrated plane for safe commercial circulation, contemporary processes of globalization would have been simply unthinkable.

The last pirates, those who resisted their integration within the disciplinary order of the Royal Navy, those who refused to settle down and return within the ranks of civilization, were the last nomadic partisans. This is not only in the sense that they were 'partisans on the move' but, especially, because *in moving* they experienced and defended a political spatiality radically different from the one for which states fought for centuries on the seas. 'Pirates,' writes Carl Schmitt, 'were pioneers of the new freedom of the sea, which essentially was non-state freedom. They were partisans of the sea' (2003: 174). They were the last partisans of the absolute freedom of the seas against the revolutionary attempt by the community of sovereign states to impose their order over the oceanic vastness. The pirates of the early eighteenth century, in other words, continued to assert the autonomy they had enjoyed and exploited in earlier times.

According to the international law crafted by the states that desired their extermination, pirates were denationalized and uprooted from their land. From the eighteenth century, therefore, those who were identified as pirates found, in the vanishing freedom of the oceans, the only space in which they could identify themselves. According to their most famous eighteenth-century chronicler, Captain Charles Johnson, when pirates hailed other vessels at sea, they often emphasized their only spatial allegiance by announcing that they came 'From the Seas'. The seas from which they came, nevertheless, were not the commercial plane of circulation that states were trying to construct in the eighteenth century, but rather the Sea as a space of exception and as a space of absolute freedom, which had existed at the margin of the international system throughout the sixteenth and seventeenth centuries. As Dominique Weber emphasizes:

> The crucial point is that pirates do not go to sea in the same way as other sailors. . . . They have left behind the world on which Man has imposed his

rule, his compass, his plumb-line, his land-registry, his lists, his civil laws. When they sail the seas, their aim is to proclaim the existence of the yawning gulf that separates the continents, the victory of water over land, of geography over civilization, of primordial order over the order imposed by engineers.

(2009: 8)

There is some truth in Janice Thomson's remark that 'the practice of privateering produced the problem of piracy' (1994: 67). In fact, it was often the very same people and the very same practices of violent plunder that, especially from the beginning of the eighteenth century, started to be *problematized* as forms of piracy that had to be eradicated. A harsher view of unregulated buccaneering and a tendency towards stricter regulation of privateering commissions emerged after the Treaty of Madrid of 1670, which, for the first time, stated that peace in Europe should also mean peace beyond the line. Nevertheless, a succession of international wars – that involved all the major European powers – caused a constant increase in the number of ships legally authorized to plunder on the high seas. During the three decades of constant warfare that closed the seventeenth century, European states relied heavily on the use of privateering commissions. Edmund Dummer, who first developed a modern system of transatlantic mail service, just after the outbreak of the War of Spanish Succession, remarked that 'it is the opinion of every one this cursed trade [privateering] will breed so many pirates that, when peace comes, we shall be in more danger from them than we are now from the enemy' (cited in Earle 2004: 159). According to contemporary sources, this is exactly what happened, once the Treaty of Utrecht established the end of hostilities. Captain Johnson, in his monumental *The General History of the Pyrates* (1724), formulated the origins of what will later be recognized as the Golden Age of Piracy in the following words, which are worthy of being quoted at length:

I Come now to the Pyrates that have rose since the Peace of Vtrecht; in War Time there is no room for any, because all those of a roving advent'rous Disposition find Employment in Privateers, so there is no Opportunity for Pyrates; like our Mobs in London, when they come to any Height, our Superiors order out the Train Bands, and when once they are raised, the others are suppressed of Course; I take the Reason of it to be, that the Mob go into the tame Army, and immediately from notorious Breakers of the Peace, become, by being put into order, solemn Preservers of it. . . . The Multitude of Men and Vessels, employ'd this Way, in Time of War, in the West-Indies, is another Reason, for the Number of Pyrates in a Time of Peace: . . . so many idle People employing themselves in Privateers, for the sake of Plunder and Riches, which they always spend as fast as they get, that when the War is over, and they can have no farther Business in the Way of Life they have been used to, they too readily engage in Acts of Pyracy, which being

> but the same Practice without a Commission, they make very little Distinction betwixt the Lawfulness of one, and the Unlawfulness of the other.
>
> (1724: 64–65)

The period immediately following the Treaty of Utrecht entered into history as 'The Golden Age of Piracy' not because plunder at sea was a novelty of the age, but because pirates were, for the first time, treated as an extraordinary phenomenon, a historical problem worthy of attention and a social issue, reflecting more profound tensions in the history of Atlantic societies. It is sufficient to flick through the fascinating bibliography of sources brought together by Philip Gosse (1926) in order to capture the amount of literary production that followed the lives of early eighteenth-century pirates. The history of the oceanic struggle between the Imperial forces of order and the pirates was reported in countless pamphlets, newspaper articles, accounts of battles, executions and confessions, chronicles and memories, sometimes reliable, other times somewhat imaginary, which slowly composed a new genre.

From the beginning, the struggle was represented in recurring epic terms: as a confrontation between the ordering power of Empire and the chaotic vitality of the pirate, between the advance of civilization and the resistance of a savage freedom, between the efficient discipline of the Navy and the joyous wastefulness of the pirate crews, between the ritualized violence of the law and the unpredictable brutality of the pirates. It was a literary representation that was ambiguous from the very beginning, since it allowed the magnification of the progressive strength of European empires but also left some space for a secret complicity with what was represented as the pirates' resistance against civilization. Already in the seminal text by Charles Johnson (1724) (since then a central reference point for conservative as much as for radical historians), an explicit praise of Empire coexists with an implicit complicity with the pirates, adopted as symbols of a more elemental freedom, which negated all the values – discipline, reason and order – celebrated by European civilization.

Many of the early pirates had been English privateers during the war, and freebooters before that. After the signing of the Peace of Utrecht, pirates with captains such as Philip Cockram, John Jennings and Benjamin Hornigold continued to affirm the immunity of the space 'beyond the line' from the sovereign declarations of peace, war and law affirmed in Europe. In their view, the oceans remained a space wholly Other, in which men retained the political freedom to choose their own struggles and their own enemies. As late as 1716, some of these former buccaneers maintained 'that they never consented to the Articles of Peace with the French and with the Spaniards' (Konstam 2008: 66). Declaring their autonomy of decision on the distinction between friend and enemy, the buccaneers effectively declared their own absolute sovereignty, their ability to decide for themselves on the essential political question. According to Carl Schmitt, only 'to the state as an essentially political entity belongs the *jus belli*, i.e. the real possibility of deciding in a concrete situation upon the enemy and the ability to fight it'

(2007a: 45). Thus, if a sovereign declares an enemy, and individuals or groups within society reject that declaration, 'the sovereign state conceived as a person is dead or at the point of dying' (ibidem). The pirates of the early eighteenth century, therefore, directly challenged the sovereign power to impose unilaterally on its subjects the decision as to the identity of the enemy. They took their lives in their own hands and went, in the abovementioned words of one of the men aboard one of those privateers-turned-pirate-ships, 'from plundering for others, to do it for themselves' (Atkins 1970: 226).

Refusing to obey the sovereign power to decide over the identity of the enemy is only one step away from the sovereign act of autonomously choosing one's own friend and enemies. And in fact, in the following years, a number of pirate crews started to decide by themselves, in absolute autonomy from the national communities they had abandoned on land, the purpose of their battle and the identity of their enemy. This stage is symbolically represented by one of the major events in the history of Caribbean piracy, which took place in 1717 when 'a multiethnic but mostly English crew of pirates overthrew Hornigold as commander because "he refused to take and plunder English vessels"' (Rediker 2004: 36). Outlawed and banned from international law – branded as an 'enemy of all nations', a vermin to be eradicated and a threat to the principle of sovereignty – a number of pirates embraced their marginality, declaring their ships to be autonomous floating republics, free as any other independent community to decide autonomously its own mode of life and the nature of its struggles.

According to a number of historians, the pirates of the Golden Age choose simply to be at war with the whole world, preying indiscriminately on all ships and all communities (Earle 2005: 12–13). Others, however, have gathered historical evidence that numerous pirate crews regarded only 'certain social groups as their enemies', while 'they got support and material assistance' from other social groups with which they felt an affinity (Rediker 2004: 83–102). In 1718, the Boston sea captain Thomas Checkley testified to the authorities that the pirates who had robbed him 'pretended to be Robbin Hood's Men' (cited in Jameson 1923: 304). A number of captured pirates, as well as different state officials, insisted that piracy was also a revolt against the extreme exploitation of labour aboard merchant vessels. Captain Francis Willis, for instance, as a member of the Royal Navy, reported to the Admiralty in London that various crews running slave ships 'were ripe for piracy. Whether it be occasioned by the masters' ill usage or their own natural inclination I must leave their Lordship to judge' (Earle 2005: 169).

As we have already seen, the maritime culture common among the sailors-turned-pirates was profoundly attached to the idea of private vengeance, legitimate retaliation and retort. Merchant ships had practised for a long time, and until fairly recently, forms of private vengeance and legalized retaliation upon the high seas. Faithful to this vanishing maritime custom, numerous pirate crews understood their violence as a form of legitimate retaliation against the world of merchants and state navies. 'Upon seizing a merchant,' writes Marcus Rediker, referencing a 1722 document from Virginia, 'pirates often administered the "Distribution of

Justice" "enquiring into the Manner of the Commander's Behaviour to their Men, and thus against whom complaint whose made" were "whipp'd and pickled"' (Rediker 2004: 86). The pirates of the eighteenth century, thus, were presented by contemporary authors, and heretofore passed into myth and history, as ambiguous 'primitive rebels' and enthralling 'social bandits'.

In Eric Hobsbawm's renowned works *Primitive Rebels* (1959) and *Social Bandits* (1972), the British historian defined social bandits as 'a cry for vengeance on the rich and oppressors, a vague dream of some curb upon them, a righting of individual wrongs' (1959: 5). What is most important in Hobsbawm's account is the stress he puts on the importance of myths and popular perceptions: social bandits are, first of all, 'those who are not or not only regarded as simple criminals by public opinion' (Hobsbawm 1972: 14). Although the historical record is greatly debated, and there is not much hope to receive at any time a factual and objective account that would forever end the debate, popular perceptions retain an autonomous significance, largely independent from the opinions of contemporary historians. The fact remains that, since the eighteenth century, pirates 'are not, or not only, regarded as simple criminals by public opinion'; instead they are portrayed sometimes as noble robbers, and more often as popular avengers whose terror actually forms part of their public image. As Hobsbawm wrote:

> they are heroes not in spite of the fear and horror their actions inspire, but in some ways because of them. They are not so much men who right wrongs, but avengers, and exerters of power; their appeal is not that of agents of justice, but of men who prove that even the poor and the weak can be terrible.
> (1972: 58)

This was the heyday of Blackbeard and Bartholomew Robers, 'Black Sam' Bellamy, of the two celebrated women pirates Anne Bonny and Mary Read. These were the pirates who, already in the eighteenth century, created a profound fascination throughout Europe. They were portrayed as rebellious figures of political significance. They were deemed to have rejected their attachment to traditional communities and to have affirmed their autonomy and independence. Charles Johnson, in the book that would influence thousands of readers and hundreds of later literary writers, relates that a pirate named Captain Bellamy made this speech to the captain of a merchant vessel who had just declined an invitation to join the pirates:

> I am sorry they won't let you have your sloop again, for I scorn to do any one a mischief, when it is not to my advantage; damn the sloop, we must sink her, and she might be of use to you. Though you are a sneaking puppy, and so are all those who will submit to be governed by laws which rich men have made for their own security; for the cowardly whelps have not the courage otherwise to defend what they get by knavery; but damn ye altogether: damn them for a pack of crafty rascals, and you, who serve them, for a parcel of hen-hearted

> numbskulls. They vilify us, the scoundrels do, when there is only this difference, they rob the poor under the cover of law, forsooth, and we plunder the rich under the protection of our own courage. Had you not better make then one of us, than sneak after these villains for employment?
>
> (1724: 54)

When the captain replied that his conscience would not let him break the laws of God and man, the pirate Bellamy continued:

> I am a free prince, and I have as much authority to make war on the whole world as he who has a hundred sail of ships at sea and an army of 100,000 men in the field; and this my conscience tells me! But there is no arguing with such snivelling puppies, who allow superiors to kick them about deck at pleasure.
>
> (1724: 55)

This passage may be taken as representative of a widespread understanding of pirates as autonomous political communities, in rebellion against traditional forms of allegiance. In *Theory of the Partisan* (2007), Schmitt holds strong to the position that pirates must be regarded as strictly non-political figures, since their 'evil deeds are focused on booty', or alternatively since 'the irregularity of the pirate lacks any relation to regularity' (2007b: 14, 70). Nevertheless, his own theory of the 'political' renders Schmitt's position on piracy untenable. In fact, if the political is 'the utmost degree of intensity of a union or separation, of an association or dissociation', and if 'the concepts of friend, enemy and struggle acquire their real meaning from the fact that they all relate, in a specific sense, to the real possibility of physical killing', then pirate crews formed a unity that was highly political, although not territorial (Schmitt 2007a: 26, 33). The 'political' alludes, in fact, to a collective identification *through* struggle. The political describes only 'the degree of intensity of an association of men, whose motives can be religious, national, economic, or of any other kind and can effect at different times different coalitions and separations' (Schmitt 2007a: 38).

There could be different motives for which pirate crews acted as robbers on the seas. They could be radical Protestants who would find in piracy an association ready to fight the Catholic powers even against the wishes of their own countries (Lane 1998). They could be Antinomians and Levellers who, after their defeat in England, sailed towards the West in search of a free space to live in communities organized according to their egalitarian principles (Hill 1986: 161–187). They could be elements of the English 'maritime proletariat' who, dispossessed of the common land, and forced to sell their labour in the British port-towns, revolted against the appalling conditions in which they were forced to live, and often die, for the sake of primitive accumulation (Rediker 2004). They could be Dutch labourers at the service of privateers and merchant companies plundering he wealth of the Malacca who would take control of the ship and set upon plundering for themselves (Lunsford 2005). They could be slaves united by nothing but their common prison (Linebaugh and Rediker 2000). Whatever the motive, even if it was 'just robbing', the ever-present threat of death to which a pirate crew was collectively exposed made it a political association, which formed itself through life and through struggle.

It would be impossible to report here the different ways in which this political association was translated and how it created micro-worlds, Foucauldian heterotopias, which could certainly mirror the institutions that dominated life in early-modern, early-capitalist states but that would also, sometimes, turn them upside down. If ships have been for centuries the greatest source of our imagination, pirate ships have been, at least since the seventeenth century, the greatest source of our *insurrectionary imagination*. A number of then unheard-of customs were practised somewhere, at some point in time, in the multitude of heterotopias that 'turned pyrate'. Historians have seen in pirate ships early forms of mutual assistance and pension funds (Rediker 2004); sexual equality and widespread homosexuality (Burg 2012), radical democratic and semi-anarchist forms of management (Wilson 2003), and ethnic intermingling and interracial relations (Williams 2001). And this is not because all of pirate ships were 'pirate utopias', but because each of them was a heterotopia, an experiment in social organization. Among the multitude of floating communities – in just the ten years between 1716 and 1726, some 5,000 people are deemed to have sailed under the Jolly Roger – historians have found 'despicable' as well as 'revolutionary' practices; nevertheless, for a genealogist, pirate communities are mirrors through which we can displace the European state and its historical evolution. Each pirate heterotopia designs a cultural line that Europe may have followed at the point in which it melted with the New World it was about to colonize.

The popular and frequently reprinted *A General History of the Pirates* carried such a vision down through the centuries as a form of mythical history. The introduction to Johnson's book begins with the consideration that many modern states arose from a collection of thieves to respectability among the nations of the world. Rome itself, 'the Mistress of the world', Johnson insists, was 'no more at first than a refuge for Thieves and Outlaws' (1724: 9). And throughout the *History of the Pirates*, Johnson insists on viewing every pirate ship as the potential beginning of an independent political community: 'if the progress of our pirates had been equal to their beginning; had they united and settled in some of those islands, they might, by this time have been honoured with the name of a Commonwealth, and no power in those parts of the world could have been able to dispute it with them' (ibidem).

One could even argue that a loose network of pirate communities emerged as a peculiar kind of political community, which was symbolically materialized and reinforced by the widespread adoption of the Jolly Roger, as well as culturally re-elaborated by the development of a distinct linguistic community forged through criss-crossing processes of *métissage* and hybridization: a diasporic pirate creole full of cursing and nautical terms, idiomatic expressions and colourful metaphors, whose appeal is paradoxically testified by the extent in which it continues to live in a globally commodified form (Mackie 2005: 24–62). When they met on the sea, pirate ships would sometimes 'greet one another and share news and drink together as when Captain Howell Davis' and Thomas Cocklin's crews met on the Sierra Leone River in April 1719' (Land 2007: 178).

Certainly, the pirates of each pirate ship constituted a strong 'community of fate' but there is a very different type of community at work in the piratical myth. There was a sense of comradeship and solidarity not only within members of the same ship, but also among different pirate crews. In 1718, an official of the Crown reported the 'alarming growth' of a 'nest of pirates' in the Bahamas, 'who already esteem themselves a community, and to have one common interest' (Rediker 1989: 265). This common interest was simply expressed by the enmity towards established states that were attempting to project their sovereign power over the anarchy of the seas. Blackbeard's crew attacked the Royal Navy in the harbour of Boston, claiming to vindicate the executions of pirates that had taken place in the preceding months (Rediker 2004: 95). When Teach's sea rovers captured a Boston ship captain, they made him report 'that if the Prisoners suffered they would Kill every Body they took belonging to New England' (Jameson 1923: 308). In September 1720, a number of pirate ships captained by Bartholomew Roberts 'openly and in the daytime burnt and destroyed . . . vessels in the Road of Basseterre', avenging the executions 'of their comrades at Nevis' (Rediker 1989: 277).

It was especially the need to establish control on the seamen's work (as sailors) and their rebellion (as pirates) that incentivized the main European powers to find a common enemy in the pirate as *hostis communis omnium*. It has been one of the main achievements of postcolonial theory to have laid bare the ways in which the community of the nation has been constructed through a mechanism of Othering that often opposed the civility of a bounded national community to the savages and barbarians roaming the planes beyond the gates (Said 1978). In a similar way, if there ever was an 'inter-national community' such as the one imagined by the fathers of international law, this was founded on the constitution of a threatening Other, whose savage freedom seemed to negate the form of loyalty on which the state ultimately rests.

The outlawed pirate ship was an early example of a nomadic state of exception, haunting the interstices of the first global *nomos*, and heralding the exceptional status of those denationalized refugees, 'outlawed and expelled from all countries', that Hanna Arendt named as 'the avant-garde of their people' (1943: 77). Its flag bore the stigma of the sovereign ban. The infamous Jolly Roger with which pirates are identified, a skull above two long bones crossed over a black field, symbolized not only the pirates' lack of concern for their own mortality, but also a threat to those merchant vessels that intended to resist, and a rejection of the nation-state as a foundation for identity and community. Informed by Agamben's theorizations on sacrality and the state of exception, we can read something more in the Jolly Roger, and perhaps hear a secret message whispered through its uncanny grin. To be declared *hostis communis omnium* meant to suffer an absolute exclusion from the political community. Eighteenth-century pirates were, even more than the common sailors described by John Flavel in *Navigation Spiritualized*, 'a third sort of persons to be numbered neither with the living nor with the dead; their lives hanging constantly in suspense before them' (1820: 206). The symbolic use of the death's head, as Walter Benjamin suggested, should be interpreted as a powerful baroque symbol: 'the single emblem that best combines the notions of fallen nature and the total historicity of the individual' (cited in Cowan 1981: 116).

Pirates were systematically demonized and described as savage beasts, cold-hearted monsters, sea wolves and demons of the oceans; or otherwise meaningless vermin to be eradicated from the sea for the efficiency of commercial circulation and the happiness of all. 'Stripped of all human characteristics,' writes Marcus Rediker, 'the pirate was now a wild fragment of nature that could be tamed only by death' (2004: 146). On 18th October 1717, in a trial that would lead to the execution of six 'persons indited for piracy', the King's attorney concluded that pirates 'can claim the protection of no Prince, the privilege of no Country, the benefit of no Law, he is denied common humanity and the very rights of Nature' (*Trials of eight person indited for piracy* 1718: 6). As outlaws at the margin of international law, pirates were understood neither as citizens guilty of a crime, nor as equal enemies to confront.

There never really was a 'war against pirates', but rather an international campaign of extermination or, in other words, a *persecutio piratarum*. 'It is fundamental to the hitherto existing interpretation of piracy,' writes Carl Schmitt:

> that the action of the pirate is not a war in the sense of international law, just as little as, conversely, the action of a state directed against the pirate is not a war . . . War owed its justice, honour and worth to the fact that the enemy was neither a pirate nor a gangster but rather a state and a subject of international law.
>
> (2011: 71, 168)

From this point of view, to name a particular group of people as pirates according to international law meant, first of all, denying the political value of their association. Pirates were motivated only by plunder, potentially at war with the entire world, and thus apolitical. This definition enabled European states to portray operations aimed at the eradication of 'pirate groups' as neutral forms of global law enforcing. The pursuit and killing of those defined as pirates was not presented as a form of political warfare, but instead as a benevolent service offered by particular Imperial states to the whole international community.

As we will see, this denial of political status, together with the form of violence it sustained and authorized, would continue to serve particular Imperial strategies. The definition of the pirate as *hostis communis omnium* and enemy of mankind, recuperated from Roman Imperial law in the eighteenth century, revealed itself an extraordinary concept of international law. Imperial states could now, in the name of humanity at large, intervene all over the earth, disposing at will of the lives of foreigners, as long as the target of their military might was convincingly portrayed as an apolitical pirate. The eradication of piracy in the eighteenth century, in other words, was paradigmatic of a form of discriminatory global violence – distinct from traditional international warfare – that would continue to haunt international law in the centuries to come. The continuity in the definition of the pirate as the 'enemy of all' – upheld by the Scholastic theologians of the School of Salamanca and then by the international lawyers of the seventeenth and eighteenth centuries – reveals the ways in which the *absolute enemy* of theology did not simply disappear, but was rather transformed in the *systemic enemy* of international law. We went from God to civilization, from the 'pirate devils' to the 'pirate brutes', and from a crusading spirit to a civilizing zeal. The narrative that opposes the absolute character of the Wars of Religion to the *guerre en forme* of the international state system obscures the fact that the international system never ceases to project its absolute enemies. War between states was limited only to the extent that the opponents recognized each other as *not* being pirates, but they also continuously branded other, minor polities as pirates to be outlawed and suppressed.

This may seem a banal consideration and yet it is often forgotten or left at the margin of studies of international relations and international law, centred as they are on the relationship that states entertain *between* themselves. For instance, it is certainly possible that modern war was, in the classic definition given by Alberico Gentili (1933), 'an armed, public and legalized conflict' (*armorum publicorum justa contentio*); and yet war was not the only type of violence that is constitutive of the state-form. The genealogy of the modern international community must take into account not only the history of international war as an institution, it must also show the ways in which Imperial violence continued to be projected at the shifting margins of the international community of states, always recreating an outside beyond international law. It is at this point that we start to glimpse in the history of Imperial campaigns against enemies of humanity and outlawed pirates *another* genealogy of war: not the glorious, codified war between equal sovereigns, but the forgotten terror of the *persecutio piratarum*.

After the hundreds of hangings of the early eighteenth century, it well may be true that the Golden Age of piracy came to an end. But the Imperial campaigns against piracy continued, although the new pirates would not enjoy the glamour of those romantic outlaws, who succeeded in capturing forever the popular imagination. In the nineteenth century, it was in defence of free trade against pirates and robbers that the United Kingdom officially intervened in the Malay archipelago (Tarling 1963). As shown by James Warren, in fact, the penetration of European commercial empires in the region coincided with the destruction of traditional networks of trade that, as it had been for centuries in the Mediterranean, were always also networks of plunder and small-scale piracy (2007). Disempowered local chieftains opposed the imposition of long-distance trade with Europe first by the Portuguese, then by the Dutch East India Company, and finally by the British Empire. British military dominance of the seas, and 'the spreading notion that the forms of sovereignty that might be possessed by non-European societies should not be permitted to interfere with the natural law of property, led to a further assumption by Great Britain of a legal authority to protect shipping lines in general' (Rubin 2006: 202). In the 1840s, the British Admiralty distributed a prize of £20 for every pirate captured or destroyed in the area, culminating in a claim of £42,000 for a single operation in 1849 in which officially, only on the first day, '1800 pirates were attacked and 400 killed with British casualties of only one man slightly wounded; and two days later an attack on 3000 Chinese pirates, killing 1700 with no British loss of life' (Fox 1973: 107–109).[2]

It was in defence of free trade that Thomas Jefferson similarly mobilized the United States in their first major military intervention abroad, declaring to uphold the universal right to commerce against 'the Barbary pirates' of Algiers in the early nineteenth century (Fisher 1974). Countless popular books today compare the Barbary Powers to modern terrorists, claiming that, 'while the Barbary War resembles today's war on terror tactically and strategically, it resonates most deeply in its assertion of free trade, human rights, and freedom from tyranny and terror' (Wheelan 2003: 25). What has been recently recuperated as 'America's first war on Terror' was characterized by the way in which the corsairs of Algiers – operating as privateers much like the ones on which America had relied only a few decades before in their war of independence – were denied the status of legitimate enemies. Here the category of the pirate anticipated and served many of the same functions that are today explicated by the ubiquitous concept of the 'terrorist', reflecting and legitimating a form of undeclared, asymmetrical warfare without borders.

Again today, in a striking turn, the universal friendship that commerce seems to create projects a threatening 'other', that undermines it from within. Counter-piracy operations, Imperial interventions conceptualized as forms of violence against pirates to be suppressed in the name of all, have a long and surprisingly neglected history. We may thus begin to ask, moving closer to our contemporary times: what is the strategic logic that governs counter-piracy operations? What do they try to achieve? How do they conceptualize global space? And, finally, what is the particular conception of humanity that seems to inform today's global system of security, at least when it takes as its operating concept of enmity the pirate as *hostis humani generis*? In short: who are the 'new pirates'? And where do they come from?

2 In order to imagine a modern-day equivalent to these sums one may start from taking into consideration the agricultural wages predominant in England at the time: in 1827 the *Commission on Emigration* estimate at £23 the annual wage of an agricultural labourer in Sussex; the Reports of the Poor Law Commissioner in 1834 show the net annual earnings of an unskilled London labourer to be circa £33 (Bowley 2014: 39).

Intermezzo: The romance of piracy

At first, the image of the pirate emerging in modern European culture from the beginning of the eighteenth century might seem startlingly contradictory. There were certainly two different mythological machines spinning incessantly the modern image of the pirate. One of them is set firmly on land and, protected by a system of fences and concrete walls, relentlessly spins a sovereign myth of bare life and absolute enmity necessary to feed and supplement the senescent apparatus of international law. The other, which is lighter and painted in dazzling colours, floats garrulous over the sea reproducing old popular songs of elemental freedom, adventure and struggle, in which those who act in defiance of the law are somehow lifted from their aberrant status and seen from a space outside law and morality, whose nature escapes us. Between them, on the shores between land and sea, at the point in which sovereign myths and popular fantasy clash into each other, is produced this wobbly shadow, this volatile outline that we call 'pirate'. The authoritative voice of international law, continuously reiterating the ancient image of the pirate as 'enemy of all', seems to clash with the proliferation of romantic and libertarian literature, which insists on picturing the pirate as a symbol of rebellion and defiance, of savage freedom and joyous camaraderie. And yet these two mythological machines, although opposed to each other, really converged on a characterization of the pirate as a figure of absolute freedom against the state. This was an image that served a constitutive role in the mythology of power as much as in the one of resistance.[1]

If, at the dawn of the eighteenth century, the pirate had already become a standard reference among international lawyers as 'the common enemy' that directly opposes and makes concrete the civilized 'community of states', it is not so paradoxical if, a century later, anarchist and romantic circles arched back to the same image in order to evoke a form of freedom over and against national loyalty

1 I take the notion of mythological machine from Furio Jesi's studies on the role and functioning of myth in modernity. The concept has been then further elaborated by Agamben in ways that do not interest us at this moment in time. On the concept see Jesi, F. *Letteratura e mito*, Einaudi, Torino 1968 and Jesi, F. *L'accusa del sangue. Mitologie dell'antisemitismo*, Morcelliana, Brescia 1992.

and state discipline. Already in the eighteenth century, as we have seen, popular literature such as Johnson's *A Complete History of the Pirates* introduced the pirate as an embodiment of popular rebellious energies, bound toward the profanation of everything sacred. In popular literature, the portrayal of pirate deeds suggested the traumatic disruption of deeply held social conventions. In *The Division of Labor in Society* (1947), the French sociologist Emile Durkheim theorized that the material harm resulting from crimes such as robbery is always secondary in importance to its symbolic value and its potential for ideological disruption. For Durkheim, the life of outlaws and criminals have the capacity to destabilize social structures, not because of the material threat they pose to established social orders, but because they demonstrate that crystallized social conventions are neither sacred nor unanimous. Because of these larger implications, crime and punishment take on a quasi-religious significance: 'penal law is not alone essentially religious in origin, but indeed always retains a certain religious stamp. It is because the acts that it punishes appear to be attacks upon something transcendent, whether being or concept' (Durkheim 1947: 100). It is the symbolic profanation of established social conventions rather than the extent of the material disruptions that elevates certain crimes to a political, mythical and even metaphysical status. In similar ways, Hobsbawm stresses the symbolical status of the outlaw in modern societies. For him, 'the bandit is not only a man, but a symbol' (1972: 112).

In fact, the pirate emerged in the early eighteenth century as a recurrent outlaw figure in popular literature. The pirate soon became a symbolic embodiment of popular fantasies of social transgression and, therefore, references to pirates often intertwined the personal and the symbolic, the historical and the mythical. What must be stressed, following Durkheim, is that the symbolic struggle surrounding the pirate, as a man and as an icon, always evoked popular fantasies of freedom and transgression as much as authoritative attempts to reaffirm the sanctity of social institutions. If the narrative representation of pirate transgression challenged the sanctity of property, law and established hierarchies, through the portrayed defeat and punishment of branded outlaws and criminals those same institutions forcefully reaffirmed themselves in the eyes of early-modern readers. It is also because of this underlying political tension that the early eighteenth century was characterized by a growing interest in the discourse of crime and punishment. In a number of European countries, and most of all in England, there was a multiplication of crime reports, criminal biographies, providence books and gallows speeches due to 'an increasingly widespread cultural perception that criminality and the law were lenses that brought into focus much of what was disturbing, and most exciting, about contemporary experience' (Gladfelder 2001: 5).

Narratives concerning the struggle between eruptions of individual and communal transgressions and the restorative power of the law gave rise to a thriving production of criminal pamphlets and broadsheets distributed before, during and after trials and executions. Consequently, from the second half of the eighteenth century, longer narrative accounts started to replace the older pamphlets and broadsheets. Collected chronicles and book-length reports that centred on the extraordinary lives and deeds of outlaws and criminals, such as Johnson's *General History*, emerged as one of the most successful, and controversial, genres of the age. The influential German literary critic Karl Muller-Fraureuth once wrote about the 'joy in seeing poor men become suddenly powerful while dukes and government officials are overthrown and hanged' as one explanation for the persistent popularity of the outlaw figure in contemporary culture (1965: 2). The long-lasting fascination with the pirate in popular literature – and especially in children's fairy tales – might be explained as an avenue for latent social desires for rebellion against internalized figures of authority. According to Jungian psychoanalysis, the pirate and the mutineer are paradigmatic figures of the insurgency of repressed desire in modern civilized societies.

> As long as . . . psychic energy finds its application in adequate and well-regulated ways . . . no uncertainty or doubt besets us, and we cannot be divided against ourselves. But as soon as one or two of the channels of psychic activity are blocked, *we are reminded of a stream that is dammed up*. The current flows backwards to its source; the inner man wants something which the visible man does not want, and we are at war with ourselves. Freud's psychoanalytic works show this process in the clearest way. The very first thing he discovered was the existence of . . . criminal fantasies which at their face value are wholly incompatible with the conscious outlook of a civilized man. *A person who was activated by them would be nothing less than a mutineer.*
>
> (Jung 2001: 207, my emphasis)

According to Jung, therefore, the figure of the pirate represents the persistent possibility of an uprising of surplus desire, breaking through the repressive apparatus of the super-ego. The pirate has the power to fascinate because he or she appears as a creature of the outside and of the margins, who abandoned repression and is able to live out the fantasies of transgression usually suppressed by the power of authority figures and the super-ego. The mutiny represents the flittering moment of the exception in which 'the power of real life breaks through the crust of a mechanism that has become torpid by repetition' (Schmitt 1985: 15); it is the triumph of corporality and joyous desire over the impositions of consciousness, reason and traditional morality. There is therefore a paradoxical convergence between the representation of pirate outlaws in popular literature and in international law: both discourses, from opposite angles, contributed to the construction of a figure defined by a Dionysian potential for profanation.

The pirate is always represented, first of all, as a transgressor of an ethical code which is considered, and enforced, as sacred and Universal: in the early sixteenth century the Christian philosophers, rooted in the Scholastic tradition, looked at English privateers such as Drake as eminent examples of heretical profaners challenging the authority of the Pope, the Church and ultimately the divine law itself. They were looked upon as enemies of the Universal Christian community; they were excommunicated and burned at the stake. Equally, the fathers of modern international law, rooted in the perspective proper to the *jus publicum europaeum*, saw pirates of the eighteenth century as a threat to the whole international system. They were therefore treated as enemies of all civilized communities: they were outlawed and hanged as barbarians and beasts of prey. As we will see, according to Hugo Grotius and Emmerich de Vattel, enlightened believers in the existence of natural law, pirates were *hostis humani generis*, enemies of humankind, since they transgressed not only the laws of civilized society but also the universal laws of nature. They were thus considered Universal criminals, monsters that challenged the well-ordered natural world. For all of humankind, the pirate must be condemned, excluded and killed in the interest of all; not because of the material damage inflicted to the victim, but rather because the pirate seemed to represent a challenge to the inviolability of the norms of the Universal Christian community, the international community of civilized states or the Universal human community of natural law.

Against these commanding voices mentioned above, pirate narratives elicit a form of carnivalesque enjoyment in showing a 'world turned upside down', in which the powerful are victimized and stripped of their authoritative position. One of the most celebrated passages in Johnson's *General History of the Pirates* reports the details of a mock trial held by Thomas Anstis and his pirate crew on an unnamed island south-west of Cuba in 1721. According to the author, the pirates often 'appointed a mock court of Judicature to try one another for piracy and he who was a criminal one day, was made a judge another' (1724: 222). The humoristic scene reflects both the carnivalesque inversion of roles typical of pirate literature and a criticism of the legal system, represented as systematically bent on reproducing established relations of power within society. As Johnson had before me, I have at hand 'an account of one of these merry trials, and as it appears diverting I shall give the reader a short account of it':

> *Attorney* An't please your Lordship, and you Gentlemen of the Jury, here is a Fellow before you that is a sad Dog, a sad sad Dog; and I humbly hope your Lordship will order him to be hang'd out of the Way immediately . . .
>
> *Judge.* Harkee me, Sirah – you lousy, pitiful, ill-look'd Dog; what have you to say why you should not be tuck'd up immediately, and set a Sun-drying like a Scarecrow? Are you guilty or not guilty?
>
> *Prisoner.* Not Guilty, an't please your Worship.
>
> *Judge.* Not guilty! Say so again, Sirrah, and I'll have you hang'd without any Tryal.
>
> *Prisoner.* An't please your Worship's Honour, my Lord, I am as honest a poor Fellow as ever went between Stem and Stern of a Ship, and can hand, reef, steer, and clap two Ends of a Rope together, as well as e'er a He that ever cross'd salt Water; but I was taken by one George Bradley [the Name of him that sat as Judge] a notorious Pyrate, a sad Rogue as ever was unhang'd, and he forc'd me, an't please your Honour.
>
> *Judge.* Answer me, Sirrah, How will you be try'd?

Prisoner. By God and my Country.

Judge. The Devil you will – Why then, Gentlemen of the Jury, I think we have nothing to do but proceed to Judgment.

Attorney. Right, my Lord; for if this Fellow should be suffer'd to speak, he may clear himself, and that's an Affront to the Court.

Prisoner. Pray, my Lord; I hope your Lordship will consider—

Judge. Consider! How dare you talk of considering?—Sirrah, Sirrah, I never consider'd in all my Life—I'll make it Treason to consider.

Prisoner. But I hope your Lordship will hear some Reason.

Judge. Do you hear how the Scoundrel prates? What have we to do with Reason? I'll have you to know, Raskal, we don't sit here to hear Reason; we go according to Law. Is our dinner ready?

Attorney. Yes, my Lord.

Judge. Then heark'ee, you Raskal at the Bar; hear me, Sirrah, hear me.–You must suffer for three Reasons: First, because it is not fit that I should sit here as Judge, and no Body be hang'd. Secondly, you must be hang'd, because you have a damn'd hanging Look. And thirdly, you must be hang'd, because I am hungry; for know, Sirrah, that 'tis a Custom, that whenever the Judge's Dinner is ready before the Tryal is over, the Prisoner is to be hang'd of Course. There's Law for you, ye Dog. So take him away Gaoler.

(Johnson 1724: 223–224)

Pirate narratives often include a closing scene centred on the conviction of the outlaw and his or her punishment, most often in the form of a violent death. Accounts of trials, when they were held, are also often included in the narrative. In contrast with the 'merry trial' presented by Johnson, nevertheless, scenes of judgment and punishment are seldom carnivalesque in their character. As Grossman has noticed, eighteenth-century pirate literature was 'rigidly shaped against the backdrop of the gallows' and often took the form of 'a teleological picaresque story that relates the graphic movement of a transgressive body, up until its final lamentable stop' (2002: 32). Accordingly, Giovanopoulos (2004) has studied pirate biographies as a narrative form singularly apt to dramatize the power of the state over the individual and to reaffirm the values of European civilization against the savage freedom of the barbarian outlaw. He suggests that pirate narratives, although centred on the life of transgressive individuals, secretly reaffirmed the values of the state and civilization, since nearly all of the published stories actually end up with the defeat of rebellion, the condemnation of the pirate and his or her death by execution.

In a similar vein, Foucault has notoriously stressed the political and ideological function of public trials and theatrical executions (1979: 1–32). The public hangings of pirates, and their representation in literature, propped up the threatened social order showing the hopelessness of revolt, and the damnation resulting from the profanation of sacred institutions. Here punishment has less to do with retribution than with the symbolic reaffirmation of the power of the law.

'When we desire the repression of crime,' writes Emile Durkheim, 'it is not that we desire to avenge personally, but to avenge something sacred which we feel more or less confusedly outside and above us' (1947: 99). The hanging body of the pirate, therefore, was a symbolic icon charged with social and political meaning, screaming to the world the sacredness of institutions such as private property and the state's monopoly of violence, but also the absolute power of the law to punish those who threaten to profane them. Eighteenth-century pirate narratives are often ambiguous because they offer the possibility of fantasizing about the unrestrained release of surplus desire and the possibility of rebellion against authority figures, but, on the other hand, they often warn against the disastrous consequences of challenging the authority of the law.

The account of the trial of George Cusack, 'the most signal Sea-Robber, that perhaps this Age hath known', reported by a self-styled 'Impartial Hand' in *The Grand Pyrate: or, the Life and Death of Capt. George Cusack the Great Sea-Robber* (1676), may be taken as representative of this recurrent aspect of pirate narratives. After having described in detail the revolt against 'God, Civilization and the Law of Nations' performed by this seventeenth-century pirate, the author exposes the apprehension and the punishment of George Cusack, turning the whole biography into a powerful reaffirmation of the inescapable power of authority. The trial begins, accordingly, with the reaffirmation of jurisdiction over the pirate, according to the Law of Nations. The rebel who excepted himself from the religious and civil order is conducted once again within the fold since the authority of the Admiralty is shown to extend 'over the British Seas; even to the very Shoars of his Neighbors' (*The Grand Pyrate* 1676: 28). In enforcing the Laws of Nations, the judge speaks in the name of the whole of civilized humanity to which are entrusted the oceans as an undivided Commonwealth. The pirate, who had explicitly meant to abandon civilized society in order to constitute a new, independent space outside traditional structures of authority, is therefore recounted within the Universal order of the Law of Nations, and he is made to suffer for his repeated profanations of Christian morality as well as international law. The statement of jurisdiction, therefore, represses the insurrection of surplus desire by showing the impossibility of escaping the social order and the power of psychic, as well as social, authority figures.

The further development of pirate literature would challenge exactly this inescapability of authority and the law. After the hundreds of hangings that effectively sanctioned the progressive disappearance of the classic figure of the pirate from the stage of history, the spectre of piracy would continue to haunt the nineteenth-century literary imagination. Romantic authors endlessly returned to the graves of eighteenth-century pirates, as pilgrims return year after year to the same symbolic sites, which are thus gradually charged with a collective psychic energy and a higher symbolic meaning. The pirate soon became the paradigmatic romantic outlaw: a towering figure embodying the awe-inspiring resistance of wild nature against industrial civilization, of sublime individuality against collective discipline, of desire against reason, of dangerous freedom against the security of urban confinement. As the pirate ship became a mythical space in which to project fantasies of freedom, a growing pirate literature grew in the heart of civilized Europe. Walter Scott's historical novel *The Pirate* (1821), Byron's epic poem *The Corsair* (1815), James Fenimore Cooper's tale *The Red Rover* (1827), Berlioz's overture *Le Corsaire* (1844), Verdi's opera *Il Corsaro* (1848), José de Espronceda's ode *Cancion del Pirata* (1835), Emilio Salgaris *I Pirati della Malesia* (1896) as well as Robert Louis Stevenson's *Treasure Island* (1883), are just a few of the most notorious nineteenth-century works expounding the Romantic pirate myth.

European Romantics saw the lawless world of piracy as an alternative to the disciplined order of the modern city dominated by its rigid laws, its dramatic inequality and its 'dark Satanic Mills' (Blake 1811: 2). They looked at the pirate outlaw as a form of subjectivity radically alternative to the grey figure of modern civilized urban man: 'independent, audacious, intrepid, and rebellious. Defying society's rules and authorities, sailing off to the unknown . . ., fearing nothing, the pirate became the ultimate symbol of freedom' (Gerassi-Navarro 1999: 2). The Romantic outlaw embodied everything that was lost in the disciplinary fabric of the modern city. They have forever broken all ties with modern society, living in a permanent state of flight and existential homelessness. And yet their mobility is not the pitiful freedom of the dispossessed vagrants that flocked toward the urban conglomerates of the early nineteenth century; it is instead a nomadic movement, an empowering form of mobility, which does not desire to settle down. Tracing their line of flight on the moving waves, the pirate is unrestrained by spatial as much as social boundaries. They have no interest in claiming an impossible integration in the expanding order of civilization, nor in taking their place on the sedentary throne of some winter palace. Their rebellion is neither a protest nor a revolution, but rather an uprising: a standing upwards in front of the hostile forces of nature and society, an affirmation of the irrepressible, constantly destructuring force of individual and collective desire.

There blindly kings fierce wars maintain,
For palms of land, when here I hold
As mine, whose power no laws restrain,
Whate'er the seas infold.
Nor is there shore around whate'er,
Or banner proud, but of my might
Is taught the valorous proofs to bear,
And made to feel my right.
My treasure is my gallant bark,
My only God is liberty;
My law is might, the wind my mark,
My country is the sea.

(José de Espronceda,
'The chant of the pirate', 1835)

Dionysus and the pirates depicting the divine punishment suffered by the pirates operating in the Tyrrhenian Sea.

Source: Mosaic of the Bardo national museum in Tunis. The pirates, creatures of the sea, are symbolically mutated by the God into dolphins and therefore banned from land and civilization.

Portrait of Sir Francis Drake (1598), a painting by Crispijn van de Passe the Elder.

Source: The Kraus Collection of Sir Francis Drake. The English is presented as 'a most noble English knight' while for the Spanish he represented the common enemy of Christendom.

Pirates Hanged at Execution Dock. A copper engraving by unknown author first published in the anonymous *A True Relation, of the Lives and Deaths of the Most Famous English Pyrats, Purser and Clinton; who lived in the Reigne of Queene Elizabeth* (1639). In the second half of the seventeenth century, when the oceans 'beyond the line' were still an alegal space in which freebooters and buccaneers dominate the scene, the suppression of piracy in the English Channel represented one of the most spectacular affirmations of sovereignty by an emerging monarchy. The bodies of the two pirates here perfectly represent the shifting border carved by sovereign violence: on this side of the line the theatre of civility, on the other side of the line the anti-civilization of the oceans.

Buccaneers of America (1678), frontispiece of the first edition published in Amsterdam by Jan ten Hoorn. The Buccaneers' violence against the Spanish is presented as literally parallel and equal to the one committed by the Spanish against the Amerindians.

Blackbeard the Pirate. A copper engraving generally attributed to James Basire and first published in Charles Johnson, *A General History of the Most Notorious Pyrates* (1724). The work of art represents one of the most mythologized pirates of the Golden Age, the notorious Edward Teach. He was killed by the Royal Navy in 1718, but his persona remains omnipresent in popular culture.

Ann Bonny and Mary Read convicted of Piracy Novr. 28th. 1720 at a Court of Vice Admiralty held at St. Jago de la Vega in ye Island of Jamaica. A copper engraving by Benjamin Cole first published in Charles Johnson, *A General History of the Most Notorious Pyrates* (1724). Both convicted of piracy in 1720, at the height of the Golden Age of Piracy, they remain two of the most famed, loved and fictionalized female pirates of all time. Their lives were recently retold by Steve Gooch's play *The Women-Pirates*, first performed by the Royal Shakespeare Company in 1978.

Thomas Anstis' Pirate Crew Holds A Mock Trial. A copper engraving by unknown author first published in Charles Johnson, *A General History of the Most Notorious Pyrates* (1724). The humoristic scene reflects both the carnivalesque inversion of roles typical of pirate literature and a criticism of the legal system, represented as systematically bent on reproducing established relations of power within society.

Silver medal commemorating the suppression of the Barbary Corsairs of Algiers, Greenwich Maritime Museum. Algiers appears as a sea-monster subjugated and killed by the divine violence of Neptune, sovereign of the seas. European imperialism is therefore equated with a process of progressive civilization culminating in the moment in which, to quote the symptomatic words of Jules Sestier, 'the glorious French flag was victoriously planted on the walls of Algiers, supreme refuge of pirates throughout the Mediterranean' (1880: 6–7).

Silver medal commemorating the first edition of the literary masterpiece *Treasure Island* by Robert Louis Stevenson (1883), Greenwich Maritime Museum. The work arched back and reinforced popular perceptions of pirates, forever associating to the pirate figure immortal images such as buried treasures, maps marked with an X, excessive drinking, anarchy, violence, the Black Spot and one-legged seamen bearing parrots on their shoulders.

Revolutionary Soviet sailors responsible for the mutiny of the Petropavlovsk – Helsinki, Summer 1917. The characteristic skull-and-bones flag carries the text: 'Death to the capitalist state.' The image singularly suggests the extent in which the romantic myth of piracy as the imposition of a real state of exception that opens up the possibility of a new freedom, and of the pirate as iconic social bandit, was profoundly rooted in the proletarian consciousness in the early twentieth century.

The Romantic pirate, like the artist and the rebellious working class of the nineteenth century, does not feel at home in the modern city. A biographer of the romantic author of *The Corsair* (1814) – who was harshly criticized for elevating 'the pirate, a criminal, an outlaw, to heroic status' and therefore 'scorning all laws that God or man can frame' (Unus Multorum 1814: 75) – perfectly describes the nature of this existential resonance: 'alienated in London, Byron was alienated in Athens. Every one of Byron's major figures turn out to be maladjusted to the point of having no country, indeed no community, they can call their own' (Sharafuddin 1996: 260). Existential homelessness is the condition that, in the nineteenth century, came to characterize both the artist and the international working class. The pirate of Romanticism sets this homelessness – this having no country of which to feel a part – in a radical new light, symbolizing a possible alternative to despair, as well as the supine acceptance of the existent.

This might be one of the reasons why, in the 1820s, Romantic poetry 'was sold in a different class of bookshops, not the elegant premises at 50 Albemarle Street but centers of the radical culture which were regularly raided and their owners fined and imprisoned' (St Clair 1990: 18). Byron in particular rapidly became a symbol and a cultural reference for most radical circles, not only in England but also throughout Europe. In the first half of the nineteenth century, Romantic literature rapidly became a symbol of defiance, increasingly associated with radical political tendencies. Leaders of both the Reform and the Chartist movements would eagerly appear in public reading Byron's works, quoting his poetry and 'even [wearing] open-necked shirts *à la* Byron' (St Clair 1990: 23).

Pirated editions, distributed by popular publishers, contributed to the dissemination of Byron's poetry to the working class, so much so that Friedrich Engels was led famously to remark that 'it is the workers who are most familiar with the poetry of Shelley and Byron. Shelley's prophetic genius has caught their imagination, while Byron attracts their sympathy by his sensuous fire and by the virulence of his satire against the existing social order' (1958: 273). According to the German author of *The Conditions of the Working Class in England*, Romantic depictions of rebellion, mutiny and the outlaw life were scandalous and profoundly shocking for the proprietary classes, but they were loved and relished by an increasingly defiant working-class: 'Byron and Shelley are read almost exclusively by the lower classes; no 'respectable' person would have the works of the latter on his desk without his coming into the most terrible disrepute' (Engels 1976: 162). This last comment may well have been autobiographical since Engels himself had been profoundly influenced by the Romantic movement, consequently coming into the most terrible disrepute with his factory-owning family. Byron's *The Corsair*, in particular, together with Shelley's poetry, had a special role in the formative years of the man who would soon become one of the central political figures of the early communist movement – so much so that Engels, in 1837, would eventually pen his very own *A Pirate Tale*, which whimsically recounts the life and death of a young Greek boy, sailing the Mediterranean with a crew of Italian corsairs in search of his father's murderer (Engels 1975: 557).

The nineteenth-century working-class fascination with the figure of the romantic outlaw and the pirate rebel went hand in hand with the growth of a profound discontent with the exploitative conditions of modern life and a growing desire for freedom and a space outside the ever-present compulsion of disciplinary apparatuses. In fact, the romantic outlaw is not simply excepted from society: their exclusion is not the one of a hopeless victim in search of a home. On the contrary, they embrace the wilderness and make it a field of projection. The pirate that we find in Romantic poetry is, after all and originally, not so much a robber but an artist. The name comes from the Greek *peiran*, meaning to test, to try, to risk. Thus, a pirate is literally someone who *is put at risk* by the seas, who is exposed to the anarchic unpredictability of its currents and its waves, but also someone that chooses risk as their dimension, leaving behind the stability of the polis in order to craft a new life. As Carl Schmitt has shown, and Agamben has more recently insisted, where extraterritoriality is imposed we are likely to find legal black holes, deadly prisons and torture chambers, ghettos of segregations and slums of poverty, obscure grey zones in which subjects are brutalized and forgotten; but invisibility can also be an art of resistance, and extraterritoriality can be, as in George Steiner's writings, 'a strategy of permanent exile' (1968: 17). This is the possibility raised by the poetry gushing from *The Corsair*'s moving ship:

O'er the glad waters of the dark blue sea,
Our thoughts as boundless, and our souls as free
Far as the breeze can bear, the billows foam
Survey our empire; and behold our home!
(Byron 1815: 10)

The empire suggested here is not one formed by the sovereign force that traces boundaries and imposes the law; it is rather a boundless force field on which the pirate moves in freedom, without a final destination. The assertion of autonomy of the outlaw, thus, finds spatial expression not only in its radical distance from the urban centres of modern civilization – where the outlaw is re-conducted only to be subjected to the law and its punishment – but also, and especially, in the outlaw's devotion to wild space. This wild space, often portrayed in Romantic literature by forests, wilderness and ruins exists in contrast to the order of agricultural fields, gardens and parks – striated by the lines of the plough and enclosed by the dominating presence of the fence – but also to the order of the walled city and the military camp. By definition, it requires a transitory condition of life, a nomadic restlessness: if the outlaw does not remain on the move, the wilderness is soon destined to bear the signs of settlement; it becomes anthropomorphous and thus no longer wild. A new law emerges and the outlaw loses their marginal status outside the city walls. The outlaw therefore, by definition, exists only in relation to what appears, to the law and to civilized men, as a wilderness (the ocean, Sherwood Forest, the Wild West, the darkness of city nights).

While civilized space, with its symmetrical straight lines and its tamed nature, is the paradigmatic space of beauty, the wilderness is pervaded by what the Romantic poets defined as the sublime. Beauty is linked to pleasure, society and the goal of reproduction. The sublime is linked to mingled pain and delight, to ideas of terror and danger, and to self-preservation. 'The passions which belong to self-preservation,' writes Burke, 'turn on pain and danger; they are simply painful when their causes immediately affect us; they are delightful when we have an idea of pain and danger, without being actually in such circumstances; this delight . . . I call sublime' (1757: 32). The sublime represents, in other words, the feeling of complete exposure to the natural elements, the impossibility to predict the future and the total dedication to the present as the only relevant dimension of time. Romantic outlaws such as Byron's piratical anti-heroes can therefore be defined by an existential attachment to the sublime – that is, by a mode of life filled with risks, uncertainties and concern with self-preservation in the here and now: 'a merry life and a short one shall be my motto,' declares Bartholomew Roberts in one of the most acclaimed passages of Charles Johnson's *A Complete History* (Johnson 1724: 214).

In fact, as much as the pirate is the paradigmatic romantic outlaw, the ocean is, according by Edmund Burke, the paradigmatic wilderness, the sublime space par excellence. The ocean combines the promise of freedom of its vast, unoccupied horizons with the terror engendered by the unpredictability of its waves and of its currents. Untouched by the civilization that people had built on land, it offered to the romantic poets the image of a space that could 'provide the opportunity for individuals and groups to reclaim a more pure humanity' (Steinberg 2001: 119). Shakespeare's play *The Tempest*, for instance, opens with the vision of a ship in the midst of hostile elementary forces, against which the King's counsellor is revealed to be utterly powerless, void of authority and reduced to their bare human status:

> What care these roarers for the name of the King? . . . You are a counsellor; if you can command these elements to silence and worke the peace of the present, wee will not hand a rope more: use your authoritie! If you cannot, give thankes you have liv'd so long, and make your selfe readie in your Cabine for the mischance of the houre, if it so happens.
>
> (2010: 3)

In the second half of the eighteenth century, in Jules Verne's science fiction the sea represents:

> the negation and antithesis of land with its police-ridden societies and its constraints. To borrow a word from the anarchist circles of the end of the nineteenth century, the sea is a 'free medium' in the highest degree. . . . It possesses the essential characteristics of 'free environments': wide horizons, freedom from governmental restraint, and the possibility of organizing social relationships with ease and flexibility.
>
> (Chesneaux 1972: 88, 96)

There is a strong anarchist element in Verne's conception of the oceans, a sentiment that must be attributed to his closeness to romantic poetry and its pirate outlaws as much as to his friendship with the anarchist geographer Elisée Reclus. The protagonist of *Twenty Thousand Leagues Under the Sea* (1870) and *The Mysterious Island* (1874), Captain Nemo, is consistently represented as an anarchic outlaw and a submarine pirate, displaced into the depths of the ocean: abyssal inhabitant of the last realm of absolute freedom after the capture of the surface of the seas by the European nations. The displaced son of a deceased Indian raja, roaming the oceans in his submarine, Nemo is driven by a thirst for vengeance and a deep-seated hatred for European imperialism, in particular the British Empire. Nothing concerning his past is revealed in the first and most notorious book, except for his loathing of all countries of the world. When asked about his nationality, he proclaims himself to belong only to the nation of the world's oppressed, and to the sea: the only space in which a man can still be free to decide his own cause:

> Yes I love the sea. The sea is everything! It covers seven-tenths of the planet. Its breath is clean and healthy. It's an immense wilderness where a man is never lonely, because he feels life astir on every side. The sea is simply the vehicle for a prodigious, unearthly mode of existence; it's simply movement and love; it's living infinity. . . . The sea doesn't belong to tyrants. On its surface they can still exercise their iniquitous claims, battle each other, devour each other, haul every earthly horror. But thirty feet below sea level, their dominion ceases, their influence fades, their power vanishes! Ah, sir, live! Live in the heart of the seas! Here alone lies independence! Here I recognize no superiors! Here I'm free!'
>
> (Verne 2010: 82)

At the end of the nineteenth century, therefore, the romantic myth of the pirate outlaw gradually spilled over into the science-fiction novel and the outlaw narrative of the American West. As the sea became increasingly an unremarkable commercial space, fantasies of freedom moved at first beneath the waves and then up into galactic spaces, or in the subterranean corners of the modern metropolis. The old pirate was duplicated and flanked by new outlaw figures: cosmopirates and urban gangsters, cowboys and *der waldganger* (Jünger 1951). Such figures were heretofore continuously reinterpreted by twentieth-century literature and then blown into mass culture by contemporary cinema, with the result of appearing increasingly worn out and commercialized. Their lasting success, nevertheless, will not cease any time soon. It will persist at least as long as there is a desire for freedom and an irrepressible impulse toward what Carl Jung described as *psychological mutiny* – that is, the desire to challenge the repressed and live out our inner fantasies, making them real in the world.

Although modern politics, since Hobbes, is founded on the establishment of an artificial space in which 'men and women must lose their natural freedom, that is their freedom of movement and their hostility against all limits' (Galli 2001: 43), the modern subject maintains a fundamental restlessness and a surplus of desire that manifests itself in a will to revolt that surfaces at every opportunity. It is this surplus desire for freedom and autonomy that has driven and still drives multitudes of children, young and adults, generation after generation, to read and wonder about pirates and outlaws. Nevertheless, when we close our romantic poetry, when we leave the cinema, when we stop revelling and we come back home, the city has not changed: its borders, its gates, its 'no trespassing!', its violence and its discipline is still there. This is why Marxist authors such as Adorno and Horkheimer never grew tired of reminding us that *escapism* and flights of the imagination do not make revolutions, but they might instead work as safety-valves, through which frustration is diffused and explosions of rebellion are kept in check (2007: 49).

In his ironic comments on the French Revolution, Marx similarly opposed revolutionary enthusiasm to the sobering 'morning after': the actual outcome of the sublime explosion of surplus desire in the streets of Paris is nothing but more repression. And yet Marx insisted that this excess of desire, which expresses itself in the most unexpected ways, although betrayed and held once more in check, is not simply abolished, but continues to be, as it were, transposed into a virtual state, 'haunting the emancipatory imaginary as a dream waiting to be realized' (Zizek 2009: 394). The anarchist neurologist Henri Laborit, in his *In Praise of Flight* (1976), expounded better than anyone else the subjective, social and political need for imaginary escapades, which can often be the only way to remain alive and continue searching for a better world:

> When a ship can not fight anymore against the wind to keep its pre-established route, it has two possibilities: heaving to, fixing the helm and the sails, which means to be drifted away according to the winds; and the flight in front of the tempest, with the wind astern and a minimum of sails. The flight is often, when we are far away from the coast, the only way to save the ship and the crew. Moreover, it brings the fugitive to discover new and unknown shores, which might appear over the horizon when the waters calm down. Unknown lands, which will remain forever ignored by those who have the illusory fortune of being able to follow the standardized routes of the cargo-ships and the tankers, the secure maritime highways imposed by our shipping companies. Maybe you have once heard of that ship, which bears the rebellious name: *Desire*.
>
> (Laborit 1976: 1)

Part II

Pirate spectres (1800–2012)

Chapter 5

The empire of free trade

Liberal Universalism and the pirate states

According to Diderot, since commerce was 'the new arm of the moral world', it was certain one day to become the base of a new world order, which would be based not upon power and plunder but upon an integrated system of competition and market exchange (Pagden 1995: 180). It was a vision shared by most Enlightenment thinkers who believed in the pacifying power of Montesquieu's 'doux commerce' (Dickey 2001: 271–317). Mirabeau's *L'Ami des hommes*, for instance, offers us the vision of a future 'universal monarchy' founded on a 'universal confraternity of trade' (1883: 101). Folded within this modern cosmopolis, a common humanity 'would work together as a single nation' (1883: 33), and the power that would have been capable of promoting and protecting this global community united by trade would be the true 'Friend of mankind, . . . establishing Universal Peace over the spherical surface of the Earth' (1883: 97). And yet, according to Mirabeu, this global power would always be forced to maintain its readiness to protect the emergent Universal order from the oppositional forces that might emerge from within. From the perspective of a completely integrated cosmopolis no external enemy could ever exist, and yet military power would be always necessary. An Imperial power should, according to this quintessential representative of the French Enlightenment, remain armed so as to suppress all challenges to the Universal order and, most of all, protect the growth of trade and interdependency. The Imperial power, thus, would not pursue war, and yet it 'might always be forced to use the Sword to support the common cause' and force the enemy of humanity to enter the universal confraternity of trade (1883: 103).

By the nineteenth century, Mirabeau's cosmopolitan dream was largely forgotten. Nevertheless, the advance of industrial capitalism, and the growing commercial integration that followed, fed new cosmopolitan projects. Especially in the British world, classical political economy promoted free trade as a new emancipatory principle that, if embraced throughout the world, would have contributed to the unification of humanity, the growth of international interdependency and, thus, the eventual demise of classical wars between nations (List 1856: 341). In the nineteenth century, following Mirabeau, classical political economy began to promote a vision whose core was the dream that England would be the centre of a cosmopolitan international economy, which would constitute the basis of a *Pax Britannica.* 'In the writings of English political economy,' writes Bernard Semmel, 'we find a vision that combines the Cobdenite promise of a cosmopolitan world economy and the self-assurance that Britain would have emerged as the metropolis of such a cosmopolis, the "workshop of the world", the "capital of trade"' (1970: 151).

In order to realize this vision, it would have been necessary to overcome the resistance of backward groups and uncivilized nations, who continued to oppose commercial integration. The perpetual war for the enforcement of market standards of civilization, therefore, did not stop with the campaign that in the first half of the eighteenth century put an end to the Golden Age of piracy. Although this remains the most recounted episode of its long history – with important historical works being produced by historians such as Peter Earle (2005), Marcus Rediker (2004), Peter Linebaugh (2000), Janice Thomson (1994), Robert C. Ritchie (1986), David Cordingly (1995) and many others – the 'war against piracy' continued well into the second half of the eighteenth century, with English and American campaigns against the piratical uses of the Barbary regencies in the northern coast of Africa; and in the nineteenth century with a sustained English campaign against widespread piracy in the Arab Gulf, in the Malay region and on the coast of India. In fact, it may be argued that the 'war against piracy' never stopped raging, and it continues today with the United Nations' campaign against piracy around the coasts of Somalia and Yemen.

In this chapter, I focus on the ways in which the concept of the pirate that first emerged in the Atlantic of the eighteenth century travelled eastward, transforming itself in the process. In the first part, I consider the further expansion of the world-market under the impulse of European industrial capitalism. I explore, in particular, the importance of British sea-power in facilitating the consolidation of global commerce, and the essential role that the protection of trade began to take in British ideology, rhetoric and military strategy. In the second part, I follow the course by which the eighteenth-century concept of the pirate as *hostis communis omnium* gradually became one of the most important operative concepts of the British Navy in the colonial world. Extra-European polities were often considered insufficiently organized to be fully recognized as modern independent states. As a consequence, a number of extra-European groups, nations and polities were condemned as 'pirate communities' on the basis of their attacks on European trade. Military action against such groups could then be seen as an option unfettered by the usual legal restraints accompanying the decision to go to war, since they were presented as 'a mere enforcement action by a "policeman" of the international order . . . for the purposes of securing universal rights to commerce' (Rubin 2006: 202). In the third part, I briefly present two important cases in which extra-European communities were consistently portrayed as 'pirate states'. In East Asia, the genocide of entire Malay communities was justified with their portrayal as 'piratical people'. In the Mediterranean, the Barbary states were increasingly stripped of their traditional legitimacy and international recognition, depicted as insufferable pirates' dens, and bombarded by the American and the British Navy, until the French Empire finally subjugated them.

World-market and global shipping: British *imperium* in the nineteenth century

The nineteenth century was a century characterized by the Industrial Revolution, the mechanization of production and the expansion of the capitalist mode of production, which first found its foremost base in England. It has also been the century in which the British Empire achieved a hegemonic position in the international system, and the British Navy 'ruled the waves' of the world's oceans, imposing its presence over the budding commerce that interconnects the local economies of the earth. These two aspects are seldom considered side by side, but they appear to constitute an indissoluble whole. The beginning of capitalism and the meteoric expansion of industrial civilization would have been unthinkable without the transformation of the oceans of the world in the greatest sphere of commerce and communication ever known to man. In his *Elements of the Philosophy of Right* [1820], Georg Friedrich Hegel argued that industry finds its natural element and its reason to expand perpetually only when the sea becomes the 'supreme medium of communication' (1991: 268). Infinite possibilities of exchange are then opened so that production and the accumulation of wealth lose their limited horizons and, for the first time, it becomes possible to think the process of social production as an endless pursuit for exchange:

> † 247. Just as the earth, the firm and solid ground is the basis of family life, so is the sea the natural and life-giving element for industry, whose relations with the external world it enlivens. By the substitution for the tenacious grasp of the soil, and for the limited rounds of appetites and enjoyments embraced within the civic life, of the fluid element of danger and destruction, the passion for gain is transformed. . . . By means of the sea, the greatest medium of communication, the desire for exchange brings distant lands into commercial intercourse, a legal relationship which gives rise to contracts. In this intercourse is found one of the chief means of culture, and in it, too, trade acquires a world-historical significance. . . . The sea binds men together.
>
> (ibidem)

For Hegel, in other words, the endless possibilities for exchange offered by the smooth spatiality of the world oceans constitute the precondition for the establishment of modern industrial capitalism. Without the possibilities offered by maritime trade, industry would remain necessarily constrained by 'limited rounds of appetites' and the logic of endless growth that sustains industrial capitalism would find no sustenance. For Marx, similarly, the initial impulse toward the establishment of the capitalist mode of production is to be found in the multiplication of possibilities for trade and exchange. Limitless possibilities of exchange stimulate the gradual transformation of local systems of production – which might initially exchange only occasional unconsumed surplus – into commercial nodes, which produce for exchange. The very structure of production is therefore gradually transformed in order to make *structural* what was initially only an *occasional* surplus. In the *Grundrisse*, Marx underlines that the possibility of reaching external markets is an essential precondition for the transition toward a system of production organized for exchange:

> The exchange of the overflow is a traffic which posits exchange and exchange value. At the beginning it extends only to the overflow and plays an accessory role to production itself. But . . . if an ongoing commerce develops, although the producing people still engages only in so-called passive trade, since the impulse for the activity of positing exchange values comes from the outside and not from the inner structure of its production, then the surplus of production must no longer be something accidental, occasionally present, but must be constantly repeated; and in this way domestic production itself takes on a tendency towards circulation, towards the positing of exchange values.
>
> (1973: 256)

Discussing the origins of industrialization and the capitalist system of production in England, Marx remarks on 'the essential, decisive role' of growing maritime trade, which provided the stimulus for the re-organization of the relationships of production:

> In England, for example, the import of Netherland's commodities . . . at the beginning of the seventeenth century gave to the surplus of wool that England had to provide in exchange, an essential, decisive role. In order then to produce more wool, cultivated land was transformed into sheep-walks, the system of small tenant-farmers was broken up etc., clearing of estates took place etc. Agriculture thus lost the character of labour for use value. . . . At certain points, agriculture itself became purely determined by circulation, transformed into production for exchange value. Not only was the mode of production altered thereby, but also all the old relations of population and of production, the economic relations that corresponded to it, were dissolved. Thus, here was a circulation in which only the overflow was created as exchange value; but it turned into a production which took place only in connection with circulation, a production which posited exchange values as its exclusive content.
>
> (1973: 257)

Primitive accumulation, therefore – that is, the expropriation of the commons, the clearing of the land, the separation of the producers from the essential means of subsistence and production – was a process by which the English system of production was gradually transformed into a mega-machine for the production of commodities destined to be sold in the world-market. Only in parallel with the acceleration of commercial circulation, and the shattering of technical and political barriers to trade, can exploitation be maximized, as Marx explains:

> The capitalist can consume cottons to a certain degree only. But now he exchanges cottons etc. for the wines and silks of foreign countries. These represent only a transformation of the surplus labour of our own population, and in this way the destructive power of the capitalist is increased beyond all bounds. Thus nature is outwitted!
>
> (1973: 417)

Marx seems to follow Hegel's suggestion that the growth of maritime trade had a fundamental role in sustaining the origin of a form of production geared toward endless growth and the systematic production of exchange-values. The growth of British industrial capitalism was, from the very beginning, strictly dependent on its access to external markets (Luxemburg 1951: 364–365).

The necessity to maintain and increase access to foreign markets was the main impulse behind Britain's growing maritime hegemony. The British Navy represented the first and essential military supplement of industrial capitalism, promoting the principles of 'free trade' and 'free seas', and enforcing respect for the juridical norms that regulate commerce in the world-market (Mowat 1939). Hegel aptly points out that while the sea appears as 'the external and life-giving principle of industry', maritime commerce is to be understood as 'a legal relationship, which gives rise to contracts' (Hegel 1991: 268). The expansion of trade intercourse is therefore also the extension of a juridical web by which maritime space is gradually transformed into a regulated space of commercial circulation. In other words, as Michel Foucault maintained: 'there was a juridification of the world, which should be thought of in terms of the organization of a market' (2008: 176).

The creation of the modern world-market required the juridification of maritime space, but the latter could only be founded on the imposition of a coercive power capable of enforcing the fundamental legal norms that sustain market mechanisms, *in primis* the respect for private property. In his history of the British Navy, the military historian Herbert Rosinski has insisted on the role of British maritime hegemony in enabling the development of international commerce in the nineteenth-century: 'industrial civilization', he writes:

> tended to underrate the significance of military strength as the basic framework that alone enabled it to attain its present preeminence. Its development . . . was furthered by the peculiar nature of the deterrent force that throughout the nineteenth century did most to maintain the peaceful atmosphere in which capitalism could flourish. This was the British Navy, whose influence was exerted not so much by the actual exercise of its power as by its mere existence. Growing up under the shield of the silent presence of sea power the

> new industrial culture was geared to peace, rather than to war, in a way that the older civilizations had never been.
>
> (1950: 11)

Rosinski's studies highlight the centrality of British sea-power in shaping the evolution of the international law governing maritime intercourse and world trade. Following an established historical tradition, he considers British naval and military hegemony essentially 'peaceful' since 'after the Napoleonic Wars major wars were avoided for almost a century, while global commerce and communication increased constantly' (1950: 16). The depiction of British maritime hegemony as a benign force, bringing peace, law and commerce to the world is hardly new; it was, in fact, already central to nineteenth-century portrayal of the state of the world. 'For its Victorian and Edwardian advocates,' writes an historian of nineteenth-century Imperial discourse, 'the *Pax Britannica* was both a modern reincarnation of the *Pax Romana* as well as its natural successor. It represented the pinnacle of civilization – by providing humanity with a hegemonic peace that was supposedly more enlightened, enduring, and exalted than anything that had preceded it' (Parchami 2009: 61). Historians have long recognized the significance of the Roman analogy in British Imperial discourse. Philippe Steinberg, for example, has argued that British maritime hegemony exported to the whole world the distinction between *dominium* and *imperium* that we found at the heart of Roman power in the Mediterranean:

> Although Britain was the overwhelming sea power for much of the eighteenth and nineteenth centuries, it never sought to claim the world ocean as part of imperial territory. Rather, like Rome before it, Britain claimed the authority to exercise its power as ocean steward in order to ensure that the world ocean remained a space for the unhindered movement of its and others' ships. Britain may have 'ruled the waves' – an act of *imperium* – but maps portraying the empire upon which 'the sun never set' indicated only land space as the territory over which British *dominium* prevailed.
>
> (2001: 146)

British sea-power, therefore, presented itself as a form of 'stewardship' or *imperium* over the common commercial routes of the world. Its military interventions were often conceptualized as forms of 'global policing', rather than classical wars, enforcing respect for presupposed norms of international law. As I argued in relation with the Pax Romana, the Pax Britannica was also essentially an Imperial order in which war was recoded and presented as an endless confrontation between 'pirates', 'international criminals', 'disturbers of the peace' and 'peace enforcers'. That violence was a persistent feature of Imperial peace is a reality recognized by Rudyard Kipling, who referred to British 'police' actions in the colonial world as 'the savage wars of peace' (1994: 334). Similarly, writing at the end of the nineteenth century, the liberal critic of imperialism John Hobson complained:

'euphemisms for war are in incessant progress. The Pax Britannica, always an impudent falsehood, has become of recent years a grotesque monster of hypocrisy, . . . fighting has been well-nigh incessant' (1902: 126). More recently Ali Parchami, analysing British gunboat diplomacy in the Indian subcontinent, stressed:

> The British exerted considerable pressure upon local rulers to open up their markets and sign unfavourable treaties with the Raj. . . . British meddling was often a self-fulfilling prophecy: undermining to such an extent the authority of local rulers, and the stability of their states, that it would necessitate direct British intervention to restore order, quell revolts and enforce the respect of commercial treaties.
>
> (2000: 144)

The Empire of the nineteenth century, therefore, was one of free trade based on an evolving international juridical order, which sustained an expanding world-market. According to the prominent naval historian Clark Reynolds:

> the British Empire came to endorse the free trade formulas preached earlier by Adam Smith and used its naval might to insure that no other nation dared to erect trade barriers to inhibit this new formula for the accumulation of wealth and profit. Also, by this trend, Britain accepted the concept of 'freedom of the seas' . . . into the mainstream of international law. This interpretation of international law met with approval throughout the Western world. . . . But Britain also interpreted her new free sea policy to include enforcing the order necessary for commerce upon the global sea lanes, so that the Royal Navy had to insure that no second-rate naval power dared to create a *Mare Clausum* in any sea and that pirates be utterly suppressed.
>
> (1974: 370)

Throughout the nineteenth century, therefore, the construction of a maritime system based on the principle of free maritime circulation was largely dependent on the hegemonic presence of the British Navy, whose operative principle was neither the defence of territorial borders nor the conquest of new territories, but rather the security of global commercial circulation. The liberal principle of *Mare Liberum*, in fact, contained from its inception the seeds of a form of Imperial violence waged in the name of international law and meant to literally free trade from the shackles of monopolistic control, antiquated resistance to foreign influences, and piratical practices (Mehta 1999). Historically, the argument for 'free seas' emerged into history as a justification for practices of violent plunder performed by vessels belonging to the Dutch East India Company in South East Asia. As noted by China Miéville, Grotius' argumentation offers a powerful justification for Dutch violence, which was presented as rightful so long as it could be conceptualized as an enforcement of the natural right to freely travel and trade on the world ocean.

> Grotius's support for equal trading access *was not* equivalent to a position for some abstract *laissez-faire* free trade, but was inextricably an argument for the right to wield coercive political power – violence – under certain circumstances. His very argument for 'free seas' is justification for an act of violent maritime plunder.
>
> (Miéville 2006: 210)

In *Security, Territory, Population* (2009) and *The Birth of Biopolitics* (2008), Michel Foucault tried to study the historical relationship between the liberal project of establishing and governing a global market governed by the principle of free and unfettered competition, and the elaboration of a new law and a new system of governmentality concerned more with the control of circulation than with the defence of clear borders. What has been less commented on is the ways in which Foucault has linked the evolution of this new system of liberal governmentality with a new spatial thinking originating in maritime law and which expressed, from its very beginnings, the necessity of a violence capable of carving out and maintaining a smooth hyperspace of flow, a space of free competition. Freedom of circulation and unfettered competition, insists Foucault, have never been considered a given by liberalism; they are not a natural state that has to be respected. Market freedom, on the contrary, is something that is constantly produced and that comes with a price:

> Liberalism is not acceptance of freedom; it proposes to manufacture it constantly, to arouse it and produce it, with of course the constraints and the problems of cost raised by this production. What then will be the principle of calculation for this cost of manufacturing freedom? The principle of calculation is what is called security.
>
> (Foucault 2009: 185)

In a similar vein, Carl Schmitt recognized that 'the principle of security of the traffic routes formulated by the British liberal empire directs itself not towards a coherent space and its inner order but rather, above all else, towards the security of the freedom of circulation of the world-market' (2011: 188). Schmitt thus opposes the principle of *national defence*, which focuses on separating an ordered inside from a hostile outside, with the liberal principle of *security*. While national defence presupposes and reinforces the idea that global space is composed of a multiplicity of separate spaces, liberal security presupposes and reinforces the idea that global space is a single plane of circulation. While national defence aims at the striation of global space through the imposition of impermeable borders, liberal security aims at establishing control over multiple processes of circulation in a single, undivided open space. While national defence operates on the principle of protecting one's people from all other peoples, liberal security operates globally safeguarding a right to freely travel and trade that is as Universal as it is only abstract. 'This freedom,' writes Schmitt, 'that is spoken in numerous English arguments regarding international law belongs by its very origin to the evolution of maritime law in the seventeenth century. These arguments reached their high point in the apology of a Universal human interest in the freedom of global commerce in the nineteenth century' (2011: 169).

Liberal security aims at the securitization of commercial exchange and, therefore, at the enforcement of the essential conditions for the existence of a world-market. And yet this is not presented as a form of imperialism by which national law is imposed on foreign territory. This form of 'route-thinking or road-thinking is characterized by the equation established between the interest of an empire founded on free trade and the interests of humanity as a whole' (Schmitt 2011: 168). This is why – while national defence has war as its most extreme instrument, either in order to establish a new border or to re-establish a threatened one – liberal security paradigmatically operates through police actions and punctual interventions against unredeemable pirates and criminals. 'The principle of security of the common traffic routes', writes Schmitt, 'can be endangered only by agents of a war against mankind. The legal consequence of all this is that war ceases to be war. For one does not conduct a war against pirates; pirates are only the object of anti-criminal or maritime police actions, which oppose the order of Empire to those who represent only chaos and disorder' (2011: 171). In the next section, therefore, I consider in detail the fundamental role played by the concept of the pirate as *hostis humani generis* in nineteenth-century international law and, in particular, as a legitimating principle of British Imperial violence in the colonial world.

The pirate as *hostis humani generis*: Uses and abuses of an Imperial concept

The concept of the pirate as *hostis communis omnium* always maintained a fundamental ambiguity: what are the limits of the human community? What characteristics or practices bond it together in a single group? And what is inimical to this grouping? It seems that this fundamental undecidability can be resolved only by punctual political decisions. As Jacques Derrida notes in *Philosophy in a Time of Terror*, definitional slippage such as that displayed by the concept of the pirate may actually be the norm rather than the exception in international law, in which it performs an essential political function:

> semantic instability, irreducible trouble spots on the borders between concepts, indecision in the very concept of the border: all this must not be analyzed as a speculative disorder, a conceptual chaos or zone of passing turbulence in public or political language. We must also recognize here strategies and relations of force. The dominant power is the one that manages to impose and thus to legitimate, indeed to legalize, the terminology and thus the interpretation that best suits it in a given situation.
>
> (Borradori 2003: 105)

As a Roman Emperor once replied to those who noted his incorrect use of a particular Latin concept: *Caesar dominus et supra grammaticam*! In other words, Imperial powers reign also over, and through, grammar. Imperial powers are those that, elevating themselves as representatives of the whole human community, pretend to single out (and set out to extirpate) those who seemingly endanger it.

The extraordinary resilience of the Latin concept of the pirate as *hostis communis omnium*, first introduced by Cicero during the first century BC, must be attributed to the unique role it plays in the very structure of international law. The figure, therefore, could be transferred from one system of international law to the following one, without losing its strategic role in the overall scheme of things. Different systems of international law – from the Roman *ius gentium*, to the Spanish *res publica Christiana* and the eighteenth-century *jus publicum europaeum* – transformed and put to use in different ways the concept of the pirate as enemy of the human community. The deep meaning of the term changed through time, reflecting significant modifications in the conception of what it is that defines the human community. In the nineteenth century, the concept of the pirate continued to have an important role in international law and international politics, especially in the colonial world. Its meaning, nevertheless, was gradually transformed, often under the influence of liberal cosmopolitanism and Illuminist conceptions of natural law.

As we have seen, in the beginning of the eighteenth century, the classical concept of the pirate as *hostis communis omnium* was revived in order to allow the suppression of denationalized pirates and the juridification of the maritime commons. Nevertheless, the concept was modified by a number of writers in a slight but symptomatic way. In an increasing number of works, the pirate was defined *hostis humani generis*. The term, which was given in Latin and was often attributed directly to Cicero, rapidly established itself as the standard epithet for pirates, displacing the original Roman formulation. In the nineteenth century, the pirate was consistently defined as the 'enemy of the human race' rather than 'enemy of all'. Although in many cases the two terms are used interchangeably, the use of one concept or the other often reveals a fundamental difference in an author's understanding of pirates and international law.

Positivist authors like Gentili tended to refer to pirates as *hostis communis omnium*, constructing them as 'enemies of all' components of the international community. Here the pirate was a *systemic enemy* of the bounded community of modern states, which had its centre in Europe. It was not an enemy of all humanity, but rather an enemy of civilization. With their actions the pirates excepted themselves from the rules that *civilized humanity* gave itself and they were therefore banned from the protection of international law. The pirates, according to authors such as Blackstone, were returned to the state of nature; they were 'outside the law' but, exactly because of that, were *not* criminals. In fact, there is no law they can possibly break or offend, since pirates have been placed outside the order of the law. According to Alberico Gentili: 'With pirates and brigands, who violate all laws, no laws remain in force' (1933: 24). The execution of the outlaw, from this point of view, is neither the restoring of the law nor the punishment of a criminal;

it is rather the highest point of an extra-legal confrontation between the sovereign and the pirate. The pirate, here, is really understood as a sovereign individual in the Foucaultian sense: they exist at the extreme limit of the diagram of international law.

However, another view of pirates was widespread in the eighteenth century. Authors like Emmerich de Vattel arched back to theories of natural law in order to think the pirate as 'monsters unworthy of the name of men' who 'should be considered enemies of the human race' (1758: 3.34). From this perspective, the pirate appeared to violate the Universal laws of nature, rather than the founding laws of the international system. It was not a *systemic enemy* of the international state system, which it endangers with its irreducible irregularity; but rather a *natural enemy* of the whole human race, violating the natural laws that regulate the life of even the most uncivilized people. Its persecution, therefore, is not conceived as being political in the Schmittian sense, but rather a form of global policing performed by a benevolent Empire, enforcing the Universal laws of nature even in the remotest corners of the world, killing in the name of humanity. Its suppression is part of a *just war*; its execution is the restoration of the law of nature.

Hugo Grotius significantly compares pirates with cannibals against whom one can wage a just war: 'Regarding such barbarians, wild beasts, rather than men, one may rightly say . . . that war against them was sanctioned by nature; and what Isocrates said, in his Panathenaic Oration, that the most just war is against savage beasts, the next against men who are like beasts' (1925: 506). Similarly, Francis Bacon considered that pirates existed as monsters, whose very existence negates the laws of nature. They are 'such routs and shoals of people, as have utterly degenerate from the laws of nature; as have in their very body and frame of estate a monstrosity; and may be truly accounted . . . common enemies and grievances of mankind; or disgraces and reproaches to human nature' (1861: 36). According to Mikkel Thorup, for philosophers and jurists writing in the tradition of natural law: 'it is evident that the pirate is in opposition to nature itself. The pirate has placed himself outside the bounds of the laws of both nature and man' (2012: 8). Following this same hypothesis, Dan Edelstein has convincingly shown that the designation of pirates as *hostis humani generis* 'continued to be justified throughout the eighteenth century, in terms of natural right' (2009: 35).

The work of Pufendorf, doubtlessly one of the most influential international legal scholars in the eighteenth century, is a case in point. As noticed by Carl Schmitt, in order to justify the status of the pirate as an enemy of humanity that must be annihilated by the civilized nations of the world, 'Pufendorf [*De jure naturae et gentium,* VIII, 6, #5] quotes approvingly Bacon's comment that specific peoples are 'proscribed by nature itself' e.g., the Indians, because they eat human flesh. And in fact the Indians of North America were then exterminated' (2007a: 54). In a prophetic quip, then, Schmitt highlights the infinite flexibility of the concept of the 'enemy of humanity': if the Spanish could deny the humanity of the Indians and then proceed to their extermination on the basis of their alleged cannibalism, and Pufendorf could justify the banishment of pirates from humankind on the base of their attacks on free trade and private property, what appellation would suffice in the future to declare men and women 'enemies of humanity' to be slaughtered in a state of exception beyond the law? Schmitt's sarcastic pessimism is here at its best: 'As civilization progresses and morality rises, even less harmless things than devouring human flesh could perhaps qualify as deserving to be outlawed in such a manner. Maybe one day it will be enough if a people were unable to pay its debts' (2007a: 55).

In natural law theory, the pirate as *hostis humani generis* often appear as the constitutive exception that founds the existence of humanity as a common league and as a political community. The most touching love for abstract humanity can thus comfortably coexist with the most radical dehumanization of particular individuals and groups. When Bacon affirms the existence of a 'supreme and indissoluble consanguinity and society between men in general', he immediately reveals the extent to which it exists only in opposition to an Other, who is radically excluded by that supreme human community. In fact, 'if there be such a tacit league of humanity sure it is not idle; it is against something, or somebody: who should they be?' (Bacon 1861: 35). The concept of an 'enemy of humanity' should not obscure the fact that it is never humanity that proclaims its enemy, but always a particular state, which takes upon itself the right to do that. In proclaiming not to fight a war but to persecute the 'enemy of humanity', therefore, a state poses as a representative and as a protector of the whole human race. In other words, it claims to act under an Imperial mantle, in conformity with the rule by which '*protego ergo obligo* is the *cogito ergo sum*' of political power (Schmitt 2007a: 52). As we have seen, from a perspective rooted in the Universal values of the *res publica Christiana* – such as the one upheld by Victoria and the Scholastic theologians of Salamanca – humanity was first of all a community of faith. Accordingly, the Treaty of Tordesillas theorized the Atlantic Ocean as an empty surface under the exclusive control of Christian nations, which were to use it in order to spread the Gospel among the savages of the New World. Any interference with this Universal right of Christian mission, expressed by Victoria in the *ius communicationis*, was therefore to be considered an attack against the whole of humanity, an act of evil against the peace sanctioned by God and the Pope. The attacks by Protestant nations against this monopolization of the oceans by the Catholic Empires of Spain and Portugal, then, were interpreted as profanations of a sacred principle and acts of piracy.

The genius of Hugo Grotius was to turn this accusation on its head, constructing the concept of the pirate according to a secularized understanding of natural law. This is why *Mare Liberum*, despite its objective complexity, rapidly became a manifesto of the liberal tradition and a battle cry for freedom of trade (Thomson, 2009: 107–130). From the new liberal perspective, humanity was not so much a community of faith but a community of trade, a multiplicity of individuals, people and nations kept together by their common interest in trade and exchange. Accordingly, Grotius constructed the sea as a space of free trade, an empty surface in which the progressive tendencies of the market were to work unfettered. Any interference with this natural right to free trade, expressed by Grotius in the formula *Mare Liberum*, was therefore to be considered an attack against the whole of humanity, an act of Universal hostility against the peace – and the distribution of wealth – sanctioned by the world-market (Thumfart 2009: 65–87). It is from this juncture, expressing a fundamental transition from the Universalism of Christian theology to the cosmopolitanism of market liberalism, that a new concept of piracy emerged.

The conventional interpretation of *Mare Liberum* is that it was written as an attack against the Portuguese and their claim to a monopoly on Indian trade based on the papal bulls of the fifteenth century (Van Ittersum 2007: 59–94). Grotius' elevation of the principle of free navigation and trade to the status of a natural right was a direct assault against the last residues of the *res publica Christiana* as an international legal order. Access to the connecting routes of the world oceans was no longer to be regulated by papal authority on the basis of the general interest of the Universal Christian community, but rather 'maritime legal arguments were deployed in favour of the burgeoning global commercial system' (Mieville 2006: 210). What is usually ignored is that Grotius' theory basically appropriated the Scholastic arguments formulated by Vitoria, Soto and Vazquez concerning the fundamental right to preach the Christian gospel for the salvation of the whole human genre (Koskenniemi 2011).

Since the eighteenth century, with the development of a liberal association of free trade with Universal peace and the common cause of humanity, the Scholastic tradition of just war theory was uprooted from its theological foundations. In the early-modern period, Vitoria's concept of a Universal right to Christian mission supervised by the Pope was transformed into a Universal right to free trade. According to Eric Wilson: 'it is easy to forget how revolutionary a concept *Mare Liberum* was within the early modern World-System, signifying a wholly capitalist approach to the issue . . . *Liberum commercium* is suffused by the presence of *ius naturale*, and the *ius gentium* operates as an ontological derivative of Natural Law' (Wilson 2008: 247). With this transformation of the *ius communicationis* into the principle of *Mare Liberum*, then, not only did Grotius develop a theological basis for market values and the rule of free trade, but also he laid the foundations for a transformation of the concept of the pirate in international law (Thumfart 2009: 65–87).

According to Martti Koskenniemi:

> The VOC [Dutch East India Company] was, then, entitled to wage war against the Portuguese in self-defence and to receive the booty it had acquired as, in part, reparation, in part, punishment. Moreover, in seeking to break the Iberian monopoly, the Dutch were supporting the interests of commerce and exchange – interests with respect to which humanity was united. Their war was thus on behalf of humanity itself.
>
> (2011: 34–35)

Grotius conceived commerce as 'a necessity for the members of the human race' and therefore concluded that acts of piracy, which interrupted free trade and limited the beneficial order of the world market, were to be considered crimes against the Universal laws of nature. In Grotius' own words: 'anyone who abolishes this system of exchange, abolishes also the highly prized fellowship in which humanity is united. He destroys the opportunities for mutual benefactions. In short, he does violence to nature herself' (1925: 303).

With this new connotation, the concept of the pirate passed through to the nineteenth century, when it was put to new uses by European Imperial powers. The concept held a central space especially in the political rhetoric of the British Empire, legitimizing the suppression of extra-European communities in the name of humanity and international law. In his monumental *The Epochs of International Law*, Wilhelm G. Grewe maintained that, in the nineteenth century, the concept of the pirate did not pertain to the laws of war, but rather it allowed Imperial powers to exercise a form of police violence, in time of peace, against extra-European communities:

> The effects of British maritime hegemony stood out even more distinctly and directly in peacetime law of the sea than they did in the nineteenth century law of naval warfare. Significantly the British fleet tended to adopt the role of an international maritime police force. The instrument of British policy in this respect was the international legal concept of piracy. Just as in previous centuries Britain had not shied away from relying on the cooperation of pirates in pursuing its overseas goals, it did not now shy away from using the struggle against piracy as an instrument for its policy of maritime dominion. (2000: 552)

Entire communities, once branded 'piratical', could be exposed to violence, persecuted and destroyed in a grey area between peace and war. In the nineteenth century, therefore, the British Empire claimed the right to determine whether a community was to be considered legitimate (and thus endowed with sovereign rights), or 'piratical' (and thus deserving to be slaughtered without further ado). In *The Magellan Pirates* case of 1853, for instance, the British Court of Admiralty claimed that a group of Chilean convicts, who had attempted to run away from a Chilean prison by capturing a British ship, were to be considered 'pirates' even though there had been no bloodshed (Phillmore 1871: 421–425). Britain not only claimed the right to treat as outlaws foreign insurgents who happened to interfere with British trade, but also suggested the possibility that entire states might be considered 'pirates' and treated accordingly. In the most extreme, and most often cited, official statement by the British court of Admiralty, it is concluded that:

> Even an independent state may . . . be guilty of piratical acts. What were the Barbary pirates of olden times? What many of the African tribes at this moment? It is, I believe, notorious, that tribes now inhabiting the African

> coast of the Mediterranean will send out their boats and capture any ships becalmed upon their coasts. Are they not pirates, because, perhaps, their whole livelihood may not depend on piratical acts? . . .
>
> (The Magellan Pirates [1853] in Scott 1906: 346)

Although the explicit tones of the decision may be exceptional, stating openly the possibility that states could be considered and treated as 'piratical', the practice of branding colonial communities *hostes humani generis* was hardly novel by this point. According to Alfred Rubin:

> the spreading notion that the forms of sovereignty that might be possessed by non-European societies should not be permitted to interfere with the natural law of property or trade, led to a further assumption by Great Britain of a legal authority to protect shipping lanes in general, eliminating the need for direct injury to a British flag vessel or national to justify military action. Such military actions could then be seen as an option of policy unfettered by the usual legal restraints on the decision to go to war . . . [since they were presented as] a mere enforcement action by a 'policeman' of the international order . . . for the purposes of securing universal rights to commerce.
>
> (2006: 202)

This mixture of motives was covered by the revival of the ancient Roman institution of *persecutio piratarum*, defined as a form of Imperial violence meant to enforce international law against unredeemable pirate outlaws. I argue that, in the nineteenth century, 'campaigns for the eradication of piracy' played an important role in the context of colonial domination, from both a material and an ideological point of view. In the next section, therefore, I turn to a brief description of British Imperial campaigns against piracy in South East Asia. According to Alfred Rubin, in fact, 'it is in this context that the shift in terminology from "war between states" to "military action to suppress piracy" must be evaluated' (2006: 203).

Imperial powers and pirate states in the colonial world

Discussing the popularity of histories, narratives and documents treating the suppression of piracy in the nineteenth century, Simon Layton remarked: 'recounting the spectacles of piracy in world history nourished a faltering vision of imperial triumph, in which the maritime violence of empires, particularly the British Empire, was seen to be a wonderful thing' (2011: 80). As the British Empire thrust into ocean space, its advance was imagined and represented as part of the forward march of European civilization, set to tame the anarchy dominating the oceans of the extra-European world. Representations of piratical feats, tribes and people reinforced the traditional image of far-away oceans as zones of lawlessness, savagery and unfettered adventure.

'Combatting piracy,' thus, as Campo aptly notices, 'was regarded by the colonial powers as part of the comprehensive programme for the transition from lawless violence to a legal order, and as the anti-piracy measures achieved success, they supposedly contributed to the legitimization of the colonial predicament' (2003: 213). Just as European merchant ventures were conceived as being at once economically profitable and culturally civilizing, contributing to the progress of backward peoples throughout the world, the protection of commerce from the predatory tendencies of omnipresent 'piratical communities' appeared as an activity simultaneously highly desirable for the maximization of economic profits and necessary for the edification of the natives in the values of honest labour, lawful commerce and respect for private property.

From the late eighteenth century:

> Britons in the east came to regard their Empire as the guardian of Indian Ocean trade, working towards the commercial Enlightenment of backward people. . . . In this way the British were able to construe their own seaborne violence as a force for modernity, at the same time as they consigned those who challenged their legitimacy to a bygone era.
>
> (Layton 2011: 82)

Piracy was represented, in accordance with a well-established tradition that could be traced back to ancient authors such as Thucydides and Strabo, as a form of economic activity characterizing primitive forms of social life. Long abandoned by European nations, vanished in the seas of Northern Europe, maintained in the Mediterranean only by the disquieting presence of the Barbary cities of Northern Africa, piracy appeared in European narratives as an unquestionable sign of extra-European backwardness (Rutter 1986). The civilizing influence of European commerce, in order to enfold its potential, had to be backed up by superior military prowess.

In the accounts of Thomas Stamford Raffles, one of the most successful and picturesque agents of European Imperialism in South East Asia, peaceful commerce could be achieved only through the eradication of piracy, an activity at once primitive and resistant to modernity:

> The prevalence of piracy on the Malayan coasts, and the light in which it is viewed as an honourable occupation, worthy of being followed by young princes and nobles, is an evil of ancient date, and intimately connected with the Malayan habits. The old Malayan romances, and the fragments of their traditional history, constantly refer with pride to piratical cruises . . . The practice of piracy is now an evil so extensive and formidable, that it can be put down by the strong hand alone.
>
> (Raffles 1965: 232)

In short, representations of persisting maritime anomy and piratical practices reinforced Imperial narratives in several ways. 'Piratical communities' were shown to need European power, in order to be redeemed and forced to undertake the modernizing path of 'useful labour' and 'honest trade'. Specularly, other groups, who were spared the damning label, 'were portrayed as spineless and helpless, and were therefore deemed to be dependent on the benevolent protection of the colonial government' (Campo 2003: 208).

Following post-colonial authors like Sugata Bose (2006), Lakshmi Subramanian (2007) and James Anderson (1995), we could say that the discourse of piracy played an important role in nineteenth-century colonial discourse, modulating the confrontation between different maritime cultures: something we might call 'piracy of the encounter'. As Stephen Greenblatt remarked in his study of the Spanish colonization of Latin America, the inclusion of indigenous communities within the embracing logic of European law only prepared the ground to their most radical exclusion, since they came to be assigned 'the marks of outlaws and rebels' (1991: 66). In the case of nineteenth-century maritime communities, the Universalization of the European laws of the sea also made their marginalization and banishment possible. Constructed during the previous century, especially in the Atlantic context, the international law of the sea appeared to be based fundamentally on the distinction between modern states and pirates, between political war and apolitical pirate violence, between legitimate taxation of trade and illegitimate plunder. As Sebastian Prange notices in colonial documents, 'Indian Ocean pirates are more likely to be portrayed as pests than as political actors' (2011: 1270).

In fact, the term 'pirates' already carries the implication of a complete lack of legitimacy and political status. As we have seen, the prevailing definition of piracy in the European legal tradition, arching back to Roman Imperial law, hinges on the fundamental distinction between legitimate war by politically established societies and piratical violence. The essential problem lies in the ambiguity of what is to be understood as a 'state', especially in the context of a complex cultural encounter between distant societies. From the perspective of European international law, centred on the model of the modern nation-state, extra-European communities often seemed to lack the necessary standards of civilization to be accepted as legitimate societies. Their violence was thus more easily constructed as 'piratical'. For instance, according to Prange's study of British colonialism in India:

> That Malabar's pirates have not been recognized as political actors is predominantly due to the pervading influence of the European historical experience, specifically the model of the nation-state and its resultant regimes of territoriality. The assumption of absent or deficient political organization has characterized the construction of Asian piracy in European sources and historiography.
>
> (2011: 1277)

Most often, colonial officials conceived piracy as an economic phenomenon rather than a political question; a problem of criminality, which threatened the natural laws sustaining early global markets: freedom of sea, freedom of commerce and respect for private property. Colonial powers would then aim at the eradication of piracy through a mixed policy consisting of ruthless violence and a spirited education to the values of liberal trade, international commerce and the Christian work ethic. When H.W. Mutinghe conducted a study of Malay 'pirate communities' for the use of the British Commissioner of Palembang and Bangka, he concluded that local participation in pirate raids was not motivated by either compulsion, innate violence or poverty of the lands but by 'unwillingness to perform useful labor' (Campo 2003: 202). Piracy, therefore, was presented as a savage alternative to hard labour in the fields and in the mines – an activity that was therefore doubly damning for European trade in the region. According to Mutinghe, the eradication of native piratical customs had as its primary aim the conversion of the natives to a way of life that would profit the British Empire. The question was not only how to limit direct attacks on trade by the pirates of Palembang, but also how to convert the pirates into labourers at the service of British commercial ventures.

Pirate narratives reinforced traditional representations of the native's indolence. According to Syed Hussein Alatas, 'it is clear that the sociological origin of the myth of the lazy Malays was based on their refusal to supply plantation labour and their non-involvement in the colonially-controlled urban capitalist economic activity' (1977: 80). The extirpation of piracy was not only a matter of restoring the validity of Euro-centric international law in the Indian Ocean; it was also part of a thorough transformation of economic life. Littoral communities were pushed into 'useful labour', which meant that they were pushed into forms of production that could be integrated in Imperial systems of trade. The coastal Gujaratis, for instance, were portrayed as culturally (and almost racially) inclined to piracy because of their supposed indolence. In 1812, the blockade of the Gulf and the escalation in the persecution of piracy officially 'sought to induce "a rapid improvement of the state of Civilization"', and it was followed by 'a marked increase in grain production . . . to be attributed to the persevering efforts of this Government in the suppression of Piracy; and thus rendering it necessary that the persons engaged in these nefarious proceedings, should have recourse to a different mode of life, to provide for their subsistence' (Trocki 1979: 164)

Native violence against European shipping, therefore, was systematically stripped of its political character and reduced to a mere economic and criminal activity, motivated by native laziness. It is among specific native communities, which refused to engage in 'useful labour' and to integrate in the global market system pioneered by the European colonial powers, that piracy flourished as a slothful alternative to civilization (Alatas 1977: 210–215). In Malaysia, nineteenth-century chronicles portrayed native societies as decadent and declining, attributing the fact to Malay indolence and moral corruption: they preferred piracy to hard labour and honest trade with European traders (Layton 2011). In actual fact, native attacks on European trade were often a reaction to earlier European plunder, ongoing monopolistic trade policies, and the negative effects on local industries of European commercial competition. As Thomas Braddell observes in his nineteenth-century study of European imperialism in the Indian archipelago, maritime trade was increasingly channelled in only a few ports under European control. The numerous native trading city-ports that had prospered for centuries in the Indian Archipelago were then either destroyed or marginalized: 'indiscriminate ruin had fallen on them all' (1858: 321).

It was the impact of European colonialism in the area that had expropriated entire communities of their traditional means of subsistence, driving many groups to piracy, both as a means of survival and as a form of political resistance. According to the British attorney-general in Singapore, British suppression of 'piratical groups' in the Indian Ocean hid much more complex dynamics, which could hardly be discarded as apolitical. Some of his considerations are worthy of quoting in full:

> Dutch and English appear to have vied with each other in enforcing, under the pretence of treaties, a more strict monopoly of commodities, . . . they forced, under a similar pretext, the production and exclusive sale to themselves of the produce of the country. This system had the effect of raising the opposition, and at last the deadly enmity of all classes of the natives. The chiefs saw their ports deserted, their revenues destroyed and their authority relaxed by the overweening arrogance and tyranny of their European visitors, while the people were reduced to a state little better than slavery. The natural resource for the chiefs was piracy. They only followed the example set by the Europeans themselves, in taking possession of whatever they were strong enough to retain. Afterwards, when the Europeans had ruined all native trading ports in the Archipelago, and had drawn all the available trade to settlements formed by themselves, they became obnoxious to the attacks of those they had driven to such courses. They then gave the name of piracy to the exact course which they had seen no impropriety in following themselves.
> (Braddell 1858: 328–329)

In Braddell's discourse, what is again central is the ambiguity of the concept of piracy: when commissioned by European merchant companies or colonial governments, compulsion and violence in the Indian Ocean were never branded as 'piracy'. Nevertheless, European powers did not abstain from plunder, the prohibition of native trade, the ban of native groups from important fishing ground, the closing of commercial ports, or killing and torture on land and at sea (Colchester 1989: 11–19). In the Atlantic-world tradition, which emerged during the seventeenth and eighteenth centuries, pirates were defined as economically driven individuals, operating independently from sovereign authorities. In the nineteenth century, European colonial powers frequently did not recognize the political authenticity and the sovereign legitimacy of extra-European communities, which could therefore be branded as 'piratical'. According to Sebastian Prange, 'the ultimate paradox of defining piracy by the absence of political organization was the attacks on so-called *pirate states*' (2011: 1289). The cases in which colonial violence was a form of international law enforcement against piratical outlaws are too numerous to be retold here. And yet, in contrast with the world of eighteenth-century pirates, historical research on nineteenth-century 'piratical communities' and their suppression by European empires has so far been sparse and seldom systematic. In the following pages, I offer an account of three counter-piracy operations carried out by the British Empire in the Indian Ocean during the 1830s and 1840s.

This is an important period in the history of piracy, when the British Empire started to make systematic use of the concept throughout the world, while considerably expanding its meaning to expose different forms of behaviour to Universal jurisdiction. The British Navy could then act officially as the military arm of the Pax Britannica and as an enforcer of international law. According to Wilhelm Grewe, 'with the end of the war against France and the War of 1812 against the United States, the main job of the British Navy shifted to protection of the growing maritime commerce of the expanding Empire. Interference with British commerce thus was denominated piracy' (2000: 205). In 1825 the head-money system, which in time of war gave monetary reward to members of the Navy for successful enemy killings, was extended to peacetime, to encourage the active suppression of piracy. This attests to the increasing confusion of war and peace in the colonial world, and the expansion of a grey legal area between the two.[1] 'Action under this statute,' remarks Grewe, 'was a major part of British imperial activity from 1825 to 1850 and the British seemed to assume they were entitled to suppress all who obstructed the expansion of British hegemony, both on the high seas and elsewhere' (ibidem).

In the Malay region in particular, the British Navy operated a continuous work of suppression, repression and annihilation of hostile groups deemed piratical. At the beginning of the nineteenth century, colonial officials like John Revenshaw repeatedly reported the necessity of violent repression: 'it may be deemed expedient to take immediate measures to compel these robbers to desist from their present views, if not totally to annihilate them' (Layton 2011: 88). In 1834, the commander of the *Samarang* was awarded £12,000 for killing 350 pirates in the Mollucus, after determining their 'hostile customs' (Tarling 1963: 101–105). In 1836, the *Andromache* ambushed 160 pirates hiding in their 'known haunt' of

1 According to Alfred Rubin, the grey area between war and peace opened by the concept of piracy, and by the practice of pirate-suppression, could also be exploited in order to circumvent democratic checks. Deploying violence internationally as mere 'pirate-suppression' allowed British officials to avoid domestic unwillingness to commit to open war: 'The need to find a legal label to justify British military activity was acute. In 1784 Parliament had forbidden Subordinate Presidencies of the Governor of India (of which Malaysia was one) to make war without express permission from the authorities in London, except in the direst emergencies. . . . It was very tempting to call Malay communities simply "large groups of pirates" and military operations against them "pirate-hunting expeditions" rather than wars' (Rubin 2006: 221).

Gallang (Tarling 1971: 94). According to the report, 'the work of slaughter began, with muskets, pikes, pistols, and cutlasses. I sickened at the sight,' recalled General MacKenzie, 'but it was dire necessity' (MacKenzie 1884: 64–65). Nevertheless, when James Brooke entered Borneo in 1839 as a private adventurer on board of the *Royalist*, after gaining control of Sarawak and obtaining endorsement by the British Empire, he complained of the soft approach maintained by British officers in their fight against piracy:

> The piracy of the Archipelago is not understood; folks, naval officers in particular, talk about native states, international law, the right of native nations to war one on another, &c., &c.; and the consequence is they are very reluctant to act, because they cannot distinguish pirate communities from native states. I would punish them if they dared to seize a trader on the high seas.
>
> (Layton 2011: 91)

The White Raja thus resolved 'to separate the piratical communities from the peaceable ones' and to suppress those he considered nothing but pirates. In his view, the people inhabiting the Sulu archipelago were to be considered and treated as 'powerful piratical nation' (ibidem). Similarly, the Sarebas were 'a powerful, wild and piratical tribe' deserving immediate suppression (ibidem). In 1845, therefore, supported by the Royal Navy, Brooke attacked the Sarebas' most important settlement, having decided to clean the seas from their uncivilized presence (Keppel 1861). According to Richard Cobden, who reported the action to the House of Commons, the steamer *Nemesis* was 'then driven among the boats, and the miserable creatures were crushed under the paddle wheels, and annihilated by the hundreds in the most inhuman manner' (Tarling 1971: 111). 'Mincemeat' was Brooke's own term to describe the scene (Layton 2011: 93). Almost 1,000 Sarebas were killed in the action. While the town was destroyed, the British suffered two killed and about six wounded. The Court of Admiralty recognized the merit of the action, paying nearly £100,000 as a reward. For Brooke, who was disturbed by 'the clamour raised by the humanity-mongers', the decision of the court, which recognized the piratical nature of the Sarebas, was sufficient to resolve any legal and moral doubts. Pirates as *hostes humani generis* could be truly killed, not only with impunity but even with pride, and money could be received for the service provided to humanity and the British Empire. Some days after the trial, Brooke wrote to his uncle, Major Charles Stuart: 'The pirate question which provoked and vexed me, is set at rest by the decision of the Admiralty Court. They are pirates, and this must justify all I have done, and more in the eyes of reasonable men' (cited in Layton 2011: 94).

In the years following independence, Indian nationalist historians challenged this discourse by 'reclaiming Indian pirates as heroic guerrilla fighters whose purported proto-nationalism induced them to oppose Western colonialism' (Prange 2011: 1290). This leaves us questioning how the figure of the pirate gained a central role in the history of Imperialism and international law. Was it, as Bose

(2006) suggests, part of a wider resistance against European colonial domination, or was it merely a conceptual spectre, haunting the fantasy of nineteenth-century Imperial agents: a ghost whose endless presence justified Imperial violence against native people? What is certain is that the concept of 'pirate communities' legitimized the destruction of societies, whose mode of existence was considered primitive and uncivilized, and in any case impermissible in the global market that was starting to enmesh the European and the colonial world in a single world-system (Colchester 1989). Countless people were captured in the temporal cracks between the demands of a rising international economic, political and legal system and those of traditional structures of authority. The result was death, or a life of imprisonment and exploitation. As a company of Sulu seamen aptly noted, after being sentenced to execution by hanging: 'If we had *not* been pirates, our own chiefs would have killed us; and, because we *are* pirates, you kill us: it is the same to us, whatever we do – either way: we die' (Mundy 1848: 241).

The concept of 'pirate states' had a fundamental role in the dynamics of British Imperialism in the Indian Ocean. Nevertheless, this was not the only area of the world that was affected by this relatively new development in the history of Imperialism and piracy. The paradoxical concept of the 'pirate community', as we have seen, could be traced back to the Mediterranean of ancient times when the Roman Empire imposed its *imperium* over that common space of trade and communication. The Romans pretended to act as enforcers of the *ius gentium*, branded entire populations as pirates – such as the Illyrians and the Cilicians – and conducted punitive military operations irrespective of traditional codes of war. After the collapse of the Roman Empire, we hear no more of 'piratical people' in the Mediterranean. It is only between the eighteenth and the nineteenth centuries that the concept travelled back to the Mediterranean Sea as part of European and American discourse, particularly against the Barbary cities of Northern Africa. The regencies of Tunis, Tripoli and Algiers, formally tributary to the Ottoman Sultan but largely autonomous from the Sublime Porte, were increasingly portrayed as uncivilized 'pirate dens', void of political legitimacy, moved only by plunder and a timeless predatory instinct, reformable only through European violence, colonial occupation and enlightened government.

Similarly to what was happening during the same years in the Indian Ocean, the concept of 'pirate communities' legitimized different forms of international violence by Western powers. What is particularly striking in the Mediterranean case is the fact that this rhetorical turn was in direct contradiction with a long diplomatic history that united the two shores of the Mediterranean. Until the eighteenth century – and in strict legal terms, even in the years immediately preceding French colonization – the Barbary cities were always considered legitimate polities. In fact, although formally part of the Ottoman Empire, they were often treated by European countries as independent sovereign states (Rubin 2006: 332). A number of official treaties were agreed between members of the European community of nations and the cities of the Barbary Coast, whose sovereignty was therefore implicitly and explicitly recognized. A form of mutual recognition grew out of a continuous conflict between the two shores of the Mediterranean. In fact, for centuries (at least from the sixteenth century), a continuous state of warfare traversed the Mediterranean Sea. This protracted, and increasingly regulated, conflict – which opposed the maritime raids organized in the Muslim ports of Northern Africa to the specular raids organized by the Christian cities, and first of all by the military and religious order of the Knights of Malta – was named *la course*. Muslim and Christian polities fought each other, delegating to private adventurers an important part in the overall conflict. Therefore, at least until the eighteenth century, the Barbary regencies were generally accepted as legitimate Muslim powers, engaged in a perpetual and mutual war with Christian powers. According to Fernand Braudel, before the eighteenth century, we rarely hear of 'piracy' in the Mediterranean. Rather this is a concept that would return to Europe only after a long colonial detour, first throughout the Atlantic and then in the Pacific and the Indian Ocean:

> In the Mediterranean, still in the seventeenth century, the concepts of 'piracy' and of 'pirates' are not normally used; people speak of *course* and of *corsairs* and the distinction, clear on a juridical level, . . . is of the utmost importance. *La course* is a legitimate war since it starts with a formal declaration of war, or otherwise by the issuing of privateering commissions, lettres de marque, passports, commissions, instructions.
>
> (Braudel 1996: 866)

As one of the most authoritative scholars of the Mediterranean in the seventeenth century has written, '*la course* has its laws, its rules, its customs and its traditions' (Bono 1964: 12–13). In this context, thus, there are no 'pirates', 'outlaws', 'enemies of all communities', certainly there are no 'enemies of the human race', but a low-intensity warfare between two distinct communities that recognize each other as inimical. Braudel suggests:

> Some readers will think that there is not much difference between corsairs and pirates: similar cruelties, similar stealing and plunder. Certainly, but there still remains a fundamental difference: *la course* is an ancient institution, grown old in the same space, with its uses, its compromises, its frequent dialogues. Not that predators and victims are always in agreement, but they are always ready to discuss and make a deal. *La course* does not belong to a single shore of the Mediterranean, to a single group. It is endemic. . . . European historians taught us to see only the Muslims, only the Barbary corsairs. Their fate overshadows the rest of the landscape. But that fate is not exclusive: Malta, Leghorn are Christian Algiers, with their prisons, their slave markets, their sordid procurements.
>
> (1996: 867)

The Mediterranean corsairs of the fifteenth and sixteenth centuries trace a distinct line in history, which runs parallel with the history of piracy we have so far retold.

As argued by Godfrey Fisher and Fernand Braudel before me, I have also tried to demonstrate that 'the Spanish in the sixteenth century had two languages: they would talk of Barbary *corsairs* in the Mediterranean and of French, English and Dutch *pirates* in the Atlantic' (Braudel 1996: 866). This is true, even if the Spanish Empire started to distinguish between the two theatres only very gradually. In the early sixteenth century, as we have seen, the Spanish would talk of Barbary corsairs and Mediterranean corsairs as two heads of the same monstrous hydra: a heretical threat to Spanish hegemony and Christian civilization. With the creation of the Oceanic amity lines in the second half of the sixteenth century, nevertheless, the history of the Mediterranean corsairs and of the Atlantic pirates drifted further apart. This does not mean that the two worlds did not communicate with each other.

Corsair crews were largely multinational, incorporating converted European renegades drifting to Northern Africa from the most disparate localities: Irish pirates, Italian exiled bandits and French fishermen often fought alongside the North African corsairs. Thousands of renegades sailing with the Barbary corsairs were men of Dutch descent who had begun their seagoing careers serving in the rebellious forces against Spanish domination of the Netherlands. Simon Danziker and John Ward were the most prominent renegades fighting for the Barbary cities in the seventeenth century (Bono 1964: 110–130). They are suspected of introducing the modern sailing ship among the Muslim corsairs and commanding the first incursions outside the Mediterranean, in the Strait of Gibraltar and beyond (Wilson 2003: 45). John Ward was a 'poore fisher's brat', 'a fellow, poore, base and of no esteeme' who was pressed into service on a ship of the Royal Navy, 'mutinied with other thirty comrades' and finally found refuge in Tunis, where he became one of the most important and esteemed Muslim corsairs of the age (Earle 2005: 28). Simon Danziker was a Dutchman from Dordrecht, who left from Marseille to join the corsairs of Algiers, where he became commander of one of the most powerful Mediterranean fleets, the first to pass the Straits of Gibraltar (Sisson and Brown 1951). Sulayman Reis De Veenboer was Dutch and an admiral of the city of Algiers, whose European crew converted to Islam and fought against the Christian powers (Vitkus 2000: 31). Before them, Ucciali made a name for himself in the sixteenth century. Born in Calabria and raised as a poor fisherman, Ucciali was enslaved by Muslims, soon converting to Islam to become one of the most powerful men in the whole Ottoman Empire. Also known as Ulug Ali (literally 'the renegade'), he was a commander in the Ottoman conquest of Tripoli, the siege of Malta, the battle of Lepanto and the rescue of Tunisia from the Spanish. He refused to return to Italy, where he was offered the title of marquis. Instead, he promoted the enslavement (or the liberation?) of hundreds of peasants and fishermen from Southern Italy, 'building a village called New Calabria and allowing them to maintain their customs and their language' (Bono 1964: 7–20).

These extraordinary renegade lives were hardly exceptional in the Mediterranean. According to Braudel:

> Algiers in 1515–1538 was a city of Berbers and Andalusians, of renegade Greeks and of Turks, thrown together pell-mell. Between 1560 and 1587, Algiers under Ucciali was becoming mainly an Italian city. After 1580–1590 and towards 1600 came the northerners, Englishmen and Dutchmen.
>
> (1996: 884)

According to Riggio, who remains the foremost authority on the subject and the main source for the latter study by Braudel, in the Calabria of the seventeenth century the oppressed population often offered itself to the corsairs, looking to the Barbary cities as the promise of a land in which, as Ucciali had demonstrated, 'the son of a fisherman could become king of Algiers' and engaging in the fight against Christianity as 'an authentic form of class struggle' (Riggio 1950: 1–30; Wilson 2003).

Historians like Paul Baepler have gone as far as arguing that 'as many as two-thirds of the Algerian corsair *reis* or captains in the seventeenth century were Christian renegades' (2000: 42). The *course* thus was not a clash between monolithic civilizations, but rather a conflict that *traversed* the Muslim and the Christian world. The characterization of the Barbary cities as 'piratical states' unilaterally preying on peaceful European powers is only a relatively late development that started in the eighteenth century. According to Braudel:

> The concept of piracy is introduced in the Mediterranean only in the late seventeenth century, when Spain wants to mark with an infamous name the depredations . . . of the Christian powers against its commerce, its power and its riches. . . . The concept may have sailed in through the Straits of Gibraltar with the Atlantic ships, but this is only a conjecture.
>
> (1996: 866–867)

The long history of the Mediterranean *course* is gradually erased in the eighteenth century: as the new maritime powers of Northern Europe penetrate this relatively enclosed world, they interpret it on the base of their Atlantic history. In the nineteenth century, the bilateral and multicultural nature of the ancient Mediterranean institution is forgotten, as is the long diplomatic history that proves the sovereign status of the North African powers. The Barbary regencies are universally damned as 'pirate states' void of international legitimacy, exposed to naval bombings by the Western powers and eventually colonized by the French.

European historiography, at least since Stanley Lane-Poole's seminal *Barbary Corsairs* (1890), have retrospectively portrayed the Mediterranean of the eighteenth century as a growing commercial arena, chronically plagued by the parasitical piracies of North African people. The two-sided nature of maritime struggle in the Mediterranean has been thus increasingly erased. European states have been presented as peaceful commercial powers harassed by bloodthirsty African mobs, which are hopelessly disorganized but strong enough to enslave thousands of innocent whites. In 1786, George Washington seemed to suggest that the

North Africans were to be considered as nothing more than outlaw pirates and *hostis humani generis*. 'Would to Heaven,' he writes in a letter to Lafayette, 'we had a navy to reform those enemies to mankind, or crush them into non-existence' (Oren 2008: 29).

In the same year, Thomas Jefferson proposed the formation of a League composed of all civilized states, in order to oppose the 'piratical states' of Northern Africa (Turner 2003). In his proposal, 'the object of the convention shall be to compel the piratical States to perpetual peace' (Jefferson 1786: 59). The international coalition of civilized states should first of all subjugate the city of Algiers, which he considered the most formidable of all 'pirate states'. Heretofore the coalition would continue to operate, in order to sanction 'other piratical states': 'When Algiers shall be reduced to peace, the other piratical States, if they refuse to discontinue their piracies, shall become the objects of this convention either successively or together, as shall seem best' (Jefferson 1786: 60). Perpetual peace would thus be realized through the construction of a system of collective security, which would systematically suppress disqualified polities, branded with the paradoxical appellation of 'piratical states'. In Jefferson's formulation – in this, not dissimilar to Immanuel Kant's original ideas (Behnke 2008) – perpetual peace is not a time void of violence; on the contrary, it requires a constant military mobilization and the armed suppression of all 'disturbers of the peace'. Perpetual peace thus appears to eliminate war, only to recode international violence as a form of global policing against 'piratical communities' and 'outlaw states'.

Although Jefferson's anti-piracy league was never realized, the aggressive European stance toward the North African Regencies grew constantly, peaking in the early nineteenth century with a series of military operations against the autonomous cities of Northern Africa. In 1805, Tripoli was attacked by land and sea by the United States. Thus the first time in history that the star-spangled banner was raised over foreign soil, it was not in a classical war but in the first of a long series of asymmetrical conflicts, the first undeclared 'war against piracy'. In 1815, it was the turn of Algiers to capitulate to American military pressures. In 1816, the British and Dutch Navies delivered a punishing nine-hour bombardment of Algiers in order to force the *dey* to accept the conditions delineated by the British Foreign Office, including cessation of all attacks on European commerce and the liberation of thousands of Christian slaves. The operation was carried out by Lord Exmouth with a mandate from the Holy Alliance, an international organization funded at the Congress of Vienna by the major European powers, which had been conceived as 'the funding block of a cosmopolitan order basically Universal, pacified, hierarchic, mono-centric and, naturally, Euro-centric' (Zolo 1997: 22). The cosmopolitan project collapsed in a decade, but in its short history it legitimized a number of interventions by the leading European powers meant to suppress local revolutions in peripheral states, including Naples and Spain (Simpson 2004: 251). Moreover, it attempted – and failed – to constitute an international police force to suppress piracy and endorsed the British expedition against Algiers, which was to be punished in the name of all nations because it was responsible for 'a shameful banditry that not only disgusts humanity but hinders trade in the most harmful manner' (Panzac 2005: 271–272).

In recent times, these asymmetrical and undeclared wars that characterized the early life of the American Republic have been celebrated as 'America's first war on Terror' (Wheelan 2003; Turner 2003). In what the media referred as 'the Barbary Analogy', American scholars and political pundits have been presenting the 'North African pirates' of the nineteenth century as the historical forebears of contemporary 'Islamic terrorists': 'terrorists by another name' (Mooney 2001). From this point of view, pirates and terrorists are nothing but 'pathogens' (Langeweische 2003: 51), 'parasites' attacking the body of humanity from the inside (Lowenheim 2003), enemies of humanity to be rooted out mercilessly (Cotler 1998; Burgess 2005). Projecting back into history the anti-terrorist zeal of contemporary American politics, an impressive number of publications have arched back to the American campaigns against the Barbary 'pirates' in order to extract useful lessons for the present War on Terror.

Richard Leiby, writing in the columns of the *Washington Post* during the first days of the American invasion of Afghanistan, suggested that 'one of the enduring lessons of the Barbary campaigns was to never give in to outlaws, whether you call them pirates or terrorists' (2001). Richard Jewett similarly remarked that, just as with today's War on Terror, the decision to undertake unilaterally the task of ridding the world from the Barbary pirates 'was bold, but the eventual victory by the tiny United States Navy broke a pattern of international blackmail and terrorism dating back more than one hundred and fifty years' (2002). Jonathan Turley, in a memo to the Congress of the United States submitted shortly after September 11, advised against the option of formally declaring war against Afghanistan. Invoking the Barbary precedent, he remarked:

> Congress did not actually declare war on the pirates, but 'authorized' the use of force against the regencies. This may have been due to an appreciation that a declaration of war . . . would have elevated their status. Accordingly, they were treated as pirates and, after a disgraceful period of accommodation, we hunted them down as pirates.
>
> (Leiby 2001: 2)

If terrorists can be equated to pirates, then it follows that the United States has a right to annihilate them wherever they are.

Similarly, British scholars have recently claimed back the history of their first bombing of Algiers, celebrating the event as 'the first humanitarian intervention' (Lowenheim 2003: 6). 'Britain engaged in a relatively costly humanitarian intervention against the Barbary pirates,' write Lowenheim, and this was 'due to her willingness to defy moral criticism and exhibit consistency with her professed moral principles. No material incentives and/or constraints influenced the British decision' (Lowenheim 2003: 23). Since the pirates were 'enemies of humanity', responsible for terrible crimes against the Universal law of nations, the bombing of Algiers was a humanitarian intervention. Following this logic, Yoni Appelbaum remarked in *The Atlantic* that Western aerial bombings of Libya in 2011 should be compared to the British bombing of Algiers:

> In the run up to this, our Third Barbary War, the case for intervention has been mounted most enthusiastically by Britain and France, and couched in terms of universal human rights. So if we must have a historical analogy, the most appropriate precedent may be the Anglo-Dutch expedition [against Algiers] of 1816, when a European armada employed overwhelming firepower to achieve humanitarian aims.
>
> (Appelbaum 2011: 17)

These recent historical representations, although openly ideological, are not wholly unsupported by eighteenth- and nineteenth-century documents. In fact, they often reflect faithfully American and European perspectives of that period, mimicking rhetorical strategies that supported and justified growing discriminations against the Barbary regencies, and eventually the colonization of Algiers. According to Ann Thomson:

> by the late eighteenth century the enlightened Europeans saw the population of Barbary as a passive mass, oppressed by despotism and sunk in barbarism, who could only be liberated by external intervention and not by their own unaided efforts. Such an attitude . . . came to characterize European appeals to act against the pirates. The need for European action was from this period onwards universally recognized by all shades of opinion and comes to be associated with the desire for conquest and colonization.
>
> (1987: 131)

When Alexander Jardine visited the Barbary Coast at the end of the eighteenth century, he reported his astonishment at the savagery of the local population and, in his *Letters from Barbary*, he complained against Europe's diplomatic treatment of the Barbary cities. He suggested that a European nation should intervene in order to encourage them to useful production, for 'to be conquered by a civilized and generous nation would be a happy event for these poor Africans' (1788: 103).

In the words of this British Officer in the Mediterranean, we find the same line of reasoning that, in the same years, was serving as a justification for the colonization of Malaysia. According to this discourse, the people of Northern Africa, just as the people of Malaysia, must be colonized – not only to stop their barbaric piratical customs, but also to teach them an alternative way of life based on labour and trade. Converging arguments in different European countries 'all pointed to the interest residing in a conquest of Algiers. . . . The result of European control of North Africa would be the replacement of piracy by agricultural development; the agricultural produce would be exchanged for European manufactured goods, and this trade would be controlled by European merchants established in Barbary' (Thomson, 1987: 134). 'American ideological leaders' similarly 'asserted that a long-term strategy was for North Africans to adopt American economic ideals' (Hunter 2010: 11). In 1821, Jefferson asserted the need to form a League of the Western powers to oppose the 'piratical states' of North Africa, but his wider goal was, in his own words, 'to change their habits & characters from a predatory to an agricultural people' (Jefferson 1786: 57–58).

In the nineteenth century, therefore, the Barbary regencies were increasingly portrayed and perceived in Europe as feral 'nests of pirates': uncivilized, lawless and piratical. The description of the cities as 'pirate states', in other words, revealed the process by which communities that had been for centuries perceived and treated as legitimate members of international diplomacy were gradually marginalized and finally excluded from it. After the British bombardment of 1816, numerous voices demanded the acquisition of the area. For two naval historians, for instance, 'the Algerines were committed by religion, custom and heredity to see life from a particular viewpoint' and would never abandon piracy and become civilized unless forced to do so; thus 'total conquest and permanent occupation' were the only solution (Thomson 1987: 137). Even in official diplomatic circles, the status of the Barbary cities was becoming more uncertain every day. In 1825, for instance, the American consul in Algiers lamented British moderation in the bombardment of 'the pirates' and insisted that, having omitted to destroy the city completely, they were responsible for the continuous existence of 'a nest of banditti, waiting only for a favourable occasion to be as mischievous as ever' (Shaler 1826: 139). To conclude, he considers that the only alternative course to complete annihilation of the pirates could be for some civilized nation to occupy the region, taking it upon itself to civilize them. The French occupation of Algiers in 1830, thus, was only the apex of a prolonged discursive colonization, by which the city had been gradually stripped of its international status and reduced to a 'nest of pirates', to be either destroyed or colonized.

The history of the criminalization and colonization of the Barbary cities of Northern Africa, thus, marks an important moment in the history of the concept of the pirate in global history and international law. The nineteenth century witnesses the modern re-emergence of the concept of the 'pirate state', which plays an important role in British Imperial politics in the Indian Ocean, and particularly in the Malay world; but this is also the century in which the idea that entire communities could be branded as 'piratical' – and therefore exposed to an Imperial violence deemed to uphold the rule of international law – returns to haunt the Mediterranean world. In a typical post-colonial trajectory, the modern concept of the pirate as 'enemy of humanity' – and of the 'pirate state' as a community stripped of its rights and marginalized from the international state system – was initially deployed in the extra-European world, only to travel back to the European centre. The application of an exogenous concept to the Barbary cities of North Africa played an important part in the erasure of a long, regional history of diplomatic exchange and international equality. The recurring condemnation of the North African cities as 'pirate dens', of their acts of war as piracies, and of their corsairs and privateers as 'pirates', certainly had the effect of preparing the ground for European colonization. It also allowed the power of the fledgling United States to present the bombing of Algiers not as a traditional act of war, but as a form of 'global policing' against illegitimate pirates.

In the next chapter, I shall show how this form of discourse further penetrated European history during the twentieth century, when Germany was repeatedly accused of acting in a piratical fashion and German military officials were branded as pirates. Also in this case, the discourse of piracy prepared the ground for the perpetuation of a grey area between war and peace, and for actions of international violence presented as a form of global policing in the service of international law. This was, as we shall see, an evolution that would have been unthinkable only a century before, but was in fact the continuation of a much longer historical trajectory. In the twentieth century, the 'pirate state' is not only outside Europe, the product of an imagined predatory inclination characteristic of little-known Asian people or 'orientalized' Muslim cities, but also *within* Europe. Equally, the form of discriminatory warfare by which 'pirate communities' have been persecuted throughout the world is no longer reserved to the colonial world, but takes a central role in the history of Europe and the whole world. In the twentieth century, therefore, exo-colonization leads to a form of endo-colonization as colonial figures, concepts and categories cast their disquieting shadows on the metropole itself (Virilio 1990: 1–30).

Chapter 6

Pirate spectres

Rightless outlaws in the age of total war

The nineteenth century represented the apex of the classical European system of international law. This was a system based on the modern state, taken as the primary institutional agent in an interstate system of relations. During the eighteenth century, control over violence was increasingly centralized, monopolized and made hierarchical (Thomson 1994). First of all, the dispersion of authority and control over violence – which was typical of the medieval and early-modern world – was contested and eventually subdued (Tilly 1985). Secondly, state-authorized non-state practices such as Atlantic privateering were brought under increased state control (Ritchie 1986). Thirdly, non-state-authorized non-state practices such as piracy were fought and suppressed (Earle 2005). As a result, in the nineteenth century, most European states appeared as absolute monopolists in the legitimate use of force over their territories (Weber 1994). Especially after the definitive abolition of privateering in 1856, legitimate state violence was unambiguously concentrated in separated institutions such as the army and the police forces. Within the state, all violence was either police violence or crime. In the open seas, similarly, all forms of non-state violence were condemned as illegitimate – a threat against which all states coalesce together as a single family: the pirate as *hostis communis omnium* – while states retained the right to use violence against one another in open and declared interstate wars.

European states recognized each other as legitimate polities endowed with the right to wage war and conclude peace on equal terms. Since there was no higher Imperial authority that could settle inter-state disputes, and decide authoritatively which of the two states in disagreement had justice on its side, a clash of interests could only be resolved by diplomatic means or through open battle. European wars were therefore limited and regulated by a growing number of legal agreements, which were meant to govern military confrontations and prepare the ground for further peace agreements. In order to limit the potential catastrophic consequences of total war, European states avoided declaring one another illegitimate and criminal. In this way, international law renounced the possibility of outlawing inter-state violence altogether, but on the other hand, it increased the possibility for compromise between the warring factions. Instead of taking the form of crusades for justice against culpable foes who must be morally punished,

European wars tended to resemble formalized duels between equal enemies. This does not mean that European wars in the eighteenth and nineteenth centuries became any less murderous and destructive. Yet, certainly, the mutual recognition between warring states guaranteed by international law always left open the possibility of an honourable settlement between parties. Moreover, it allowed other states to remain neutral between the warring factions, without being accused of playing the unacceptable part of the 'repulsive choir of angels who were neither rebels nor faithful to God' (Dante [1321] 1918: 29).

As we have seen, nevertheless, this limitation of hostilities did not extend into the colonial world. The same European states that recognized each other as equal members of a single civilization most often denied a similar recognition to extra-European polities. It is in this context that the figure of the pirate continued to play an important role in global history well after the end of the Golden Age of Atlantic piracy. The image of the pirate constructed in eighteenth-century literature and international law was projected by European Imperial powers over disparate individuals, groups and communities throughout the world. The concept was singularly useful to Imperial rhetoric, since it seemed to activate a space of exception at the heart of international law. Once labelled as pirates, native subjects could be persecuted as stateless outlaws and their destruction presented as a service to humanity and civilization. The concept was not employed only in the context of naval policing; instead entire polities were depicted as 'piratical' and thus cast in a dubious status at the extreme edge of international law. The statehood of Malay sultanates was openly denied whence they were portrayed as 'piratical communities', or at least seriously questioned when paradoxically condemned as 'pirate states'. Similarly, the sovereignty of the Barbary regencies, which had been previously recognized by a number of European states, was definitely put in disrepute in the years preceding the colonization of Algiers.

In this chapter, I consider the ways in which this form of Imperial rhetoric, and the practice of asymmetrical warfare correlated to it, returned to Europe during the twentieth century. In the first part, I consider the crisis of the classical *jus publicum europaeum* and its gradual transformation under the influence of liberal cosmopolitan ideas. In the second part, I continue to reflect on the transformation of international law through an investigation of the heated debates that accompanied German submarine warfare during the first half of the century. I consider the framework of ideas that, breaking with the classical tradition of international law, eventually enabled the denunciation of German submarines as 'piratical vessels' subjected to Universal jurisdiction. Focusing on the Nyon Conference of 1937, which addressed attacks on international shipping in the Mediterranean Sea during the Spanish Civil War, I consider the symptomatic significance of the charge of piracy against official German military agents. In the third part, I look at the continuous use of the figure of the pirate in the early development of international criminal law, investigating in particular the role of the pirate image in the writings of cosmopolitan legal scholars such as Hans Kelsen, Georges Scelle and Hersch Leuterpacht.

World War I: The colonial *persecutio piratarum* returns to Europe

Throughout the eighteenth and the nineteenth centuries, Europe was governed by the so-called 'balance of power system', which found a legal expression in the principles of the *jus publicum europaeum* (Luard 1992). The fundamental norms of this Euro-centric international system were meant to strictly regulate warfare among European states. It was accepted that European society was divided into a plurality of independent and sovereign states *superiorem non recognoscentes*. It followed that war among the members of this society of states was considered fully legitimate, at least as long as it was waged according to the limits and forms codified in the *jus in bello*. On the other hand, the polities that were not recognized as legitimate members of international society were marginalized, and their violence was considered automatically illegitimate. The European Continent was therefore increasingly conceptualized as a geographical and political space composed of a plurality of modern states, each fully sovereign over the territory under its control and free to settle international disputes with other states by various diplomatic means, which included strictly regulated military confrontations.

In this classical European order, thus, there was no single power (or international institution) invested with the Imperial authority to interpret international law, settle international disputes and enforce its decisions in the name of all members of society. *Rex in regno suo est imperator* (every sovereign is an emperor in their own realm) but, at the international level, there was no Imperial authority (Bartelson 1995: 99–100). For over two centuries, the ideal of an Imperial constitution capable of eliminating war and establishing a cosmopolitan legal system was effectively cast aside. The normal state of international relations is not an Imperial peace reflecting an unchangeable order dictated by God, nature or even history, but rather a dynamic balance between forces: 'an international political-military physics in which variable forces interact with one another, the one against the other, through violent and aleatory clashes of power' (Robinet 1994: 235–236). Between the many states that compose international society, in other words, there is no natural peace, but rather a sort of permanent military mobilization and a fragile political equilibrium between powers. Together with permanent diplomatic apparatuses – meant to make and unmake precarious alliances in order to prevent excessive concentrations of power – military coercion is an instrument constantly available in the hands of the state and embodied in large armies in perpetual mobilization. European states are always ready to make war against one another, but they do this not in order to enforce international law, to punish another state or to eradicate evil from humanity. War is conceived as a valuable instrument to maintain the balance of power *between* states, and not as a means to protect humanity against evil 'pirate states'. International law, accordingly, serves the need to regulate warfare, but it is never a justification for punitive expeditions against other states (Koselleck 2000: 17–68).

For the first time, then, the *jus publicum europaeum* established a strict separation between *military power* and *police power*. Operations of law enforcement are the exclusive competence of police forces within the state, while outside the state there are only wars, which are neither just or unjust, but are simply the way in which states resolve international controversies in an anarchical international system. Modern war 'is here no longer *bellum iustum*. It is *bellum contra iustum hostem*, a duel against equally worthy adversaries; it is a *bellum utrimque iustum* because it is fought among *hostes aequaliter iusti*' (Galli 2009: 199). This means that in case of armed conflict between states, no one can claim to wage a *just war* only because it declares to enforce international law and to act as a bastion of civilization against a disqualified other; nevertheless both sides can claim to wage a *regular war* as long as they follow the established protocols.

The Clausewitzian theory, according to which 'war is the continuation of politics by other means', was the perfect mirror of that particular model of politics that first emerged in early-modern Europe in the seventeenth century (Clausewitz 2009). War was thus thought of and practised as a rational action, the result of heartless calculations performed by the state-machine. It was nothing but the cold execution of state interests according to a strict logic of accumulation of power, compelled by a competitive environment with its all-imposing systemic logic. This is, according to Carl Schmitt (2003), the *triumph of modern rationality* that – imposing a distinction between inside and outside, enemy and criminal, military and civilian – realized a historical temporality that strictly separated war and peace. And yet this was a triumph of rationality, a triumph of the state computing-machine, not of man. War could be excluded from morality and thus isolated from any notion of *justa causa*, but only at the price of wars being pursued even more coldly and mechanically in an escalating spiral of passionless, bureaucratic horrors (Mumford 1974: 35–56).

The enemy was not demonized any more, but only because it was now only a disembodied variable to be taken into consideration when determining state interests and state politics. Wars were regularly pursued for the simple maximization of state interest, or to redress the growing power of one of the units in the international system. The competitive dynamics of the system, moreover, stimulated the constant growth of military power, the accumulation and perfection of technologically advanced means of mass destruction, and the subjection of hundreds of thousands of people to military discipline for the regimented release of violence in war (Buzan and Herring 1998). In 1789, on the eve of the French Revolution, Friedrich Schiller would summarize the paradoxical and self-destructive character of European equilibrium with the following prophetical words:

> peace is now kept by an ever-armoured war and the self-love of one state makes it a guardian of the other's wealth. The society of European States seems to have been transformed into one large family. . . . Should we not define this peace a sort of constant war since it can be maintained only thanks to millions of armed slaves constantly trained for aggression?
>
> (1940: 3–11)

In the nineteenth century, the constant increase in military capabilities and technological means of mass destruction was combined with the aggressive tendencies of a rampant nationalism and a voracious capitalism constantly in search of new markets (Anderson 2006; Luxemburg 1951). At this point, the juridical limitations imposed on total war by the international system appeared as a precious and fragile glass lid on a boiling cauldron.

The destructive power of the new professional military institutions was first unleashed outside Europe, in the colonial wars of the nineteenth century (La Vergata 2005: 125–171). These Imperialist ventures, as we have seen, can only be defined as 'colonial wars' in a very vague sense, since they were fundamentally different from what was defined as 'war' in Euro-centric international law. In fact, war could exist in its pure form only within Europe, since it was defined as a regulated clash between independent and sovereign states. In the colonial world, European powers most often did not recognize native polities as equal members of an enlarged system of international law. Instead, the colonized were portrayed either as disorganized multitudes of savages – whose only hope was to be civilized by European rule – or as piratical societies, to be punished for their disregard of Universal and natural norms (such as respect for private property as defined by the Europeans). In both cases, outside Europe the rules and regulations that defined symmetrical warfare did not apply, and nationalist fervour, capitalist 'insatiable appetite for surplus labour' (Marx 1976: 375), and the pure destructiveness of advanced military technologies truly had free rein. As Carl Schmitt noticed, 'according to classic, European international law, war possesses its own laws, its own honour and its own dignity only because the enemy is not taken as a pirate or a gangster, but as a State and a subject of international law' (1938: 48).

Since the natives did not organize their social life in states moulded on the European model, their armed resistance to European Imperialism was never accepted as a legitimate form of warfare. As we have seen, it was more often portrayed as the product of a natural disposition toward piracy and plunder, itself part of a mythologized anthropological hostility against integration in the market economy. In the colonial world, then, European empires did not wage limited and strictly regulated wars; rather they 'civilized', they 'administered punishments', they 'enforced international or even natural law', they 'protected humanity' from the monstrous practices of the barbarians. The *ius in bello* – that is, the rules for the correct military engagement between European states – had no value in such unilateral campaigns. This is one of the lessons that the history of the pirate concept in the colonial world may teach us: if the 'other' is not accepted as an equal enemy in a limited dispute but it is instead portrayed as an outlaw against international law, or worse, a monster against natural law, all limits to violence are at risk of being washed away by hatred. After making, in his own words, 'mincemeat' of the Sarebas people of Borneo, James Brooke could light-heartedly conclude: 'They are pirates, and this must justify all I have done, and more in the eyes of reasonable men' (Layton 2011: 94). Imperial campaigns of this kind are always at risk of turning into genocide. They have a horrific tendency to escalate into punitive massacres, operations of ethnic cleansing justified as clashes of good against evil.

Within the *jus publicum europaeum*, juridical limitations to war served the primary goal of allowing the future establishment of peace, but in the colonies, where the other was portrayed as an intolerable being – that must be either reformed or eliminated altogether – any agreement between the parties became logically impossible. While unrestricted and total warfare in Europe was seen as a catastrophe to be avoided at all costs, the same was not true in the colonial world. This was not only because the colonized were systematically dehumanized, but also because the difference in military capacity was often so great that the Europeans had no reason to fear forms of unrestricted warfare without legal limitations. European powers thus rapidly abandoned all juridical limitations to give free rein to their vast military machines. As convincingly argued by Carl Schmitt:

> If the weapons are conspicuously unequal then decades the symmetrical concept of war, in which the opponents fight one another as equal. It is in fact essential to war that both sides have a certain chance, a minimum of possibility for victory. Once that ceases to be the case, the weaker opponent becomes nothing more than an object of suppression. Then the hostility between the warring parties is increased exponentially. . . . The vanquished are displaced into a *bellum intestinum* (internal war). The victors consider their superiority in weaponry to be an indication of their *justa causa*, and declare the enemy to be a criminal. The discriminatory concept of the enemy as a criminal and the attendant implication of *justa causa* run parallel to the intensification of the means of destruction. The intensification of the technical means of destruction opens the abyss of an equally destructive legal and moral discrimination.
>
> (2003: 320–321)

In Europe, the endless escalation of violence that attends the demonization of the other had to be restrained in order to avoid mutual destruction. In the colonial world, instead, European military superiority was soon translated into an imaginary moral superiority. Paradoxically, technological perfection in the debased science of killing other human beings seemed to reassure the colonizers of their intellectual and even moral superiority. Thus, there could be no symmetrical war between the Imperial powers of Europe and the savage 'piratical states' of the rest of the world, neither on a material nor on a conceptual level. At the material level, European military operations are too often unilateral slaughters, with little or no possibility for the Europeans to suffer anything approaching a defeat. If mutual hatred escalates, the Imperial powers remain shielded behind their overwhelming military might. At the conceptual level, Imperial interventions are portrayed as counter-piracy operations, whose aim is to enforce international law and civilize the inferior people that populate the colonial world.

In the nineteenth century, European Imperialist expansion was made possible by an exceptional military superiority (Headrick 1979). Without this essential technological factor, the reiterated subduing of millions of people by infinitely smaller groups of colonizers would have been simply unthinkable. Military technologies had to be utilized to their full potential, beyond all juridical or moral limitations. The methods of 'total warfare' that would devastate the European Continent in the twentieth century were first introduced and tested in the colonies. Machine guns, aerial bombings and chemical warfare were first developed in the colonial world (Traverso 2010: 31–56). Frequently, new weapons considered too cruel to be deployed in war against fellow Europeans were deemed legitimate and necessary for the punishment and civilization of non-European peoples. The lethality of the machine gun, for instance, reached an unprecedented level in 1897 with the patenting of the dum-dum bullet, by one Captain Bertie-Clay of the Indian ammunition centre at Dum-Dum (Spiers 1975). This particular ammunition, capable of expanding upon impact, was designed to cause larger, untreatable wounds, and it was unanimously judged too cruel to be employed in European warfare. Nevertheless, the English and American armies insisted on the appropriateness of its continuous use in the colonies.

During the Hague Convention of 1899, the English delegation, headed by Sir John Ardagh, opposed all demands for the abolition of the dum-dum bullets in the colonies, explaining the differences between the calm rationality of regulated war with civilized soldiers and the horror of fighting fanatical barbarians (Lumsden 1974: 15–20). According to the English representative, the use of exceptional forms of violence in the colonies only reflected the exceptional nature of the savage people roaming the extra-European world, whose irrational stubbornness and monstrous vitality seemed to defy certain death when wounded by normal bullets:

> The civilized soldier when shot recognizes that he is wounded and knows that the sooner he is attended to the sooner he will recover. He lies down on his stretcher and is taken off the field to his ambulance, where he is dressed or bandaged. Your fanatical barbarian, similarly wounded, continues to rush on, spear or sword in hand; and before you have the time to represent to him that his conduct is in flagrant violation of the understanding relative to the proper course for the wounded man to follow – he may have cut off your head.
>
> (Tuchman 1966: 62)

This passage is noteworthy for several reasons – first of all, because it shows in a clear way the process by which the decision to use the most frightful means of warfare required the dehumanization and demonization of the colonial Other. The use of exceptional means of violence could not be presented as part of normal symmetrical wars. In order to justify the full unleashing of the technological demons awakened by incessant military competition and research in Europe, colonial violence had to be presented as an asymmetrical confrontation between good and evil: a clash of humanity and civilization against the barbarism of savage pirates and enemies of humankind. Anticipating the indiscriminate bombing of

European cities in the two world wars, the Imperialist 'non-wars' ignored the distinction between civilians and combatants. A European military official such as General Bugeaud in Algeria, then, could exhort his soldiers to forget the principles of the *jus in bello* that were taught in the European academies, since 'in the colonial context they were not fighting against an opposing *army*, but against an hostile *people*' (Etemad 2001: 113). It is in this sense that, according to Enzo Traverso, 'colonial wars contained already the fundamental principle of that Total War that would rage throughout Europe in the twentieth century' (2010: 78).

The strict separation between the European order and the colonial disorder was finally overcome during the First World War, which represented at once the apogee and the definitive crisis of the *jus publicum europaeum*. This conflict sanctioned the end of an international order that had been essentially based on the interaction between multiple sovereign states, each possessing the freedom to declare war according to its own reasons (*jus ad bellum*), and to wage it according to shared rules of engagement (*jus in bello*). And yet, paradoxically, this first, revolutionary global war began in July 1914 as a classic European international conflict (Hobsbawm 2010: 320). All major international powers were gradually dragged into the conflict by various strategic calculations. On 28 July, the conflict opened with the Austro-Hungarian invasion of Serbia, followed by the German invasion of Belgium, Luxembourg and France, and a Russian attack against Germany. Heretofore, several military alliances formed over the previous decades were invoked, so within weeks all the major powers exercised their sovereign *jus ad bellum*. Through their colonies, the conflict finally spread throughout the world.

According to the principles of the *jus publicum europaeum*, the war was supposed to involve only the European states and their military apparatuses. Its aims should not have been social, ethical or religious, but strictly political and strategic. Its violence should not have directly involved the civilian populations. The progression of the war, nevertheless, rapidly showed that the classic idea of inter-state warfare, and the conception of international equilibrium that was directly connected to it, could hardly be sustained in the new industrial context. War could no longer be controlled and used as an instrument of rationally calculated foreign policies, since it could no longer be limited to a clash between separate armies. The state-machine, fuelled by an injection of unprecedented nationalist fervour, had now reached a titanic power of control and direction of the whole social sphere. The martial efforts were not limited to any one section of society, but instead followed a logic of *total mobilization*, by which the entire national economy was integrated into a single system sustaining the war effort (Horne 2002: 4–21). The distinction between military corps and civilian multitudes, that could be considered extraneous to the hostilities, slowly started to be erased as every productive member of society, directly or indirectly, was summoned on the battlefield. More than 70 million people directly suffered and died in the gigantic armies that fought the first technological/industrial war, but an infinitely higher number would participate indirectly in the war. Entire populations were rapidly absorbed in the national war-machines, integrated as essential components in complicated martial mechanisms, and thus also taken as military targets by the opposing forces. As Ernst Junger wrote shortly after the conclusion of the war in which, like many others, he was profoundly involved:

> The times are long gone when it sufficed to send a hundred thousand enlisted subjects under reliable leadership into battle – as we find, say, in Voltaire's Candide; and when, if His Majesty lost a battle, the citizen's first duty was to stay quiet. . . . The image of war as armed combat merges into the more extended image of a gigantic labour process. In addition to the armies that meet on the battlefields, originate the modern armies of commerce and transport, foodstuffs, the manufacture of armaments: the army of labour in general. In the final phase, which was already hinted at toward the end of the last war, there is no longer any movement whatsoever – be it that of the homeworker at her sewing machine – without at least indirect use for the battlefield. In this unlimited marshalling of potential energies, which transforms the warring industrial countries into volcanic forges, we perhaps find the most striking sign of the dawn of the age of labour. It makes the World War a historical event superior in significance to the French Revolution.
> (1993: 126)

The Great War represented the theatre in which the extraordinary violence evoked by the new nation-state, with its industrial means of mass production and mass destruction, finally broke free of the juridical limitations that the *jus publicum europaeum* had imposed on war (Traverso 2010: 80–95). As had happened before in the colonial world, in Europe also the escalation of violence dictated by the inclusion of entire populations in the dynamics of war soon required a parallel rhetorical escalation. As the war mutated from a regulated confrontation between disciplined armies on empty battlefields into a total clash, virtually without borders, between entire social systems; as the destruction of the enemy forces required no longer only the defeat of enemy battalions, but the wholesale disruption of the social and economic forces sustaining them; as total war required not only justifications for the killing of soldiers, but also for the bombing of cities, the sinking of merchant ships, the slaughter of unarmed men, women and children, sometimes hundreds of miles away from the closest battlefront; in short, as the magnitude and brutality of industrial war came to the fore, new justifications for violence arose and new discriminatory images of the enemy emerged. A process of mutual demonization rapidly intensified, paradoxically supported by the cosmopolitan interpretations of international law that had risen in popularity in the decades immediately preceding the war (Zolo 2008: 1–32).

It is in this context that the spectre of piracy unexpectedly returned to haunt Europe. Its return was at once a symptom of, and the most powerful implement for, the collapse of classic Euro-centric international law. Nevertheless, returning from its colonial exile, the pirate image, at first, could not but reappear in its most natural element: at the waterfront. This is generally considered a secondary theatre of the First World War but, in fact, the ocean was arguably the decisive arena of the whole conflict. In the previous two centuries, growing commercial integration had a severe impact on European national economies and, by the beginning of the war, most industries were strongly dependent on the global market for their survival (Halpern 1995: 110–120). Access to the world oceans was therefore essential, not only in order to maintain industrial production, but also to feed the civilian population. The German Empire relied on imports for food and domestic food production, and the United Kingdom relied heavily on imports to feed its population (Herwig 2000: 189). Both required raw materials to supply their industrial production. The two powers aimed, therefore, to blockade one another. On 27 January, 1917 Admiral David Beatty of the Royal Navy observed that 'The real crux of the war lies in whether we blockade the enemy to his knees, or whether he does the same to us' (ibidem).

In fact, already very early in the war, a British blockade seriously crippled the German economy. By 1915, German imports were more than halved and critical shortages gravely damaged all major industries. The production of arms and munitions, essential for the continuation of the war, was slowed down by shortages in industrial fuels. Agriculture was affected by the impossibility to access foreign fertilizers. But most important of all, Germany could not feed itself even before the war, and the British blockade made it almost impossible to import food from overseas. Malnutrition affected many and real starvation loomed. A study sponsored by the Carnegie Endowment for International Peace in 1940 estimated that 'a thorough inquiry has led to the conclusion that the number of civilian deaths traceable to the blockade was 424,000, to which number must be added about 200,000 deaths caused by the influenza epidemic' (Howard 1993: 167).

Without a surface fleet strong enough to challenge the Royal Navy's Grand Fleet, the German government was soon left with only two conceivable courses of action: either accept the inevitability of long-term defeat or deploy its submarine fleet in order to cut off Britain's sea-lanes. Considering the island's heavy reliance on imports from America and the colonial world, this might have forced the British out of the war. The German decision to employ unrestricted submarine warfare nevertheless damaged the economic interests of neutral countries and endangered the lives of sailors and travellers from all countries. Moreover, the German attempt to disrupt the world market by capturing the oceans of the world was in direct contrast with the fundamental interests of the United States. Submarine warfare was meant to undermine the oceanic lanes of trade, threatening the fundamental infrastructures of global commerce. The philosophy of the new American Navy, on the other hand, was summarized by Alfred Tbayer Mahan, its greatest admiral and theoretician as essentially centred on the protection of free trade, which he sensed would give the United States an ever-growing global influence: 'The new Monroe Doctrine, really conformed to the new liberal age, for Alfred Mahan was: free reign to the world market, which presupposed a great naval power, capable to protect all lanes of communication and the scattered bases of a global oceanic Empire' (Schmitt 1942: 176; Bull 1976: 1–9).

On 19 April 1916, Woodrow Wilson officially gave an ultimatum to Germany. The revolutionary significance of the forthcoming American intervention was emphasized by the general tone of the note, in which the President of the United States did not speak in the name of the American people, but rather on behalf of the moral rights of humanity. The note stressed the 'principles of humanity as embodied in the law of nations', and condemned the 'inhumanity of submarine warfare' (Seymour 2003: 61). He ended by stating that the United States, while reluctant to enter the war against Germany, felt compelled to act '[on] behalf of humanity and the rights of neutral nations' (ibidem). The fundamental idea that American military violence would be deployed not only to protect the country's particular strategic, commercial and social interests, but also to enforce international law and uphold the Universal rights of mankind, was also the main theme of a speech delivered two days previously:

> America will have forgotten her traditions whenever upon any occasion she fights merely for herself under such circumstances as will show that she has forgotten to fight for all mankind. And the only excuse that America can ever have for the assertion of her physical force is that she asserts it in behalf of the interests of humanity.
>
> (Garett 1955: 203)

On 2 April 1917, Woodrow Wilson finally announced to the world that the United State had decided to enter the war against Germany. The American power revoked its neutrality to enforce the right of all nations to freely travel and trade in the oceans of the world. It entered the war against Germany in order to stop the inhuman violence of submarine warfare, which Wilson declared to be a war against mankind. From now on, therefore, the First World War would no longer be a military confrontation between equal nations; it was instead a war that opposed mankind to the *hostes humani generis* responsible for unrestricted attacks against all nations, which 'cut to the very roots of human life' (Wilson 2004: 13):

> The present German submarine warfare against commerce is *a warfare against mankind*. It is a war against all nations. American ships have been sunk, American lives taken, in ways which it has stirred us very deeply to learn of, but the ships and people of other neutral and friendly nations have been sunk and overwhelmed in the waters in the same way. There has been no discrimination. The challenge is to all mankind.
>
> (ibidem)

Like the 'Barbary pirates' against whom the United States had waged their first undeclared war almost a century before, Germany was accused of violating the Universal law of nations and denying the free use of the common oceans of the world:

> International law had its origin in the attempt to set up some law which would be respected and observed upon the seas, where no nation had right of dominion and where lay the free highways of the world. This minimum of right the German Government has swept aside under the plea of retaliation and necessity, and because it had no weapons which it could use at sea except these.
>
> (ibidem)

The revolutionary significance of declaring Germany a 'pirate state' responsible of crimes against humanity and international law was not lost on Wilson. Looking forward, he envisaged a new world order emerging from the war, destined to substitute the classic Euro-centric *jus publicum europaeum*. No longer could sovereign states expect to act in an anarchical international system; the new order would be inscribed in international law and enforced by a new benign Imperial power. Taking upon itself the burden to punish the piratical practices of the German state, the United States projected the world into a new historical phase:

> We are at the beginning of an age in which it will be insisted that the same standards of conduct and of responsibility for wrong done shall be observed among nations and their governments that are observed among the individual citizens of civilized states.
>
> (Wilson 2004: 14)

With these words, the traditional dynamics of international law were profoundly twisted. It was a historical turn that reflected three fundamental historical trends. First of all, the reduction of Germany to a 'pirate state' signposted the definitive crisis of the *jus publicum europaeum* and the overcoming of the classic separation between a civilized Europe, in which wars are maintained lawful and symmetrical, and the colonial world, in which violence remains asymmetrical and out of bounds. Secondarily, the war exposed the emergence of the United States as a new global Imperial power, which claimed to protect humanity from evil. Finally, Wilson's declaration – that proclaimed war as the foundation of a new international law in which sovereign states would be like 'individual citizens of civilized states' – anticipated the emergence of new, global institutions like the League of Nations. In the next section, I shall consider how the pirate analogy continued to play an important role throughout the inter-war period, justifying the assertion of a practice of global policing in the name of humanity and international law.

Between war and peace: Germany as a pirate state

The American intervention in the First World War had an important impact on international politics, both symbolically and materially. The war raged for another 19 months, causing over 37 million deaths (Hobsbawm 1995: 21–53). Then, under the combined pressures of governmental demands for further war efforts and widespread deprivation due to the British blockade, German society collapsed. In November 1918, after a number of failed local insurrections, a nationwide revolution successfully overthrew the government of Kaiser Wilhelm II, seized power and proclaimed a new constitution. Imperial Germany was dead, a new Germany had been born: the Weimar Republic (Henig 1998: 1–15).

Nevertheless, the Allies maintained a punitive attitude against Germany for over eight months after the armistice, until the signing of the Treaty of Versailles (Bane 1942). Throughout this period, suspended between war and peace, the embargo was maintained in order to ensure German compliance. In March 1919, Winston Churchill said in the House of Commons:

> We are enforcing the blockade with rigour, and Germany is very near starvation. All the evidence I have received from officers sent by the War Office all over Germany show: firstly, the great privation which the German people are suffering; and, secondly, the danger of a collapse of the entire structure of German social and national life under the pressure of hunger and malnutrition.
> (Neilson 1954: 210)

In this dramatic context, the *Law Quarterly Review*, in its 35th issue, published what at first view can only appear as a most untimely article, titled: 'Piracy and the Barbary Corsairs'. Behind the scholarly title, the essay presented a strong argument in support of treating Germany as a 'pirate state', and all German officials as 'pirates', subject to Universal jurisdiction. It was signed by no less than the Quain Professor of Comparative Law at the University of London, J.E.G. De Montmorency, then one of the most influential legal authorities in the English-speaking world. Beginning with a review of the *Lusitania* trial, recently held in November 1918 in New York, the English scholar recollected the fact that 'District Judge Mayer, after an exhaustive examination of the evidence in the case, decided that the act of the German submarine commander in sinking the *Lusitania* was an illegal act' (De Montmorency 1919: 142). Then he added:

> That that crime would have been piracy if it had been an uncommissioned act no lawyer could doubt. The United States Court says that the act is not justified by the fact that the agent was commissioned. Hence the Government which directed the act is responsible for a piratical act. In other words, the members of the German Imperial Government were *pirates*. Whether they will be charged with that or any offence is no doubt a matter that the Peace Conference will decide, but whatever the decision may be, it will surely be unsatisfactory unless it definitely recognizes that a justiciable crime was committed, and thus create a precedent for future international guidance.
> (ibidem)

According to De Montmorency, 'so far from the submarines being the enemy solely of a particular state, they were strictly *hostes humani generis*' (ibid: 134). The article thus justifies the punitive treatment of Germany, and suggests that German officials should be considered denationalized individuals who, having lost the protection of their state, might be punished by all nations. It states in clear terms: 'In these circumstances the nations of the world are dealing with a Pirate State, and the agents of that state are pirates who cannot shelter themselves under the commission of a sovereign who has chosen to fly the black flag with the skull and crossbones above his national colours' (ibid: 135). De Montmorency, then, remembered the long colonial history of the pirate concept, praising in particular its use against the Barbary cities of Northern Africa:

> It may be said that it is difficult to create precedents; that there is no precedent for Pirate States. But in fact there is one great precedent, which is written large across the history of Europe during a period of at least three centuries. . . . The case of the corsairs who flew the flags and carried the commissions of the sovereign Barbary States. No one doubted that these corsairs' were pirates, no nation intervened to prevent their summary execution, and yet they were the commissioned agents of sovereign powers who made treaties on terms of international equality with the proudest states of Europe.
>
> (ibid: 136)

Numerous jurists and lawyers, complains De Montmorency, recognized the importance of the pirate concept in recent colonial history and yet seemed appalled by the idea of applying the very same concept in a European context. He recognized that these systematic inconsistencies were rooted in history, but he insisted that they had to be overcome in order to affirm the Universality of international law and protect civilization from the German threat. In his view, the long history of Imperial interventions against non-European 'pirate states' seemed to indicate a single course of action:

> If Liberia had suddenly issued its orders to the world, and threatened the navies of the world with destruction without a trace if it were disobeyed, the great nations would have declared it to be a Pirate State, and would have executed as pirates every Liberian sea-captain and his crew on capture. It was only the fact that it was a great nation like Germany, with notable traditions, which caused and causes jurists and lawyers to falter.
>
> (ibid: 135)

With an original twist of perspective, De Montmorency rejected the classic Eurocentric approach that saw international relations in Europe as the normative model from which it becomes possible to judge the colonial world. Instead, he looked at the colonial use of the pirate concept as a model, which should be universally applied in order to reform the structure of international law and order. For too long the illusion of German sovereign rights had prevented members of the German army and government from being identified for what they really were:

pirates to be executed on capture. The idea that a sovereign member of the international community could not be *hostis humani generis* impeded a prompt coalition of all civilized states against the German threat. To 'prevent the repetition of such a mistake', according to De Montmorency, was 'the great object of the Paris Conference', which the following month would have sanctioned the definite end of the war (ibid: 141). In order for this to be achieved, a novel cosmopolitan conception of international law had to be imposed: 'It is submitted that this end can only be secured by the definite formulation of an International Criminal Law, and by the specific recognition of the capacity of a sovereign state to commit crime' (ibidem).

De Montmorency's suggestion of policy did not go unheard. Articles 227 and 231 of the Treaty of Versailles required Germany to renounce its jurisdiction over the Kaiser, hand him over to the Allies and witness his trial. The Allied and Associated powers sought to judge Wilhelm II publicly under the accusation of 'a supreme offence against international morality and the sanctity of treaties' (Kelsen 1947: 155). In the consultations of the Paris Peace Conference, it was American delegates who insisted the most on describing German warfare as a crime against international law and German state agents as criminals. Although the Netherlands eventually refused to comply with the compulsory extradition of Wilhelm, the decision represented the first attempt to construct and enforce an international criminal law that would expose official representatives of recognized sovereign states to Universal jurisdiction. According to L.C. Green, 'it seems to be generally believed that the movement for the recognition of an international criminal code and jurisdiction is a product of the First World War and the provisions in the Treaty of Versailles for the trial of the Kaiser' (1976: 570).

The pirate category is therefore the fundamental conceptual basis on which the whole structure of modern international criminal law has been built. As we have seen, the pirate was the first subject to be considered an 'enemy of humanity', a denationalized subject abandoned by the protection of their state of origin and thus subjected to Universal jurisdiction. Projecting the image of the pirate over Germany, De Montmorency is able to evoke an absolute negativity, against which the international system and humanity at large are called to coalesce. To describe indiscriminate submarine warfare (or anything else) as 'piracy' means condemning those responsible as pirates, foes against whom no one can claim neutrality. As observed by Louis Sohn:

> the first breakthrough towards an international system for punishing global crimes occurred when international law accepted the concept that pirates are 'enemies of mankind'. Once this concept of an international crime was developed in one area it was soon applied by analogy to other fields.
>
> (1980: 11)

There is, therefore, a fundamental evolution in the use of the concept of piracy and a parallel extension of Universal jurisdiction, which threatens to undermine a global order of sovereign states by allowing one state to reach into the affairs of another. Far from being a concept without history, from the beginning of modern international law until today the meaning of Universal jurisdiction has fundamentally changed. Having retraced the history of the exercise of Universal jurisdiction against pirates in the last three centuries, we could venture to submit that this was an institution originally *complementary* to a Euro-centric international system of states. Subsequently, when European Imperialism posed the problem of differentiating between sovereign states partaking of the international community and groups unworthy of the honour, Universal jurisdiction started to play a *constitutive* role in relation to the international system. Finally, in the twentieth century, Universal jurisdiction became essentially an *alternative* to the classical, absolute sovereignty of the state. Let us briefly review these three moments.

As we have seen, Universal jurisdiction emerged as an institution that was largely *complementary* to the Westphalian order of territorial states. In the eighteenth century, the Commercial Revolution transformed the oceans of the world in the most important space of global circulation. Nevertheless, this was a zone subtracted from the sovereign power of every single state, which asked the question of how the fundamental rules sustaining a market could be upheld. The question posed itself dramatically during the Golden Age of Piracy, when hundreds of multinational pirate crews, independent from any recognized state, provoked a crisis in international commerce. Eighteenth-century pirates refused to subject themselves to the state order and revolted against the extension of international legal norms to the oceans of the world, up to that point conceived as an anomic sphere beyond the Euro-centric international law of the *jus publicum europaeum*.

Universal jurisdiction was introduced for the first time in modernity in order to confront this challenge. Oceanic space was conceptualized as a space of free trade, which does not belong to any single state but is instead common to all members of the international community. Since pirates defied private property and the international law meant to protect it, they were considered *hostis communis omnium*, so that any state was entitled to punish them in the name of all. In early modernity, thus, Universal jurisdiction was an exceptional institution of international law, since it allowed a sovereign to sanction people that not only were outside of its territory, but also who were not its subjects. And yet it seemed to complement rather than challenge the sovereignty of the state. In fact, following Schmitt, we could say that the *jus publicum europaeum* existed as the combination of an international order of territorial states (in Europe) and an oceanic zone (outside of it). Throughout this liquid frontier, increasingly traversed by a commerce that gives rise to contracts, the enforcement of international law depended on the exercise of Universal jurisdiction.

In the nineteenth century, the classic pirate image was recuperated and transformed by European imperialist powers in order to serve as a fundamental conceptual tool in the colonization of much of the world. For instance, Malay communities resisting European commercial penetration were not recognized as sovereign members of the international community. Instead they were labelled as 'pirate states', and persecuted as malevolent congregations of 'enemies of humanity' united by a common hostility to civilization, peaceful labour and trade. Likewise, the sovereignty of the Barbary cities of Northern Africa was questioned by the European powers, who considered their corsairs to be nothing but pirates. The attacks on trade by the Barbary corsairs were not accepted as legitimate acts of war, performed by official agents of a sovereign state. Instead they were denounced as piracies, crimes against international law that required all civilized nations to coalesce. The United States assaulted Tripoli in what would be their first undeclared war, while the British presented the bombing of Algiers as a humanitarian operation. Finally, the French conquest of Algiers was celebrated as necessary for the civilization of the inhabitants, and the extirpation of their piratical customs.

In all these examples, the concept of the pirate is part of the struggle to define the limits of the international community. Separating legitimate political communities, worthy of being part of the international system, from illegitimate communities of outlaw pirates is a political operation in itself, by which the limits of an international order are negotiated. What differentiates a 'sovereign state' from a 'pirate state'? Who is a legitimate privateer (acting as a representative of a political community) and who is a pirate (acting as a member of a piratical community)? Rather than simply complementing the international state system, the exercise of Universal jurisdiction seems as much to help constitute it. It is always an Imperial power that, taking the decision to exercise Universal jurisdiction against what it defines as a 'piratical community', proves the latter's exclusion from the international community.

Finally, in the twentieth century, the introduction of international criminal law transformed the relation between sovereignty and Universal jurisdiction. If, in the eighteenth century, Universal jurisdiction with respect to piracy reinforced an international order based on state sovereignty over enclosed territorial spaces; and in the nineteenth century, the exercise of Universal jurisdiction against sea rovers pertaining to various indigenous polities was the essential moment in which the latter's membership of the international community was denied; in the twentieth century, Universal jurisdiction seems to undercut state sovereignty. It allows one sovereign to judge members of another state, according to its particular understanding of international law. In the most extreme and paradoxical case, foreshadowed by the proposed trial of Wilhelm II of Germany, it may allow one sovereign member of the international community to judge another. The enemy of all, thus, is no longer someone willingly outside of the international community, nor someone who is part of a polity not accepted within the community of civilized nations; it is instead a member of the international community that must be forcefully cast outside of it. In this case, Universal jurisdiction is really an *alternative* to sovereignty, since it preludes a cosmopolitan Imperial order in which those who were once absolute sovereigns, recognizing no superior authority, are now subjected to judgments and sanctions according to international law. In short, the piracy analogy has underpinned the whole movement towards the twentieth-century revival of Universal jurisdiction, which today is posed as the foundation stone of a global police order.

After the war: Schmitt 'the pirate' and the origins of international criminal law

The Treaty of Versailles was already an important step toward the constitution of a cosmopolitan community ruled by international criminal law. It demanded the extradition of the German Emperor, but also it founded the first international organization whose principal mission was to maintain world peace: the League of Nations. Formally constituted in 1920, the League of Nations was – after the Holy Alliance discussed in the previous chapter – the second modern attempt to protect global peace through the institution of an international authority (Zolo 1997: 20–27). After the conclusion of the war, the victorious powers not only redrew the world map according to the new balance of power, they also established an international organization meant to protect the new order from future disputes. The League of Nations was supposed to enforce and protect the international order agreed by the major power at the end of the war. This included the economic expiation and political marginalization of Germany: a potential factor of crisis that was exorcised only through specific dispositions imposing the permanent disarmament of that country (Macmillan 2003: 35–46).

The new international order naturally presupposed and elicited a revision of classical theories of international law. In order to sustain an international legal order that would be independent, binding and superior to state sovereignty, it was essential to reject the idea that the only source of international law is the contractual self-obligation of states, which can thus at any time subtract themselves from the international community. The idea of a new global order that would be institutionalized, supra-national and ecumenical guided the minds of a new generation of cosmopolitan theorists, who conceived a new way to think of the nature of international law. In works such as Kelsen's *The Problem of Sovereignty and the Theory of International Law* (1920), Georges Scelle's *Précis de droit de gens* (1932) and Hersch Lauterpacht's *The Function of Law in the International Community* (1933), a cosmopolitan interpretation of international law supports the political project of a new global order; a *civitas maxima* regulated by a Universal common law and a global police power, whose role would be to maintain the constituted order and suppress all violators of international law.

In his essay *Das Problem der Souveranitat und die Theorie des Volkerrechts* (1920), Hans Kelsen outlined his theory of international law for the first time. Symbolically contemporary with the institution of the League of Nations, the volume conceives the international legal system as a Universal order encompassing a number of subordinate legal systems. Kelsen takes as the ultimate foundation for his legal positivism the existence of a 'Universal legal community of human beings' superior and independent from contingent historical conditions – that is, the plurality of nation-states (1920: 319). The existence of a Universal human community governed by a cosmopolitan legal order, according to Kelsen, had been only recently forgotten and cast aside. He shows how, before modern international law came into being, its existence was widely recognized in the notion of *imperium* and in the ancient theological idea of *civitas maxima* (1920: 271–274; Zolo 1998: 309). Now, with the end of the First World War and the inauguration of the League of Nations, Kelsen's pure theory of law argues for the necessity once again to interpret international law as a 'world or universal legal system' (ibidem). Finally, since he understands international law as a supreme legal order, Kelsen rejects the idea that states possess an absolute sovereignty. This is both a descriptive and a prescriptive theory of international law. According to Kelsen, in fact, since international law is in its essence a superior legal order which gives form and validity to all subordinate legal systems, state sovereignty can only be a temporary and primitive phase before the re-establishment of a cosmopolitan Union:

> It is only temporarily, by no means forever, that contemporary humanity is divided into states, formed in any case in more or less arbitrary fashion. Its legal unity, that is the *civitas maxima* as organization of the world: this is the political core of the primacy of international law.
>
> (1920: 319)

Kelsen's retrieval of classic juridical cosmopolitanism had an immediate impact in twentieth-century perceptions of international law. His was a timely intervention, which responded to the new political perspectives opened by the institutionalization of the League of Nations as a potentially supra-national legal order. It was thus followed by a stream of writings that directly challenged the old pluralist conception of international law, now depicted as both scientifically incorrect and politically disastrous. Two of the most influential writers in this sense were Georges Scelle and Hersch Lauterpacht (Koskenniemi 2001: 327–338, 353–411). Notwithstanding the profound differences between the two writers, they both sustained the primacy of the statute of the League of Nations over any other source of law, including direct agreements between sovereign states. They both considered the League of Nations 'a purposeful instrument in the process of political integration of mankind' (Lauterpacht 1936: 54). Politically they advocated an evolution of the international legal community from its classic anarchical, horizontal and state-centric configuration to a more hierarchical and vertical structure, centred on the League of Nations. From the writings of these representative liberal theorists transpires a common cosmopolitan ideal: a Universal and depoliticized society that would embrace humanity within a single legal system, of which the League of Nations would be nothing but the embryo (ibid: 424–436).

In the cosmopolitan system of international law that these liberal theories claim to glimpse in the present, and definitely evoke for the future, the concept of war must of necessity disappear. In the new international order, in fact, war becomes strictly inconceivable: either international violence is unauthorized by the League of Nations and therefore is a crime against international law; or it is authorized as a legal sanction, which means that it is a form of global police (Zolo 2008). According to Hans Kelsen, for instance:

> a military action against a Member State which, contrary to the institution, has attacked another member of the league is, from the point of view of the ideology of the league, not 'war' . . . but a sanction, i.e., a reaction against a violation of law directed at a delinquent member. The purpose of stipulating such a sanction is to prevent war, to maintain peace within the League.
>
> (2008: 53–54)

In short, if there is a unitary legal system at the global level, there can be no *alegal* warriors, but only policemen and criminals.

The most interesting fact – which emerges as a disquieting prophecy in the midst of what are otherwise cosmopolitan theories infused with optimism for the future – is that the space left open by the elimination of the classic concept of war is immediately occupied by the emergence of a new form of global violence, which is an elaboration of the ancient Roman concept of the *persecutio piratarum*. Significantly, this is the only precedent for the non-wars sanctioned by the League of Nations to which Kelsen can arch back: just as the cosmopolitan reaction to the violation of international law by a delinquent state is not a war, equally 'the capture and punishment of a pirate' is not a war but 'the execution of a sanction provided by a norm of international law' (2008: 55–56). The homology should not be surprising, considering that the cosmopolitan order prefigured by the League of Nations, always according to Kelsen, is essentially a re-edition of the ancient Roman concept of Empire (Zolo 1998).

This cosmopolitan peace, therefore, remains essentially a form of Imperial peace, which can extinguish war only by recoding violence in new forms. As already pointed out by Carl Schmitt, who was particularly concerned with the cosmopolitan international legal theory attending the erection of the League of Nations, the point from which this revolutionary re-codification of international violence becomes possible is the concept of the pirate as *hostis humani generis* – which has its origin in the cosmopolitan outlook of Roman Imperial law, but which was then recuperated by international law in its classic period and deployed in the oceanic and colonial spaces outside Europe. 'It should not be forgotten,' Schmitt writes:

> that the concept of piracy, which suddenly has become once again topical, has been for a long time a unique problem of international law, which on the one hand appears as a trifle, today interesting only from a theoretical point of view; but on the other turns out to be the single point of irruption for a completely novel international law, which shatters in a thousand pieces the concept of the State.
>
> (1937: 353)

The reason why the pirate analogy is continuously evoked in this particular historical phase is because it represents an ideal point of transition from the old system of international law to the new. Its significance is therefore infinitely multiplied: in the old system of international law, as Schmitt remarked, the pirate concept was a unique anomaly, which opened perspectives of Universal jurisdiction, global policing, humanitarian intervention and dehumanization of the Other (Heller-Roazen 2009). Nevertheless, it was an anomaly that remained for a long time marginal to the classic system of international law: its significance and *raison d'être* localized in the oceans of the world and, especially, in the colonial world. From Schmitt's acute but strictly Euro-centric perspective, then, the figure of the pirate initially appears a theoretical conundrum of little practical impact (Hesse 2011). And yet, in the twentieth century, the concept of piracy became the device by which the discriminatory practices of global policing previously characteristic of the colonial world were imported into Europe. The pirate image, in other words, was turned into a *semiotic machine*, which could be projected on different subjects of international law with the result of transferring them into an Imperial legal system that is global, hierarchical and thoroughly juridified.

The significance of the pirate analogy is only confirmed in the years immediately preceding the conflagration of the Second World War. In 1922, the idea that those responsible of fundamental violations of international law should be treated as denationalized pirates subject to Universal jurisdiction was included in the Treaty of Washington, which laid down strict rules for the use of submarines and concluded:

> [a]ny person in the service of any Power who shall violate any of those rules, whether or not such person is under orders of a governmental superior, shall be deemed to have violated the laws of war and shall be liable to trial and punishment as if for an act of piracy and may be brought to trial before the civil or military authorities of any power within the jurisdiction of which he may be found.
>
> (Finch 1937: 660–661)

The provision was part of the new international order established by the League of Nations. Submarine crews accused of violating international law (even when they did so as official agents of a sovereign state) were considered pirates according to international law and therefore subject to Universal jurisdiction. The treaty thus affirmed the superiority of international law over all national laws, to the point that soldiers – following the laws of their country – might appear as pirates in front of international law. Although symptomatic, the Treaty had little practical impact in the immediately following years – at least, until 22 November 1936, when the cruiser *Miguel De Cervantes* was unexpectedly hit by a torpedo launched by an unidentified submarine. The military ship belonged to the government of the Spanish Republic, then embroiled in a bitter civil war. We now know that the anonymous submarine belonged to the Italian Navy, which had begun its secret campaign in support of the Spanish reactionary *coup* (Frank 1990). In the following months, German and Italian submarines haunted the Mediterranean, trying to cut off all imports to the Spanish Republic. Careful to keep their identity unknown, they attacked a number of merchant ships of various nationalities, without any warning and regardless of the fate of passengers and crews.

In November 1937, to offer a united response to the rising threat to international security and Mediterranean commerce, France and Great Britain summoned an international conference to be held in Nyon (Maiolo 1999: 55–76). The final arrangements of the international conference judged the anonymous attacks to be 'violations of the rules of international law' (Heller-Roazen 2011: 24). Moreover, the illegal submarine assaults were proclaimed to 'constitute acts contrary to the most elementary dictates of humanity, which should be justly treated as piracy' (ibidem). As a result, the anonymous submarines were open to Universal jurisdiction, although initially exercised only by France and Britain (Finch 1937). The significance of this agreement lay less on its limited practical impact on the events surrounding the Spanish Civil War, than in the coherent way in which it tried to apply the ideas of world order and international criminal law that had been proclaimed since the institution of the League of Nations almost 20 years before. It was immediately apparent to all the major actors involved that this was the first historical test of the cosmopolitan declination of international law that had emerged from the Paris Conference (Ruschi 2009).

In the following months, a veritable intellectual battle took place around the use of the accusation of piracy in the Treaty of Nyon (Rech 2012). At a superficial level, the issue was limited to a dispute regarding the legitimacy of such an accusation; on a deeper level, the question revolved around the use of the pirate analogy as a way to establish international criminal law. International legal theorists that remained faithful to the categories of classical international law accused the Nyon diplomats of being simply mistaken in their use of the 'pirate concept' (Genet 1938: 53–63). They maintained that only private subjects – motivated by desire for plunder and acting independently from any sovereign state – could be accused of piracy. The cosmopolitan innovators, nevertheless, were eager to assimilate submarine warfare to piracy in order to affirm the superiority of international law over national legislation (Wilcox 1938). If German and Italian submarines could be analogized to pirate ships, their crews could have been apprehended and punished for crimes against international law, even if they were acting under the sovereign command of a nation-state. This would have created a precedent for international criminal law, coherent with the international order established after the First World War. In the debate surrounding the question of piracy, two personalities stood out for clarity of vision and deep awareness of the fundamental issues at stake: one was Hersch Lauterpacht, who would become one of the leading international legal scholars of the twentieth century and an inspirer of the United Nations; the other was Carl Schmitt.

In his *Insurrection et piraterie* (1939), Lauterpacht called for a wide application of Universal jurisdiction against serious violators of international law. As noticed by Walter Rech:

> Lauterpacht ultimately aimed to extend the concept of piracy to public enemies in order to submit them to Universal jurisdiction. He believed it useful that, at this early stage of international criminal law, international criminals be labelled as pirates and 'enemies of mankind' in order to legitimate their prosecution and punishment before the international community. . . . The radical outcome of this reasoning was that piracy *jure gentium* included any offence that states agreed to name so and to counter by means of Universal jurisdiction.
>
> (2012: 4)

Lauterpacht therefore suggested that by establishing an analogy with eighteenth-century pirates, states could subject *any* offence against international law to Universal jurisdiction, beginning with unrestricted submarine warfare. Grave violators of international law, once equated to pirates, would be 'denationalized, deprived of the guarantees normally conceded to criminals by municipal law, and denied the status of lawful belligerents' (Rech 2012: 22). Matti Koskenniemi called attention to Lauterpacht's decisive contribution to the erection of contemporary international criminal law. Focusing mainly on his important role in the preparation of the Nuremberg trials and the way in which he has moulded the concept of 'crimes against humanity', Koskenniemi convincingly portrays him as 'the last century's most influential international lawyer' (2004: 810; 1997). Yet it must be stressed that Lauterpacht's concept of 'crimes against humanity' can only be understood in continuity with his interwar reflections on the concept of piracy. Following Lauterpacht's intellectual parable, it emerges once more that the pirate figure has been the most powerful inspiration and historical precedent for nascent international law.

Diametrically opposed to Lauterpacht's cosmopolitan interpretation of international law, Carl Schmitt was the first and most authoritative voice to speak out against the Nyon Conference. In 'The Concept of Piracy' (1937), he reasserted that originally, in the eighteenth century, only stateless individuals acting independently from all states were labelled as pirates. Since they were not recognized as legitimate political communities but only as multitudes of individuals moved by egoistic interests, they were denied the status of legitimate enemies. Instead they were considered *hostis communis omnium*, systemic enemies of the entire international system of states (1937: 352). As their action was considered apolitical, so too was their repression. According to Schmitt, since pirates are denationalized they can only be considered in two ways by international legal theory: either they are *outlaws* banned from international law and cast into a space of exception radically void of legal rights and duties, or they are *criminals* responsible for some grave offence against some kind of Universal or natural law. In both cases, the suppression of pirates 'is not a war, but either criminal justice, according to the English understanding, or a measure of international security, according to the Continental one' (1937: 353).

Schmitt insists that the classic, eighteenth-century pirate figure has disappeared for almost a century, following the exponential increase in state's powers of control over the whole world. He notes that in the classical tradition of international law 'an essential trait of the modern concept of piracy was the fact that the pirate inhabited the empty space outside the state, he was existentially part of a reality radically alien to the modern state' (1937: 352). Then he wonders where the pirate 'would find today that juridical empty space totally free from the state', since modern technologies 'enormously augment the capacity of control of modern states', even at sea (1937: 353). In fact, he concludes, while the space occupied by the geometrical ordering of the state 'appears every day more close on itself . . . the empty space of freedom required by the old concept of piracy becomes every day smaller and finally insignificant' (1937: 353). Schmitt thus explains the disappearance of the classic pirate figure from the stage of world history with the fact that no space can be any longer considered a 'juridical empty space'. Not only are there no more colonial zones 'beyond the line', radically excepted from the rule of international law, but there is no space in which pirates can hope to operate truly independently from one or more official governments. In the twentieth century, suggests Schmitt, it is hard to believe that a pirate crew may operate in the oceans of the world against the combined will of all states: either pirates are protected and supported by a state – in which case they are effectively state agents – or they are destined to be annihilated.

Schmitt thus notices that 'given the equation between the state and the political', actions directly performed by state agents – or even by revolutionaries whose aim is to become agents of a transformed state – would not be normally considered acts of piracy (1937: 353). From this point of view, the portrayal of German and Italian submarines as pirates *jure gentium* represents a radical departure from classic international law. Schmitt nevertheless does not criticize the decision reached in Nyon as simply 'incorrect'. He does not consider the denunciation of submarine warfare as a 'piratical action' to be a naïve mistake that might be corrected by the enlightened intervention of academic scholars well versed in the history of concepts. Instead, he looks at the 'Conference on Piracy' as a political operation by which a number of actors have tried to affirm a new international order, an order in which sovereign states could be held accountable of crimes against international law, just as individuals are held accountable of their crimes against national norms. According to Schmitt, the contemporary resurgence of the pirate figure in international law, and the tendency to expand its meaning by analogy, 'relate to the impulse to replace war with collective arrangements of various types (international police, criminal punishment, proscriptions and sanctions), and to create some power capable of acting "in the name of humanity"' (1937: 354).

Among the many critics of the Conference of Nyon, Schmitt was one of the few to stress that the alteration of the concept of piracy was a sign of epochal transformations in the world of public order. The conference, in fact, not only reiterated the classical conception of piracy, but added something radically new. According to the acts of the conference, 'any person, whether or not such person is under a governmental superior' who makes himself responsible for attacks against merchant free trade 'is to be considered guilty as if for an act of piracy' (Sato 2011: 39–40). For the first time, Universal jurisdiction was enforced not against stateless individuals but against people acting under the authority of a sovereign European state. In this way, the absolute authority of a European state over its citizens was radically put in question. As argued by De Montmorency 20 years before, Schmitt too believes that German and Italian submarine crews are thus cast in the same position as the Barbary corsairs of the nineteenth century. They are the official agents of a 'pirate state':

> The concept of piracy displaces the whole [submarine] question on a universalistic and ecumenical level. Indeed, the pirate is marked, more than anything else, by the fact that he is 'denationalized' and abandoned by the state to which he presumably belongs. It represents thus a breach in the structure of international law, which is important also because it is susceptible to be remarkably enlarged by super-national and Universalistic interpretations. They make it possible to treat entire states and nations as pirates and to evoke anew the concept of the *pirate state* (itself a term thought for a century to have become totally obsolete) at a level of increased intensity.
>
> (2011: 68)

In Schmitt's view, by instituting forms of international policing against German and Italian submarines and treating them as piratical vessels, the signatories at Nyon had radicalized the trend toward a discriminating concept of war. One side claims to represent humanity while the other is demonized and cast as an irredeemable enemy of humankind. If successful, this attempt would have also contributed to the construction of a global order in which war would be banned, only to be substituted by police operations, moral disqualification and economic sanctions, suspended in a grey area between war and peace, and carried out in the name of humanity. The consequence, writes Schmitt, is that any person portrayed as a 'pirate' would immediately 'pass into that empty space foreign to the state that up to now was the fundamental premise for the very notion of piracy. . . . The state would be forced to abandon the people held responsible' (1937: 354). Thus the concept of the pirate – that in the past *presupposed* a place exempt from the law – now seemed to be capable of *recreating* that space, at least insofar as states were asked to withdraw their protection from citizens identified as *hostes humani generis*. The outside of the international state order therefore was not 'beyond the line' any more, but *within* a global order that seemed to have no more stable, identified outside.[1]

The analyses offered by Carl Schmitt and Hersch Lauterpacht are diametrically opposed, but effectively convergent. They both consider the pirate concept an exception within the classical order of international law. Both regard the pirate analogy as an important device that can be used by the major powers in order to enlarge the scope of Universal jurisdiction and gradually bend the structure of international law toward a more cosmopolitan configuration. Both consider the criminalization of war to be an essential part of the transition to a new liberal global order, in which state sovereignty would be decisively limited by superior norms of international law. And yet, although they appear to share similar expectations, Schmitt and Lauterpacht have opposed opinions about the desirability of such a profound transformation of international law.

Lauterpacht considered that a world organized in a plurality of independent and sovereign nations was destined to yield to 'a supra-national Federation of the World, which must be regarded as the ultimate postulate of the political organization of man' (1950: 46). In November 1938, on the eve of the Second World War, he could still boldly proclaim that the recent progress of international law would eventually lead to a Universal political organization of mankind:

> Nobody who has paid any attention to the peculiar features of our present era will doubt for a moment that we are living a period of the most wonderful transition which tends rapidly to accomplish that great end to which indeed all history points – the realization of the unity of mankind.
>
> (1938: 587)

After the war, Lauterpacht actively participated in this historical transition, both as a scholar and as an international lawyer. In 1945 he became a member of the British War Crimes Executive; he was also part of the British delegation to the Nuremberg Trials and wrote drafts for Britain's Chief Prosecutor Sir Hartley Shawcross (Koskenniemi 1997: 243–246). In the same years, he was one of the most recognized authorities in the discussions leading to the definition of the Charter of the United Nations, and his proposals left an important trace in the constitution of the supranational organization (ibidem).

1 The pirate, both in its classical forms and in the multifarious forms it can take by analogy, is the paradigmatic denationalized individual. Accordingly, when in 1926 the League of Nations codified the status of pirates in international law, it considered them 'enemies of the human race and . . . outside the law of peaceful people'. It stressed that they were to be considered denationalized subjects, stripped of all belongings: 'By committing an act of piracy, the pirate and his vessel *ipso facto* lose the protection of the State whose flag they are otherwise entitled to fly. Persons engaged in the commissions of such crimes obviously cannot have been authorised by any civilised state to do so' (Matsuda and Committee of Experts for the Progressive Codification of International Law 1926: 225).

In his scholarly work, Lauterpacht continued to stress the fact that, given the criminalization of war after the founding of the UN, humanity would be eventually united under a single cosmopolitan legal order, enforced by a supra-national organization endowed with a global monopoly of violence:

> The disunity of the modern world is a fact; but so, in a truer sense, is its unity. The essential and manifold solidarity, coupled with the necessity of securing the rule of law and the elimination of war, constitutes a harmony of interests. . . . The ultimate harmony of interests that, within the State, finds expression in the elimination of private violence is not a misleading invention of nineteenth century liberalism.
>
> (1941: 26)

In Lauterpacht's vision, the future supra-national Federation of the World would determine fundamental laws and norms for the whole of humanity, which states would be obliged to implement. Conflicts would be settled by international judges and decisions enforced by a global police under their orders. This global police would act only for the benefit of humanity and in order to suppress pirates and enemies of mankind. In short, as argued by Matti Koskenniemi, 'Lauterpacht's Utopia is a world ruled by lawyers' (1997: 256).

In the years leading to the Second World War, and even more clearly in the second half of the twentieth century, Carl Schmitt offered a radically divergent, apocalyptic interpretation of global integration (Schmitt 2003; Galli 1996). His views cannot be clearly separated from the personal, lived experience of the effects of international criminal law during the Nuremberg Trials. Just like Lauterpacht, Carl Schmitt participated directly in the military tribunals instituted by the Allies for the prosecution of prominent members of Nazi Germany. But while Lauterpacht sat amidst the prosecutors, Schmitt was a suspected criminal before international law. He was therefore infinitely more inclined to observe the more disquieting elements of the global order that emerged after the war. In *Ex Captivitate Salus* (1950), the series of diaries written while he was held in custody awaiting his judgment 'in the desolate vastness of a narrow cell' (ibid: 4), he admits experiencing the end of classical international law as a suspected pirate in the hands of victorious captors. In these desperate diaries, Schmitt finds himself accused of crimes against humanity: a contemporary *hostis humani generis* waiting for execution, in a legal limbo suspended between war and peace. In his writings, thus, the pirate ship emerges as a 'situation-symbol' of the legal limbo in which the enemy of humanity is abandoned, removed from the protection of the state of which he is part (1999: 129). 'I am the last, conscious representative of the jus publicum Europaeum, its last teacher and researcher in an existential sense, and I experience its end just as Benito Cereno experienced his capture on the pirate ship' (1950: 4).

Significantly, this is the same Carl Schmitt who only a few years before – in the infamous lecture *Volksgruppen: nicht Minderheitenrecht* held in Flensburg in April

1938 – had pointed out that, following denationalization the 'Jew as citizen of the world' (*Jude als Weltburger*) was effectively in the same positions as 'the pirate, who does not have the protection of any state and who is not authorized by any state' (quoted in Bojanic 2011: 213).[2] According to Schmitt, the genocide of the Jewish people in the Nazi camps was therefore performed in the same legal limbo normally utilized for the persecution of pirates: all Jews were conceived as rightless outlaws who were literally abandoned in a feral space outside the law. And yet, as in a Dantesque *contrappasso*, the figure of the pirate as a denationalized individual, stripped of all legal protections, returned to haunt those who had evoked it in order to create the preconditions for the horror of the Nazi camps. After the end of the Second World War, the legal limbo evoked by the figure of the pirate was not faced as a dramatic problem, but instead became a useful instrument for the continuous policing of humanity and the punishment of individuals and groups considered dangerous to mankind.

In *The Nomos of the Earth* (2003), Schmitt's most important contribution to a theory of international law, he confirms his diffidence toward the idea of a 'world state' that would absorb the multiplicity of modern independent polities, erect itself as protector of the whole of mankind and institute a global police as an alternative to war. In Schmitt's view, the institution of a supra-national organization such as the United Nations eliminates international war only to make way for the advent of an even more terrible 'global civil war' (ibid: 296). The end of classic interstate war, according to Schmitt, will lead not to a state of perpetual peace but only to a radicalization of violence at the global level. In the new world inaugurated by the erection of the United Nations, humanity will be exposed to a permanent state of emergency suspended between war and peace.[3] In other words, Lauterpacht's supra-national federation will be permanently traversed by intestine conflicts, which will resemble the *persecutio piratarum* that thousands of years before traversed the enclosed totality of the Roman Empire.

According to Schmitt, the hegemonic powers will pretend to act as global policemen, using their superior military violence in the name of humanity in order to suppress 'outlaw pirates' and 'disturbers of the peace' (2003: 44; 309–311). Paradoxically, the policing of a contested peace may become even more murderous and violent than classic interstate war. In fact, 'given that war has been transformed into a police action against troublemakers, criminals, and pests, justification of the methods of this "police bombing" must be intensified. Thus, one is compelled to push the discrimination of the opponent into the abyss' (2003: 321). The violence

2 This is a comment that echoes Hannah Arendt's reflections on the infinite vulnerability of 'refugees outlawed and expelled from all countries' (1943: 77; but see also Policante 2012c).

3 As Hans Kelsen has noticed, from the Charter of the United Nations that finally introduces 'a system of international security characterized by a high degree of centralization', the idea and even the term 'war' has completely disappeared, systematically substituted by the phrase 'use of armed force' (2008: 26–40).

haunting the future world order will not be a limited war likely to end with some definitive treaty of peace, but rather a 'permanent civil war' opposing a global police force, determined to impose its control over the entire planet, against those accused of endangering the unity of mankind: new pirates and *hostes humani generis*. The emergence of a cosmopolitan society is therefore strictly correlated with the imposition of a permanent state of emergency; humanity must be perpetually defended from threats that are always exceptional perturbations in an otherwise immobile peace. In the introduction to a new collection of his early writings published for the first time in the early 1970s, Schmitt would thus conclude: 'Today humanity is conceived as a unitary society, substantially already pacified; . . . thus, in place of a world politics, what today may emerge is a world police' (1971: 25).

In the last chapter, I turn to the new forms of global violence that have emerged in the years since the end of the Second World War. I focus in particular on the terrible chain of conflicts that has characterized the first two decades after the collapse of the Soviet Union and the end of the Cold War, when dreams and fears of global integration have returned once more to the centre of international politics. I thus consider the ways in which the opposed and symmetrical prophecies launched by Carl Schmitt and Hersch Lauterpacht have been able to envisage many of the conundrums of today's world, in all its enthralling ambiguity. In order to perform this daunting task, I consign myself once more to the figure of the pirate, who I trust to guide me in the *perpetuum mobile* of late capitalist 'liquid modernity' (Bauman 2000). Following this thread, I discuss the many ways in which the spectre of the pirate continues to daunt international law, projecting itself over ever-changing subjects, taking newfangled clothes and names, disguising itself in different forms. Looking at the origins of contemporary figures such as the 'criminal against humanity', the 'terrorist', the 'illegal combatant', the 'failed state' and the 'rogue state', I consider to what extent they have been constructed on the base of more established concepts such as the 'pirate' and the 'pirate state'. I find the pirate sitting centre-stage in all the non-wars fought in humanity's name, and I ask myself what the image of humanity is that guides those who assume the task of killing in the name of mankind and its preservation. I therefore look at the way in which the contemporary *persecutio piratarum*, in its different manifestations, legitimizes the expansion of ever more lethal military technologies and ever more stringent forms of global policing.

Chapter 7

Terrorists and pirates

Global police and *humanitas afflicta*

The following pages are dedicated to an analysis of the ways in which the figure of the pirate continues to haunt our present. In the first part, I reflect on the juridical transformations that, after the conclusion of the Second World War, have affected the traditional state-centric configuration of the international order. In particular, I focus on the ways in which, in the last 20 years, economic globalization has been supplemented by an accelerating institutional integration, which points toward new global juridical structures. Flirting with Hegel, we may say that the oceanic spaces of the world-market are today a source of juridical paradigms that tend to project a single supra-national figure of political power. As we have seen, it is in the borderless commons of the world that Universal jurisdiction moved its first modern steps as a necessary support for growing international trade. Similarly today, new cosmopolitan juridical figures attend the globalization of productive networks and sustain an ever more all-embracing market. Following Hardt and Negri, it may be maintained that, 'in postmodernity the notion of right should be understood again in terms of Empire' (2000: 12).

The central role that the concept of the pirate as *hostis humani generis* – whose genealogy I traced back to Rome's Imperial law – has assumed in the last 20 years is the most powerful symptom of these tendencies. It is precisely by taking upon itself the burden of fighting those who were represented as 'common enemies of all human communities' that Rome claimed an Imperial role throughout the ancient world. Only by depicting Imperial violence not as war, but as the persecution of outlaw groups (*persecutio piratarum*), could the Roman Emperor be presented as a global peace-enforcer (*pacator orbis*). Similarly today, war has disappeared only to make space for global police actions against terrorist networks, criminal mafias, rogue states and pirate outlaws.

In the second part, I thus consider the essential role played by the figure of the pirate in the rhetorical and juridical construction of new 'enemies of the human race'. Both 'criminals against humanity' and 'global terrorists' have been recently construed as *hostis humani generis*, relying on a systematic analogy with classical pirates (Kontorovich 2004; Greene 2008). In order to protect humanity from their threatening presence, new practices of global security and global policing have been introduced and fundamental norms of international law have been suspended, while 'humanitarian bombings', 'surgical strikes' and 'targeted killings' have been legitimized as exceptional but necessary forms of violence. Meanwhile, post-colonial states accused of harbouring or supporting 'terrorists' have been branded as 'rogue'. Like the Barbary 'pirate states' of the nineteenth century, they have been stripped of their sovereign right and exposed to punitive bombings, military occupations and civilizing reconstructions. In this section, I briefly follow some of the key historical moments in the genealogy of the contemporary concept of 'the terrorist' from the early twentieth century until today, focusing in particular on the discourses surrounding the persecution of 'anarchist terrorism', 'Palestinian terrorism' and 'Islamic terrorism'.

In the last part, I look at the ways in which maritime piracy has been recently constructed as a global security threat, in response to which a transnational system of security seems to be emerging. An unprecedented military coalition, which cuts across traditional geopolitical rivalries, has been given a single common purpose and a single common enemy by the perceived pirate threat to global commercial circulation; moreover, new transnational institutions are constructed in an attempt to limit threats to global market exchange. As opposed to the 'War on Terror', the current global mobilization against pirates seems to be politically uncontroversial. Until today, we have not seen mass mobilizations against either the 'targeted killings' of suspected pirates caught in action nor against the innocent victims always shadowing military operations, and which usually come under the name of 'collateral damage'. The indifference toward these deaths has not been the result of insufficient mass media coverage of the events; instead, it is revealing of the hegemonic function of classic historical narratives and the extent to which violence is banalized as an effective tool of global policing. The pirate, thus, continues to be the figure that most perfectly embodies the idea of an apolitical pest, whose killing is offered to humanity as a simple, neutral, righteous and legally sound form of global policing.

Globalization and the 'humanitarian exception': The return of Empire?

In the summer of 1944, the Second World War was about to end, leaving behind millions of victims caught in the midst of an endless escalation of violence that reached its apex in the horror of the Nazi camps – where 6 million stateless Jews were exterminated as 'pirates, who do not have the protection of any state and who are not authorized by any state' (Schmitt 1938, as cited in Bojanic 2011: 213). In preparation for the end of the hostilities, the representatives of the United States, Great Britain, China and the Soviet Union convened in Dumbarton Oaks in order to draw the outline of the new world order emerging from the war. On 26 June 1945, the Charter of the United Nations was introduced as the fundamental backbone of a global order that was meant to guarantee a new international stability and the banishment of war (Fassbender 2009: 1–12). The entire structure of the United Nations was conceived with the fundamental aim of centralizing the legitimate use of force in the hands of the new international organization, and away from the individual sovereign states that compose the international community (Kunz 1951: 529–534). Classic international war, thus, was openly proscribed already in the opening words of the Charter, in which it is defined as a 'scourge'.

Nevertheless, the definitive banishment of war was not meant to be equivalent with the abolition of military forces, the elimination of all means of mass destruction and the declaration that all violence is ultimately illegitimate and unjustifiable. At the opposite, the fact that violence can be deployed legitimately was confirmed, although this privilege was transferred from the hands of the sovereign states to those of the United Nations. The Charter establishes a 'regime of international peace and security' in which 'armed force shall not be used, *save in the common interest*' (United Nations 1945). Article 39 of the Charter, in fact, empowers the Security Council of the United Nations – effectively controlled by the five powers that had won what was supposed to be the last war of humanity – with the legal authority to punish violations of international law that engender the stability of the international order (ibidem). In order to clad this legal authority with the iron gloves necessary to enforce it, the United Nations needed to concentrate in its hands an overwhelming violence capable of breaking any hope of resistance in those condemned for grave violations of international law.[1] It was necessary, in other words, to transform the means of war accumulated by the major powers in a *global police force* that would enforce the decisions of the new international authority. To this end, Article 47 of the United Nations' Charter decreed the institution of a permanent army directly under the control of the Security Council, and directed by the military Chiefs of Staff of the five major powers. This was meant to be a global police power endowed with absolute military supremacy, and capable of annihilating any form of unauthorized resistance to the decisions imposed by the Security Council (Houck 1993: 1–70).

In the following years, nevertheless, Article 47 was never implemented and remained dormant, although it was never formally abolished. The increased animosity between the United States and the Soviet Union, in fact, prevented any such centralization of power. The absence of a global police force under the direct orders of the United Nations has thus legitimated the outsourcing of policing functions to different groups of states, which are authorized to deploy their sovereign violence – the power to kill or let live – not in the classic institutional forms dictated by the concept of symmetrical warfare but in police operations meant to 'maintain or restore international peace and security' (United Nations

1 As noted by Koskenniemi: 'For a sanction to be effective, it must be able to break the resistance of its target. For national criminal law, that was normally no problem and if it is, then revolution was at hand. Internationally, the presence of overwhelming public force was an exception, however, and in the normal situation different interpretations confronted each other with some amount of force on each side' (2001: 458).

1945). Luigi Condorelli has ironically pointed out that in the first 67 years of its activity, the United Nations has relied on its power to distribute global letters of marque, such as the ones that European states used to distribute to their privateers until the late nineteenth century (quoted in Zolo 2002: 90). Just as in the sixteenth century, when private entrepreneurs such as Francis Drake could legitimize their violence thanks to the explicit authorization of their sovereign, today a number of states have legitimized their violence thanks to the authorization of the United Nations. Just as sovereign powers could convert illegal acts of piracy into legitimate acts of privateering through their concession of special authorizations, equally today the United Nations has the power to convert illegal wars of aggression into legitimate operations of global policing. This happened for the first time in the 1950s when the USA intervened in the Korean Civil War, flying the flag of the United Nations. After the end of the Cold War, UN-authorized interventions dramatically multiplied, with actions taking place in Iraq, Somalia, Haiti, Yugoslavia and Kosovo (Zolo 2009). In every single instance, the United Nations has legitimized the use of military violence by member states, including the use of semi-nuclear weapons of mass destruction and the killing of hundreds of thousands of unarmed civilians.[2]

Nevertheless, it would be incorrect to portray any of these events in terms of classic warfare. Today, UN-authorized interventions are not dramatic ruptures in the global social order but an integral part of it: they 'maintain or restore international peace and security' (United Nations 1945). In the new international order prefigured by the United Nations Charter, in fact, there is no space left for the traditional concept of war as an armed struggle between equal states (Beck 2005: 1–7). War is simply unthinkable, since it is impossible for any human group to exercise violence without entering into some relation with the global order. At a formal level, either violence is unauthorized by the United Nations and it can then only be a crime against its order, or it is authorized by it and thus it is part of a collective form of law enforcement for the preservation of that same order. If, according to Hugo Grotius, the essential principle of the classic international order was *inter pacem et bellum nihil medium* (between war and peace there is no middle condition), here we should rather say *inter praedones et lictores nihil medium* (between outlaws and police enforcers there is no middle condition). The notion of war is replaced by the binary concepts of law-breaking and law-enforcing violence, while the ambiguous figure of the warrior is forced to disappear from the world stage. In his place, once again, are evoked more characterized,

2 For instance, Operation Desert Storm – the first global police operation of the 1990s, waged by a UN-authorized, US-led coalition force from 34 nations, in response to Iraq's illegal war against Kuwait – has caused the death of over 200,000 Iraqis and 500 members of the UN expedition force (Adams 1991; Clark 1992: 59–84). In the 42 days of action the coalition used a quantity of explosives superior to the one used by the Allies in the entire Second World War, including several semi-nuclear bombs i.e. fuel-air explosives (Zolo 1997: 68; Clark: 38–84).

unambiguous figures such as pirates and peace-enforcers, terrorist outlaws and global policemen.

The metamorphosis of war is only confirmed by the vanishing of the traditional concepts of neutrality (Franck and Patel 1991). In fact, if it was once possible to maintain one's impartiality between two warriors – and continue to live, labour and think untainted by their mutual hatred – today this freedom is on the point of disappearing. Confronted by the total clash between global policemen and global outlaws, a detached indifference or a stance of compassionate understanding for both parts is a precarious position to take. In a veritable re-edition of the *interdiction acquae et ignis*, by which the Roman Empire prohibited excessively kind-hearted people from providing water and fire to those banished from its order, Article 2(5) of the United Nations commands us to 'refrain from giving assistance to any State against which the United Nations is taking preventive or enforcement action' (United Nations 1945). To avoid ambiguities, during the drafting session of the UN Charter, France suggested including in the text that membership in the organization is 'incompatible with the status of neutrality' (Werner 2004: 159). In the context of the 1991 bombings of Iraq, the president of Austria similarly affirmed the doctrine by which 'when the members of the United Nations act against an aggressor, there can be no question of neutrality, only of solidarity' (Lahodynsky 1992: 24). What Junger prophetically identified as the central characteristic of Total War – that is, the willing or unwilling involvement of the whole German nation in the mechanism of war – is therefore cast at the global level as the whole of humanity is summoned to participate directly or indirectly in the suppression of the outlaws. As the chief rapporteur to the Drafting Committee of the United Nations Charter once observed, the new organization 'renders sacred the obligation of all states to participate in its [military] operations' (Lepard 2003: 258).

During the Cold War years, the capacity of the United Nations to act as the central institution of an emerging global order was seriously undermined. And yet it is unquestionable that 'the notion of right defined by the UN Charter also points toward a new positive source of juridical production, effective on a global scale – a new centre of normative production that can play a sovereign juridical role' (Hardt and Negri 2000). The many ways in which the transition from the classic international state order towards the global police order promised by the Charter is far from being completed are obvious and there is no need to describe them in detail (Callinicos 2007). And yet, despite its many shortcomings and limitations, the United Nations, as pointed out recently by Thomas Franck and Faiza Patel:

> is the most ambitious organic entity ever created by states. Its central purpose is to replace the outmoded, dangerous national self-reliance on unilateral force with a workable global police system, capable of . . . responding quickly with levels of force appropriate to a specific circumstance of lawlessness.
> (1991: 73)

At the end of a devastating war, the constitution of the United Nations represented the most decisive attempt to include the entire world under a single juridical order. Without the slightest ambiguity, the supra-national institution was erected as an alternative to the form of interstate order that had dominated European modernity. It was at once pre-modern and post-modern in its form. In its Universal, boundless aspiration, it resuscitated the dream of a Universal Empire capable of embracing the whole of humanity under a single law and a single sword, which had animated the writings of European jurists, philosophers and poets up until the eighteenth century. Yet it also responded to powerful material processes that tend to integrate the entire world into a single commercial system ceaselessly engendering contracts (that must be guaranteed) and conflicts (that must be resolved). In the last 20 years, these powerful tendencies toward the constitutionalization of a supranational power that were first inscribed into the United Nations' Charter, and then partially held back during the Cold War years, have emerged once again in all of their revolutionary potential.

As we have seen throughout the last chapters, after each major conflict of the last two centuries the victorious powers have always tried to establish a cosmopolitan peace that would police the established order. The Holy Alliance, the League of Nations and the United Nations all emerged with this same explicit aim. After the conclusion of the Cold War, it was the United States that declared the emergence of a 'new world order' – a novel global configuration of power in which, in the words of George H.W. Bush, 'the United Nations, freed from cold war stalemate, is poised to fulfill the historic vision of its founders' (Kerton-Johnson 2010: 32). At the centre of this emerging order the notion of *global security* has gradually emerged, elaborated in documents such as the 1992 *National Security Strategy of the United States* (Intriligator and Coulomb 2008).

At the heart of this concept operates the idea that growing interdependence – and the accelerating speed with which merchandise and information, but also violence and factors of crisis, travel around the world – requires new forms of *global policing*. Disorder and lawlessness can no longer be tolerated, even when they are localized in a particular state, or in stateless areas like the oceans of the world. The Western 'way of life', in fact – especially in the major Western metropolitan conglomerates – is dependent on systems of production and consumption that are increasingly global.

> The economic systems of the major Industrial nations have become more vulnerable. They depend on the free and regular access to energy sources and raw materials located throughout the world, on free and secure maritime and aerial commercial lanes, on the stability of international markets and global financial hubs.
>
> (Zolo 1997: 43)

As Tony Blair clearly put it, in his speech 'Doctrine of the International Community', which was symptomatically delivered during the bombing of Serbia in April 1999:

> We are all internationalists now, whether we like it or not. We cannot refuse to participate in global markets if we want to prosper. . . . We cannot turn our backs on conflicts and the violation of human rights within other countries if we want still to be secure.
>
> (Fairclough 2005: 54)

In the last 20 years, in other words, there has been a growing demand for the creation of apparatuses of security and control that would be immediately operative at the global level, by-passing traditional national borders. The necessity to enlarge traditional concepts of national defence has been based on an increasingly hegemonic narrative, which assumes that accelerating processes of commercial exchange, human circulation and inter-cultural communication have been eroding the power of traditional barriers, so that it becomes impossible to isolate the state from outside flows (Brand 2005). In order to open the state to the world-market, all sorts of human and commercial circulation must be allowed to traverse state borders (Foucault 2009: 33–34). As Thomas Friedman, arguably the leading popular guru of globalization in the United States, breathlessly put it: 'globalization involves the inexorable integration of markets, nation states and technologies to a degree never witnessed before' (1999: 7). The very concept of globalization projects a coming-into-being of 'the globe' as a new integrated system inhabited by a finally united human species. And yet this is presented, from the very beginning, as a human community that must be perpetually secured and defended (Policante 2010). While traditional statements of *national defence* justified military spending, and the necessity for organized violence, on the basis of the necessity to defend the enclosed order of the state from the rest of humanity, the contemporary concept of *global security* justifies the organization and deployment of violence on the basis of the necessity of defending humanity from multifarious, ever-present 'security threats' (Zolo 1997: 133; Hardt and Negri 2004: 18–25).

Partly as a consequence of such thinking, much effort has been made to develop a doctrine of 'sovereignty as responsibility', whereby state sovereignty becomes conditional upon respect for international law and fundamental human rights (Nolte 2005: 389–392). In case of violations, state sovereignty has been suspended by appeal to a 'humanitarian exception'. Military interventions in formal violation of international law, and without authorization from the UN, have been therefore legitimized on a number of occasions (Elden 2006). The humanitarian exception, in this sense, suspends the *jus cogens* norm of international law that protects sovereign nation-states from external military aggressions. Especially during the 1990s, a number of scholars have argued that a new customary law was emerging from the practice of states, which would legitimate the use of military violence in the name of human welfare (Orford 1999). International lawyers such as Antonio Cassese have asserted that, in response to 'egregious crimes against humanity', states can legitimately confer on themselves the role of global policemen, even without the authorization of the Security Council (1999a; 1999b: 799). Similarly, Michael Glennon has advocated the complete abandonment of traditional rights of sovereign immunity, in order to affirm an international law aimed at 'alienating the disorderly' in order to construct 'a more orderly world' (1999: 7), while Lee Feinstein and Anne Marie Slaughter (2004) have argued that lawful states should feel free to treat 'rogue states' in an unequal manner, since they have already sacrificed their rights through criminal behaviour. Similar arguments in support of unauthorized police actions have fuelled an endless stream of writings. Authors such as Fernando Tesón (1992; 1995; 2005), Geoffrey Robertson (2000), Thomas Weiss (1999), Thomas Franck (2001) and Michael Ignatieff (2002) have all, in different forms, supported the right of major powers to act outside traditional norms of international law in case of emergencies that threaten the welfare of humanity.

In most of these works, the affirmation of various 'humanitarian exceptions' somehow obscures the fundamental question of who is to determine when, in concrete terms, an emergency exists. What global authority is entitled to speak in name of humanity and thus determine the identity of the 'rogue states' that can be lawfully bombed, invaded and civilized? What global authority is entitled to point out who are the 'criminals against humanity' to be punished in the name of the species? These questions remain suspended in an ontological instability that cannot be resolved within the internal logic of international law. Ultimately the question posed by the category of *hostis humani generis* may only be answered through the exogenous intervention of a sovereign decision at the global level. In fact, as we have seen, the suspension of standard norms of international law regulating sovereign jurisdiction – which was introduced in order to allow the major European power to persecute pirates all over the world, regardless of their nationality – has been interpreted and used in radically different ways, by different powers, in different historical and geographical contexts. Throughout the centuries different Imperial powers have claimed the authority to determine who might be labelled a pirate, and thus an 'enemy of humanity'. In fact, the concept of the pirate as *hostis humani generis* has always maintained a fundamental ambiguity: what are the limits of the human community? What characteristics or practices bond it together in a single group? And what is inimical to this grouping? Who is, in concrete terms, the 'common enemy'? Who is to decide this? These essential questions have been posed time after time throughout modernity by the figure of the pirate; today they are posed, in an even more dramatic form, by the current affirmation of a 'humanitarian exception' that would allow the use of devastating violence in the name of humanity.

It seems today that international law is more and more taking the form of an Imperial constitution (Hardt and Negri 2000). The discourse surrounding contemporary humanitarian interventions affirms the existence of a single global legal order, which is meant to regulate human coexistence throughout the world. The affirmation of global norms, nevertheless, implies also the appearance of global outlaws who systematically violate them. If the idea of a 'humanitarian exception', which systematically justifies the suspension of traditional norms of sovereign immunity triumphs as a general view in international law, then there will be no doubt about the fact that we have entered a new historical phase. During the NATO intervention in Kosovo, Jürgen Habermas described the bombing of Belgrade as a 'pure anticipation of a future cosmopolitan state that it also seeks to promote' (2000: 61). Similarly, Ulrich Beck has argued that traditional international law is in the course of being supplanted by 'a global domestic policy', which involves 'a new kind of postnational politics of military humanism' based on 'the use of transnational military power with the aim of enforcing the observance of human rights' (1999: 985–987).

What remains to be determined is where global sovereignty resides today – in other words, who has the authority to interpret international law and decide on the 'humanitarian exception'. Who can convincingly and legitimately invoke the right to use violence in order to protect humanity? A multiplicity of actors have recently justified violence in humanitarian terms, including: the United Nations, the NATO coalition, the United States and a plethora of other sovereign states, but also individuals such as Ted Kaczynski, who considers humanity to be threatened by the rise of an integrated technological system destined to become a space of total control (2005). Convinced of his vision, this professor of mathematics concluded that the necessity to save humanity from 'technological slavery' justified the use of violence against those supporting its tyrannical dominion. Between 1978 and 1995, Kaczynski engaged in a bombing campaign against modern technology, planting or mailing numerous home-made bombs, killing three people and injuring 23 others (Waits and Shors 1999: 1–12). An essay in *The New Yorker* by Cynthia Ozick described Ted Kacynzski as America's 'own Raskolnikov – the appealing, appalling, and disturbingly visionary murderer of *Crime and Punishment* – . . . a philosophical criminal of exceptional intelligence and humanitarian purpose, who is driven to commit murder out of an uncompromising idealism' (1997: 114).

This extreme story illuminates many of the dangers implicit in every discourse that evokes humanity as an endangered global population which must be protected. First of all, it is clear that those who claim to act in defence of humanity can justify the most terrible violence in its name: in the humanitarian mind, the choice is between murder and passive acceptance of even more terrible catastrophes. As a supporter of NATO bombings of Serbia and Kosovo, which involved the killing of over 5,000 people, puts it, 'the choice is between using force for the greater good or inaction . . . the morality of humanitarian intervention is in many ways unquestionable' (Merriam 2001: 125). Secondarily, it becomes clear the extent in which humanity is nothing but an empty signifier, which must be endlessly filled by shifting 'mythical structures of signification' (Barthes 1973: 115–143; Policante 2011a: 465–471). In short, we must recollect that 'with every significant concept the important thing is, who interprets, defines and uses it; who, through a concrete decision, decides what is to count as peace and disarmament; who decides what intervention, public peace and security is' (Schmitt 1929: 112). Who is entitled to determine what threatens humanity and how to protect it? If anyone (or at least any sovereign state) is entitled, then we are exposed to a global civil war in which opponents will fight one another in the name of their particular conception of what humanity needs. Otherwise, humanitarian discourses hide the fundamental fact that only the major Western powers are entitled to speak in the name of humanity, while the post-colonial world is left to play the role of either the victim to be saved or the monster to be destroyed.

Since the days of the Roman Empire, the claim to serve humanity, extirpating those who threaten its welfare, has played a fundamental role in Imperial rhetoric. Stable Imperial orders left little ambiguity about who possessed the authority to name and fight the *hostes humani generis*. In the Roman Empire, it was the Emperor and no one else who possessed the authority of *pacator orbis*. He was the 'global peace-enforcer', entrusted with the authority to determine when the Imperial peace had been broken, and by whom. He was the one empowered to persecute pirates in the name of all communities and enforce the *ius gentium*. Centuries later, the *res publica Christiana* recognized a similar authority to the Holy Roman Emperor, who was meant to protect the House of Christianity from heretics and enemies of the faith. The unity of the Christian Commonwealth was assured by the influence of papal authority, which guaranteed that a particular claim to *imperium* would be recognized by all Christian crowns. Thus, when the papal authority was openly challenged by the 'Protestant corsairs' of the sixteenth century, the whole Imperial order rapidly collapsed.

This is why Carl Schmitt described the pirate as 'a Universal and core concept of enmity' (2003: 65). Looking at the history of antiquity, the German philosopher correctly stressed how in Imperial times the concept of pirate as 'common enemy of the human race', 'not only obtained its meaning from, but affirmed the existence of the concrete order of the international law of an Empire' (ibidem). We must add, nevertheless, that in periods of transition, the concept of piracy inevitably loses its relation with the historical reality of a comprehensive spatial order; a struggle to define who is 'the common enemy' may then emerge, opposing alternative hegemonic forces. Today, the questions surrounding the pirate as *hostis humani generis* continue to represent the international correlative of the decision on the state of exception and, as such, might reveal a dynamic struggle for hegemony, or the crystallization of a stable Imperial order. If there is a tendency toward the formation of an Empire – that is, a single juridical order that strives to impose its validity throughout the world – certainly this is still an Empire that has no Emperor. There is no global sovereign figure that has been able to impose over all people its authority to speak and fight in the name of humanity.

During the transition from a Republican to an Imperial constitution, Rome increasingly presented itself as an Imperial power imposing respect for a sacred peace (the Pax Romana) and a Universal law (the *ius gentium*), a force imposing the *ius gentium* against disqualified communities of pirates (Domingo 2010: 3–11). The Empire appeared simultaneously as a cosmopolitan power whose might was at the service of a crystallized peace, as an enforcer of international law and as a steward of the Mediterranean commons. Its violence, since it was deployed against groups portrayed as pirates and 'enemies of all', was elevated as a service performed in the name of all mankind.

Today, similarly, humanitarian interventions have been presented as operations aimed at protecting humanity from monstrous enemies of the human race. Countless interventions, bombings and deaths have been justified as necessary in order to annihilate ubiquitous 'criminals against humanity' and 'terrorists'. After 2001, in particular, the figure of the 'terrorist' rapidly became ubiquitous in a number of interrelated discourses throughout the world. After the suicidal attacks on the World Trade Center, the United States' declaration of a global 'War on Terror' has justified extraordinary security measures including: military attacks against 'rogue states', 'surgical bombings', 'targeted killings', 'extraordinary renditions' and torture, as well as the limitation of free speech and other civil liberties. In less than a decade, the figure of the terrorist has acquired an unprecedented, world-historical significance. It is to an investigation of this fundamental concept, and the ways in which its genealogy intertwines with the classic concept of the pirate as enemy of the human race, that I shall now turn.

The War on Terror: A contemporary *persecutio piratarum*?

As we have already seen, the origins of Universal jurisdiction must be found in the particular spatiality of the world oceans. In this space, removed from the sovereignty of any single state, Universal jurisdiction was a legal instrument that allowed European states to persecute piracy worldwide, irrespective of the nationality of the individuals accused. It was an institution that became particularly prominent in the eighteenth century, when the expansion of international commerce demanded a firm legal ground for the global protection of private property. As Friedrich Hegel (1993), Michel Foucault (2008), Gilles Deleuze and Félix Guattari (2004) have argued (although in very different ways), the oceans of the world were the first area of the world that was thought of as a worldwide space of free circulation organized according to a number of legal principles, which were necessary for the enforcement of contracts, for the defence of property and, in general, for the correct functioning of market institutions. In relation to the suppression of piracy, 'we can say that there was a juridification of the world, which should be thought of in terms of the organization of a market' (Foucault 2008: 176). Universal jurisdiction was born as an institution complementary to the Westphalian order of states, and meant to organize the maritime side of the *jus publicum europaeum* (Schmitt 2003: 179).

For hundreds of years, thus, Universal jurisdiction only applied to the crime of piracy. In *An Introduction to International Law*, Mark W. Janis affirms: 'the Universal principle is perhaps best illustrated by the jurisdiction that every state has over pirates' (Janis 2003: 82); *The Princeton Principles on Universal Jurisdiction* describe piracy as 'a crime that paradigmatically is subject to prosecution by any nation based on principles of universality, and it is crucial to the origins of universal jurisdiction' (Macedo and Robinson 2001: 45). Louis Sohn, in the introduction to

Benjamin Ferencz's *An International Criminal Court: A Step Toward World Peace*, reiterates:

> The first breakthrough towards an international system for punishing global crimes occurred when international law accepted the concept that pirates are 'enemies of mankind'. Once this concept of an international crime was developed in one area it was soon applied by analogy to other fields.
>
> (1980: 11)

According to the *Princeton Principles on Universal Jurisdiction*, which is a sort of restatement of current debate on the right to humanitarian intervention: 'The notion of "enemy of humanity" first constructed in relation to the crime of piracy is crucial to the origins of Universal jurisdiction' (Macedo and Robinson 2001: 15).

In the nineteenth century, when piracy was no longer a serious threat to the world-market and the juridical order sustaining it, the figure of the pirate maintained a historical significance in the 'savage wars of peace' that traversed the colonial world. Since it evoked a form of asymmetry that allowed European powers to portray their violence as a service offered to humanity, while it disqualified the armed resistance of native communities and groups, the figure of the pirate remained at the centre of a number of European discourses that legitimized imperialism and colonization. Moreover, the spectre of piracy continued to serve a role whenever European powers needed to expose to Universal jurisdiction individuals who would have been otherwise difficult to prosecute. England, for instance, utilized the exception opened in international law by the figure of the pirate in order to gain jurisdiction over slave-traders from all countries. This served the cause of suppressing the slave trade in a rapid and effective campaign. Nevertheless, it also legitimized the English claim to act as a global maritime police, further entrenching its hegemonic position in the oceans of the world (Grewe 2000: 554–558).

In the twentieth century, the spectre of the pirate was repeatedly evoked in the context of a sustained campaign for the coordinated suppression of the international anarchist movement. It is in this context that the contemporary figure of the terrorist, as an absolute foe against whom extraordinary measures are both necessary and justified, began to emerge. Between 1881 and 1914, individuals and groups associated with anarchist ideals were responsible for the assassination of numerous monarchs and heads of state throughout the world. In 1878: in Germany, Max Hödel attempts to assassinate Kaiser Wilhelm I; in Italy, Giovanni Passannante tries to kill King Umberto I; while in Russia Sergey Stepnyak-Kravchinsky stabs to death General Nikolai Mezentsov, head of the Tsar's secret police. In 1879: Alexander Soloviev attempts to assassinate Tsar Alexander II of Russia, while Grigori Goldenberg assassinates Prince Dmitri Kropotkin, the Governor of Kharkov in the Russian Empire. In 1881: Tsar Alexander II of Russia is killed in a bomb blast by Narodnaya Volya, an anarchist group with its base in

Switzerland. In 1882: Alexander Berkman tries to kill the American industrialist Henry Clay Frick, publicly in retaliation for the seven steelworkers killed during the violent suppression of the Homestead Strike. In 1893: Auguste Vaillant throws a nail bomb in the French National Assembly, causing disruptions but no deaths. In 1894: Sante Geronimo Caserio stabs to death Sadi Carnot, the President of France. In 1897: Michele Angiolillo kills Spanish Prime Minister Antonio Cánovas del Castillo. In 1900: Gaetano Bresci shoots the Italian King Umberto I dead, seeking revenge for the Bava-Beccaris massacre in Milan. In 1901: Leon Czolgosz shoots US President William McKinley at the Pan-American Exposition in Buffalo, New York. On 14 September of the same year, McKinley dies in hospital and Czolgosz is executed by electric chair (Suskind 1971: 14–48).

It is at this point that Theodore Roosevelt, suddenly elevated to the Presidency, called for an international crusade for the eradication of the anarchist movement. In the previous years, the threat that anarchist violence posed to sovereigns, monarchs and the ruling classes of all nations had pushed a number of governments to cooperate against the common enemy (Jensen 2001). Cooperative efforts to share law enforcement information and establish stricter controls on transnational anarchist groups were put in place late in the nineteenth century. In his first message to Congress, Roosevelt advanced the proposal to declare anarchism a crime against the law of nations and the anarchist an 'enemy of the human race' against whom all governments would be justified to exercise Universal jurisdiction:

> Anarchy is a crime against the whole human race; and all mankind should band against the anarchist. His crime should be made an offense against the law of nations, like piracy and that form of man-stealing known as the slave trade; for it is of far blacker infamy than either. It should be so declared by treaties among all civilized powers. Such treaties would give the Federal Government the power of dealing with the crime.
>
> (Roosevelt 1901: 7)

The international anarchist movement was to be considered, just as the pirate networks that haunted the Atlantic of the eighteenth century, as a danger posed to all organized states. They were denationalized groups, hostile to all nations. Roosevelt, therefore, called for the introduction of extraordinary measures for the suppression of terrorism: freedom of the press should have been limited and special legislation should have guaranteed the infliction of punishments 'proportioned to the enormity of the offense against our institutions' (ibidem). Moreover, at least according to the President, the anarchist creed of McKinley's assassin would have justified the criminalization of the whole anarchist movement. In fact, the intrinsic criminality of anarchist doctrines meant that 'no man or body of men preaching anarchist doctrines should be allowed at large', and that 'anarchist speeches, writings and meetings are essentially seditious and treasonable' (Roosevelt 1901: 6). Ultimately, no distinction could be made between the assassin and anarchist writers, speakers and thinkers throughout the world:

> For the anarchist himself, whether he preaches or practices his doctrines, we need not have one particle more concern than for any ordinary murderer. He is not the victim of social or political injustice. There are no wrongs to remedy in his case. The cause of his criminality is to be found in his own evil passions and in the evil conduct of those who urge him on.
>
> (ibidem)

All anarchists, thus, independently from their individual actions, ought to be condemned and, since no remedy could alleviate their evil, they had to be expelled from the healthy body of the nation. To avoid further metastasis, the United States Congress:

> should take into consideration the coming to this county of anarchists or persons professing principles hostile to all governments and justifying the murder of those placed in authority. Such individuals as those who not long ago gathered in open meeting to glorify the murder of King Humbert of Italy perpetrate a crime, and the law should ensure their rigorous punishment. They and those like them should be kept out of this country; and if found here they should be promptly deported to the country whence they came; and far-reaching provisions should be made for the punishment of those who stay.
>
> (ibidem)

Paradoxically, violence against the anarchists is justified since their beliefs are evil, and they are evil because they justify violence. In the following years, the persecution of anarchist groups in the USA escalated to the point that the Secretary of Commerce and Labour instructed the immigration officials 'to rid the country [through deportation] of alien anarchists' (Jensen 2001: 34). Finally, on 4 March 1908, the *New York Times* announced: 'The United States has declared open war on Anarchists' (ibidem).

Marcus Rediker has described the eighteenth-century clash between European maritime Empires and the multinational pirate crews that disrupted commerce throughout the Atlantic world as 'a tale of two terrors' (2004: 4). In his words, the public executions of pirates were theatrical representations of 'a clash of two different kinds of terror. One was practiced by rulers as they sought to eliminate piracy. . . . The other kind of Terror was practiced by common seamen like William Fly who sailed beneath the Jolly Roger' (2004: 5). Similarly, the electrocution of Leon Czolgosz was a theatrical representation – reproduced on film and screened in American cinemas – which symbolically embodied a clash of two terrors (Porton 1999: 16–17). On the one hand, there was the anarchist assassin who thought, arching back to a long tradition that may be traced back to Cicero, that tyrants were *hostes humani generis* from whom humanity must be defended at all costs.[3] On the other hand, there was Theodore Roosevelt, who thought, arching back to another long tradition that may be traced back to Cicero, that pirates and now anarchists were *hostes humani generis* from which humanity must be defended at all costs. This mode of thinking was so entrenched that, months after Roosevelt compared the suppression of anarchism to the persecution of pirates, Emma Goldman compared Czolgosz to Marcus Junius Brutus the slayer of tyrants (1901: 471–477). In both cases, the claim that the protection of humanity requires the extirpation of monsters in human form justifies an exceptional violence that escapes all controls.

The events surrounding the wave of anarchist violence, which at the beginning of the last century shook the world and unveiled the mechanisms of an escalating dialectics of terror, echo our contemporary predicament in many ways. Since the beginning of the new millennium, a spiral of violence has risen from the ashes of the World Trade Center. In reaction to this act of terror, the leaders of the American super-power immediately declared a 'global war on terror'. This is a global military, legal and ideological struggle, targeting both 'terrorist organizations' and the 'rogue states' accused of supporting them. It initiated with the invasion of Afghanistan in 2001, and it continued with the invasion of Iraq in 2003. It has involved the occupation of both countries for almost a decade, until today, as well as a series of military operations, surgical bombings, extraordinary renditions and targeted strikes throughout the world. This is no longer a war in the classical sense, a symmetrical interstate conflict governed by defined rules of engagement, with limited objectives and a clear temporal frame separating war from peace. Rather, the 'War on Terror' resembles the *persecutio piratarum* that traversed the Mediterranean world in the days of the Roman Imperial *pax*. It is a form of violence that cannot be contained in well-marked battlefields, but rather traverses the entire Imperial space. It is not a rupture in the international order that is likely to terminate with the establishment of a new order, but a form of police violence that is fully internalized to the global order.

3 As we have seen, Cicero argued that the tyrant, like the pirate, was a threat to the whole human community. Just as in the case of pirates, this meant that Roman power was justified to act throughout the world to liberate humanity from tyrants. Similarly, within the Christian Commonwealth the Emperor possessed the authority to fight and depose tyrants (Schmitt 2003: 65). With the fall of the Christian Empire, nevertheless, the question posed by the pirate category was equally posed by the category of the tyrant: *Qui judicabis?* Who can take upon himself the authority to identify and punish tyrants? This was a question that occupied political philosophers of the liberal and of the anarchist tradition for a long time (Jaszi and Lewis 1957). Theories of natural law in particular often justified tyrannicide as the execution of a higher law. Saint-Juste justified the execution of Louis XVI with reference to both natural law and the law of nations, which he argued had been the basis also for the execution of Charles I in England (Edelstein 2009: 147–148). Anarchists often arched back to the same tradition of natural law, which tended to project a Manichean worldview of good versus evil (Newman 2001: 47–50).

In November 2001, George W. Bush depicted the new scenario in a speech to the United Nations: 'Civilization itself, the civilization we share, is threatened. . . . The only alternative to victory is a nightmare world where every city is a potential killing field' (Shomura 2010: 53). This is, in other words, a violence that cannot be stopped by peace treaty but must be perpetually reiterated in order to maintain the very conditions on which peace and order exist. As Vice President of the United States, Dick Cheney explained in 2006: 'I don't think it's possible to negotiate any kind of settlement with terrorists. . . . I think you have to destroy them. It's the only way to deal with them' (Fattah 2006: 3). The 'War on Terror' can and must be a war of extermination, since the 'other' has nothing in common with us: there can be neither dialogue, nor common understanding. The limitless character of the 'war on terror' therefore reflects itself on the abstract, undecipherable figure of the 'terrorist'. In the US National Security strategy from September 2002, in fact, the construction of a terrifying figure of the 'terrorist' appears as the necessary precondition for an effective military campaign. The first step towards the realization of a perpetual 'humanitarian exception' is 'using the full influence of the United States, and working closely with allies and friends, to make clear that all acts of terrorism are illegitimate so that terrorism will be viewed in the same light as slavery, piracy or genocide; behaviour that no respectable government can condone or support and all must oppose' (Bush 2002: 4).

This form of political rhetoric – which denies any symmetry or common ground between 'us' and 'them'; which portrays 'humanity' not as a community traversed by conflict, but as a single front under attack; which banishes the other from civilization and the human race, and therefore evokes into being a total war from which no one can withdraw – is rooted in centuries of anti-pirate discourse. It is not surprising, then, if the contemporary figure of the 'terrorist' bears many of the characteristics, and serves many of the functions, that the 'pirate' had in a number of past Imperial formations. With its threatening, fleeting and ungraspable presence, the terrorist, like the pirate, legitimizes the Imperial sword as necessary for the preservation of peace and the protection of humanity. Moreover, a number of state lawyers and legal scholars have recently proposed placing terrorists in the same legal black hole that was first developed for pirates in the eighteenth century and, since then, has served as a dumping ground for countless people (Halberstam 1988; Detter 2007; Vlasic 2011). The spectre of piracy has been evoked in particular in the context of debates regarding the legitimacy of targeted killings, extraordinary renditions and tortures.

In fact, the War on Terror has not only embroiled countries like Afghanistan and Iraq, which were classified as contemporary 'pirate states' and thus stripped of their sovereign immunity, invaded, occupied, civilized and reconstructed. It has taken as its fields of operation the entire earth, without geographical barriers or limitations (Policante 2011b). Even countries that might appear at peace cannot be considered immune from the global logic of security and, in a number of them, the apparatuses of global policing have already suddenly appeared in order to kill. In Pakistan, for instance, peace did not prevent US drones from killing, according to data compiled by the New America Foundation, 'an estimated 3,225 people since 2004, of which 2,769 were reported to be militants' (Cockburn 2012: 12). The use of 'targeted killings' in countries officially at peace has escalated since 2009, offsetting hopes that the election of Barack Obama to the Presidency of the United States would be sufficient to end this practice (Krishnan 2009: 83). Quite to the contrary, in April 2011, John O. Brennan, the Assistant to the President for Homeland Security and Counterterrorism, publicly defended the American right to kill suspected terrorists wherever they are: 'the United States is in an armed conflict with al-Qa'ida, the Taliban, and associated forces . . . there is nothing in international law that prohibits us from using lethal force against our enemies outside of an active battlefield' (Chiesa and Greenawalt 2012: 1387). According to this view, the United States would be entitled to intervene throughout the world in order to kill anyone who has been classified as a 'terrorist'. A number of legal scholars have justified this view on the basis of the 'pirate precedent': if terrorists, like pirates, can be categorized as 'enemies of the human race', then 'targeted killing' would be nothing but an effective execution of Universal jurisdiction (Sinor and Blackwood 2005; Burgess 2005, 2008, 2010; Colangelo 2007; Detter 2007; Vlasic 2011; Hickman 2011).

The recent tendency to extend Universal jurisdiction to those labelled 'terrorists' is not completely unprecedented. In the last 20 years, the argument has had persistent appeal for countries such as the United States and Israel, who strive to open an avenue that would allow them to kill 'terrorists' based in other countries, and with whom they are not willing to begin an open war. In February 1978, for instance, the *Israel Law Review* published an article by Shalev Ginossar entitled 'Outlawing Terrorism'. The author argued that 'every terrorist is an enemy of mankind, *humani generis hostis*, and as such he must be treated. . . . The apprehension and suppression of its perpetrators is not only within the *power* of every State, but it becomes for them a *duty* they owe to the family of nations' (Ginossar 1978: 155–156). Moreover, he insisted that international law should consider as terrorists not only those responsible of acts of violence but all the people associated with a terrorist organization: 'their individual guilt is so enormous that the mere fact of belonging to a terrorist movement calls for the same penalty as that incurred by its leader' (ibid: 157).

In the last pages, the article assumes darker tones when the author considers that 'the enemies of humanity have succeeded in penetrating into what was meant to be the very citadel of civilization . . . we have even seen a terrorist organization being granted official status in the governing bodies of the United Nations, including the International Civil Aviation Organization itself!' (Ginossar 1978: 155). Although never named, the reader cannot but infer that the mysterious terrorist organization that has penetrated the citadel of civilization is nothing but the Palestine Liberation Organization, which was then recognized as the 'sole legitimate representative of the Palestinian people' by the United Nations and over 100 states with which it holds diplomatic relations (Brynen 1990). The conclusions of the article risk being truly terrorizing and genocidal: since the PLO is a terrorist organization and all those associated with it must be considered terrorists, and since terrorists are 'enemies of the human race', one is not too far from suggesting that all Palestinians are in fact *hostes humani generis* who can be persecuted wherever they are found. One month after the publication of this article, Israel invaded Lebanon with the declared intent of destroying Palestinian bases in that country (Norton and Schwedler 1993). The conflict resulted in the deaths of 20 Israeli and almost 2,000 Lebanese and Palestinians, most of them civilians. Between 100,000 and 250,000 people were forcefully displaced (Chomsky 1983: 192). Finally, Lebanese sovereignty was denied and transformed into a borderless ocean which the Israeli army could penetrate in order to enforce its right to persecute Palestinian 'terrorists'.

The line of reasoning first pioneered by Ginossar reappears today in the context of the global war on terror. In fact, after the humanitarian interventionism of the 1990s, the war against terrorism has become the new pivot around which international relations turn. And yet both of these global discourses appeal to this forgotten legal category of 'enemy of the human race' that finds its underpinning in the oceanic free space of circulation, and its genealogy in the ways in which piracy has been discussed and problematized since the beginning of Roman Imperial Law. In September 2001, the terrorist attack on New York's Twin Towers opened up a new global stage in which the piratical category was to become fundamental. Since the beginning of the global 'War on Terror', the spectre of the pirate as *hostis humani generis* has been evoked in order to justify the practice of 'targeted killings' of suspected terrorists throughout the world. Moreover, it has also served the aim of justifying the right to ignore the Geneva Convention in exceptional spaces like Guantanamo and Abu Ghraib. In 2004, for instance, the then Deputy Assistant Attorney General of the White House John Yoo, complaining against the protests of human rights activists, asked:

> Why is it so hard for people to understand that there is a category of behavior not covered by the legal system? What were pirates? They weren't fighting on behalf of any nation. . . . Historically, there were people so bad that they were not given protection of the laws. There were no specific provisions for their trial, or imprisonment. If you were an illegal combatant, you didn't deserve the protection of the laws of war.
>
> (quoted in Thorup 2009: 409)

And the following year Yoo contended that 'War has different rules for a nation and different rules for people who choose to fight kind of like pirates who are outside the control of a nation' (ibidem). On these bases, Yoo has argued for the exclusion of 'terrorists' – but also of soldiers serving states condemned as 'failed' or 'rogue' – from the protection of the Geneva Convention (Yoo and Delahunty 2002). Moreover, he has supported the right of the US President to order torture, meaning the infliction of suffering 'equivalent in intensity to the pain accompanying serious physical injury, such as organ failure, impairment of bodily function, or even death' (quoted in Annas 2005: 2128; Yarwood 2008).[4] Finally, in June 2012, after a CIA drone strike had killed 15 suspected terrorists in North Waziristan, Yoo publicly complimented Obama's choice and, in the *Wall Street Journal*, invited the President to consistently declare terrorists 'enemies of mankind' whom 'no one should mourn the death of':

> According to press reports, aides claim the president is a student of St. Augustine and St. Thomas Aquinas who brings their views to targeting choices. But . . . just-war theory should broaden, rather than limit, the use of force against terrorists. The work of the Catholic theologians drew upon traditions stretching back to the ancient world that would have considered terrorists to be *hostis humani generis*, the enemy of all mankind, who merited virtually no protections under the laws of war. A return to first principles such as *hostis humani generis* may prove a better guide for a nation at war than a president's day-to-day instincts.
>
> (Yoo 2012)

This exceptional violence, that obliterates all legal and moral limits, is part of a discourse that portrays the tortured subjects as people who, through their actions, have excluded themselves from humanity and, therefore, from the protection of all human laws. It is part of a discourse that portrays humanity as a victimized population with no autonomous political agency and continuously threatened by bestialized 'enemies of the human race'. The War on Terror is thus legitimized as a service offered to mankind, a form of violence that exceeds the fundamental norms of the international legal order in order to respond to the ever-present 'terrorist emergency'. As a consequence, the doctrine of 'humanitarian exception' – developed during the humanitarian wars of the 1990s as an emergency power to suspend fundamental norms of international law, in a particular locality and for a limited time, in order to

4 Paradoxically, the turn toward the use of Universal jurisdiction enabled by the invocation of the figure of the pirate as 'enemy of the human race' has been favoured both by those invested in prosecuting torture and human rights violations, and by those seeking to justify engaging in them. For instance, supporters of the War on Terror have justified the use of torture against 'terrorists' on the basis of their exceptional status as 'enemies of the human race'. In 1980, nevertheless, the United States Court of Appeals in *Filártiga v. Peña-Irala* concluded that 'the torturer has become – like the pirate before him – *hostis humani generis*, an enemy of all mankind' (cited in Samuels 2010). This legal chaos suggests two things. First of all, there is a definite tendency toward the extension of the traditional 'pirate exception'. Second, there is a dynamic struggle over who can legitimately decide who, in concrete terms, is a 'enemy of the human race'. The result is an international order that is really the worst disorder, in which those who claim to protect humanity from the 'enemy of the human race' are themselves accused of being 'enemies of the human race'.

prosecute 'egregious crimes against humanity' (Cassese 1999b: 791) – is generalized and transformed. The War on Terror, in fact, removes all temporal and spatial limitations that were initially imposed on the 'humanitarian exception': the persecution of the terrorist 'enemy of the human race' is a continuous source of Universal jurisdictional powers by which those claiming to fight for the protection of humanity can intervene anywhere at any time. The function of global policing – which now may be activated with or without the authorization of the Security Council (Glennon 1999: 5; Cassese 1999b: 791–793) – thus becomes 'a nowhere tangible, all pervasive, ghostly presence' which 'intervenes for security reasons in countless cases' outside and even against the law (Benjamin 1996: 267).

The concept of 'the terrorist' today serves, at a global level, a similar role to the one that has been historically played by the concept of 'the pirate' in the oceans of the world. It is an empty signifier that offers itself to interpretation. If it is to be accepted that terrorists, like pirates, are to be considered *hostis humani generis*, nothing can stop the escalation of violence and eventually the coming into being of a global civil war of devastating consequences. Two current barriers to 'surgical strikes', 'humanitarian bombings' and 'targeted killings' would be removed: jurisdiction and sovereignty. Anyone labelled as a 'terrorist' would have no place in the world, since they would be threatened everywhere by a violence that is capable of surpassing all borders. No state could protect the 'terrorist' since its territory would turn into a sea in which any army – acting in the name of humanity – would be entitled to operate. The protection of today's peace would then justify continuous military interventions, anti-piracy operations and anti-terrorism strikes. The 'humanitarian exception' would no longer be a temporary and localized exception to the norms of international law, but would truly be global and permanent. No barrier could stop bombings in the name of humanity occurring in any place at any time, for the persecution of ubiquitous 'enemies of the human race' hiding among the innocents. In the words of Saul Newman, it would then appear 'a space of exception – a "no man's land" between legality and illegality – in which law is both preserved and transgressed through the very violence and arbitrariness with which it is enforced' (2004: 579). The land would be submerged in a borderless ocean in which the distinction between pirates and privateers, authorized state agents and terrorists, blurs in a grey zone of conceptual indistinction. Paradoxically, exactly when the process of decolonization and statification of the world seems to have forever eradicated the borderland from the world map, the latter in fact becomes ubiquitous. The ocean is no longer an untameable outside but a space of indistinction that can emerge everywhere, at any moment.

Security, commons and Somali pirates: Towards a global biopower?

The current global mobilization against piracy, epitomized by the unparalleled coalition of navies involved today in joint anti-piracy patrols around the Horn of

Africa, becomes an interesting phenomenon at this point. One might see, in a sense, the whole history of piracy repeated today on a miniature scale. After the collapse of the Somalian State, the lack of sovereign controls was translated in the existence of a juridical void, a space of exception 'beyond the line' that became immediately the occasion for imperialist practices, open plunder and primitive accumulation or, in David Harvey's words, 'accumulation by dispossession' (Harvey 2005). In a second phase, when the exceptional freedom dictated by the absence of sovereignty gives rise to practices that appear to endanger the smooth working of the global market, Universal jurisdiction legitimizes forms of Imperial intervention in the name of humanity, which take the form of global police operations against denationalized pirate outlaws. The imposition of an Imperial *pax*, today enacted in the name of the United Nations, thus rapidly replaces lawless imperialist plunder as the dominant form of interventionism in the region.

Today the United Nations Convention on the Law of the Sea (UNCLOS) defines piracy as 'any illegal acts of violence or detention or any act of depredation, committed for private ends by the crew or the passengers of a private ship' (Rubin 2006: 440) and is limited to the high seas and places 'outside the jurisdiction of any State' (ibidem). Because piracy is considered to be a violation of the law of nations, any state has the authority to seize a pirate ship and dispose of the pirates according to its own legal and political will. The pirates are denationalized and thus stripped of the protection normally afforded by their nationality (Matsuda and Committee of Experts for the Progressive Codification of International Law 1926: 225). Over the last decade, the number of maritime piracy attacks has increased steadily. In 2008, 293 incidents of piracy were officially reported, an increase of 11% from the previous year. In the last three years, over 1,290 incidents were reported, but many more remained probably unreported due to fear of rising insurance costs (International Chamber of Commerce 2012). In only a few years, then, piracy has been again turned from a marginal economic problem into the centre of a rising system of security that is both global in scope and transnational in its organization.

The rise in pirate attacks in the proximity of the Horn of Africa and particularly off the Somali coast contributed to rising international concern over the issue of piracy. Since the early 2000s, then, major powers in the international system have been working towards turning piracy into a problem of international security. This process reached its first climax in early 2007, when the United States pushed forward the proposal for a 'Global Maritime Partnership', an ambitious programme of international military cooperation against piracy and terrorism, which included the vision of a '1000-ship navy' composed of vessels 'from all willing nations', destined to become the first materialization of a transnational police force in the service of the safety of global trade (Kraska and Wilson 2009a). On 2 June 2008, the Security Council at the United Nations adopted Resolution 1816, the first ever to deal explicitly with piracy. It was rapidly followed by other three resolutions, all issued in 2008, which provided authorization for exceptional measures against piracy. Resolution 1851, in particular, urged all members of the international community to 'undertake all necessary measures that are appropriate in Somalia for the purpose of suppressing acts of piracy and armed robbery at sea' (Ploch 2010: 13).

In response to the call of the United Nations for international cooperation towards the enforcement of international criminal law, the United States created a 'Maritime Security Patrol Area' in the Gulf of Aden, involving a coalition of navy warships and aircraft which patrols the waters and airspace of the area (Onuoha 2009). Meanwhile the European Council announced the decision to work toward the inauguration of the first joint European naval operation, a collective venture for the suppression of piracy under the name of *Operation Atalanta* (Van Rooyen 2011). The European mandate, today in its fourth year, has been recently extended to December 2014 and it now explicitly calls for the targeting of pirate bases on shore and for further direct intervention in the region. Nevertheless, *Operation Atalanta* constitutes only one of the three major multilateral operations in the area together with the US-led *Combined Maritime Force* and the NATO's mission *Ocean Shield*. The three multilateral operations are coordinated by a single operative framework, which is also inclusive of the Chinese military forces in the area (Homan and Kamerling 2010). Overall, at least 37 states are directly involved in military operations against piracy, including, in a single effort, traditional geopolitical rivals such as China, India, Iran, Japan and Russia (Kraska 2009b).

For many states, involvement in these collective counter-piracy operations have been motivated as much by political signalling – flaunting a munificent willingness to deploy military violence for the protection of humanity – as by any determination to suppress piracy. Moreover, counter-piracy operations have proved to be an effective disguise for states willing to expand their influence in a strategically significant region (Willett 2011). And yet this unprecedented cooperative military effort is revealing of the ways in which international law remains a profoundly undemocratic juridical system, whose interpretation and enforcement is most often dependent on the interests of only the most powerful international actors (Miéville 2006). If one compares the complete absence of international action to stop the waste-dumping and over-fishing that daily despoils the oceanic commons with the multi-layered, organized response to eradicate piracy, the sense of imbalance becomes glaring.

In fact, for over 30 years now the Gulf of Aden has been the theatre of forms of corporate crime that are responsible for an incalculable destruction of common wealth and human lives. However, before the emergence of Somali piracy, the vacuum of power left behind by the profound crisis of Somali institutions was not only ignored but, in fact, was systematically exploited by international capital (Panjabi 2009). In lawlessness, business interests initially saw opportunity for vast profits, and took advantage of the situation. According to a report by the United Nations Environmental Program, 'heavily armed foreign boats have often tried to exploit the breakdown of law and order in Somalia since the overthrow of President Mohammed Siad Barre in 1991 by fishing in the rich Somali waters, thus depriving coastal communities of resources' (UNEP 2005: 133). Moreover, the

UNEP has been denouncing, at least since the early 1980s, 'countless shipments of illegal nuclear and toxic waste of industrial provenance dumped along the coastline' (UNEP 2005: 134). In 1995, leaders of all 12 major Somali political factions – in one of the first and only joint statements in recent years – complained formally to the United Nations and the European Union about the environmental problems caused by extensive illegal fishing and the dumping of toxic waste by foreign vessels in Somali waters (Panjabi 2009). In 2000, several UN agencies revealed massive pollution by nuclear and hazardous waste (including chemical contaminants and radioactive uranium) caused by illegal dumping of dangerous materials originating in Europe (Hamblin 2008).

In the last decade, European and American fishing industries illegally plundered an estimate of US$300 million of tuna, shrimp and lobster every year from the Somali coastal region – roughly three times the sum proved to have been paid out to pirates by the shipping industry – reducing one of the richest fishing grounds in the world to a deserted toxic garbage heap (Lehr 2008, 2009; Panjabi 2009). The incursions of foreign vessels provoked some fishermen in the late 1990s into forming armed vigilante groups to guard their coastlines (Panjabi 2009). Early on, Somali representatives complained to the United Nations, appealing for help against the illegal activities being perpetrated in the oceans. They complained not only about the over-fishing by industrial means but also of having been actively prevented from fishing (Achieng 1999). The devastating effect of this type of corporate-led primitive form of capital accumulation cannot be overstated in a region where, according to the most recent reports of the UNEP, over 30 million people depend on maritime and coastal resources for their daily livelihood (Clifford 2004).

On a more general level, the systematic over-exploitation of the oceanic commons by major transnational corporations is increasingly threatening the world's marine ecosystems (Madeley 1999: 80–87). As Mancur Olson (2000) has argued, distant water fleets and mobile trawlers regularly operate as roving bandits, lacking any attachment to particular maritime environments, which appears from their perspective to be only a standing-reserve of economic value to be extracted. The effects of this form of accumulation by dispossession have proved devastating – not only for local communities, whose 'traditional ways of life, which for centuries have been sustained by fisheries are collapsing' (Madeley 1999: 82), but also for the entire inter-species ecosystem. An international team of maritime scientists has argued that 'human-dominated marine ecosystems are experiencing accelerating loss of population and species, with largely unknown consequences' (Worm et al. 2006: 786). They contend that 'a new dynamic has arisen in the globalized world: new markets can develop so rapidly that the speed of resource exploitation often overwhelms the ability of local institutions to respond' predicting that unless global policies change 100% of sea-food-producing species stocks will irremediably collapse by 2048' (ibidem).

Nevertheless, no state has so far acted forcefully in order to implement the United Nations Conventions on the Law of the Sea, which banishes both over-fishing and toxic dumping in oceanic waters. This form of illegality – despite the environmental disruption and the high cost in human life it implied – is largely left unchecked, despite the protests of local institutions and environmental organizations. Only when piracy appeared in the region was the lack of effective sovereign control over the Gulf of Aden problematized. Piracy rapidly propelled Somali coastal communities to the forefront of global concerns, leading to an impressive naval response by the armed forces of over 40 major countries: an international military mobilization that represents only the most visible point of a global security assemblage under construction.

The magnitude of the intervention with which the major military powers are attempting to control and govern this space of flow is hardly surprising. Up to 50% of the world's trade by volume travels through the Gulf of Aden and the Suez Canal. By one estimate, approximately 20,000 ships traverse Somali waters annually. These vessels carry minerals, gas and huge containers filled with every type of consumer product. Even more strategically momentous, over 40% of the world's oil is moved through the Gulf of Aden (French and Chambers 2010). A number of military analysts have argued that the escalation of piracy in the region could bring not only commerce but also industrial production to a standstill (Stavridis and LeBron 2010). Nevertheless, the Center for Strategic and International Studies estimated that losses due to pirate attacks in the whole of 2011 were equivalent to US$16 billion, which, compared to the US$7.8 trillion representing the total yearly value of international maritime trade, constitutes a minuscule fraction (Scheffler 2010: 3). The fear of piracy therefore has very real effects but, as Julian Reid and Michael Dillon have noted, 'the governmental hysteria around, and the mobilization of new strategies for the protection of critical infrastructures, tells us more about liberal regimes' fears over the fragility of their infrastructures than about the actual extent of the material threats posed to it' (Dillon and Reid 2009: 37).

What is certain is that – while neither fear for the livelihood and security of coastal populations nor concern for environmental destruction were perceived as a problem of security sufficiently threatening to activate any significant response by the international state system – even a limited threat to the safety of commercial circulation was immediately constructed as an overwhelming global security threat (Bueger 2010: 25–26). Prior to the rise of the pirate threat off the Somali coast, no other issue could have brought the navies of the United States, the EU nations, NATO, China, Japan, Iran and Russia to identify a single common enemy and a single common cause. Symptomatically, this common cause has been combating the interruption of international commerce. The only common enemy so far has been the pirate. From this perspective on security – emerging from the very unequal treatment of corporate and environmental crimes versus piracy in the Gulf of Aden – the sea is neither a productive place nor a natural environment, but rather a smooth space of flow, a network of super-highways and lanes of trade; to 'cleanse the sea' has nothing to do with pollution and water purity, but means removing the blockages in circulation and restoring the unimpaired speed of commercial exchange. Finally, the concept of global security does not take into consideration the necessities of different local economies, but instead seems uniquely concerned with the preservation of global commercial patterns necessary for the sustenance of a heavily market-dependent liberal way of life (Dillon and Reid 2009).

As opposed to the War on Terror, the current global mobilization against pirates seems to be politically uncontroversial. Until today, we have not seen mass mobilizations against either the 'targeted killings' of suspected pirates or the innocent victims, or the 'collateral damage' of military operations. This has not been the result of insufficient mass media coverage of the events; instead, it is revealing of the hegemonic function of classic historical narratives and the extent to which violence is banalized as an effective tool of global policing. The apparent absence of international political controversy is reflected in the fact that the war on piracy has readily gained backing from the United Nations, inducing a common military effort from such mutually antagonistic states as the USA, Iran, Russia, China, Saudi Arabia, India, Pakistan, Japan and the European Union.

The global military mobilization against pirates is made to appear as a neutral, righteous and legally sound form of global policing, therefore closing all possibilities of dialogue with the other. A self-righteous attitude that is already producing monsters – as if those who take upon themselves the right to name and fight the 'enemy of human civilization' are led, in a sort of Dantesque *contrappasso*, to lose their own civility in the process. Ralph Peters could thus write, in the famed columns of the *New York Post*:

> Pirates must be punished fiercely and comprehensively. Attack their harbors with land, sea and air power. Kill pirates, sink their vessels (including those dual-use fishing boats) and wreck their support infrastructure. The clans behind the pirates must feel sufficient pain to rein in their young thugs. And we don't need to stay to rebuild Somalia. We need to leave while their boats are still burning down to the waterline.
>
> (Peters 2009: 11)

As interest in the activities of Somali pirates continued to grow, nevertheless, a counter-narrative emerged from the public claims of local Somali communities that all of a sudden gained a voice in Western media. Repeatedly, the pirates presented themselves as coastguards and defenders of the Somali people from foreign criminal activities off the coast of Somalia (Dawdy 2011). Often condemned as a strategic discourse meant to justify pirate crimes, it certainly attempted to displace the exceptional character of pirate violence, making it instead the visible part of a much wider, invisible system of violence. Interviewed Somalis, in Africa and abroad, again and again stressed the connection between the rise in piracy and the crisis lived by coastal communities. In a telephone interview to the *New York Times*, the pirate spokesman Sugure Ali declared: 'We don't consider ourselves sea bandits. We consider sea bandits those who illegally fish in our seas and dump waste in our seas and carry weapons in our seas' (Gettleman 2008b). In another interview to the CNN, a young man similarly stated: 'Since the ocean is our government, we got into the deep and took possession of cargo ships. There is no law that allows us to do that. But what motivates us is life, since we are the people who used to work at sea' (Boyah 2008).

Authorities have expressed concern about the power of this narrative from below, even when condemning it as 'partial' or 'false'. 'It's true that the pirates started to defend the fishing business; and illegal fishing is a real problem,' said Mohamed Osman Aden, the diplomatic representative for Somalia in Kenya, 'but since then they got greedy' (cited in Gettleman 2008a). Bronwyn Bruton, a member of the US Council of Foreign Relations, commented that 'Somali awareness of how foreign countries are profiting from their country's misery has increased the pirate's popular support' (Gathii 2010: 22). The interviews collected by Reclaim the Seas, a German organization that followed the pirate trials that took place in Hamburg between 2011 and 2012, for instance, are extremely significant in giving us direct ethnographic access to how the pirate crisis is understood by the Somali public. From the eyes of the interviewed, mostly Somali refugees in Germany, Somalia emerges as the theatre stage of a terrible clash of illegalities, a dialectic of terror, in which the pirates embody the enraged violence of the dispossessed. The first of the collected interviews begin:

> I remember when I was in Somalia in the beach you see dead fish, some bad things they threw in our sea, so sometimes you see a lot of dead fish, so they get angry and they talk to each other and they say we become pirates. That's why they are pirates but not me, I am a refugee. If I would be pirate I would have money and I would be alive in Somalia. . .
>
> (Reclaim the Seas 2011)

The human cost of the current global war on piracy is difficult to estimate. SOS, an organization lobbying to promote tougher policies against piracy and funded by global shipping corporations, has claimed that 64 seafarers have been killed by Somali pirates since 2007 (Jablonski and Oliver 2012). The sailors and maritime workers that suffered the most from the resurgence of piracy are often Filipinos, Bangladeshis and Pakistanis, who compose a great section of the global shipping workforce. They are often underpaid, exploited and work in extremely difficult conditions, suffering hundreds of deaths every year from unsafe and under-regulated working conditions (Fink 2011: 145–202). Marginal and forgotten, working all of their lives unseen, these workers have become victims in need of protection only as part of a discourse meant to justify further military violence. On the other hand, coalition naval forces have been accused of targeting fishermen mistaken for pirates. Although it is extremely difficult to estimate the number of 'collateral murders' caused by the international military campaign against piracy, a few anecdotes have emerged in the media. At least eight Somali fishermen are still missing from vessels that were allegedly attacked by foreign warships in

February 2012 (Bridger 2012: 2). Fishermen operating close to Mogadishu repeatedly complained about harassment by coalition warships (Panjabi 2009: 22). On 15 February 2012, two Indian fishermen were shot dead off the coast of southern India by Italian marines who believed them to be pirates, sparking a diplomatic incident between the two countries (Kumar 2012). On 12 March, two Somali fishermen were killed after an unknown naval vessel – later reported to be a US Navy ship – opened fire on their boat (Bridger 2012: 4).

These civilian deaths are symptomatic of the indiscriminate use of force by international naval forces; but they also raise serious questions about the exceptional status of those who are targeted as 'pirates'. In fact, notwithstanding the catch-and-release policy applied by a number of states that participate in the global mobilization against piracy – a policy motivated primarily by the resistance posed by many states to the cost of deporting the suspects in order to give them a fair trial, and highly criticized in academic circles as a sign of 'inefficiency' and 'excessive concern with human rights' (Carafano et al. 2009) – military corps have in fact killed a number of people because they were suspected of planning acts of piracy. According to a report from Jack Lang, the UN's Special Adviser on Legal Issues related to Piracy off the Coast of Somalia, since 2007 at least 300 pirates have been reported killed – with 111 reported killings in 2011 – while probably many more died unreported (Hurlburt 2012).

Hundreds of people have been killed with neither due process nor respect for the Geneva Convention. These deaths have been rarely discussed, never mourned and often celebrated as a sign of 'effective policy'. In 2010, for instance, the *Wall Street Journal* published an article that sums up the reasoning behind this tendency; it was aptly titled: 'Put Pirates to the Sword: Targeted killings are a necessary, justified and legal response to high-seas piracy' (Gopalan 2010: 13). The global military mobilization against piracy is therefore operating in an ambiguous legal threshold threatening to pry open a state of exception in international law. As it has been argued in relation to the novel and ubiquitous category of the 'terrorist', the 'pirate' is a concept that seems to prefigure the danger of a global security system operating beyond the law for reasons of 'extreme necessity', 'pressing security' and 'exception'. What constitutes a 'question of global security' and who is to be identified, in concrete terms, as 'a pirate', 'a terrorist' or 'an enemy of humanity' is never a technical question, but rather a fundamental political issue concerning the life and death of a growing number of people.

The contemporary global *persecutio piratarum* and the War on Terror reveal the same fundamental biopolitical logic. In both cases violence is not presented as a weapon in a confrontation between equal enemies, but as an instrument meant to serve and protect humanity. In this sense, we might be witnessing the first steps of a global biopolitical logic, which goes beyond traditional national paradigms. As Michel Foucault has shown, during the nineteenth century the creation of the notion of 'the Nation', as an organic entity that must be continuously protected by state power, stimulated the formation of a new form of violence. 'The new discourse,' writes Foucault, 'the hegemonic discourse, does not say: "we have to defend ourselves against society" but rather "we have to defend society against all internal threats"' (Foucault 2003: 62). In nationalist rhetoric throughout the world, the 'Nation' has become 'the pure source of every identity but must, however, continually be redefined and purified through exclusions' (Agamben 1998: 178). As we have seen, the Nazi State brought this genocidal logic to its most extreme conclusions: promoting the denationalization of Jews, their expulsion from the body of the nation and, ultimately, their extermination (Foucault 2003). A recurrent theme in Nazi anti-Semitic propaganda was that Jews spread diseases; that they were, in fact, 'disease incarnate' (Savage 2007: 416). Therefore they had to be removed by the national body, in order to foster its healthy growth. In a 1936 lecture on radiotherapy, SS radiologist Hans Holfeder showed students an image that sums up the fundamental genocidal logic of aggressive nationalism: 'a slide in which cancer cells were portrayed as Jews, and X-rays launched against them as Nazi storm troopers' (Savage 2007: 422).

Today it is no longer the protection of 'the Nation' but of 'Humanity' that is invoked, at the global level, as a rationale for emergency measures that suspend international law. To paraphrase Foucault (2003), we could say that the new hegemonic discourse no longer says 'we have to defend our nation from the rest of humanity' but rather 'we have to defend humanity from all internal threats'. In discourses that try to support the use of military violence for the protection of humanity against 'terrorists' and 'criminals against humanity', humanity becomes 'the pure source of every identity but must, however, continually be redefined and purified through exclusions' (Agamben 1998: 178). The War on Terror brings this global biopolitical logic to its most extreme conclusions when it produces arguments that equate 'terrorists' to 'pirates' and 'pirates' to 'enemies of the human race'.

Carl Schmitt could not avoid noticing that German Jews, once denationalized by the racist dispositions of the Nuremberg laws, found themselves in the same state of exception that had been previously reserved for pirates 'who do not have the protection of any state' (Schmitt 1938). As we have seen throughout this work, the status of the pirate as *hostis humani generis* implies not only its denationalization but, even more radically, its symbolic banishment from humanity itself. The extermination of pirates, and today the killing of terrorists, is therefore often equated with operations of pest control or the surgical removal of cancerous cells. In the words of the seventeenth-century author of *News from sea* – the pamphlet in celebration of the hanging of George Cusack and his pirate crew – pirates are '*Humani Generus hostes*, Publique Enemies to Mankind whom every one was obliged to oppose and destroy, as we do Common vermine that Infest and trouble us' (*News from sea* 1674: 3). Similarly, according to Paul Johnson, writing in the 1986 anthology *Terrorism. How the West can Win* edited by the later Israeli Prime Minister Benjamin Netanyahu:

> terrorism is the cancer of the modern world. No state is immune to it. It is a dynamic organism which attacks the healthy flesh of the surrounding society.

> It has the essential hallmark of malignant cancer: unless treated, and treated drastically, its growth its inexorable, until it poisons and engulfs the society on which it feeds and drags it down to destruction.
>
> (1986: 31)

Therefore, the relationship with the 'other' is recast. We pass from a political relationship of enmity and war to a biological relationship of pest control: 'The enemies who have to be done away with are not adversaries in the political sense of the term; they are threats, either external or internal, to the population and for the population' (Foucault 2003: 255–256). When the agonistic plurality of states characteristic of the classic international system is subverted by a perspective fixed on the unity of humanity, the classic concept of war is also transformed. While traditional interstate wars took the form of a clash of identities, now a new form of global violence tends to emerge. This appears not as a clash between two equal subjects, but rather as a practice of immunization against the multitude of viral threats menacing the global body of the human population. Sovereignty, understood as the power over life and death, does not fade away; instead we witness a transformation of its logic from the political to the biopolitical. The state continues to kill, therefore exercising what for Foucault is the fundamental act of sovereignty, and yet state murder is less and less the result of a political decision on the friend/enemy distinction; it is instead the 'collateral effect' of a biopolitical *practice* aimed at maximizing the welfare of humanity. Humanitarian bombings, targeted killings and surgical strikes certainly kill and destroy, but with the declared aim of fostering the life of abstract humanity. Throughout history the evocation of the pirate spectre, the paradigmatic *hostis humani generis*, has served a fundamental role in Imperial law, theory and rhetoric. Once more, the hanging body of the pirate 'enemy of the human race' legitimizes and glorifies the violence of Empire.

Conclusion

This book has tried to reflect upon the history of the piracy from antiquity until today. We have looked at the pirate as a legal category and as a semiotic construction, focusing on the role it played in different Imperial discourses. In the first chapter, we considered the different ways in which the Roman Empire legitimized its hegemonic role in the ancient Mediterranean world. The claim to serve as a bastion of law and order against the omnipresent threat of pirate groups, inimical to all organized societies, was a constitutive part of Imperial discourse: the demonic figure of the pirate specularly glorified the pacifying might of Empire. All Mediterranean communities, therefore, were called to unite as a single front under the authority of Rome, in order to confront the 'common enemy' and preserve the safety of the common Mediterranean routes.

In the second chapter, we analysed the transformation of this form of Imperial discourse in the context of the sixteenth-century European Wars of Religion. After the discovery of America, the crisis of the Christian Commonwealth was accelerated by the escalating conflict that opposed the supra-national authority of the Catholic Church to the revolutionary zeal of the Protestant nations. In this context, the Pope entrusted the colonization of the New World to the Spanish and Portuguese Empires. The Iberic powers were meant to civilize the New World and convert the natives to the Christian faith. Since conquest was understood as a mission in the name of the entire Christendom for the spiritual salvation of the natives, those who interfered with it were excommunicated and treated as heretic foes. In the sixteenth century, thus, the Lutheran corsairs that plundered the Spanish throughout the Atlantic appeared as the systemic enemies of a Universal Christian community centred in Rome.

Only in the second half of the century was a strict division between Europe and the colonial world established. While a *jus publicum Europaeum* emerged in order to moderate warfare among modern European states, the colonial vastness beyond the line was reduced to an anomic state in which might made right and imperialist plunder could operate freely as the main lever for processes of primitive accumulation on a global scale. Starting from Marx's critique of the so-called primitive accumulation of capital and Schmitt's analysis of the role of amity lines in the seventeenth century, we looked at the ways in which piracy and Imperialist plunder were legitimated by early international law as an exceptional activity beyond the line. We then observed how the freedom to plunder beyond the line was increasingly exploited by mutineers and pirates who, slipping from the forms of control that made them functional to imperial projects, went 'from plundering for others, to do it for themselves' (Atkins 1970: 226). This is the argument of the third chapter, in which I considered the world-historical significance of piracy for early-modern imperialism, and the exceptional status of the Atlantic freebooters and the outlaw buccaneers.

The fourth chapter reflected upon the transition between the classic age of primitive accumulation and the creation, in the eighteenth century, of a worldwide oceanic market based on a number of legal principles. Starting from a line of research first suggested by Michel Foucault, we argued that the formation of a stable world-market and the growth of a colonial economy based on the exploitation of slave labour necessitated the suppression of piracy, and the normalization of the exceptional spaces beyond the line. We have looked at the ways in which the pirate was reduced to the status of an 'enemy of mankind', against whom a revolutionary Universal jurisdiction legitimates exceptional measures that suspend traditional norms of international law. In the fifth chapter, we saw how this form of exceptional violence against pirates and 'enemies of mankind' was effectively employed, in the nineteenth century, to legitimate forms of Imperial interventionism. We considered, in particular, the case of the British campaign against 'the Malay pirates', the American bombing of Tripoli and the French conquest of Algiers. In the last two chapters, I have shown how, in the twentieth century, the exceptional figure of the pirate played a fundamental role in the genesis of international criminal law. I have shown how concepts originally engendered in the colonial world – such as 'the enemy of the human race', the 'pirate state' and the idea of 'global policing' – were key to a gradual transformation of international law. The consolidation of the world-market, as a single global space of human interaction, was paralleled by the emergence of a global legal order. In the last chapter I have shown how this global order is taking shape in the context of the global War on Terror and the global military campaign against piracy.

As we have seen, throughout history, Imperial powers always presented their violence as being in the service of humanity and international law. The concept of Empire evokes a power that conceives itself as global in scope and Universal in its vocation. This is why Imperial discourse projects humanity as a single united totality, which must be continuously protected and purified in an endless *persecutio piratarum*. The War on Terror, as well as the contemporary global mobilization against piracy, perfectly embodies this new global Imperial logic. The invocation of humanity in the fight against rogue states, pirates and terrorists reveals the extent to which the liberal peace emerging within the space of the world-market continues to be nothing but 'a coded global civil war'- that is, a civil war pursued behind and through a global law that absolutely and simultaneously affirms and negates the common unity of the human race.

The pirate is a figure that evokes, and brings into being, a grey zone between war and peace. The contemporary resurgence of concepts whose genealogy can be traced back to the Imperial Roman institution of the pirate as *hostis humani generis* is symptomatic of the persistence of this grave and momentous danger. Those who today are labelled as 'terrorists', 'unlawful combatants' or 'pirates' are threatened with a violence that claims to operate in the name of humanity and therefore can strike anywhere at any time, in a permanent state of exception beyond international law. Ultimately, the spectre of the pirate can appear anywhere and at any time; it can be evoked by different powers in contrasting ways; it potentially exposes anyone to be sacrificed in the abstract name of humanity. This exceptional semantic instability, nevertheless, is constantly at risk of escaping the limits posed by hegemonic narratives. Modern states have often displayed pirates in order to evoke the persistence of a threatening anarchy beyond the border, which must be at once feared, disdained and ridiculed. And yet, pirates have also captured the popular imagination, offering a body on which to project the fantasy of a life beyond the constituted order of the state. Today, the pirate figure continues to be appropriated and turned upside-down by countless literary, social and political movements throughout the world. Pirate flags are omnipresent in political protests as symbols of rebellion, defiance and radical desire. Pirate fictions are consumed in libraries, theatres and cinema halls. Pirate images crowd popular culture, evoking a space in which the exception has become the norm, not to threaten life but to multiply freedoms. Pirate fictions evoke the possibility of 'another anarchy': a new spatiality beyond the sovereign order of the modern state, whose meaning can not be determined in advance. In their bewildering radicality, popular fantasies about pirates at once mirror and transfigure the radical fears projected by political and legal discourses on pirates as paradigmatic enemies of humanity lurking off the coast. Michel Foucault once wrote that the 'ship is the heterotopia par excellence', since it 'has been not only the greatest instrument of economic development, but also the greatest reserve of the imagination' (Foucault 1986: 27). Pirate ships, forever suspended in a highly-contested polysemic ambiguity, continue to be the greatest reserve of our political imagination: they chase us, they question us, they force us to think anew the fundamental categories of our political life in common. In other words, if there is a ghost haunting Empire today, this is undoubtedly the ghost of a pirate.

Bibliography

The list includes only the text directly cited. All quotes from works in Italian, German, French, Spanish and Latin have been directly translated by the author, unless otherwise stated.

'A Campaign of Piracy and Pillage', *The Times* (London, 16 March 1915), p. 5.

Achieng, J. (1999) 'Somalia: Local Fishermen Battle Foreign Trawlers', *Somali Ctr. for Water and Env't*, Accessed at http://www.somwe.com/fishmen.html [14 September 2012].

Adams, J. (1991) 'Iraki Toll Could Be 200,000 Dead', *London Time*, 3 Marzo, pp. 1–2.

Adorno, T. and Horkheimer, M. (2007) *Dialectic of Enlightenment*, Stanford, CA: Stanford University Press.

Agamben, G. (1998) *Homo Sacer: Sovereign Power and Bare Life*, Stanford, CA: Stanford University Press.

Agamben, G. (2001) 'Security and Terror', *Theory and Event*, 5(4): 1–2.

Agamben, G. (2002) *Il Regno e la Gloria; per una genealogia teologica dell'economia e del governo*, Torino: Bollati Borringhieri.

Alatas, S.H. (1977) *The Myth of the Lazy Native: A Study of the Image of the Malays, Filipinos and Javanese from the 16th to the 20th Century and its Function in the Ideology of Colonial Capitalism*, London: Frank Cass.

Amirell, S.E. (2005) 'Piracy: A Critical Perspective', *IIAS Newsletter*, 36 (March): 1.

Anderson, B. (2006) *Imagined Communities: Reflections on the Origin and Spread of Nationalism*, London: Verso.

Anderson, J.L. (1995) 'Piracy and World History: An Economic Perspective on Maritime Predation', *Journal of World History* 6(2): 175–99.

Andrews, K.R. (1984) *Trade, Plunder, and Settlement: Maritime Enterprise and the Genesis of the British Empire, 1480–1630*, Cambridge: Cambridge University Press.

Andrews, K.R. (2011) *Elizabethan Privateering: English Privateering During the Spanish War, 1585–1603*, Cambridge: Cambridge University Press.

Annas, G.J. (2005) 'Unspeakably Cruel – Torture, Medical Ethics, and the Law', *New England Journal of Medicine*, 352(20): 2127–2132.

Appelbaum, Y. (2011) 'The Third Barbary War', *The Atlantic*, 11(3), Available at http://www.theatlantic.com/international/archive/2011/03/the-third-barbary-war/72749 [21 October 2012].

Arend, A.C. (1992) 'United Nations and the New World Order', *Georgetown Law Journal*, 81: 491–522.

Arendt, H. (1943) 'We Refugees', *Menorah Journal* 3(1): 69–77. Republished in: Robinson, M. (1994) *Altogether Elsewhere: Writers on Exile*, Boston: Faber and Faber.

Aristotle (1992) *The Politics*, London: Penguin Books.

Aristotle (1996) *The Politics and the Constitution of Athens*, London: Cambridge University Press.

Arnold, A.J. (2007) 'From Piracy to Policy: Exquemelin's Buccaneers and Imperial Competition in America', *Review: Literature and Arts of the Americas*, 40(1): 9–20.

Atkins, J. (1970) *Voyage to Guinea, Brazil and the West Indies in H.M.S. 'Swallow' and 'Weymouth': With Remarks on the Gold, Ivory and Slave Trade*, London: Frank Cass Publishers.

Avidov, A. (1997) 'Were the Cilicians a Nation of Pirates?', *Mediterranean Historical Review*, 12(1): 5–35.

Azubuike, L. (2009) 'International Law Regime Against Piracy', *Annual Survey of International & Comparative Law*, 15: 43–81.

Bacon, F. (1861) 'Advertisement Touching an Holy Warre', in Spedding, J., Ellis, R.L. and Heath, D.D. (2011) *The Works of Francis Bacon*, vol. 7: 1–36. London: Cambridge University Press.

Badian, E. (1952) 'Notes on Roman Policy in Illyria (230–201 B.C.)', *Papers of the British School at Rome*, 20(1): 72–93.

Baepler, P. (2000) 'Introduction', in Baepler, J. (ed.), *White Slaves, African Masters: An Anthology of American Barbary Captivity Narratives*, Chicago, IL: University of Chicago Press.

Baldry, H. (1965) *The Unity of Mankind in Greek Thought*, Cambridge: Cambridge University Press.

Bane, S.L. (1942) *The Blockade of Germany after the Armistice 1918–1919*, Stanford, CA: Stanford University Press.

Bartelson, J. (1995) *A Genealogy of Sovereignty*, Cambridge: Cambridge University Press.

Barthes, R. (1973) *Mythologies*, London: Jonathan Cape.

Bauman, Z. (2000) *Liquid Modernity*, Cambridge, MA: Polity Press.

Beck, U. (1999) 'Uber den postnationalen Krieg', *Blatter fur deutsche und Internationale Politik*, 8(1): 984–990.

Beck, U. (2005) 'Neither Order nor Peace: A Response to Bruno Latour', *Common Knowledge*, 11(1): 1–7.

Beckles, H. (2001) ' "The 'Hub of Empire": The Caribbean and Britain in the Seventeenth Century', in Canny, N. (ed.), *The Oxford History of the British Empire: Volume I: The Origins of Empire: British Overseas Enterprise to the Close of the Seventeenth Century*, Oxford: Oxford University Press, pp. 218–240.

Behnke, A. (2008) 'Eternal Peace as the Graveyard of the Political: A Critique of Kant's Zum Ewigen Frieden', *Millennium – Journal of International Studies*, 36(3): 513–531.

Belgrave, C. (1966) *The Pirate Coast*, London: G. Bell and Sons.

Benjamin, W. (1996) [1921] 'Critique of Violence', in Bullock, M. (ed.), *Selected Writings Vol. 1 1913–1926*, Cambridge, MA: Harvard University Press, pp. 259–280.

Benton, L. (2009) *A Search for Sovereignty: Law and Geography in European Empires, 1400–1900*. Cambridge: Cambridge University Press.

Bey, H. (2003) *Taz*, New York: Autonomedia.

Blackstone, W. (1827) *Commentaries on the laws of England*, London: J. Grigg.

Blake, W. (1811) *Milton a Poem*, London: William Blake.

Bland, J. (1660) *Trade Revived, Or, A Way Proposed to Restore, Increase, Inrich, Strengthen and Preserve the Decayed and Even Dying Trade of this Our English Nation, in Its Manufactories, Coin, Shiping and Revenue: Set Forth by a Wel-wisher to the Nation and Its Prosperity*, London: T. Leach.

Bodin, J. (1992) *On Sovereignty*, Cambridge: Cambridge University Press.

Bojanic, P. (2011) 'The Figures of (A)simmetry: Pirates', *Filosofia Politica*, 25(2): 207–214.

Bono, S. (1964) *I corsari barbareschi*, Torino: ERI.

Boot, M. (2003) *The Savage Wars Of Peace: Small Wars And The Rise Of American Power*, London: Basic Books.

Borradori, G. (2003) *Philosophy in a Time of Terror: Dialogues with Jürgen Habermas and Jacques Derrida*, Chicago, IL: University of Chicago Press.

Bose, S. (2006) *A Hundred Horizons: The Indian Ocean in the Age of Global Empire*, Cambridge, MA: Harvard University Press.

Boucher, P.P. (2007) *France and the American Tropics to 1700: Tropics of Discontent?*, New York: JHU Press.

Bowley, A. (2014) *Wages in the United Kingdom in the nineteenth century*, Cambridge: Cambridge University Press.

Boxer, C.R. (1965) *The Dutch Seaborne Empire, 1600–1800*, London: Hutchinson.

Boyah (2008) 'No Way to Stop Us, Pirate Leader Says', Interviewed by Garowe Online for CNN, [TV] Eyl, Somalia, 25 November 2008. Available at http://www.youtube.com/watch?v=4cjpZmcyD64 [28 August 2012].

Braddell, T. (1858) 'The Europeans in the Indian Archipelago in the 16th and 17th Centuries', *JIAEA*, 11(4): 328–342.

Brading, D.A. (1988) 'The Two Cities: St. Augustine and the Spanish Conquest of America', *Revista Portuguesa de Filosofia*, 44(1): 99–126.

Brand, U. (2005) 'Order and Regulation: Global Governance as a Hegemonic Discourse of International Politics?', *Review of International Political Economy*, 12(1): 155–176.

Braudel, F. (1992) *Civilization and Capitalism, 15th–18th Century, Vol. II: The Wheels of Commerce*, Berkeley, CA: University of California Press.

Braudel, F. (1996) *The Mediterranean and the Mediterranean World in the Age of Philip II*, Berkeley, CA: University of California Press.

Braund, D. (1995) 'Piracy under the Principate and the Ideology of Imperial Eradication', in Rich, D.J. and Shipley, G. (eds), *War and Society in the Roman World*, London: Routledge.

Brewer, J. (2002) *The Sinews of Power: War, Money and the English State 1688–1783*, London: Routledge.

Bridger, J.M. (2012) 'The EU's Misguided Move to Fight Pirates Onshore', *Marine Waves*, 8(5): 2–7.

Brynen, R. (1990) *Sanctuary and Survival: The PLO in Lebanon*, Boulder, CO: Westview Press.

Buchanan, R. (1938) 'Theodore Roosevelt and American Neutrality, 1914–1917', *The American Historical Review*, 43(4): 775–790.

Bucharin, N. (1916) 'The Imperialist Pirate State', in Gankin, O. and Fisher, H. (1940), *The Bolsheviks and the World War: The Origin of the Third International*, Stanford, CA: Stanford University Press.

Bueger, C. (2010) 'Security as Performation: Securitization, Piracy and the United Nations Security Council', Paper presented at the bi-annual conference of the Standing Group for International Relations of the ECPR, Stockholm.

Bull, H. (1976) 'Sea Power and Political Influence', *The Adelphi Papers*, 16(122): 1–9.

Burg, B. (2012) *Sodomy and the Pirate Tradition: English Sea Rovers in the Seventeenth-Century Caribbean*, New York: NYU Press.

Burgess, D.R. (2005) 'Hostis Humani Generi: Piracy, Terrorism and a New International Law', *University of Miami International & Comparative Law Review*, 13(1): 293–321.

Burgess, D.R. (2010) *The World for Ransom: Piracy is Terrorism, Terrorism is Piracy*, New York: Prometheus Books.

Burgess, D.R. (2008) 'Piracy is Terrorism', *New York Times*, p. 5. Available at http://www.mtholyoke.edu/~dewar20e/International%20Security%20Research/burgess.pdf [24 September 2012].

Burke, E. (1757) *A Philosophical Enquiry into the Origin of Our Ideas of the Sublime and Beautiful*, London: R. & J. Dodsley.

Bush, G.W. (2002) *The National Security Strategy of the United States of America*, Washington, DC: The White House.

Buzan, B. and Herring, E. (1998) *The Arms Dynamic in World Politics*, Boulder, CO: Lynne Rienner Publishers.

Byron, G. (1815) *The Corsair: A Tale*, London: John Murray.

Callinicos, A. (2007) 'Does Capitalism Need the State System?', *Cambridge Review of International Affairs*, 20(4): 533–549.

Campo, J. (2003) 'Discourse without Discussion: Representations of Piracy in Colonial Indonesia 1816–25', *Journal of Southeast Asian Studies*, 34(02): 199–214.

Carafano, J., Weitz, R. and Andersen, M. (2009) 'Maritime Security: Fighting Piracy in the Gulf of Aden and Beyond', *Heritage Special Report*, 59(2): 1–28.

Cassese, A. (1999a) 'Ex iniuria ius oritur: Are We Moving Towards International Legitimation of Forcible Humanitarian Countermeasures in the World Community?', *European Journal of International Law*, 10(1): 23–30.

Cassese, A. (1999b) 'A Follow-up: Forcible Humanitarian Countermeasures and Opinio Necessitatis', *European Journal of International Law*, 10(4): 791–799.

Castellanos, J. (1921) *Discurso de el Capitán Francisco Draque*. Madrid: Instituto de Valencia de D. Juan.

Cavazzuti, L. (2004) 'La Pirateria nella Navigazione Antica', in Giacobelli, M. (ed.), *Lezioni Fabio Faccenna II. Conferenze di Archeologia subacquea*, Bari: Edipuglia srl, pp. 45–58.

Cesare Ottaviano Augusto (1991) *Res gestae divi Augusti*, Pordenone: Edizioni Studio Tesi.

Chesneaux, J. (1972) *The Political and Social Ideas of Jules Verne*, London: Thames & Hudson.

Chiesa, L.E. and Greenawalt, A.K.A. (2012) 'Beyond War: Bin Laden, Escobar, and the Justification of Targeted Killing', *Wash & Lee Law Review*, 69(2): 1371–1759.

Chomsky, N. (1983) *The Fateful Triangle: The United States, Israel and the Palestinians*, Boston: South End Press.

Chomsky, N. (2002) *Pirates and Emperors, Old and New: International Terrorism in the Real World*, London: Pluto Press.

Cicero, M.T. (1856) *Flaccus* in *Three Orations on the Agrarian Law, the Four Against Catiline, the Orations for Rabirius, Murena Sylla, Archias, Flaccus, Scaurus, etc.* London: H.G. Bohn, pp. 424–470.

Cicero, M.T. (1992) *Verrine Oration*, Detroit, MI: Wayne State University Press.

Cicero, M.T. (2006) *De Officiis*, New York: ReadHowYouWant.

Cipolla, C. (1965) *Guns and Sails in the Early Phase of European Expansion 1400–1700*, New York: Collins.

Clark, R. (1992) *The Fire This Time*, New York: Thunder's Mouth Press.

Clausewitz, C. (2009) *On War*, New York: Wildside Press LLC.

Clavel-Léveque, M.(1976) 'Brigandage et piraterie: representations idéologiques et pratiques impérialistes au dernier siécle de la République', *Dialogues d'histoire ancienne*, 4(1): 17–31.

Clendinnen, I. (1987) *Ambivalent Conquests: Maya and Spaniard in Yucatan, 1517–1570*, Cambridge: Cambridge University Press.

Clifford, S. (2004) 'Multi Million Dollar Fund to Cease Western Indian Ocean Pollution', *Edition News*. Accessed at http://www.edie.net/news/news_story.asp?id=8575 [27 August 2012].

Clulow, A. (2009) 'European Maritime Violence and Territorial States in Early Modern Asia, 1600–1650', *Itinerario*, 33(3): 72–94.

Cockburn, P. (2012) 'How US Drones Forge as Many Foes as They Kill', *The Independent*, 28 October, p. 12.

Colangelo, A. (2007) 'Constitutional Limits on Extraterritorial Jurisdiction: Terrorism and the Intersection of National and International Law', *Harvard International Law Journal*, 48(1): 121–144.

Colchester, M. (1989) *Pirates, Squatters, and Poachers: The Political Ecology of Dispossession of the Native Peoples of Sarawak*, Selangor: Petaling Jaya.

Colucci, L.C. (2012) *The National Security Doctrines of the American Presidency: How They Shape our Present and Future*, Santa Barbara, CA: ABC-CLIO.

Cooper, J.F., (1827) *The Red Rover*, London: Henry Colburn.

Cordingly, D. (1995) *Life Among the Pirates: The Romance and the Reality*, London: Little, Brown & Co.

Cotler, I. (1998) 'Towards a Counter-terrorism Law and Policy', *Terrorism and Political Violence*, 10(2): 1–14.

Cowan, B. (1981) 'Walter Benjamin's Theory of Allegory', *New German Critique*, 22(4): 109–122.

Cranch, W., Peters, R., Wheaton, H., Howard, B.C. and Black, J.S. (1820) *Reports of Cases Argued and Adjudged in the Supreme Court of the United States*, New York: John Conrad and Co.

Croft, P. (1972) 'Englishmen and the Spanish Inquisition 1558–1625', *The English Historical Review*, 87(343): 249–268.

Dante, A. (1918) *The Divine Comedy*, Cambridge: Harvard University Press.

Davis, R. (1954) 'English Foreign Trade, 1660–1700', *The Economic History Review*, 7(2): 150–166.

Dawdy, S.L. (2011) 'Why Pirates Are Back', *Annual Review of Law and Social Science*, 7(1): 361–385.

de Espronceda, J. (1835) 'The Chant of the Pirate', in Walsh, T. (ed.) (1920), *Hispanic Anthology: Poems Translated from the Spanish by English and North American Poets*, New York: Putnam's Sons.

De Martino, F. (1965) *Storia della costituzione romana*, Naples: Edizioni Jovene.

De Montmorency, J.E.G. (1919) 'Piracy and the Barbary Corsairs', *Law Quarterly Review*, 35: 133–142.

De Sousa Santos, B. (2007) 'Beyond Abyssal Thinking: From Global Lines to Ecologies of Knowledges', *Eurozine*, 1(1).

De Souza, P. (1995) 'Greek Piracy', in Powell, A. (ed.), *The Greek World*, New York: Psychology Press.

De Souza, P. (1999) *Piracy in the Graeco-Roman World*, London: Cambridge University Press.

de Vattel, E. (1758) *Le droit des gens ou Principes de la loi naturelle appliqués à la conduite et aux affaires des nations et des souverains*. London: Published by E. Vattel. [Translated as Vattel, E. (1883) *The Law of Nations or the Principles of Natural Law Applied to the Conduct and to the Affairs of Nations and of Sovereigns*, Philadelphia, PA: T. & J. Johnson].

Deane, P.M. (1980) *The First Industrial Revolution*, Cambridge: Cambridge University Press.

Defoe, D. (1725) *An account of the conduct and proceedings of the late John Gow alias Smith, captain of the late Pirates executed for Murther and Piracy*, London: John Applebee.

Deleuze, G. and Guattari, F. (2004) *A Thousand Plateaus: Capitalism and Schizophrenia*, London: Continuum.
Detter, I. (2007) 'The Law of War and Illegal Combatants', *George Washington Law Review*, 75(5): 1049–1421.
Dickey, L. (2001) '*Doux-commerce* and Humanitarian Values: Free Trade, Sociability and Universal Benevolence in Eighteenth Century Thinking', *Grotiana*, 22(3): 271–317.
Dillon, M. and Reid, J. (2009) *The Liberal Way of War: Killing to Make Life Live*, London: Routledge.
Domingo, R. (2010) *The New Global Law*, London: Cambridge University Press.
Drummond, S.K. and Nelson, L.H. (1994) *The Western Frontiers of Imperial Rome*. London: M.E. Sharpe.
Du Tertre, J.B. (1671) *Histoire générale des Antilles habitées par les Francais*, Paris: Thomas Jolly.
Durkheim, E. (1947) *The Division of Labor in Society*, New York: Free Press.
Duverger, M. (1980) 'Le concept d'Empire', in Duverger, M. (ed.), *Le Concept d'Empire*. Paris, PUF, pp. 1–23.
Earle, P. (2005) *The Pirate Wars*, London: Thomas Dunne Books.
Edelstein, D. (2009) *The Terror of Natural Right: Republicanism, the Cult of Nature, and the French Revolution*, Chicago IL: University of Chicago Press.
Elden, S. (2006) 'Spaces of Humanitarian Exception', *Geografiska Annaler: Series B, Human Geography*, 88(4): 477–485.
Engels, F. (1958) *The Condition of the Working Class in England*, New York: Macmillan.
Engels, F. (1975) 'A Pirate Tale', in Marx, K. and Engels, F. (eds), *Marx/Engels Collected Works Volume 2*, London: Lawrence & Wishart, pp. 557–572.
Engels, F. (1976) 'Letters from London', in Marx, K. and Engels, F. (eds), *On Literature and Art*, Moscow: Progress Publishers.
Ennis, D. (2002) *Enter the Press-Gang: Naval Impressment in Eighteenth-Century British Literature*, Newark, DE: University of Delaware Press.
Eppstein, J. (2012) *The Catholic Tradition of the Law of Nations*, London: The Lawbook Exchange.
Etemad, B. (2001) *La possession du monde. Poids et mesures de la colonisation*, Bruxelles: Complexe.
Exquemelin, A. (1684) *The History of the Buccaneers of America*, London: B.B. Mussey & Co.
Fairclough, N.L. (2005) 'Blair's Contribution to Elaborating a New Doctrine of International Community', *Journal of Language and Politics*, 4(1): 41–63.
Fassbender, B. (2009) *The United Nations Charter As the Constitution of the International Community*, The Hague: Brill Academic Publishing.
Fattah, H.M. (2006) 'U.S. Rejects Truce Offer From Bin Laden', *The New York Times*, p. 3.
Feinstein, L. and Slaughter, A.M. (2004) 'A Duty to Prevent', *Foreign Affairs*, 83(1): 136.
Fenn, P.T. (1925) 'Justinian and the Freedom of the Sea', *The American Journal of International Law*, 19(4): 176–192.
Fichte, J.G. (2012) *The Closed Commercial State*, New York: Suny Press.
Finch, G.A. (1937) 'Piracy in the Mediterranean', *The American Journal of International Law*, 31(4): 659–665.
Fink, L. (2011) *Sweatshops at Sea: Merchant Seamen in the World's First Globalized Industry, from 1812 to the Present*, Chapel Hill, NC: University of North Carolina Press.
Fisher, S. (1974) *Barbary Legend: War, Trade, and Piracy in North Africa, 1415–1830*, Westport, CT: Greenwood Press.
Fitzpatrick, P. (1992) *The Mythology of Modern Law*, London: Routledge.

Flavel, J. (1820) *The Whole Works of John Flavel: Late Minister of the Gospel at Dartmouth, Devon*, London: W. Baynes and Son.

Florus, L. (2009) *Epitomae de Tito Livio Bellorum Omnium Annorum*, New York: BiblioBazaar.

Flynn, G. (1966) 'Padre Las Casas, Literature, and the Just War', *Revista de Historia de América*, (61/62): 57–72.

Foucault, M. (1977) 'Nietzsche, Genealogy, History', in Bouchard, D. (ed.), *Language, Counter-Memory, Practice: Selected Essays and Interviews*. Ithaca, NY: Cornell University Press.

Foucault, M. [1977] (2000) 'Lives of Infamous Men', in Faubion, J.D. (ed.), *Power: Essential Works of Foucault 1954–1984*. New York: The New Press, pp. 157–175.

Foucault, M. (1979) *Discipline and Punish: The Birth of the Prison*, New York: Vintage Books.

Foucault, M. (1986) 'Of Other Spaces', *Diatrics*, 16(1): 22–27.

Foucault, M. (2001) *Madness and Civilization: A History of Insanity in the Age of Reason*, London: Routledge.

Foucault, M. (2003) *Society Must Be Defended. Lectures at the College de France 1976*, London: Penguin Books.

Foucault, M. (2008) *The Birth of Biopolitics: Lectures at the Collège de France, 1978–79*, New York: Palgrave Macmillan.

Foucault, M. (2009) *Security, Territory, Population: Lectures at the Collège de France 1977–1978*, New York: Picador.

Fox, G.E. (1973) *British Admirals and Chinese Pirates, 1832–1869*, London: Hyperion Press.

Francalanci, G. and Romanò, D. (1994) *Lines in the Sea*, Amsterdam: Martinus Nijhoff Publishers.

Franck, T.M. (2001) 'When, If Ever, May States Deploy Military Force Without Prior Security Council Authorization', *Washington University Journal of Law & Policy*, 5(1): 51–68.

Franck, T.M. and Patel, F. (1991) 'UN Police Action in Lieu of War: "The Old Order Changeth"', *The American Journal of International Law*, 85(1): 63–74.

Frank, W.C. (1990) 'Politico-military Deception at Sea in the Spanish Civil War, 1936–39', *Intelligence and National Security*, 5(3): 84–112.

French, P. and Chambers, S. (2010) *Oil on Water: Tankers, Pirates and the Rise of China*, London: Zed Books.

Friedman, T. (1999) *The Lexus and the Olive Tree: Understanding Globalizations*, New York: Ferrar, Straus and Giroux.

Galiani, F. (1782) *De doveri di principi neutrali verso i principi guerreggianti, e di questi verso i neutrali*, Naples: Franco Moirano.

Galli, C. (1996) *Genealogia della politica: Carl Schmitt e la crisi del pensiero politico moderno*, Bologna: Il Mulino.

Galli, C. (2001) *Spazi politici: L'età moderna e l'età globale*, Bologna: Il Mulino.

Galli, C. (2009) 'On War and on the Enemy', *CR: The New Centennial Review*, 9(2): 195–219.

Garett, G. (1955) *The American Story*, Houston, TX: Ludwig von Mises Institute.

Garlan, Y. (1987) 'War, Piracy and Slavery in the Greek World', *Slavery & Abolition*, 8(1): 7–21.

Gathii, J. (2010) 'The Use of Force Freedom of Commerce, and Double Standards in Prosecuting Pirates in Kenya', *Legal Studies Research Paper Series*, 8(1): 59–91.

Genet, R. (1938) 'The Charge of Piracy in the Spanish Civil War', *The American Journal of International Law*, 32(2): 253–263.

Gentili, A. (1933) *De iure belli libri tres*, London: Humphrey Milford.

Gerassi-Navarro, N. (1999) *Pirate Novels: Fictions of Nation Building in Spanish America*, Durham, NC: Duke University Press.

Germond, B. and Smith, M.E. (2009) 'Re-thinking European Security Interests and the ESDP: Explaining the EU's Anti-piracy Operation', *Contemporary Security Policy*, 30(3): 573–593.

Gettleman, J. (2008a) 'Somali Pirates Tell Their Side: They Want Only Money', *The New York Times*, 1 October, p. 12.

Gettleman, J. (2008b) 'Somalia's Pirates Flourish in a Lawless Nation', *The New York Times*, 31 October, p. 7.

Ginossar, S. (1978) 'Outlawing Terrorism', *Israeli Law Review*, 13(1): 150–159.

Giovanopoulos, A. (2004) 'Captain Kidd and the King: Piracy and Politics in Restoration England', in Fludernik, M. and Olsen, G. (eds.), *In the Grip of the Law: Trials, Prisons, and the Space Between*, Frankfurt: Peter Lang.

Girard, R. (1986) *The Scapegoat*, Baltimore, MD: John Hopkins University Press.

Gladfelder, H. (2001) *Criminality and Narrative in Eighteenth Century England: Beyond the Law*, Baltimore, MD: John Hopkins University Press.

Glennon, M.J. (1999) 'The New Interventionism: The Search for a Just International Law', *Foreign Affairs*, 78(2): 2–7.

Goldman, E. (1901) 'The Tragedy at Buffalo', in Falk, C. (eds.) (2003), *Emma Goldman: A Documentary History of the American Years, 1890–1919, Volume 1: Made for America, 1890–1901*, Berkeley, CA: University of California Press, pp. 471–477.

Goodwin, J.M. (2006) 'Universal Jurisdiction and the Pirate: Time for an Old Couple to Part', *Vanderbilt Journal of Transnational Law*, 39(1): 973–1012.

Gopalan, S. (2010) 'Put Pirates to the Sword: Targeted Killings are a Necessary, Justified and Legal Response to High-seas Piracy', *The Wall Street Journal*, January 18: 13–14.

Gordon, R. (1997) 'Saving Failed States: Sometimes a Neocolonialist Notion', *American University Journal of International Law & Politics*, 12(6): 903–912.

Gormley, W.P. (1963) 'Development and Subsequent Influence of the Roman Legal Norm of Freedom of the Seas', *The University of Detroit Law Journal*, 40(1): 561–584.

Gosse, P. (1926) *My Pirate Library*, London: Ayer Publishing.

Gosse, P. (2006) *The Pirates' Who's Who. Giving Particulars of the Lives & Deaths of the Pirates & Buccaneers*, Teddington, MA: Echo Library.

Gould, E.H. (2003) 'Zones of Law, Zones of Violence: The Legal Geography of the British Atlantic, circa 1772', *The William and Mary Quarterly*, 60(3): 471.

Graeber, D. (2004) *Fragments of an Anarchist Anthropology*, Cambridge: Prickly Paradigm Press.

The Grand Pyrate: or, the Life and Death of Capt. George Cusack the Great Sea-Robber (1676), London: Jonathan Edwin [Anonymous Author].

Green, L.C. (1976) 'International Criminal Code – Now', *An. Dalhousie Law Journal*, 3(2): 560–592.

Greenblatt, S. (1991) *Marvelous Possessions: The Wonder of the New World*, London: Oxford University Press.

Greene, J. (2008) 'Hostis Humani Generis', *Critical Inquiry*, 34(4): 683–705.

Grewe, W.G. (2000) *The Epochs of International Law*, London: Walter de Gruyter.

Gros, F. (2006) *États de Violence*, Paris: Gallimard.

Grossman, J. (2002) *The Art of Alibi: English Law Courts and the Novel*, Baltimore, MD: John Hopkins University Press.

Grotius, H. (1646) *De iure belli et pacis*, Amsterdam: Apud Johannem Blaev.

Grotius, H. (1925) *The Laws of War and Peace*. New York: Bobbs-Merrill.

Grotius, H. (2001) *The Freedom of the Seas, Or, the Right Which Belongs to the Dutch to Take Part in the East Indian Trade*, New York: The Lawbook Exchange.

Habermas, J. (2000) 'Bestialitat und Humanitat', in Merkel, Reinhard (ed.) (2000), *Der Kosovo-Krieg und das Volkerrecht*, Frankfurt am Main: Suhrkamp, pp. 51–65.

Halberstam, M. (1988) 'Terrorism on the High Seas: the Achilla Lauro, Piracy and the IMO Convention on Maritime Safety', *American Journal of International Law*, 82(2): 269–310.

Halpern, P.G. (1995) *Naval History of World War I*, Washington, DC: Naval Institute Press.

Hamblin, J. (2008) *Poison in the Well: Radioactive Waste in the Oceans at the Dawn of the Nuclear Age*, Rutgers, NJ: Rutgers University Press.

Hansen, S.J. (2008) 'Modern Piracy as a Subject of Academic Enquiry', e-International Relations. Accessed at http://www.e-ir.info/2008/12/19/modern-piracy-as-a-subject-of-academic-enquiry [11 May 2012].

Hanson, F. (1792) 'Introduction', in Hanson, F., Wood, W. and Edward, B., *Laws of Jamaica*, San Jago de la Vega: Alexander Aikman.

Hardt, M. and Negri, A. (2000) *Empire*, Cambridge, MA: Harvard University Press.

Hardt, M. and Negri, A. (2004) *Multitude: War and Democracy in the Age of Empire*, New York: The Penguin Press.

Haring, E.P. (1910) *The Buccaneers in the West Indies in the Seventeenth Century*, London: E.P. Dutton.

Harries, J. (2001) *Law and Empire in Late Antiquity*, Cambridge: Cambridge University Press.

Harris, W.V. (1985) *War and Imperialism in Republican Rome: 32–70 B.C.*, London: Oxford University Press.

Harris, W.V. (1999) 'Demography, Geography and the Sources of Roman Slaves', *The Journal of Roman Studies*, 89(1): 62–75.

Hart, J. (2001) *Representing the New World: The English and French Uses of the Example of Spain*, London: Palgrave Macmillan.

Harvey, D. (2005) *The New Imperialism*, London: Oxford University Press.

Headrick, D.R. (1979) 'The Tools of Imperialism: Technology and the Expansion of European Colonial Empires in the Nineteenth Century', *The Journal of Modern History*, 51(2): 231–263.

Hegel, G.W.F. (1991) *Elements of the Philosophy of Right*, London: Cambridge University Press.

Hegesippus (2004) 'On Halonnesus', in Philipps, D. (ed.), *Athenian Political Oratory: Sixteen Key Speeches*, London: Routledge, pp. 139–164.

Heller-Roazen, D. (2009) *The Enemy of All: Piracy and the Law of Nations*, New York: Zone Books.

Heller-Roazen, D. (2011) 'Introduction to "The Concept of Piracy"', *Humanity: An International Journal of Human Rights, Humanitarianism, and Development*, 2(1): 23–25.

Henig, R.B. (1998) *Weimar Republic, 1919–1933*, New York: Psychology Press.

Herwig, H. (2000) 'Total Rhetoric, Limited War: Germany's U-boat Campaign, 1917–1918', in Chickering, R. and Forster, S. (eds), *Great War, Total War: Combat and Mobilization on the Western Front, 1914–1918*, London: Cambridge University Press, pp. 189–206.

Hesse, B. (2011) 'A Creolization of the Political', in Lionnet, F. and Shih, S. (eds), *The Creolization of Theory*, Durham, NC: Duke University Press, pp. 37–51.

Hickman, D.J. (2011) 'Terrorism as a Violation of the "Law of Nations": Finally Overcoming the Definitional Problem', *Wisconsin International Law Journal*, 29: 447–642.

Hill, C. (1975) *The World Turned Upside Down: Radical Ideas During the English Revolution*, Harmondsworth: Penguin Books.

Hill, C. (1986) 'Radical Pirates?', in *The Collected Essays of Christopher Hill. Volume 3: People and Ideas in 17th Century England*. Brighton: Harvester Press, pp. 161–187.

Hill, C. (1996) *Liberty Against the Law: Some Seventeenth-Century Controversies*, London: Penguin Books.

Hixson, W. (2002) *The Atomic Bomb in History and Memory*, London: Routledge.

Hobbes, T. (2010) *Leviathan*, New York: Broadview Press.

Hobsbawm, E. (1995) *Age of Extremes: The Short Twentieth Century 1914–1991*, London: Abacus.

Hobsbawm, E. (2010) *Age Of Empire 1875–1914*, London: Hachette.

Hobsbawm, E.J. (1959) *Primitive Rebels: Studies in Archaic Forms of Social Movements in the 19th and 20th Century*, New York: Norton.

Hobsbawm, E.J. (1972) *Bandits*, London: Pelican.

Hobson, J.A. (1902) *Imperialism: A Study*. New York: James Pott and Co.

Hoffner, J. (1969) *Kolonialismus und Evangelium*, Trier: Paulinus-Verlag.

Homan, K. and Kamerling, S. (2010) 'Operational Challenges to Counterpiracy Operations off the Coast of Somalia', in Van Ginkel, B. and Van der Putten, F. (eds), *The International Response to Somali Piracy: Challenges and Opportunities*. Leiden Martinus Nijhoff Publishers, pp. 65–103.

Homer (2004) *The Homeric Hymns*, Baltimore, MD: Johns Hopkins University Press.

Hopkins, K. (1983) 'Introduction', in Garnsey, P., Hopkins, K. and Whittaker, C.R. (eds), *Trade in the Ancient Economy*, London: Chatto & Windus.

Horace (1882) *The Odes and Carmen Saeculare*, London: George Bell and Sons.

Horder, M. (1975) 'An Elizabethan Sailor', *Blackwood's Magazine*, 318: 266–270.

Horkheimer, M. and Adorno, T. (2007) *Dialectic of Enlightenment*, Stanford, CA: Stanford University Press.

Horne, J. (2002) *State, Society and Mobilization in Europe During the First World War*, Cambridge: Cambridge University Press.

Houck, J.W. (1993) 'Command and Control of United Nations Forces in the Era of Peace Enforcement', *Duke Journal of Comparative & International Law*, 4: 1.

Howard, N.P. (1993) 'The Social and Political Consequences of the Allied Food Blockade of Germany, 1918–19', *German History*, 11(2): 161–188.

Hunter, M. (2010) 'Patriots and a Menace: American Values and the Pirate Paradox, 1776–1827', *Journal for Maritime Research*, 12(1): 1–26.

Hurlburt, K. (2012) 'The Human Cost of Somali Piracy' [online], *Oceans Beyond Piracy*. Available at http://oceansbeyondpiracy.org/sites/default/files/human_cost_of_somali_piracy.pdf [13 June 2012].

Ignatieff, M. (2002) 'Intervention and State Failure', *Dissent*, 12(1): 115–124.

International Chamber of Commerce: International Maritime Bureau (2012) *Piracy and Armed Robbery Against Ships*, Annual Report, 1 January–31 December 2011. Available at http://www.icc-ccs.org/piracy-reporting-centre [12 September 2012].

Intriligator, M.D. and Coulomb, F. (2008) 'Global Security and Human Security, in Jacques Fontanel', in Chatterji, M. (ed.), *War, Peace and Security*, Bingley: Emerald Group Publishing, pp. 53–66.

Jablonski, R.S. and Oliver, S. (2012) 'The Political Economy of Plunder: Economic Opportunity and Modern Piracy', *Journal of Conflict Resolution*. Available at http://jcr.sagepub.com/content/early/2012/07/10/0022002712448907 [25 November 2012].

Jameson, F. (2005) 'Notes on the *Nomos*', *The South Atlantic Quarterly*, 104(2): 199–204.

Jameson, J.F. (1923) *Privateering and Piracy in the Colonial Period, Illustrative Documents*, New York: Augustus M. Kelly.
Janis, M.W. (2003) *An Introduction to International Law*, New York: Aspen Publisher.
Jardine, A. (1788) *Letters from Barbary, France, Spain, Portugal*, London: T. Cadell.
Jaszi, O. and Lewis, J. (1957) *Against the Tyrant: The Tradition and Theory of Tyrannicide*, Glencoe IL: The Free Press.
Jefferson, T. (1786) 'Proposals for Concerted Operation Among the Powers at War with the Piratical States of Barbary', reprinted in Jefferson, T. (1829) *Memoirs Correspondence and Private Papers of Thomas Jefferson: Late President of the United States*, London: Colburn and Bentley, pp. 55–58.
Jensen, R. (2001) 'The United States, International Policing and the War Against Anarchist Terrorism, 1900–1914', *Terrorism and Political Violence*, 13(1): 15–46.
Jesi, F. (1968) *Letteratura e mito*, Torino: Einaudi.
Jesi, F. (1992) *L'accusa del sangue: Mitologie dell'antisemitismo*, Brescia: Morcelliana.
Jewett, T. (2002) 'Terrorism in Early America: The U.S. Wages War Against the Barbary States to End International Blackmail and Terrorism', *Early America Review*, 4(1): 6–15.
Johnson, A., Coleman-Norton, P. and Bourne, F. (2003) *Ancient Roman Statutes: A Translation with Introduction, Commentary, Glossary, and Index*, New York: The Lawbook Exchange.
Johnson, C. (1724) *A General History of the Pyrates*, London: T. Warner.
Johnson, P. (1986) 'The Cancer of Terrorism', in Netanyahu, B. (ed.) (1986), *Terrorism: How the West can Win*, London: Weidenfeld & Nicholson, pp. 31–37.
Jung, C. (2001) *Modern Man in Search of a Soul*, London: Routledge.
Junger, E. (1951) *Der Waldgang*, Frankfurt: Klostermann.
Junger, E. (1993) *Total Mobilization. In The Heidegger Controversy: A Critical Reader*, Baltimore, MD: MIT Press, pp. 119–140.
Justice, A. (1724) *A General Treatise of the Dominion of the Sea*. London: T. Page and F. Mount.
Kaczynski, T. (2005) *Industrial Society And Its Future*, Minneapolis, MN: Filiquarian Publishing, LLC.
Kelsen, H. (1920) *Das Problem der Souveränität und die Theorie des Völkerrechts. Beitrag zu einer Reinen Rechstlehre*, Tübingen: Mohr.
Kelsen, H. (1947) 'Will the Judgment in the Nuremberg Trial Constitute a Precedent in International Law?', *International Law Quarterly*, 1(1): 153–171.
Kelsen, H. (1952) *Principles of International Law*, New York: The Lawbook Exchange, Ltd.
Kelsen, H. (2008) *Peace Through Law*, New York: The Lawbook Exchange, Ltd.
Keppel, H. (1861) *The Expedition to Borneo of H. M. S. Dido for the Suppression of Piracy: With Extracts from the Journal of James Brooke, Esq., of Sarawak (Now Agent for the British Government in Borneo)*, New York: Harper and Brothers.
Kerton-Johnson, N. (2010) *Justifying America's Wars: The Conduct and Practice of US Military Intervention Since 1990*, London: Taylor & Francis.
Killingray, D. (2004) 'Introduction. Imperial Seas: Cultural Exchange and Commerce in the English Empire, 1780–1900', in Killingray, D., Lincoln, M. and Rigby, N. (eds), *Maritime Empires: British Imperial Maritime Trade in the Nineteenth Century*, Rochester, NY: Boydell Press.
Kipling, R. (1994) *The Collected Poems of Rudyard Kipling*, London: Wordsworth Editions.
Koebner, R. (1961) *Empire*, New York: Cambridge University Press.
Konstam, A. (2008) *Piracy: The Complete History*, Oxford: Osprey Publishing.
Kontorovich, E. (2004) 'The Piracy Analogy: Modern Universal Jurisdiction's Hollow Foundation', *Harvard International Law Journal*, 45(1): 183–222.

Koselleck, P.R. (2000) *Critique and Crises: Enlightenment and the Pathogenesis of Modern Society*, Cambridge, MA: MIT Press.

Koskenniemi, M. (1997) 'Lauterpacht: The Victorian Tradition in International Law', *European Journal of International Law*, 8(2): 215–263.

Koskenniemi, M. (2001) *The Gentle Civilizer of Nations: The Rise and Fall of International Law 1870–1960*, Cambridge: Cambridge University Press.

Koskenniemi, M. (2004) 'Hersch Lauterpacht and the Development of International Criminal Law', *Journal of International Criminal Justice*, 2(3): 810–825.

Koskenniemi, M. (2011) 'Empire and International Law: The Real Spanish Contribution', *University of Toronto Law Journal*, 61(1): 1–36.

Kraska, J. (2009a) 'Coalition Strategy and the Pirates of the Gulf of Aden and the Red Sea', *Comparative Strategy*, 28(3): 197–216.

Kraska, J. (2009b) 'Fresh Thinking for an Old Problem: Report of the Naval War College Workshop on Countering Maritime Piracy', *Naval War College Review*, 62(4): 66–67.

Kraska, J. and Wilson, B. (2009) 'The Global Maritime Partnership and Somali Piracy', *Defense & Security Analysis*, 25(3): 223–234.

Krishnan, A. (2009) *Killer Robots: Legality and Ethicality of Autonomous Weapons*, Farnham: Ashgate Publishing.

Kumar, S. (2012) '2 fishermen Shot Dead on High Seas', *The Hindu* (16 February). Available at http://www.thehindu.com/news/states/kerala/article2899651.ece [17 September 2012].

Kunz, J.L. (1951) 'Bellum Justum and Bellum Legale', *The American Journal of International Law*, 45(3): 528–534.

Laborit, H. (1976) *Éloge de la fuite*, Paris: Éditions Robert Laffont.

Lafargue, P. (1975) *The Evolution of Property from Savagery and Civilization*, London: New Park Publications.

Lahodynsky, O. (1992) 'The Changing Face of Austrian Neutrality', *Nato Review*, 40(6): 24–28.

Land, C. (2007) 'Flying the Black Flag: Revolt, Revolution and the Social Organization of Piracy in the Golden Age', *Management & Organizational History*, 2(2): 169–192.

Lane, K.E. (1998) *Pillaging the Empire: Piracy in the Americas, 1500–1750*, New York: M.E. Sharpe.

Lane-Poole, S. (1890) *The Barbary Corsairs*, London: Allen and Unwin.

Langeweische, W. (2003) 'Anarchy at Sea', *Atlantic Monthly*, 9: 50–80.

Latimer, J. (2009) *Buccaneers of the Caribbean: How Piracy Forged an Empire*, Cambridge, MA: Harvard University Press.

Lauterpacht, H. (1933) *The Function of Law in the International Community*, Oxford: Clarendon Press.

Lauterpacht, H. (1936) 'The Covenant as the "Higher Law"', *British Yearbook of International Law*, 12(1): 54–65.

Lauterpacht, H. (1938) 'The League of Nations', in Lauterpacht, E. (ed.) (1973), *International Law, Being the Collected Papers of Hersch Lauterpacht*, vol. 3, London: Cambridge University Press, pp. 582–587.

Lauterpacht, H. (1939) 'Insurrection et piraterie', *Revue Generale de Droit International Public*, 4(2): 513–549.

Lauterpacht, H. (1941) 'The Reality of the Law of Nations', in Lauterpacht, E. (ed.) (1973), *International Law, Being the Collected Papers of Hersch Lauterpacht*, vol. 2, London: Cambridge University Press, pp. 21–28.

Lauterpacht, H. (1950) *International Law and Human Rights*, London: F.A. Praeger.
La Vergata, A. (2005) *Guerra e Darwinismo Sociale*, Soveria Manelli: Rubbettino Editore.
Layton, S. (2011) 'Discourses of Piracy in an Age of Revolutions', *Itinerario*, 35(2): 81–97.
Lefèbvre, H. (1991) *The Production of Space*, Oxford: Wiley-Blackwell.
Lehr, P. (2008) 'Off the Lawless Coast of Somalia, a Question of Who is Pirating Who', *Chicago Tribune*, 10 October.
Lehr, P. (2009) 'You are Being Lied to about Pirates', *The Independent*, January 5.
Leiby, R. (2001) 'Terrorists by Another Name: The Barbary Pirates', *Washington Post*, 15 October: 1–2.
Leiner, F.C. (2006) *The End of Barbary Terror: America's 1815 War Against the Pirates of North Africa*, Oxford: Oxford University Press.
Lepard, B.D. (2003) *Rethinking Humanitarian Intervention: A Fresh Legal Approach Based on Fundamental Ethical Principles in International Law and World Religions*, University Park, PA: Penn State Press.
Lewontin R.C., Rose S. and Kamin, L.J. (1985) *Not in our Genes: Biology, Ideology, and Human Nature*, New York: Pantheon Books.
Linebaugh, P. (1991) *The London Hanged: Crime and Civil Society in the Eighteenth Century*, London: Penguin.
Linebaugh, P. and Rediker, M. (2000) *The Many-headed Hydra: Sailors, Slaves, Commoners, and the Hidden History of the Revolutionary Atlantic*, Boston, MA: Beacon Press.
List, F. (1856) *National System of Political Economy*, Philadelphia, PA: Lippincott.
Lowenheim, O. (2003) 'Do Ourselves Credit and Render a Lasting Service to Mankind: British Moral Prestige, Humanitarian Intervention, and the Barbary Pirates', *International Studies Quarterly*, 47(1): 23–48.
Luard, E. (1992) *The Balance of Power: The System of International Relations, 1648–1815*, London: Macmillan.
Lumsden, M. (1974) 'New Military Technology and the Erosion of International Law: The Case of the Dum-Dum Bullets', *Instant Research on Peace and Violence*, 4(1): 15–20.
Lunsford, V.W. (2005) *Piracy and Privateering in the Golden Age Netherlands*, Basingstoke: Palgrave.
Lupieri, E. (2011) *In the Name of God: The Making of Global Christianity*, Amsterdam: Eerdmans Publishing.
Luxemburg, R. (1951) *The Accumulation of Capital*, London: Routledge & Kegan Paul.
Macedo, S. and Robinson, M. (2001) *The Princeton Principles on Universal Jurisdiction*, Princeton, NJ: Princeton University Press.
Mackenzie, H. (1884) *Storms and Sunshine of a Soldier's Life: Lt General Colin Mackenzie 1825–1881*, Edinburgh: David Douglas.
Mackie, E. (2005) 'Welcome the Outlaw: Pirates, Maroons, and Caribbean Countercultures', *Cultural Critique*, pp. 24–62.
Macmillan, M. (2003) *Peacemakers: The Paris Conference of 1919 and Its Attempt to End War*, London: John Murray.
Madeley, J. (1999) *Big Business, Poor Peoples: The Impact of Transnational Corporations on the World's Poor*, London: Palgrave Macmillan.
Mainwaring, H. (2008) *The Life and Works of Sir Henry Mainwaring*, London: Lightning Source Incorporated.
Maiolo, J.A. (1999) 'Deception and Intelligence Failure: Anglo-German Preparations for U-boat Warfare in the 1930s', *Journal of Strategic Studies*, 22(4): 55–76.
Maltby, W. (1971) *The Black Legend In England, The Development of Anti-Spanish Sentiment, 1558–1660*, Durham, NC: Duke University Press.

Marsden, P. (2011) *The Levelling Sea: The Story of a Cornish Haven in the Age of Sail*, London: HarperCollins.
Martin, R. (1971) *Recherches sur les agronomes latins et leurs conceptions économiques et socials*, Paris: Les Belles Lettres.
Marx, K. (1955) 'On Proudhon: Marx to JB Schweitzer (24 January 1865)', in Marx, K., *The Poverty of Philosophy*, London: Lawrence & Wishart, pp. 169–172.
Marx, K. (1973) *Grundrisse: Foundations of the Critique of Political Economy*, London: Penguin Classics.
Marx, K. (1976) *Capital: A Critique of Political Economy – Vol. I*, London: Penguin Classics.
Marx, K. (1988) 'Theories of Surplus Value', in Marx, K. and Engels, F. (eds), *Marx/Engels Collected Works Volume 30*, London: Lawrence & Wishart.
Marx, K. (2007) *Capital: A Critique of Political Economy – Vol. III, The Process of Capitalist Production as a Whole*, New York: Cosimo, Inc.
Mastino, A. and Ibba, A. (2006) 'L'imperatore pacator orbis', *Tradizione Romana*, 1(5): 1–12.
Mathew, D. (1924) 'The Cornish and Welsh Pirates in the Reign of Elizabeth', *The English Historical Review*, 39(155): 337–348.
Matsuda, M. and Committee of Experts for the Progressive Codification of International Law (1926) 'Questionnaire no. 6: Piracy', *American Journal of International Law*, 20(3): 222–229.
Mattingly, G. (1963) 'No Peace Beyond What Line?', *Transactions of the Royal Historical Society*, 13(2): 145–162.
Mattox, J.M. (2006) *St. Augustine and the Theory of Just War*, London: Continuum International Publishing Group.
Means, P. (1935) *The Spanish Main, Focus of Envy, 1492–1700*, London: Scribner's Sons.
Mehta, U.S. (1999) *Liberalism and Empire: A Study in Nineteenth Century British Liberal Thought*, Chicago, IL: University of Chicago Press.
Meijer, F. (1986) *A History of Seafaring in the Classical World*, Beckenham: Croom Helm.
Menefeee, S.P. (1993) 'Case of the Castle John, or Greenbeard the Pirate: Environmentalism, Piracy and the Development of International Law', *California Western International Law Journal*, 24(1): 1–42.
Menefeee, S.P. (1993b) 'Case of the Castle John, or Greenbeard the Pirate: Environmentalism, Piracy and the Development of International Law', *California Western International Law Journal*, 24(1): 1–37.
Merriam, J.J. (2001) 'Kosovo and the Law of Humanitarian Intervention', *Case Western Reserve Journal of International Law*, 33(1): 111–138.
Merrien, J. (2003) *Histoire Des Corsaires*, Paris: Ancre de Marine Editions.
Merriman, R. (1962) *The Rise of the Spanish Empire in the Old World and in the New*, New York: Cooper Square Publishers.
Miéville, C. (2006) *Between Equal Rights: A Marxist Theory of International Law*, London: Haymarket Books.
Mirabeau, V.R. (1883) *L'Ami des homes*, Paris: Albert Rouxel.
Miramontes y Zuazola, J. (1978) *Armas Antárticas*, Caracas: Biblioteca Ayacucho.
Mo, J. (2002) 'Options to Combat Maritime Piracy in Southeast Asia', *Ocean Development & International Law*, 33(3): 343–358.
Mohamed, A.E. (2001) 'Somalia's Degrading Environment: Causes and Effects of Deforestation and Hazardous Waste Dumping in Somalia', *Somali Ctr. for Water and Env't.* Available at http://www.banadir.com/a.htm [27 September 2012].

Mommsen, T., Krüger, P., Schoell, R. and Kroll, W. (eds) (1954), *Corpus Iuris Civilis*, Berlin: Apud Weidmannos.

Monaco, L. (1996) *Persecutio piratarum: Battaglie ambigue e svolte costituzionali nella Roma repubblicana. Vol. 1*, Napoli: Jovene.

Montesquieu, C. (2011) *The Spirit of Laws*, New York: Cosimo, Inc.

Mooney, C. (2001) 'The Barbary Analogy', *American Prospect Online*, 16 October. Available at *http://www.prospect.org/webfeatures/2001/10/mooney-c-10-16.html* [12 March 2011].

Mowat, R.B. (1939) 'British Sea Power and World Peace', *Royal United Services Institution Journal*, 84(533): 52–56.

Muller-Fraureuth, C. (1965) *Die Ritter und Rauberromane: Ein Beitrag zur Bildungsgeschicte des Deutschen Volkes*, Hildesheim: Georg Olms.

Mumford, L. (1968) *The City in History: Its Origins, Its Transformations, and Its Prospects*, New York: Harvest Books.

Mumford, L. (1974) *The Pentagon of Power*, New York: Harcourt Brace Jovanovich.

Mundy, R. (1848) *Narrative of Events in Borneo and Celebes, Down to the Occupation of Labuan: from the Journals of James Brooke, Esq. Rajah of Sarawak, and Governor of Labuan*, London: John Murray.

Murphy, M. (2007) 'Contemporary Piracy and Maritime Terrorism', *Adelphi Papers*, 47 (388): 1–88.

Negri, A. (2008) 'Sovereignty: That Divine Ministry of the Affairs of Earthly Life', *Journal for Cultural and Religious Theory*, 9(1): 96–100.

Neilson, F. (1954) *The Churchill Legend*, London: C.C. Nelson.

Newman, S. (2001) *From Bakunin to Lacan: Anti-authoritarianism and the Dislocation of Power*, Lanham, MD: Lexington Books.

Newman, S. (2004) 'Terror, Sovereignty and Law: On the Politics of Violence', *German Law Journal*, 5(1): 569–584.

News from sea or, the takeing of the cruel pirate, being a full and true relation how Captain Cewsicke, alias Dixon, alias Smith, an Irish-Pyrate took an English ship of 500. Tuns culled the Saint Anne (1674), London: printed for R.W. [Anonymous Author].

Nolte, G. (2005) 'Sovereignty as Responsibility', *American Society of International Law Proceedings*, 99(2): 389–392.

North, D.C. (1968) 'Sources of Productivity Change in Ocean Shipping, 1600–1850', *Journal of Political Economy*, 76(5): 953–970.

Norton, A. and Schwedler, J. (1993) '(In)security Zones in South Lebanon', *Journal of Palestine Studies*, 23(1): 61–79.

O'Connell, D.P. (1982) *The International Law of the Sea*, Oxford: Clarendon Press.

Olson, M. (2000) *Power and Prosperity: Outgrowing Communist and Capitalist Dictatorships*, Oxford: Oxford University Press.

Onuoha, F. (2009) 'Sea Piracy and Maritime Security in the Horn of Africa: The Somali Coast and Gulf of Aden in Perspective', *African Security Studies*, 18(3): 31–44.

Oren, M.B. (2008) *Power, Faith, and Fantasy: America in the Middle East: 1776 to the Present*, London: W.W. Norton & Company.

Orford, A. (1999) 'Muscular Humanitarianism: Reading the Narratives of the New Interventionism', *European Journal of International Law*, 10(4): 679–711.

Ormerod, H.A. (1996) *Piracy in the Ancient World*, Baltimore, MD: Johns Hopkins University Press.

Ozick, C. (1997) 'Dostoyevsky's Unabomber', *The New Yorker*, pp. 114–121.

Pagden, A. (1987) *The Fall of Natural Man: The American Indian and the Origins of Comparative Ethnology*, Cambridge: Cambridge University Press.

Pagden, A. (1995) *Lords of All the World: Ideologies of Empire in Spain, Britain and France c. 1500–1800*, Yale, CT: Yale University Press.
Panjabi, R. (2009) 'Pirates of Somalia: Opportunistic Predators or Environmental Prey', *The William & Mary Environmental Law and Policy Review*, 34: 377–491.
Panzac, D. (2005) *Barbary Corsairs: The End of a Legend, 1800–1820*, Leiden: Brill.
Parchami, A. (2009) *Hegemonic Peace and Empire: The Pax Romana, Britannica and Americana*, London: Taylor & Francis.
Parry, J.H. (1971) *Trade and Dominion: The European Overseas Empires in the Eighteenth Century*, New York: Praeger Publishers.
Pascal, B. (1995) *Pensées*, Harmondsworth: Penguin.
Peters, J.S. (2005) 'A Bridge over Chaos: "De Jure Belli", "Paradise Lost", Terror, Sovereignty, Globalism, and the Modern Law of Nations', *Comparative Literature*, 57(4): 273–293.
Peters, R. (2009) 'The Audacity of Rope: Crush All the Pirates – Now', *New York Post*, p. 11.
Petty, W. (1899) *The Economics Writings of Sir William Petty Together with the Observations Upon the Bills of Mortality*, London: Cambridge University Press.
Phillipson, C. (1911) *The International Law and Custom of Ancient Greece and Rome*, London: Macmillan.
Phillmore, R. (1871) *Commentaries Upon International Law*, vol. 1, London: Butterworths.
Philo (1971) *Embassy to Gaius*, Cambridge: Harvard University Press.
Ploch, L. (2010) *Piracy Off the Horn of Africa*, Darby, PE: DIANE Publishing.
Plutarch (1923) *The Parallel Lives*, Cambridge, MA: Harvard University Press.
Plutarch (1998) *De Alexandri Magni Fortuna aut virtute*, Napoli: M.D'Auria.
Policante, A. (2010) 'War Against Biopower: Timely Reflections on an Historicist Foucault', *Theory & Event*, 13(1): 87–103.
Policante, A. (2011a) 'Of Cameras and Balaclavas: Violence, Myth, and the Convulsive Kettle', *Globalizations*, 8(4): 457–471.
Policante, A. (2011b) 'Game of Drones: Cubicle Warriors and the Drudge of War', *Nyx*, 7: 110–116.
Policante, A. (2012a) 'Foucault, Subjectivity and Flight: Witchcraft, Possession and the Resistance of the Flesh', *Material Foucaultiani*, 1(1): 235–259.
Policante, A. (2012b) *I Nuovi Mercenari: Mercato Mondiale e Privatizzazione della Guerra*, Verona: Ombre Corte.
Policante, A. (2012c) 'The Pirate Camp: An Heterotopia for the 21st Century?', in *The Pirate Camp Reader*, Torino: Kanichen-Haus, pp. 17–23.
Policante, A. (2012d) 'Vampires of Capital: Gothic Reflections Between Horror and Hope', *Works and Days*, 59(3): 213–230.
Pollock, F. (1901) 'The History of the Law of Nature: A Preliminary Study', *Columbia Law Review*, 1(1):11–32.
Polybius (1922) *The Histories*, Cambridge, MA: Harvard University Press.
Porton, R. (1999) *Film and the Anarchist Imagination*, London: Verso.
Prange, S.R. (2011) 'A Trade of No Dishonor: Piracy, Commerce, and Community in the Western Indian Ocean, Twelfth to Sixteenth Century', *The American Historical Review*, 116(5): 1269–1293.
Proudhon, P.J. (1994) *What is Property?*, Cambridge: Cambridge University Press.
Quesada, S. (2011) *Espejo de Paciencia*, Madrid: Linkgua digital.
Raffles, T.S. (1965) *The History of Java*, 2 vols, Kuala Lumpur: Oxford University Press.
Randall, K.C. (1988) 'Universal Jurisdiction Under International Law', *Texas Law Review*, 66(1): 785–798.

Rappaport, S. (1989) *World Within Worlds: The Structure of Life in Sixteenth-Century London*, Cambridge: Cambridge University Press.
Rech, W. (2012) 'Rightless Enemies: Schmitt and Lauterpacht on Political Piracy', *Oxford Journal of Legal Studies*, 32(2): 235–263.
Reclaim the Seas (2011) 'Somali Voices' [online], *Reclaim the Seas*. Available at http://reclaim-the-seas.blogspot.co.uk/p/somali-voices.html [13 June 2012].
Rediker, M. (1981) '"Under the Banner of King Death": The Social World of Anglo-American Pirates, 1716 to 1726'. *The William and Mary Quarterly*, 38(2): 203–227.
Rediker, M. (1989) *Between the Devil and the Deep Blue Sea: Merchant Seamen, Pirates and the Anglo-American Maritime World, 1700–1750*, London: Cambridge University Press.
Rediker, M. (2004) *Villains of All Nations: Atlantic Pirates in the Golden Age*, London: Verso.
Reppy, A. (1950) 'The Grotian Doctrine of the Freedom of the Seas Reappraised', *Fordham Law Review*, 19(3): 243–285.
Reyes, A. (2009) *Can't Go Home Again Sovereign Entanglements and the Black Radical Tradition in the Twentieth Century*, Dissertation submitted in partial fulfillment of the requirements for the degree of Doctor of Philosophy in the Literature Program in the Graduate School of Duke University.
Reynolds, C. (1974) *Command of the Sea: The History and Strategy of Maritime Empires*, New York: William Morrow.
Riggio, A. (1950) *Gli stati barbareschi e la Calabria (1535–1816)*, Firenze: La Nuova Italia.
Ritchie, R.C. (1986) *Captain Kidd and the War Against the Pirates*, Cambridge, MA: Harvard University Press.
Robertson, G. (2000) *Crimes Against Humanity: The Struggle For Global Justice*, London: Penguin.
Robinet, A. (1994) *G. W. Leibniz. Le meilleur des mondes par la balance de l'Europe*, Paris, Presses Universitaires de France.
Rodger, N. (1986) *The Safeguard of the Sea: A Naval History of Britain 660–1649*, London: Norton & Rodgers.
Roosevelt, T. (1901) 'State of the Union Address (December 3, 1901)', in *State of the Union Addresses of Theodore Roosevelt* (2007), Teddington, MA: Echo Library.
Rosello, P.L. (1962) 'Res communes omnium', *Revista de Derecho Puertorriqueno*, 2 (1): 1–27.
Rosinski, H. (1950) *The Evolution of Sea Power*, Newport, RI: Naval War College.
Rubin, A.P. (2006) *The Law of Piracy*, Honolulu, HA: University Press of the Pacific.
Ruschi, F. (2005) 'Leviathan e Behemoth. Modelli egemonici e spazi coloniali in Carl Schmitt', *Quaderni fiorentini per la storia del pensiero giuridico moderno* (XXXIII/XXXIV), pp. 379–462.
Ruschi, F. (2009) 'Communis hostis omnium. La pirateria in Carl Schmitt', *Quaderni fiorentini per la storia del pensiero giuridico moderno*, 38(2): 1215–1276.
Rutter, O. (1986) *The Pirate Wind: Tales of the Sea-Robbers of Malaya*, Singapore: Oxford University Press.
Said, E.W. (1978) *Orientalism*, New York: Pantheon Books.
Salgari, E. (1896), I Pirati della Malesia, Genova: Donath.
Samuels, J. (2010) 'How Piracy Has Shaped the Relationship Between American Law and International Law', *American University Law Review*, 59(5): 1231–1265.
Savage, R. (2007) '"Disease Incarnate": Biopolitical Discourse and Genocidal Dehumanisation in the Age of Modernity', *Journal of Historical Sociology*, 20(3): 404–440.
Scelle, G. (1932) *Précis de droit des gens; principes et systématique*, Paris: Librairie du Recueil Sirey.
Scheffler, A. (2010) 'Piracy: Threat or Nuisance?', *NATO Defence College Research Paper*, 56: 1–12.

Schiller, F. (1940) *Samtliche Werke*, Stuttgart and Berlin: J.G. Cotta.
Schmitt, C. (1929) 'Wesen und Werden des faschistischen Staates', in *Schmollers Jahrbuch fur Gesetzgebung, Verwaltung und Volkswirtschaft*, 9(1): 107–115, now republished in Schmitt, C. (1994), *Positionen und Begriffe*, Berlin: Duncker & Humblot: 124–130; Italian translation now available as: Schmitt, C. 'Essenza e divenire dello stato fascista', in Schmitt, C. (2007), *Posizioni e concetti in lotta con Weimar–Ginevra–Versailles. 1923–1939*, Milano: Giuffrè.
Schmitt, C. (1937) 'Der *Begriffe* der *Piraterie*', *Völkerbund und Völkerrecht*, 4(3): 351–354. Now translated in English as: Schmitt, C. (2011) 'The Concept of Piracy (1937)', *Humanity: An International Journal of Human Rights, Humanitarianism, and Development*, 2(1): 27–29.
Schmitt, C. (1938) *Die Wendung zum diskriminierenden Kriegsbegriff*, Munich: Duncker & Humblot.
Schmitt, C. (1941) 'Sovranità dello Stato e Libertà dei Mari', in Schmitt, C. (1994) *L'unità del mondo e altri saggi*, Roma: Pellicani.
Schmitt, C. (1942) 'La lotta per i grandi spazi e l'illusione Americana', *Lo Stato* 13(1): 173–180.
Schmitt, C. (1950) *Ex Captivitate Salus, Erfahrungen der Zeit 1945/47*, Köln: Greven Verlag.
Schmitt, C. (1955) 'Die geschichtliche Struktur des heutigen Welt-Gegensatzes von Ost und West: Bemerkungen zu Ernst Jungers Schrift, "Der Gordische Knoten"', in Mohler, A. (ed.), *Freundschaftliche Begegnungen*, Frankfurt: Klostermann, pp. 135–167.
Schmitt, C. (1971) 'Premessa', in *Le categorie del Politico*, Bologna: Il Mulino, pp. 9–26.
Schmitt, C. (1985) *Political Theology: Four Chapters on the Concept of Sovereignty*, Cambridge, MA: MIT Press.
Schmitt, C. (1991) *Völkerrechtliche Großraumordnung mit Interventionsverbot fur raumfremde Mächte*, Berlin: Duncker & Humblot.
Schmitt, C. (1997) *Land and Sea*, London: Plutarch Press.
Schmitt, C. (1999) 'Letter to Ernst Junger', in Junger, E. and Schmitt, C. (eds), *Ernst Junger-Carl Schmitt. Briefe 1930–1983*, Stuttgart: Helmuth Kiesel, pp. 129–130.
Schmitt, C. (2003) *The Nomos of the Earth in the International Law of the Jus Publicum Europaeum*, New York: Telos Press.
Schmitt, C. (2007a) *The Concept of the Political*, Chicago, IL: University of Chicago Press.
Schmitt, C. (2007b) *Theory of the Partisan: Intermediate Commentary on the Concept of the Political*, New York: Telos Press.
Schmitt, C. (2011) *Writings on War*, New York: Polity.
Scott, J.B. (1906) *Cases of International Law*, St. Paul: West Pub. Co.
Scott, J.B. (2000) *The Spanish Origin of International Law: Francisco de Vitoria and His Law of Nations*, London: The Lawbook Exchange Ltd.
Scott, W. (1821) The Pirate, Edinburgh: Archibald Constable and Co.
Sebastianelli, P. (2012) *Il Diritto Naturale dell'Appropriazione: Ugo Grozio Alle Origini del Pubblico e del Privato*, Bologna: Emil di Odoya.
Semmel, B. (1970) *The Rise of Free Trade Imperialism: Classical Political Economy and the Empire of Free Trade and Imperialism (1750–1850)*, New York: Cambridge University Press.
Semple, E. (1911) *Influences of Geographic Environment: On the Basis of Ratzel's System of Anthropo-Geography*, New York: Holt Publisher.
Senior, C.M. (1976) *A Nation of Pirates: English Piracy in its Heyday*, New York: David and Charles.
Sestier, J.M. (1880) *La piraterie dans l'antiquité*, Paris: A. Marescq.
Seymour, C. (2003) *Chronicles of America: Woodrow Wilson and the World War 1921*, New York: Kessinger Publishing.

Shakespeare, W. (2010) *The Tempest*, London: Cricket House Books.
Shaler, W. (1826) *Sketches of Algiers*, Boston, MA: Cummings, Hilliard and Company.
Sharafuddin, M. (1996) *Islam and Romantic Orientalism: Literary Encounters with the Orient*, London: I.B.Tauris.
Shomura, C. (2010) ' "These Are Bad People" – Enemy Combatants and the Homopolitics of the "War on Terror"', *Theory & Event*, 13(1): 21–32.
Simpson, G. (2004) *Great Powers and Outlaw States: Unequal Sovereigns in the International Legal Order*, London: Cambridge University Press.
Simpson, G. (2006) 'Enemies of Mankind', in Gunning, J. and Holm, S. (eds), *Ethics, Law, and Society*, Farnham: Ashgate Publishing, pp. 85–94.
Sinor, M.L. and Blackwood, R.M. (2005) 'Confronting Nomadic Terrorism', *Naval Law Review*, 52(1): 98–121.
Sisson, C.J. and Brown, A. (1951) 'The Great Danseker: Literary Significance of a Chancery Suit', *The Modern Language Review*, 46(3/4): 339–354.
Smith, A. (1818) *An Inquiry into the Nature and Causes of the Wealth of Nations*, London: Cooke & Hale.
Sohn, L. (1980) 'Introduction', in Ferencz, B., *An International Criminal Court, a Step Toward World Peace: A Documentary History and Analysis*, Dobbs Ferry, NY: Oceana Publications.
Spiers, E.M. (1975) 'The Use of the Dum Dum Bullet in Colonial Warfare', *The Journal of Imperial and Commonwealth History*, 4(1): 3–14.
St Clair, W. (1990) 'The Impact of Byron's Writings: An Evaluative Approach', in Rutherford, A. (ed.), *Byron: Augustan and Romantic*, London: Macmillan.
Stavridis, J. and LeBron, R. (2010) 'Taming the Outlaw Sea', *The Naval War College Review*, 63(4): 73–84.
Steinberg, P.E. (1999a) 'Lines of Division, Lines of Connection: Stewardship in the World Ocean', *Geographical Review*, 89(2): 254–264.
Steinberg, P.E. (1999b) 'Navigating to Multiple Horizons: Toward a Geography of Ocean-space', *The Professional Geographer*, 51(3): 366–375.
Steinberg, P.E. (2001) *The Social Construction of the Ocean*, Cambridge: Cambridge University Press.
Steiner, G. (1968) *Extraterritorial*, London: Faber.
Stevenson, R.L. (1883) *Treasure Island*, London: Cassell & Company.
Stirner, M. (1995) *The Ego and its Own*, London: Cambridge University Press.
Storr, V. (2004) *Enterprising Slaves and Master Pirates: Understanding Economic Life in the Bahamas*, Oxford: Peter Lang.
Story, J. (1833) 'Commentaries on the Constitution', in Kurland, P.B. and Lerner, R. (eds) (1987), *The Founders' Constitution*, vol. 3, Chicago, IL: University of Chicago Press.
Strabo (1856) *Geography*, London: H.G. Bohn.
Subramanian, L. (2007) 'Of Pirates and Potentates: Maritime Jurisdiction and the Construction of Piracy in the Indian Ocean', in Ghosh, D. and Muecke, S. (eds), *Cultures of Trade: Indian Ocean Exchanges*, Newcastle: Cambridge Scholars Publishing.
Suetonius (1997) *Lives of the Twelve Caesars*, London: Wordsworth Editions.
Suskind, R. (1971) *By Bullet, Bomb, and Dagger: The Story of Anarchism*, London: Macmillan.
Tarling, N. (1963) *Piracy and Politics in the Malay World: A Study of British Imperialism in Nineteenth-century South-east Asia*, Melbourne: F.W. Cheshire.
Tarling, N. (1971) *Britain, the Brookes and Brunei*, Kuala Lumpur: Oxford University Press.
Tarwacka, A. (2009) *Romans and Pirates. Legal Perspective*, Warszawa: Wydawnictwo Uniwerystetu Kardynala Stefana Wyszynskiego.

Tenenti, A. (1961) *Venezia e i corsari*, Bari: Laterza.

Tesón, F.R. (1992) 'The Kantian Theory of International Law', *Columbia Law Review*, 92(1): 53–102.

Tesón, F.R. (1995) 'Collective Humanitarian Intervention', *Michigan Journal of International Law*, 17(3): 323–372.

Tesón, F.R. (2005) 'Ending Tyranny in Iraq', *Ethics & International Affairs*, 19(2): 1–20.

Thomas M.F. (2003) 'Interpretation and Change in the Law of Humanitarian Intervention', in Holzgrefe, J.L. and Keohane, R.O. (eds), *Humanitarian Intervention: Ethical, Legal, and Political Dilemmas*, London: Cambridge University Press, pp. 204–231.

Thomson, A. (1987) *Barbary and Enlightenment: European Attitudes Towards the Maghreb in the 18th Century*, Leiden: Brill.

Thomson, E. (2009) 'The Dutch Miracle, Modified. Hugo Grotius's Mare Liberum, Commercial Governance and Imperial War in the Early-Seventeenth Century', *Grotiana*, 30(1): 107–130.

Thomson, J.E. (1994) *Mercenaries, Pirates, and Sovereigns: State-Building and Extraterritorial Violence in Early Modern Europe*, Princeton, NJ: Princeton University Press.

Thorup, M. (2006) '"Delinquents, Troublemakers, Pirates and Gangsters": New Wars in the Postpolitical Borderland', *Theoria*, 53(110): 97–124.

Thorup, M. (2009) 'Enemy of Humanity: The Anti-Piracy Discourse in Present-Day Anti-Terrorism', *Terrorism and Political Violence*, 21(1): 401–411.

Thorup, M. (2012) *An Intellectual History of Terror: War, Violence and the State*, London: Routledge.

Throop, S.A. and Hyams, P.R. (2010) *Vengeance in the Middle Ages: Emotion, Religion and Feud*, Farnham: Ashgate Publishing.

Thucydides (1962) *History of the Peloponnesian War*, London: W. Heinemann.

Thumfart, J. (2009) 'On Grotius's Mare Liberum and Vitoria's De Indis, Following Agamben and Schmitt', *Grotiana*, 30(1): 65–87.

Tilly, C. (1985) 'War-making and State-making as Organized Crime', in Evans, P., Rueschemeyer, D. and Skocpol, T. (eds), *Bringing the State Back In*, Cambridge: Cambridge University Press, pp. 169–191.

Todorov, T. (1984) *The Conquest of America: The Question of the Other*, Norman, OK: University of Oklahoma Press.

Traverso, E. (2010) *La violenza nazista. Una genealogia*, Bologna: Il Mulino.

Trials of eight persons indited for piracy: Of whom two were acquitted, and the rest found guilty. At a justiciary Court of Admiralty assembled and held in Boston within His Majesty's province of the Massachusetts-Bay in New-England, on the 18th of October 1717. And by several adjournments continued to the 30th. Pursuant to His Majesty's commission and instruction, founded on the act of Parliament made in the 11th. & 12th of King William IIId. Intituled, An act for the more effectual suppression of piracy (1718) Boston, MA: B. Green & John Edwards [Anonymous Author].

Trocki, C.A. (1979) *Prince of Pirates: The Temenggongs and the Development of Johor and Singapore*, Singapore: Singapore University Press.

Tuchman, B.W. (1966) *The Proud Tower: A Portrait of the World Before the War, 1890–1914*, London: Hamish Hamilton. Available at http://148.201.96.14/dc/ver.aspx?ns=000283553 [2 November 2012].

Turner, R.F. (2003) 'State Responsibility and the War on Terror: The Legacy of Thomas Jefferson and the Barbary Pirates', *Chicago Journal of International Law*, 4(2): 121–142.

Ullmann, W. (1955) *The Growth of Papal Government in the Middle Ages: A Study in the Ideological Relation of Clerical to Lay Power*, New York: Taylor & Francis.

United Nations (1945) *Charter of the United Nations*, 1 UNTS XVI. Available at http://www.unhcr.org/refworld/docid/3ae6b3930.html [22 September 2012].

United Nations Environmental Program (2005) 'After the Tsunami Rapid Environmental Assess', *UNEP Official Reports*. Available at: www.unep.org/tsunami/reports/TSUNAMI_report_complete.pdf [accessed on 10 April 2013].

Unus Multorum (1814) 'To Lord Byron', *The Morning Post* (16 February). Reprinted in: *The Spirit of the Public Journals for 1814* (1815), London: Ridgway [Anonymous Author].

Van Ittersum, M.J. (2007) 'Mare Liberum in the West Indies? Hugo Grotius and the Case of the Swimming Lion, a Dutch Pirate in the Caribbean at the Turn of the Seventeenth Century', *Itinerario Leiden*, 31(3): 59–94.

Van Rooyen, F. (2011) 'Flotsam and Jetsam: Towards Ending Somali Piracy on Shore', *Strategic Analysis*, 35(2): 237–247.

Verne, J. (1870) *Vingt mille lieues sous les mers*, Paris: Éditions Hetzel. Translated in English as: Verne, J. (2010) *Twenty Thousand Leagues Under the Sea*, New York: Forgotten Books.

Verne, J. (1874) *L'Île mystérieuse*, Paris: Éditions Hetzel.

Versluis, A. (2006) *The New Inquisitions: Heretic-Hunting and the Intellectual Origins of Modern Totalitarianism*, Oxford: Oxford University Press.

Villiers, P. (2007) *Les corsaires: des origines au traité de Paris du 16 avril 1856*, Paris: Editions Jean-Paul Gisserot.

Vincent, C.P. (1985) *The Politics of Hunger: The Allied Blockade of Germany, 1915–1919*, Athens, OH: Ohio University Press.

Virilio, P. (1990) *Popular Defense & Ecological Struggles*, New York: Semiotext(e).

Vitkus, D.J. (2000) *Three Turk Plays from Early Modern England: Selimus, A Christian Turned Turk, and The Renegado*, New York: Columbia University Press.

Vitoria, F. (1917) *De Indis at de Ivre Belli Relectiones*, Washington: Carnegie Institute.

Vlasic, M.V. (2011) 'Assassination and Targeted Killing: A Historical and Post-Bin Laden Legal Analysis', *Georgetown Journal of International Law*, 43(2): 259–292.

Vodola, E. (1986) *Excommunication in the Middle Ages*, Berkeley, CA: University of California Press.

Waits, C. and Shors, D. (1999) *Unabomber: The Secret Life of Ted Kaczynski*, Helena, MT: Helena Independent Record.

Warren, J.F. (2007) *The Sulu Zone, 1768–1898: The Dynamics of External Trade, Slavery, and Ethnicity in the Transformation of a Southeast Asian Maritime State*, Singapore: National University of Singapore Press.

Weber, D. (2009) 'Piratical Transgressions, Political Transgressions. Re-reading Carl Schmitt's "Theory of the Partisan"', *Esprit*, 7(9): 12–23.

Weber, M. (1994) 'The Profession and Vocation of Politics (1919)', in *Weber: Political Writings*, London: Cambridge University Press, pp. 309–369.

Weinreb, L. (1987) *Natural Law and Justice*, Cambridge, MA: Harvard University Press.

Weiss, T.G. (1999) 'Principles, Politics, and Humanitarian Action', *Ethics & International Affairs*, 13(1): 1–22.

Werner, W.G. (2004) 'From Justus Hostis to Rogue State: The Concept of the Enemy in International Legal Thinking', *International Journal for the Semiotics of Law*, 17(2): 155–168.

Westover, J. (1998) 'The Impressment of Billy Budd', *The Massachusets Review*, 39(3): 361–384.

Wheelan, J. (2003) *Jefferson's War: America's First War on Terror 1801–1805*, New York: Carroll & Graf Publishers.

Wilcox, F. (1938) 'The League of Nations and the Spanish Civil War', *Annals of the American Academy of Political and Social Science*, 198(1): 65–72.
Wilkes, J. (1995) *The Illyrians*, New York: Blackwell Publishers.
Willett, L. (2011) 'Pirates and Power Politics', *The RUSI Journal*, 156(6): 20–25.
Williams, D. (2001) 'Refuge Upon the Sea: Captivity and Liberty in the Florida Pirate', *Early American Literature*, 36(1): 71–88.
Wilson, E.M. (2008) *The Savage Republic: De Indis of Hugo Grotius, Republicanism, and Dutch Hegemony Within the Early Modern World-system (c. 1600–1619)*, Leiden: Brill.
Wilson, P.L. (2003) *Pirate Utopias: Moorish Corsairs & European Renegadoes*, New York: Autonomedia.
Wilson, W. (2004) *Why We Are At War*, Whitefish, MO: Kessinger Publishing.
Woolf, G. (1992) 'Imperialism, Empire and the Integration of the Roman Economy', *World Archaeology*, 23(3): 283–293.
Worm, B., Barbier, E., Beaumont, N., Duffy, J., Folke, C., Halpern, B., Jackson, J., Lotze, H., Micheli, F., Palumbi, S., Sala, E., Selkoe, K., Stachowicz, J. and Watson, R. (2006) 'Impacts of Biodiversity Loss on Ocean Ecosystem Services', *Science*, 314(5800): 787–790.
Yarwood, L. (2008) 'Defining Torture: The Potential for Abuse', *Journal of the Institute of Justice and International Studies*, 8(3): 324–351.
Yoo, J. (2012) 'Obama, Drones and Thomas Aquinas', *The Wall Street Journal*, June 7, p. 6.
Yoo, J. and Delahunty, R. (2002) 'The President's Constitutional Authority to Conduct Military Operations Against Terrorist Organizations and the Nations that Harbor or Support Them', *Harvard Journal of Law and Public Policy*, 25(1): 487–515.
Zahedieh, N. (1986) 'Trade, Plunder, and Economic Development in Early English Jamaica, 1655–89', *The Economic History Review*, 39(2): 205–222.
Zahedieh, N. (1990) 'A Frugal, Prudential and Hopeful Trade. Privateering in Jamaica, 1655–89', *The Journal of Imperial and Commonwealth History*, 18(2): 145–168.
Zizek, S. (2009) *In Defense of Lost Causes*, London: Verso.
Zolo, D. (1997) *Cosmopolis: Prospects for World Government*, London: Polity Press.
Zolo, D. (1998) 'Hans Kelsen: International Peace Through International Law', *European Journal of International Law*, 9(2): 306–324.
Zolo, D. (2002) *Invoking Humanity: War, Law and Global Order*, London: Continuum International Publishing Group.
Zolo, D. (2008) 'La profezia della Guerra Globale', in Schmitt, C. (ed.), *Il Concetto Discriminatorio di Guerra*, Roma: Laterza.
Zolo, D. (2009) *Terrorismo umanitario. Dalla guerra del Golfo alla strage di Gaza*, Reggio Emilia: Diabasis.

Index

Page numbers in *italics* refer to illustrations.

Kolibri 360 GmbH
Ferdinand-Jühlke-Straße 7
99095 Erfurt, Deutschland
produktsicherheit@kolibri360.de